Grotesque Figures

PARALLAX  RE-VISIONS OF CULTURE
AND SOCIETY

Stephen G. Nichols, Gerald Prince, and Wendy Steiner

SERIES EDITORS

Grotesque Figures

Baudelaire, Rousseau, and the
Aesthetics of Modernity

Virginia E. Swain

The Johns Hopkins University Press
Baltimore and London

© 2004 The Johns Hopkins University Press
All rights reserved. Published 2004
Printed in the United States of America on acid-free paper
9 8 7 6 5 4 3 2 1

The Johns Hopkins University Press
2715 North Charles Street
Baltimore, Maryland 21218-4363
www.press.jhu.edu

Library of Congress Cataloging-in-Publication Data

Swain, Virginia E., 1943–
  Grotesque figures : Baudelaire, Rousseau, and the aesthetics
of modernity / Virginia E. Swain.
      p.   cm.—(Parallax, re-visions of culture and society)
Includes bibliographical references and index.
ISBN 0-8018-7945-0 (hardcover : alk. paper)
    1. Baudelaire, Charles, 1821–1867—Criticism and
interpretation.   2. Rousseau, Jean Jacques, 1712–1778—
Influence.   3. Grotesque in literature.   I. Title.   II. Parallax
(Baltimore, Md.)
PQ2191.Z5S88 2005
841′.8—dc22

                                      2003027926

A catalog record for this book is available from the
British Library.

To Harry
and
To Hannah, Jessica, Samuel, and Katelyn
with love

Contents

Illustrations

Acknowledgments

Determining the extent and nature of Rousseau's contribution to the *Petits poèmes en prose* has always been a thorny problem for Baudelaire scholars, and I have thoroughly experienced the difficulty of this undertaking. I am very much indebted to the numerous colleagues, students, family members, and friends whose advice, criticism, confidence, and support have enabled me to overcome many moments of frustration and bring this project to completion.

I am especially grateful to Ross Chambers and Richard Stamelman, who each read pieces of this work at an early stage in its conceptualization. Their generosity and kindness buoyed me when I was floundering, and their insightful and rigorous scholarship set the standard to which I have aspired here. E. S. Burt, Katharine Conley, Julie Hayes, Lynn Higgins, Marianne Hirsch, Lawrence Kritzman, Barry Scherr, Donald Spence, Roxana Verona, and the late Susanne Zantop all commented on portions of the book in various stages of its evolution, and I thank them too for their interest and help. Susan Bibeau, Margaret Darrow, Mary-Jean Green, John Rassias, and Sally Sedgwick deserve credit for providing professional advice and moral support along the way.

Two librarians at Dartmouth College's Baker Library—Robert Jaccaud, the former reference librarian, and Patricia Carter, the interlibrary loan specialist— made my research not only easier, but fun.

The energy and the enthusiasm of my student research assistants—Lauren Ambrose, Heather Charles, Shane Leahy, Rebecca Leffler, Jessica Lyons, and Christopher von Ginoven—were a wonderful tonic. I hope their involvement in this project has inspired them to carry out similar projects of their own one day.

I would also like to express my appreciation to Tessa Murdoch of the Victoria and Albert Museum and to Gene Garthwaite for last-minute help with the illustrations, and to the journals that have allowed me to reuse elements of articles I originally published in them. Specifically, I thank Dominique Jullien for permission to use portions of an article on "Le Vieux Saltimbanque" and "Une Mort héroïque" published in *Romanic Review* 73 (1982): 452–62; the

xi

Trustees of Boston University for permission to reproduce portions of an article that appeared in *Studies in Romanticism* 26, no. 4 (1987): 573–90; and the Modern Language Association for permission to use parts of an essay on Rousseau and personification that appeared in the volume *Approaches to Teaching Rousseau's Confessions and Rêveries d'un promeneur solitaire,* edited by John C. O'Neal and Ourida Moustefai, published in 2003.

Thanks also go to the Ramon and Marguerite Guthrie Fund of Dartmouth College and the Guthrie Fund Committee for support of this publication, and to Stephen G. Nichols, who sponsored the book for the Parallax series.

Finally, I want to acknowledge the all-important support of my husband, Harry Beskind, whose love, understanding, and belief in me made this book possible. I'm grateful, too, that my mother has not only lived to see the book finished but is ready and able to celebrate it with us.

Abbreviations

Baud., *Corr.*   Charles Baudelaire, *Correspondance,* ed. Claude Pichois and Jean Ziegler (Paris: Gallimard, 1973)

Baud., *OC*   Charles Baudelaire, *Oeuvres complètes,* ed. Claude Pichois (Paris: Gallimard, 1976)

Encyclopédie   *Encyclopédie; ou, Dictionnaire raisonné des sciences, des arts et des métiers,* ed. Denis Diderot et al. (Paris: Briasson, 1751–80)

Proud., *OC*   P.-J. Proudhon, *Oeuvres complètes,* ed. C. Bouglé and H. Moysset (Paris: Librairie Marcel Rivière, 1923–59)

Rouss., *CW*   Jean-Jacques Rousseau, *The Collected Writings of Rousseau,* ed. Roger D. Masters and Christopher Kelly (Hanover, N.H.: University Press of New England, 1990–)

Rouss., *Julie*   Jean-Jacques Rousseau, *Julie, ou la Nouvelle Héloïse,* in *Oeuvres complètes* (Paris: Gallimard, 1964); *Julie, or the New Heloise,* trans. Philip Stewart and Jean Vaché, in Rouss., *CW,* vol. 6 (1997).

Rouss., *OC*   Jean-Jacques Rousseau, *Oeuvres complètes* (Paris: Gallimard, 1959–95)

Grotesque Figures

Introduction

Why did Charles Baudelaire invoke Jean-Jacques Rousseau in a title he proposed for the prose poem collection now known as *Les Petits Poèmes en prose,* or *Le Spleen de Paris?* Although the title—"Le Promeneur solitaire" (The solitary walker)—was never used, the apparent reference to Rousseau's autobiography "Les Rêveries du promeneur solitaire" is surprising, for Baudelaire rarely alluded to his predecessor in his letters, criticism, and poetry. And why would he choose to bring up another author, let alone one whom he seldom discussed, in connection with his own new—and innovative—poems?

Baudelaire was not normally averse to sharing his critical opinions about other writers, having extolled the talents of Edgar Allan Poe and written with enthusiasm about Théophile Gautier and other contemporaries; and if he was affected by the style or ideas of Rousseau, he could have joined the frequent literary and political debates about Rousseau's legacy. However, he did not spell out his reaction to Rousseau in writing. Baudelaire's sporadic references to the eighteenth-century author do not yield a coherent explanation of his views. Baudelaire mentions Rousseau favorably in his *Salon de 1846,* choosing Rousseau's supposed suicide as an example of a singularly modern phenomenon. However, in the 1850s, Baudelaire's cursory remarks about him are full of scorn. Rousseau is an "auteur sentimental et infâme" ("a sentimental and vile author"), a liar who has the audacity to claim that he puts truth above life.[1] As if that were not enough, he is undoubtedly one of those fools who believe in the innate goodness of man,[2] and an abhorrent author given to public confessions.[3] Yet, Baudelaire also makes notes in his journals recognizing himself in

some of Rousseau's actions,[4] and in 1861 and 1863, he tells his mother that when his own "book about [him]self" is published, "J[ean]-J[acques]'s *Confessions* will appear pale" by comparison.[5] In sum, Baudelaire's infrequent and contradictory comments offer precious little information that would illuminate his intentions regarding "Le Promeneur solitaire." We can only turn to the poems themselves for answers.

Indeed, in the last several decades, scholars have noted significant borrowings from Rousseau in prose poems such as "Le Gâteau," as well as phrases and attitudes reminiscent of Rousseau in "L'Etranger," "Le *Confiteor* de l'artiste," "La Chambre double," "Le Mauvais Vitrier," "Les Foules," "Le Joujou du pauvre," "La Solitude," and "Les Fenêtres," among others.[6] Not all of these cases have been studied in depth, but when they have been analyzed, they have generally been interpreted as manifestations of Baudelaire's hostility toward "Jean-Jacques." (Jean Starobinski asserts, for example, that Baudelaire rereads Rousseau "in order to refute him with his own images.")[7] However, it has always seemed to me that, in the absence of a comprehensive investigation, it was important not to foreclose the questions raised by the proposed title and the more general question of Baudelaire's relationship to Rousseau. This book is my attempt to provide a more systematic treatment of this poorly understood aspect of Baudelaire's work. Nonetheless, it is not my aim to provide a definitive interpretation. Rather, I hope my efforts will encourage further research and discussion, from which our understanding of Baudelaire and modernity can only benefit.

I have uncovered many previously undetected borrowings from Rousseau in *Les Petits Poèmes en prose*; and as a result, this book presents six completely new readings of prose poems, based on Baudelaire's hidden, yet extensive, rewritings of Rousseau. At the same time, my research and analysis have convinced me that many of the central characters in the poems, not just "The Solitary Walker" of the proposed title, are caricatures of Rousseau drawn from the ideological debates about the post-Revolutionary identity of France that marked the nineteenth century. If Rousseau was not just a source of textual material for Baudelaire, but also a recurrent character in his prose poem collection, as I believe, then I could only conclude that, contrary to the closely held opinion of Baudelaire scholars, the poems were intended to be more than random vignettes of Paris life.

My study grew in unexpected ways and took on broader significance still when I made the surprising discovery that the common ground on which Baudelaire and Rousseau meet is the unstable terrain of the grotesque. The

idea that anyone would consult Rousseau to learn about the grotesque is itself novel and startling. Baudelaire's insight into this unsuspected element of Rousseau's work has given me a new appreciation of both authors' breadth. More important, however, as I read their works together, I became aware that their convergence and disagreement concerning the grotesque was a key moment in the development of a modernist aesthetic. Reading Baudelaire with Rousseau shows how the modern grotesque is historically rooted, structurally unchanging, and yet radically new. By focusing on these two authors, both of whom influenced the course of European literature, this book thus seeks to shed light on a major aesthetic shift that continues to have repercussions for art in our time.

The history of the grotesque is usually described as falling rather neatly into two distinct moments. The trauma of the French Revolution and its aftereffects throughout Europe, which also divide Baudelaire from Rousseau, can be seen as a watershed between the two.[8] Grotesque productions of the earlier period, extending from the Renaissance through the mid-eighteenth century, bear the stamp of the carnivalesque, described by Mikhail Bakhtin as "a festive perception of the world." In France, Italian theater (or commedia dell'arte), street theaters and fairs, opera, and the arabesque paintings so preponderant in interior decor recall the "folk festivities of the carnival type, the comic rites and cults, the clowns and fools, giants, dwarfs, and jugglers" that Bakhtin associates with the carnivalesque. They all contain elements of the "culture of folk carnival humor," and they call for "ever changing, playful, undefined forms." In this early period, the grotesque "consecrate[s] inventive freedom, . . . permit[s] the combination of a variety of different elements and their rapprochement, . . . liberate[s] from the prevailing point of view of the world, from conventions and established truths, from clichés, from all that is humdrum and universally accepted."[9] In sum, the early grotesque has a carefree, utopian flavor.

In contrast, the grotesque that arises after the French Revolution is anything but happy-go-lucky or optimistic. Bakhtin observes that in the nineteenth century, "Laughter loses its gay and joyful tone [and its positive regenerating power]."[10] In Wolfgang Kayser's view, interest in the grotesque arises in periods of insecurity, when "the belief . . . in a perfect and protective natural order cease[s] to exist." Basing his understanding largely on literary works from the romantic period to the twentieth century, Kayser asserts that the grotesque is "the estranged world," a world that has ceased to be reliable and therefore instills fear. The post-Revolutionary grotesque, then, is not an ex-

tension of the carnival spirit; it does not evoke feelings of freedom and the possibility of change. If anything, it may "carry the [artist] away, deprive him of his freedom, and make him afraid of the ghosts which he so frivolously invoked." At best, according to Kayser, the later grotesque represents the artist's struggle to overcome feelings of "helplessness and horror" by "attempt[ing] to invoke and subdue the demonic aspects of the world."[11]

This is the historical paradigm that would normally segregate Baudelaire from Rousseau and place the former squarely in the modern camp. But the Baudelaire–Rousseau relationship is not susceptible to this kind of dichotomous reading. In the first place, Baudelaire's work is on the cusp where the pre-Revolutionary and the later grotesque meet. His prose poetry is a liminal case, partaking of both the early and the modern styles. The juxtaposition is obvious at a glance. Baudelaire mobilizes the themes and actors of the carnivalesque in texts that have a world-weary or melancholic tone. He produces joyful scenes of street fairs and mimes alongside down-and-out characters and ironic narrators representing the inescapable misery of the real world. But it is in his poetic response to Rousseau, in particular, that Baudelaire offers us the opportunity to witness the shift within the grotesque from the artistic inventiveness of the rococo to the manifestation of forces that threaten to render the artist helpless. Baudelaire sees beyond the epiphenomena of the grotesque (its themes and styles) and locates the real grotesque in the realm of language. For him, the real grotesque arises as a folly or madness of language, which threatens to override the poet's control. This grotesque is apprehended in the vertiginous experience of reading, and Baudelaire comes to this awareness in reading Rousseau.

Reading Baudelaire reading Rousseau, then, I address both the specific features that make Baudelaire's poetry a distinctive example of the modern grotesque and the underlying principles that attach his work unmistakably to the unchanging or eternal grotesque. In his dialogue with Rousseau, Baudelaire serves not just as an example of a new grotesque style but as a point of entry into the grotesque as a timeless phenomenon.

The visual signifiers of the grotesque in the rococo period, the political and aesthetic connotations of the Paris Opéra in the mid-eighteenth century, the debates over "Rousseau" and the identity of "France" between 1848 and 1861, and the role of (social and allegorical) types in caricature in the mid-nineteenth century are among the subjects discussed in this book. In its fusion of historical, cultural, and rhetorical elements, my work thus differs from the writings of the critics who discuss Baudelaire's use of allegory or even his rela-

tion to Rousseau. By emphasizing the grotesque over the allegorical in Baudelaire's poetry, and by linking his modernist aesthetic to Rousseau's rejection of the grotesque, I bring forward the connections between Baudelaire's art and the visual and literary styles of the eighteenth century, as well as the differences that make Baudelaire's work new.

The book's seven chapters pursue my argument from several different points of view. Chapter 1 establishes the structural link between Baudelaire's ideas about allegory, grotesque figures, and fetishes. Briefly reviewing the commonly held ideas about the grotesque, I disregard the numerous differences of value and historical emphasis among scholarly texts on the subject and focus instead on the traits on which all agree. I then consider the similarities between the grotesque, as it has been defined, and the traditional view of allegory as a restricted figure or trope. By positing the structural affinity between grotesque and allegory I pave the way for a new understanding of the grotesque as an unchanging feature of language. Finally, basing my own analysis on Baudelaire's "De l'essence du rire" ("Essay on Laughter") and selected verse poems, I establish the crucial premise that Baudelaire's grotesque is both traditional and new, inasmuch as for him, allegory is not a restricted but rather an open and unpredictable "grotesque figure."

Chapter 2 takes up the visual elements of the decorative allegorism (or grotesque style) of the rococo and shows how this visual style becomes a figure for modern poetry in "Le Poème du hachisch." Baudelaire elaborates on his ideas about allegory in this "Poème," likening the open figure to the painted arabesques of the rococo. Here he not only sets out the equation between intoxication and reading but also catches us up, as readers, in the delirious experience of allegory as it spirals out of control. Since the "Poème" is also the first text in which Rousseau figures as a character—the prototype of modern man, it foreshadows the use to which Baudelaire puts Rousseau in the prose poems he published the following year. There is thus a logical link between "Le Poème du hachisch" and the prose poems discussed in the last four chapters of the book.

However, in Chapter 3, in order to establish how and why Rousseau came to personify modern man in Baudelaire's poems, I address the thorny subject of Rousseau's reception in nineteenth-century France, specifically the ideological debates over the legacy of the French Revolution and its meaning for the identity of France. I demonstrate that between 1845 and 1865, "Rousseau" is already in use as an allegorical figure, a personification of the good or evil effects of the Revolution—the "god" or "devil" of modern France. Inasmuch as

"Rousseau" exemplified and focused the nineteenth century's preoccupation with the past, "he" encapsulated the ethos of the present, an essential aim of Baudelaire's modernity. Baudelaire makes ample use of the Rousseau caricatures put into circulation in the ongoing ideological debates. But the poet also turns to "Rousseau" to express his alienation from the values of his time. By taking up the images of Rousseau made available by contemporary discourse and appearing to endorse the dominant conservative view of the eighteenth-century author, Baudelaire both points to and cagily covers over his extensive engagement with Rousseau.

Beginning with Chapter 4, I turn specifically to Rousseau's role in Baudelaire's prose poem collection and its relation to the modern grotesque. I argue that types are the nexus where allegory, the grotesque, and caricature converge in Baudelaire's poetry. Baudelaire's long-standing interest in caricature and his desire to create a poetic version of the popular *Physiologies* make themselves felt in his use of "Rousseau" as a prototype of various social outcasts who traverse the prose poems and in "Rousseau"'s role as an overarching figure for the poems as a whole. Analyzing this insistent presence of "Rousseau" in the poems, I suggest that "Rousseau" personifies the grotesque for Baudelaire. This hypothesis is borne out by a close reading of Baudelaire's poem "Le Mauvais Vitrier," which relies on Rousseau's theory and practice of personification. In particular, the "Huitième Promenade," the eighth of Rousseau's *Rêveries du promeneur solitaire,* shapes Baudelaire's understanding of the generative function of the modern grotesque.

In making "Rousseau," an actual historical figure, the personification of the grotesque in his prose poems, Baudelaire brings together the real and the grotesque, which Rousseau fought hard to keep rigorously separate. Rousseau criticizes the excessive use of allegory, and allegory itself as an excessive (or grotesque) figure; and, for reasons that have to do with his desire to reform society, he calls for a more restrained use of rhetoric in the service of the real. Baudelaire learns from Rousseau's critical statements about the grotesque and even borrows extensively from them, but he does not completely adopt them. In Chapter 5, on realism and the modern grotesque, I continue my investigation of the aesthetic debate between the two authors, arguing that Baudelaire builds on and yet departs from Rousseau's theory and practice to create a new, modernist idiom. After examining in some detail Rousseau's satirical letter on the Paris Opéra in his novel *Julie, ou la Nouvelle Héloïse,* which indirectly lays out Rousseau's definition and critique of the grotesque, I show how Baudelaire puts textual and rhetorical elements of this letter to work in new ways in his

poems "Le Vieux Saltimbanque," "Le Crépuscule du soir," "Une Mort héroïque," and "La Corde."

My analysis of Rousseau's theory of the grotesque continues in Chapter 6, which extensively compares Rousseau's dictionary article "Opéra" and the Baudelaire poem that painstakingly rewrites it, "Les Yeux des pauvres." "Opéra" is the text that most fully explains Rousseau's position on the grotesque, complementing, in a much more serious vein, the comic treatment of it in *Julie*. Although both texts make clear the affiliation of the grotesque with the luxury and excesses of the absolute monarchy, they eventuate in rather different political positions, and in Chapter 6, I take up these sociopolitical implications of the grotesque. Both Baudelaire and Rousseau wrote under repressive governments whose censorship practices affected them directly, and both adopted a stance toward the grotesque that reflected their opposition to these regimes. But if Rousseau wanted to do away with the grotesque and, implicitly, the absolute monarchy that sponsored it, Baudelaire welcomed the grotesque, which he understood as a principle of instability or a destabilizing force. For Baudelaire, the grotesque was a subversive force in oppressive times.

Finally, in Chapter 7, I review "Rousseau"'s function as Baudelaire's grotesque figure or fetish. In his essay on laughter, Baudelaire uses the term "grotesque figure" to refer to allegory as an eroded language, an arbitrary or conventional sign, giving as an example the goddess Venus. With the advent of Christianity and the loss of her pagan powers, Venus became a comical icon or, as Baudelaire puts it, an "extravagant fetish." As a fallen revolutionary idol, "Rousseau" is just such a degraded sign or fetish for Baudelaire and his era. Of course, the fetish, in Freudian terms, is an object to be collected, a sign standing in for the lost object of the child's desire and a way of warding off his fear of castration. This sense of the fetish is equally applicable to Baudelaire's relation to Rousseau. Like his contemporaries, Baudelaire was at once fascinated and repelled by Rousseau, whom he saw as both an inspiration and a threat. The prose poem "Le Vieux Saltimbanque," which tells the story of the narrator-poet's emotional encounter with an "old man of letters" who has outlived the generation he once amused, perfectly captures this stance.

In mid-nineteenth-century France, and in Baudelaire's prose poems in particular, "Rousseau" is the unforgettable sign of a past that haunts the present and prevents it from coming into its own. Although this dilemma presents itself to his contemporaries as the traumatic effect of the French Revolution, Baudelaire inscribes it in his prose poems as the trauma of reading. On one level, the poem "Le Vieux Saltimbanque" dramatizes this trauma as the psy-

chological shock to the poet's system resulting from his encounter with Rousseau's works. But on another level, this autobiographical tale is yet another example of the personification so central to Baudelaire's poems. Analyzing "Le Vieux Saltimbanque" in relation to its primary Rousseau intertext, the ninth of the *Rêveries du promeneur solitaire,* I show how the poem acknowledges and tries to compensate for the shock of reading, which unleashes both the creative force and deadly threat of the grotesque.

1 The Grotesque
Definitions and Figures

Charles Baudelaire was bent on creating an art for his era. Indeed, many believe that it was Baudelaire who brought about the literary revolution that established modern art. But although we know Baudelaire as the poet of modernity, the poet of alienation and melancholy who describes the grim reality of city life, his poetry, even the last and most modern of his works, retains the imprint of what went before.

Baudelaire's relation to the past is more complex than is often acknowledged. In his important essay on modernity "Le Peintre de la vie moderne" ("The Painter of Modern Life"), Baudelaire draws a parallel between fashion and the artistic representation of the present; he makes the point that decorative or stylistic elements that are often dismissed as superficial may in fact hold the key to the moral, psychological, and aesthetic climate of the times ("la morale et l'esthétique du temps"). Yet he also understood that the frequent "metamorphoses" of the present make its representations, like styles in dress, quickly passé.[1] Styles in art or fashion stamp beauty with the mark of time, simultaneously tying it to the present and subjecting it to decay. Paradoxically, however, styles also allow the past to come back to life. An eighteenth-century garment, for example, may seem stiff and funny when viewed objectively; but it becomes lively and serious when we imagine it worn by a person or see it animated by an actor in the theater:

> L'imagination du spectateur peut encore aujourd'hui faire marcher et frémir cette *tunique* et ce *schall.* Un de ces jours, peut-être, un drame paraîtra sur

un théâtre quelconque, où nous verrons la résurrection de ces costumes . . . et s'ils sont portés et animés par des comédiennes et des comédiens intelligents, nous nous étonnerons d'en avoir pu rire si étourdiment. (Baud., *OC*, 2: 684)

The spectator's imagination can still today make this tunic and this shawl walk and tremble. One of these days, perhaps, a drama will appear on some stage or other, where we shall see the resurrection of these costumes . . . and if they are worn and animated by intelligent actresses and actors, we shall be astonished that we were able to laugh at them so thoughtlessly.

Just as an old garment can be given a new life in a subsequent age, the past can be resuscitated—animated or personified: "Le passé, tout en gardant le piquant du fantôme, reprendra la lumière et le mouvement de la vie, et se fera présent" ("The past, while retaining the piquancy of a phantom, will once again have the light and movement of life, and will make itself present"). If the present is always passing, the past is always on the verge of coming alive. Baudelaire's modernity is the uneasy negotiation between the two.

This book examines the way the phantomatic past of the eighteenth century "makes itself present" in Baudelaire's modernity. I argue that Baudelaire looked to eighteenth-century aesthetics to help him develop his theory of the grotesque, which is the basis of his modern art. Baudelaire may have founded a new era in French literature, and a new style that inspires artists even today, but that era and that style are beholden to the eighteenth-century art of the rococo and to eighteenth-century reflections on it. This book, then, is about Baudelaire's grotesque as it relates to the previous century's esthetic theory and practice. The grotesque dominated the literary and visual arts in France throughout much of the eighteenth century—at least until the philosophes, led by Jean-Jacques Rousseau, attacked the rococo aesthetic in their campaign against the Paris Opéra.[2] Baudelaire was well aware of this history and had studied both the eighteenth-century applications of the grotesque and Rousseau's criticism of it. Not only does Rousseau's essay on the Paris Opéra inform Baudelaire's theory of the grotesque, but "Rousseau" also appears as the representative of the grotesque in Baudelaire's poems. Taking up "Rousseau" in his own poetry, Baudelaire uses the traits of a historical personality (a historical figure) to give a human form (an allegorical figure or personification) to the grotesque (itself bound up with figuration). The grotesque figures to which the title of this book refers are thus multiple, both historical and rhetorical, and thoroughly interconnected.

Defining the Grotesque

The grotesque is a slippery term, which has defied definition.[3] Depending on which authority one consults, the grotesque may designate either the lively mood and social inversion of the carnival (Mikhail Bakhtin) or the bleak fantasies and ironic expression of the alienated individual (Wolfgang Kayser). Scholars also disagree about the grotesque's history. It may span several centuries or several millennia, beginning in antiquity, the Middle Ages, or the Renaissance, and continuing today—indeed, one commentator (Bernard McElroy) notes "an affinity which makes the grotesque not only typical of [twentieth-century] art, but perhaps its most characteristic expression."[4] Yet despite their varying assessments of the use, tone, and history of the grotesque, critics agree on several of its characteristics. First and foremost, the grotesque refers to the improbable "fusion of different realms."[5] Grotesque images are "double, tense, and contradictory."[6] Monstrous or chimerical, they interweave heterogeneous forms in creative ways that have no obvious model; they ignore nature and the hierarchical ordering of the world.[7] Indeed, the grotesque is removed from any origin or foundation that might undergird it. The opposite of "the indisputable and stable,"[8] it opens "an abyss . . . where we thought to rest on firm ground."[9] The "pure product of the imaginary," the grotesque is "exactly the antithesis of . . . representation."[10] Another important trait of the grotesque, whether condensed in an individual figure or written out in an extended narration, is the relation to time.[11] Like the terra-cotta figurines of "senile, pregnant hags" that Bakhtin describes, grotesque images incorporate a temporal gap that is often responsible for the illusion that not just time but "species boundaries" have been "overleaped."[12] Grotesque figures can thus be read "as images of instantaneous process, time rendered into space, narrative compressed into image."[13] The grotesque keeps us balancing tentatively at the limit between "death and rebirth, insanity and discovery, rubble and revelation." By virtue of its double nature and its defiance of logic, the grotesque strands our understanding "in a 'liminal' phase, for the image appears to have an impossible split reference, and multiple forms inhabit a single image."[14] Depending, it seems, on the author's tolerance for disorientation, the grotesque is therefore judged to be either "ridiculous" or "terrifying," if not both at once.[15]

Striking as they may be, these basic criteria scarcely limit the number and types of images and subjects that are grouped under the heading of the grotesque. Books on the grotesque tend to spread in all directions, drawing into

their purview many apparently distinct phenomena, although, here again, certain examples receive universal assent. Examples of the grotesque in art and literature that are repeatedly cited by critics include literary and visual depictions of demons; the sketches of the seventeenth-century artist Jacques Callot (particularly his Italian actors); the productions of the commedia dell'arte, with their dizzying repartee, extraordinary gymnastics, and "masks" or stock characters; caricature; fair performances; puppet shows; and human beings reduced to "puppets, marionettes, and automata, . . . their faces frozen into masks."[16]

Nonetheless, despite these points of agreement, the grotesque continues to appear as a catchall term lacking any precision.[17] As Geoffrey Golt Harpham observes: "Curiously, [the grotesque] remains elusive despite the fact that it is unchanging."[18] One of the principal difficulties surrounding discussions of the grotesque, I submit, is that the term refers both to a specific artistic and literary style and to a condition of language that is associated with the "demonic" and perceived as "an impersonal force, an alien and inhuman spirit" inhabiting (or haunting) the productions of art.[19] Grotesque imagery or grotesque narrative may hint at this other grotesque, conceived as condition or force, but the two do not (and cannot be made to) completely cohere. Any attempt to make sense of the phenomenon called the grotesque must first untangle these two.

Baudelaire, for his part, understood this problem. He knew that the grotesque is not just a style or a mood but also an intangible process, which can only be represented indirectly, in the most improper of terms. For Baudelaire the grotesque is not only a visual phenomenon, apprehensible as "graphic play" or a "painter's dream."[20] Although it may be associated with endless, spiraling forms and implausible hybrids (monstrous chimeras, mutant bodies, and the like), it is not reducible to them. Instead, this overt playfulness, this evocation of illogical or unnatural fantasy, seeks to express the "other" grotesque—what I call the generative play of language—the "non-thing" that resists representation.[21] "The grotesque image reflects a phenomenon in transformation, an as yet unfinished metamorphosis,"[22] and the changing forms or visible shapes can only hint at this invisible and never-ending process.

For Baudelaire, the grotesque names the paradox of allegory, which is central in the texts and visual productions of the rococo, as it is throughout the poet's own work.[23] Without delving into Baudelaire's theory at this point, it is sufficient to recall rhetoricians' descriptions of allegory to see that the structural elements of the grotesque on which critics generally agree are quite similar to the structure of allegory as it has traditionally been understood. First,

allegory, like the grotesque, is double and disparate. César Chesnau Du Marsais (1676–1756), who contributed articles about grammar and rhetoric to the *Encyclopédie* until his death, said of allegory:

> L'allégorie est un discours, qui est d'abord présenté sous un sens propre, qui paraît tout autre chose que ce qu'on a besoin de faire entendre, et qui cependant ne sert que de comparaison pour donner l'intelligence d'un autre sens qu'on n'exprime point. . . . dans l'allégorie tous les mots ont d'abord un sens figuré; c'est-à-dire que tous les mots d'une phrase ou d'un discours allégorique forment d'abord un sens littéral qui n'est pas celui qu'on a dessein de faire entendre.

> Allegory is a discourse that is first presented under a proper meaning, which appears to be something completely other than what one needs to convey, and that nonetheless only serves as a comparison to make clear another meaning that one doesn't express. . . . in allegory, all the words have first a figural meaning; that is, all the words of an allegorical phrase or discourse first form a literal meaning that is not the meaning one intends to convey.[24]

Proposing two dissimilar meanings with a single expression, allegory is perpetually and constitutionally different from itself. Allegory literally designates the speech of the "other" (in Greek, *allos*), and otherness is its very structure.

Furthermore, if the grotesque's heterogeneity requires us to unpack its temporal structure in order to recapitulate the evolution of a species or imagine the possible violence that might have thrown disparate elements together, allegory's doubleness, too, requires a double understanding, which, pragmatically speaking, can only be arrived at sequentially. Explicating this passage from Du Marsais, Tzvetan Todorov writes: "[I]ci, tous les mots . . . semblent bien former un premier sens littéral; mais, *dans un deuxième temps,* on découvre qu'il faut chercher un sens second, allégorique" ("[H]ere, all the words . . . seem to form a first literal meaning; but, *in a second time,* one discovers that one must seek a second, allegorical meaning").[25] Allegory requires us to read in "two times" in order to comprehend its double, differential meaning. In other words, in the world of allegory, as in the world of the grotesque, "time is the originary constitutive category." "Allegory designates primarily a distance in relation to its own origin," Paul de Man argues, and "it establishes its language in the void of this temporal difference."[26]

Finally, allegory is anything but stable and well-grounded. The confusion over "sens propre," "sens figuré," and "sens littéral" evident in Du Marsais's

definition, which Todorov's reformulation attempts to eliminate (by directly inverting the terms), hints at the uncertainty allegory promotes. Pointing toward an "object" or meaning that it cannot name or present ("l'objet principal . . . disparaît entièrement dans l'allégorie"),[27] allegory is both "illustrative" (as sign or basis of comparison) and resistant to illustration. The difference and deferral of meaning within the figure guarantee that allegory will always chase after itself, in a movement of perpetual regression.[28] As a figure, allegory has the same enigmatic or elusive quality as the grotesque.

In the pages and chapters that follow, I show how Baudelaire's idea of allegory (which builds upon but goes beyond the rhetoricians' traditional definitions) converges with his idea of the grotesque. In our common parlance we may speak of a thing or a situation as "grotesque," meaning odd, deviant, or morally dubious,[29] and Baudelaire himself sometimes uses the word in this loose way. In this book, however, I reserve the term "grotesque" for the visual and operatic art of the rococo (which was regularly called "the grotesque" in the eighteenth century and which informs Baudelaire's practice) and for the well-thought-out theory of the grotesque propounded by Baudelaire.

Baudelaire's Theory of the Grotesque

Since Baudelaire does not elaborate his theory of the grotesque in any systematic fashion, it must be gleaned and pieced together from various sources, including verse poems such as "Le Masque," the prose "poem" on hashish, and the essays on caricature, as well as from his reflections on the essence of laughter ("De l'essence du rire" [1857]), where it is available to us in its most complete form. This chapter and the next take up all these sources, but here I want to turn first to "De l'essence du rire."

In the course of this short piece, which began as thoughts about caricature and grew into a work on the grotesque, Baudelaire draws on examples as heterogeneous as the English romantic novel (notably *Melmoth the Wanderer*) and German literature of the fantastic (the novellas of E. T. A. Hoffmann), lithographs in the style of the French illustrator Gavarni, Jacques Callot's seventeenth-century drawings of Italian actors, English mime theater in the tradition of the commedia dell'arte, and bronze figurines, masks, and phallic objects from Greek antiquity. The broad sweep of these illustrations recalls, perhaps a bit too much, the endemic problem that seems to characterize books on the grotesque. But Baudelaire's examples do more than suggest the far-ranging implications of the grotesque, its thematic affiliations, and its associa-

tion with various genres. Taken together, the illustrations help us come to terms with the function and effects of this "unnamable" condition,[30] which Baudelaire also calls "the absolute comic" ("le comique absolu").[31] Through an examination of some of these examples, we can begin to fathom Baudelaire's idea of the grotesque and why he considered it the highest achievement of art, an unsettling performance at the top of the comic scale.

Baudelaire first uses the word "grotesque" in the essay on laughter when he proposes the comic example of some "grotesque figures" of antiquity. His discussion aligns the grotesque with figures, masks, and "monstrous apparatuses of generation," all of which have lost their initial meaning or seriousness with the passage of time:

Quant aux figures grotesques que nous a laissées l'antiquité, les masques, les figurines de bronze, les Hercules tout en muscles, les petits Priapes à la langue recourbée en l'air, aux oreilles pointues, tout en cervelet et en phallus,—quant à ces phallus prodigieux sur lesquels les blanches filles de Romulus montent innocemment à cheval, ces monstrueux appareils de la génération armés de sonnettes et d'ailes, je crois que toutes ces choses sont pleines de sérieux. Vénus, Pan, Hercule, n'étaient pas des personnages risibles. On en a ri après la venue de Jésus, Platon et Sénèque aidant. Je crois que l'antiquité était pleine de respect pour les tambours-majors et les faiseurs de tours de force en tout genre, et que tous les fétiches extravagants que je citais ne sont que des signes d'adoration, ou tout au plus des symboles de force, et nullement des émanations de l'esprit intentionnellement comiques. Les idoles indiennes et chinoises ignorent qu'elles sont ridicules; c'est en nous, chrétiens, qu'est le comique. (Baud., *OC*, 2: 533–34)

As for the grotesque figures left to us by antiquity, the masks, the bronze figurines, the muscle-bound Herculeses, the little Priapuses with their tongues curled in the air and their pointy ears, all cerebellum and phallus,—as for those prodigious phalluses on which the white daughters of Romulus innocently ride, those monstrous apparatuses of generation decked out with bells and wings, I think that all those things are full of seriousness. Venus, Pan, Hercules, were not laughable characters. We laughed at them after the coming of Jesus, with Plato and Seneca helping. I believe that antiquity was full of respect for the drum-majors and for those who accomplish all sorts of feats of strength or skill [tours de force], and that all the extravagant fetishes that I cited are only signs of adoration, or at the most symbols of force, and not at all emanations of an intentionally comic spirit. Indian and Chinese idols do not know that they are ridiculous; the comic is in us Christians. (my translation)

This dense example proposes a preliminary explanation of the grotesque as a turn of events in which one (mythological) signifying system is supplanted by another (focused on the Christian deity). The substitution causes the original seriousness or meaning of the pagan beliefs to fall away and brings about the laughter that marks this loss (one diagnostic sign or symptom of the grotesque).[32] In the Christian world, Venus and Hercules no longer act as forces, as they once did; instead of bringing an idea of beauty or strength into being, their names merely connote it. Formerly viewed as supernatural entities endowed with power, movement, and life, the gods have been stripped of their subjectivity and reduced to material objects of misplaced adoration; they have become, to use Baudelaire's phrase, "extravagant fetishes." As inanimate or artificial objects whose value arises not out of any inherent power, but from the irrational or arbitrary attribution of supposed power, the fetishes are conventional signs, functioning in a system where inner properties are no longer the key to meaning.[33]

Although as a result of long habit, "Venus" and "Hercules" still stand for beauty and strength, this remnant of meaning is a poor substitute for the omnipotence that was once their essence. The original, proper meaning of the names, which designated superhuman beings, is replaced by an eroded, conventional meaning, with at best a limited power. Although not all ideation is lost, what remains of the proper name is a shadow of its former self: not a revered god, but an allegorical figure (Venus, Hercules, Pan, Priapus). Baudelaire presents allegory under the guise of "grotesque figures" that once had a sacred fullness of meaning but that function now as comic "fetishes" or conventional signs. Allegory is a fallen or lapsed language, consonant with the acknowledged vanity of the gods.[34]

Baudelaire is thus not taking up unchanged the grotesque figures of the past. Although the essay on laughter puts forward several of the grotesque images typically associated with Renaissance and rococo art, we should not be misled by their familiarity. Unlike the half-animal, half-human forms frolicking in the arabesque scrolls of a rococo painting, Baudelaire's "grotesque figures" suggest that the grotesque is not the monstrous union of two disparate bodies—a physical hybrid—but a cleavage within a proper name or a sign.

As the example of the grotesque figures suggests, Baudelaire's essay on laughter is concerned primarily with rhetoric. Although he draws several of his illustrations from the visual and dramatic arts, Baudelaire is ultimately writing about the aesthetic categories and laws that govern his own poetic production. Thus, when he turns his attention to the example of a troop of English mimes

working in the commedia dell'arte style, he laments the impossibility of capturing their play with "pale and glacial" words: "Comment la plume pourrait-elle rivaliser avec la pantomime? La pantomime est l'épuration de la comédie; c'en est la quintessence; c'est l'élément comique pur, dégagé et concentré" ("How could the pen rival pantomime? Pantomime is the purification of comedy; it's the quintessence of comedy; the pure comic element, detached and condensed") (Baud., *OC*, 2: 540). Watching the pantomime play, Baudelaire has his own poetry in mind. His poignant comment on the mimes reveals his own desire as a poet, even as it underscores the constraints that handicap all poetry. The mimes represent what Baudelaire wishes most to capture on the page, but his enthusiasm for their "marvelous" aura is matched by his acute sense of his own impotence. Poetry can never reproduce the atmosphere that attends the mime's silent play. At best, words can suggest the grotesque indirectly; they cannot bring it to the page.

Baudelaire is reduced to giving a written resume of the mime sketch, which, in and of itself, is germane to the poetic problem at hand. Not only does the poet suffer from a sense of impotence as he recognizes the discrepancy between his medium and that of the silent players, but the mime play also dramatizes and reinforces the themes of discrepancy and loss. In the mimes' sketch, Pierrot is punished for thievery by being guillotined on stage. After "struggling and bellowing like a bull approaching a slaughterhouse," he undergoes his fate. His detached head rolls onto the floor, revealing the bloody wound, the severed vertebra, and "all the details of a piece of meat at a butcher shop recently cut up for display." Suddenly, moved by an "irresistible monomania," Pierrot's torso snatches up his head "like a ham or a bottle of wine," thrusts it deep into his pocket, and carries on as before. Pierrot's head loses its seriousness as the seat of intellect and becomes merely another material object to be collected—or consumed. This transformation and degradation recalls the fate of the pagan gods, which became objects of ridicule or fetishes when they lost their religious meaning. But the mime story does not merely repeat the radical cleavage that transforms the sign into a grotesque figure; it relates this metamorphosis to the loss of rational control.

Pierrot's physical comedy embodies the transgression of natural laws. Cut in two, the dead body goes on living, with a mind of its own, as it were, independent of its cranium. Matter, which first seemed as ordinary and natural as beef cattle and ham, now operates like a machine moved by its own laws, which are not those of organic nature. Pierrot's character, his "monomania," continues to find expression in a body without a head. In "death" (which re-

fuses to be a conclusion), Pierrot's body takes over from his mind and continues to inscribe ambiguous gestures in space. The "dead" Pierrot practices automatic writing. Pierrot is not so much a "person" as an automaton, mechanically generating figures without reference to an origin or end.[35] His fate dramatizes the untimely demise of the poetic subject or intentionality that might have controlled this astonishing play. The public's laughter springs from the unsettling shock of this discovery.[36]

Pierrot's story reveals allegory to be a kind of "graphic play"—a runaway form of writing, propelled by and compensating for a fearful loss. Like the spirals of the painted arabesque, allegory is "a rhetorical mode of exuberant representation whose signs, because they can never reach the object they designate, move in random, arbitrary, and extravagant patterns. . . . No coincidence with an origin controls them or keeps their meanings from slipping, blurring, or sliding."[37] The example of the guillotined Pierrot carrying on as if nothing has happened makes a powerful statement about what is at stake in the grotesque. Pierrot's severed head dramatically underscores the anxiety and sense of impotence Baudelaire expresses in his presentation of this exhilarating play.[38]

The example of the English pantomime players exposes the "impersonal force," the "alien and inhuman spirit," that inhabits the productions of the grotesque. The grotesque is not a simple point of origin, an event arising at a single moment in time, or even a narrative—although it is often experienced as "narrative compressed into image" or written out as the history of consecutive moments (before and after, then and now, early and late). Baudelaire himself frequently has recourse to this narrative doubling, as this very example proves. Yet he also insists that the grotesque is "une espèce une, et qui veut être saisie par intuition" ("an indivisible species, which must be grasped by intuition").[39] Pierrot brings out the grotesque's paradoxical character: simultaneously "one" (Pierrot is always and ever "Pierrot" by virtue of his ongoing "monomania"), "double" (the guillotine cuts him in two but leaves him equally "dead" and "alive"), and capable of the endless generation of extraordinary effects.

Neither an object nor an entity, the grotesque cannot serve as a ground or an origin, of which allegory would be the re-presentation or copy. Rather, it is an impersonal force impelling allegory, beyond the reach of the poet's will. The grotesque is the condition of language that makes allegory both the antithesis of representation and a principle of poetry—the "center of poetic play and appearance."[40]

A *"Monstrous Apparatus of Generation"*

Baudelaire's verse poem "Le Masque" (1859) makes a similar point with respect to "an allegorical statue in the Renaissance taste." The poem is of particular relevance to the present study for several reasons. First, by virtue of its stated subject (the allegorical statue in the Renaissance style), it acknowledges the historical link between allegory and the aesthetics of the rococo (considered as the outgrowth or culmination of the Renaissance baroque). Second, as an allegory of allegory, it offers an opportunity to evaluate specifically the difference between allegorical representation and the principle of the grotesque that drives it. And, finally, as a complex series of perpetually regressive layers, it provides further evidence of the temporality of allegory—its structure of perennial belatedness or yearning—which is so important in understanding Baudelaire's relation to Rousseau.

The sculpture the poem describes represents a beautiful woman, whose stunning face turns out to be "un masque, un décor suborneur" ("a mask, a seductive decor") (v. 20). The statue is double: Behind the beautiful features it initially presents to the viewer is a second, "atrociously contorted" face, dissolved in tears (v. 22)—the face of a woman grieving over the tragedies of life, mourning what she has lost. Conforming to the traditional understanding of allegory as a double figure, which points beyond itself to its ultimate object, the statue conveys the lesson that Beauty (or allegory) is a deception, a dressed-up death.[41] For all intents and purposes, Beauty is a grotesque figure.

If we stop with this first idea of the poem as a (paradoxically) literal rendition of allegory, however, we miss its other face. Like the statue, Baudelaire's poem is also double. "Le Masque" recreates the experience of two spectators (the poet-guide and an interlocutor), who discover this "two-headed monster" (v. 19) as they "turn around" it (v. 16). The poem traces their evolving reactions to the immobile figure. During their initial moments of contemplation, when the beautiful face is all they have seen, the poet's friend manifests his unease. Commenting on Beauty's "mocking glance" and her "conquering attitude" (vv. 10, 12), he expresses the sense that the allegorical figure is a threat to her admirers (v. 30). This threat is borne out, but only partially, by the statue's deception.

As they gradually recover from the shock of their discovery, the poet begins to identify with the statue's sorrow. The figure becomes increasingly animated through the poet's interpretation of "her" plight, until the distance between this conquering beauty and her admirers is replaced by the identification that

concludes the poem. Beauty has come down off her pedestal; in the poet's mind "she" is "like us" (v. 36). Unlike his companion, who continues to be impressed by this "perfect beauty" (v. 29), the poet is drawn to the statue's "human" side. This becomes obvious when he domesticates the "monster," separating it into "a lying mask" and "a sincere face" (v. 23). Dismissing the beautiful mask as an ornament or "ruse," he can then recover the security of truth and meaning. He seeks in this way to guarantee the authority of his interpretation. Indeed, his haughty attitude toward his companion, whom he calls "crazy" or "stupid" ("insensé" [v. 32]), effectively silences the other speaker, and the poem concludes with the poet's uncontested statement of the allegory's "true" meaning.

Like the examples of the pagan gods and Pierrot, whose stories involve two sequential moments of perception or understanding, "Le Masque" seems to conform to the received idea of allegory as a double figure that requires two readings, which can be characterized in terms of right and wrong, reason and delusion. Through its vocabulary of truth and lies, of transparency and masks, the poem falls into line with the long-standing view of allegory as a relation between "decor" and ideas, which Angus Fletcher summarizes as follows:

> [I]n allegory there is clearly a disjunction of meanings. *Allegoria* manifestly has two or more levels of meaning, and the apprehension of these must require at least two attitudes of mind. When, for example, one witnessed a court masque with decor by Inigo Jones, one no doubt lavished considerable attention on the mere ornament of the play, on the costumes, the decor, the dancing, the music, and so on, and to shift from this kind of sensuous world to the world of ideas must have engaged a secondary train of thought.[42]

Baudelaire writes out these "two attitudes of mind" as different voices or speakers and thus underscores the duplicity—the doubleness and deceptiveness—implicit in allegory. But in fact the poem, like the story of the comic mime, goes well beyond this dualism.

What it takes some acuity to realize is that the poem undermines the felicitousness of the poet's "true" interpretation, just as the statue destroys the happiness its divine body initially seems to promise (v. 18). The classical ideal of unity and harmony, which applies to texts and their interpretation, just as it does to sculptures, is undone by the difference that is permanently inscribed in—and constitutes—this work of art. This fact becomes clear when we step back from the description of the statue to examine the poem in itself.

The division inherent in the statue finds a counterpart in the poem, in the relationship between the two speakers. Although they are never explicitly named, we identify these two voices as those of the fictional poet and his reader,[43] whose unequal relation is apparent in the poet's high-handed rejection of the reader's ideas. But the poet's consecutive responses to the statue (one blinded, the other supposedly true) do not entirely obscure the reader's reaction, which continues to emphasize the strength and beauty of the statue despite its tears (vv. 29–31). Rather than writing off the beautiful face as a mere mask in order to focus on the statue's "human" qualities and reducing the figure to a single (trite, if pathos-ridden) meaning, the reader sees the figure as a vitiated "whole." He wonders what possible "mal" (illness, defect or evil) could infect allegory from within. We might say that this reader proposes a more comprehensive view of allegory, which takes its forceful beauty into account, in contrast to the poet's humanizing approach, which focuses only on allegory's relation to life and death. The two speakers represent two different and incompatible understandings of the enigmatic figure.

By incorporating the two viewers, who supplement the two faces of the statue and allegorize the experience of reading, the poem sets in motion a second-order phenomenon that invites other interpretations in turn. The two viewers-readers double the allegorical statue's own doubleness and provide for the possibility of yet other readings to come. Their movement in space as they "turn around" the statue—a movement equivalent to our (double) reading of this poem—sets into motion the figural spin through which the immobile statue generates multiple and often contradictory meanings. Like the masks and figurines of antiquity that did not change in and of themselves but became grotesque when they were read differently, "Le Masque" differs from "itself," depending on whether we take it as a (literal) description of an (allegorical) statue, accept it as the "poet"'s (one-sided) interpretation, or view it as a complex work about allegory's (multiple) effects.

By virtue of its own irreconcilable differences, the poem undoes the hierarchical idea of allegory, which opposes a sensuous ornament or decor to the world of ideas.[44] It would be difficult to say with any certainty which of the poem's various aspects is "primary" and which "secondary," according to the traditional idea of the figure. Baudelaire does depict allegory as a "two-headed monster," according to the traditional view of the figure; but he does not subscribe to the traditional understanding of allegory as the opposition of primary and secondary, surface and depth.[45] In "Le Masque," the "poet"'s decision to set aside the mask by labeling it a "ruse" or a "seductive decor" is revealed to

be arbitrary, a deliberate silencing of the "crazy" possibility that allegory is an intrinsically open-ended and uncontrollable figure. In this poem, the grotesque is not one side of the allegorical figure (its distorted or disfigured "face") or even its monstrous "bicephalism," but rather allegory's potential for limitless proliferation, which Richard Stamelman calls "the monstrosity of rhetoric." The grotesque, then, is a name for the constitutive instability of the figure; it opens the text to "an endless succession of interpretations which undo each other. . . . There is no original head which is true once and for all."[46]

As the examples of Pierrot and "Le Masque" show, Baudelaire understands the grotesque as a dynamic and unnamable force of language that regularly wears (allegorical) masks. But these allegorical "faces" can never do more than cover a void, where the grotesque—which is neither a being nor a thing—has never "been." The grotesque is the principle of allegory, its engine or "monstrous apparatus of generation." As an elusive aspect of language that we might call its "play,"[47] the grotesque names the *differance* that constitutes allegory, both its eternal divergence from its (hypothetical) proper meaning and the temporality of desire or bereavement that this divergence institutes. Grotesque figures—signs of modernity for Baudelaire—are always out of synchrony with the present.[48]

Personifying the Grotesque

As a powerful yet intangible force, the grotesque does not yield itself up to direct representation. However, as Baudelaire's examples attest, it is often personified. In their silent play, Pierrot, Arlequin, and Columbine enact language's own surprising turns and unpredictable antics, the very mobility that no written text can directly present. According to Baudelaire, their action is set in motion when the "breath of the marvelous" ("le souffle merveilleux") wafts over the stage and transforms them into zany comic types.[49] Volition is wrested from the players, and they are propelled by an unnamable energy into their new existence ("ils se sentent introduits de force dans une existence nouvelle"). As if by magic, the mimes become different from themselves. The effect is palpable and yet the change itself is imperceptible. The actors' transformation occurs through a strange wrenching, which can only be designated in the airiest or most surreal terms and experienced as dizziness and disorientation.[50] Language has no proper terms to convey the force that affects the performers. (Only vocabulary borrowed from the "marvelous" genres—seventeenth- and

eighteenth-century fairy tales, operas, and other representations of the super-natural—can approximate the unsettling unfamiliarity of the moment.) The subtle metamorphosis that overtakes these "persons" renders the moment when the grotesque takes hold of the sign and whirls the viewer-reader away into a new, irrational world.

Similarly, "Le Masque" describes a statue of a seductive woman who per-sonifies allegory and makes it seem human, just as the poem's own personifi-cations seduce us in turn. Typical interpretations of "Le Masque," which give the full weight of authority to the "poet"'s last words, verify the pull of the per-sonal. The ultimate statement of the statue's "true" meaning is compelling be-cause it simultaneously makes the statue and the poetic voice human. By iden-tifying allegory as a woman and then identifying with the woman's tragic plight, the poetic voice itself takes on human qualities, becoming the more sympathetic (as well as the more authoritative) speaker of the two. The poem catches us up in a proliferating allegory, in which the two sides of the statue are multiplied by the two voices; yet it tempts us to arrest this multiplication by choosing sides and fixing allegory in its most human posture—the posture that makes the figure most "like us." Pretending to stabilize and concretize what is inherently unstable and evanescent, personification claims to make present, lively, and real what has neither presence nor life.

Many different "faces," both beautiful and comic (Venus and Beauty, but also Pan, Priapus, and Pierrot), come to incarnate the grotesque for Baude-laire. In the poems he published between 1859 and 1865, he added yet another face to this list: the figure of "Rousseau." In the nineteenth century, "Rousseau" was both the name of a historical and literary personage (whose work exemplifies a modern, but conflicted, idea of allegory) and a cliché—a conventional sign evoking the cataclysm of the late eighteenth century, the French Revolution. Thanks to Rousseau's reputation as the author whose writ-ings had precipitated and informed the Revolution, the name "Rousseau" had become a metonym for the great social upheaval that post-Revolutionary France wanted either to extend or repress. However, by the time of the coup d'état that instituted the Second Empire in 1852, the name "Rousseau" had lost its heroic aura; to the conservatives in power, it connoted only the worst ex-cesses of the Terror. Thus "Rousseau" was already a degraded figure when Baudelaire adopted "him" for his own ends. Stripped of subjectivity, reduced to a cliché, Baudelaire's "Rousseau" is not the living, breathing man whom many in the eighteenth century revered. Rather, like the pagan gods who be-

came "extravagant fetishes" or "grotesque figures" with the passage of time, "Rousseau" is the fallen idol of an outmoded cult, which Baudelaire's contemporaries had turned into an object of ridicule or revulsion. It is this "Rousseau" that Baudelaire takes up as a ready-made "poncif," or commonplace, in his last poetic works.[51]

In Baudelaire's "Poème du hachisch" and in his prose poetry, "Rousseau" is a caricature of his former self, a sign brought forward from the previous century to stamp the present with its mark—not as an object of intrinsic value, a dense remnant of the past, but rather as a kind of curio, invested with a new and ambivalent meaning by the current age. As a grotesque figure, "Rousseau" does not convey any truth of his era or his own life to his nineteenth-century descendants; instead, he adds to the delineation of the present, as an object of its fascination. "Rousseau" is a kind of collector's item in the nineteenth century, a rather ambiguous fashion of Baudelaire's time.[52]

This book examines how "Rousseau" functions as the grotesque figure or fetish that fascinates Baudelaire. In the "Poème du hachisch" and in the *Petits Poèmes en prose,* Baudelaire utilizes Rousseau's writing as an essential intertext and "Rousseau" as the personification of the grotesque. As I have already suggested, Rousseau's view of the grotesque informs Baudelaire's own. Baudelaire both learns from and contests Rousseau's use of allegory. Whereas Rousseau is acutely aware of, but fights to limit, allegory's unruliness, Baudelaire espouses and occasionally delights in the untamable force of the grotesque. By taking up "Rousseau" as his grotesque figure, then, Baudelaire is both acknowledging Rousseau's formative role in his own poetry and establishing his difference from his predecessor. Thus "Rousseau" is in several ways the "other" of Baudelaire's allegory. Although it goes almost without saying that "[t]he 'other' named by the term *allos* in the word 'allegory' is not some other hovering above the words of the text, but the possibility of an otherness . . . inherent in the very words on the page,"[53] in Baudelaire's prose poetry this otherness is represented by the "person" of "Rousseau." "Rousseau" is simultaneously the pre-text of Baudelaire's allegory, a historical and textual past that Baudelaire's poetry envelops, but with which it can never coincide, and the personification of his poetry's modernity.

Baudelaire's "faces" of allegory reveal the tricks of personification, the ability of an impersonal trope to masquerade as a "human" figure. Like the contemporary performer who puts on an eighteenth-century shawl and makes us forget its stiffness, personification acts out a role and "brings it to life." Yet in its impersonal, mechanical way, it also defies the natural and organic. In

fact, allegory's primary device, personification, kills as it resuscitates, conveying an impression of life to which the chill of death clings. (Thus when Baudelaire evokes the potential resurrection of the past in "Le Peintre de la vie moderne," he observes that it will always have "le piquant du fantôme.") At the intersection of life and death, past and present, personification is at the heart of the modernist dilemma—and, for Baudelaire, "Rousseau" is its principal figure.

2 ∎ *Rococo Rhetoric*

Figures of the Past in "Le Poème du hachisch"

A woman is caught in a gilded cage. It's evening; the setting sun glints off the golden bars that keep her in. She admires the way it illuminates the clear rivers and green landscape surrounding her prison. Brilliant tropical birds fly by, singing an arresting metallic song. Overhead, monkeys frolic and satyrs mock her, while mythological gods smile encouragingly, urging her to be patient. She dreams of Sleeping Beauty in her enchanted woods, of necessary expiations and future deliverance.

The woman is on a drug trip. She's been experimenting with hashish and is spending the night at an old chateau owned by her friends. The room in which she is to sleep is a faded but charming boudoir in an uninhabited section of the building, decorated in the rococo style of the eighteenth century. Her experience of being in a beautiful cage is a drug-induced distortion of the room's arabesque decor. In reality, the boudoir is a narrow little space. At the level of the cornice, the ceiling is rounded off into a vault; the walls are covered with long mirrors, separated by panels of painted landscapes. Running around the room near the ceiling are various allegorical figures, and above them brightly colored birds and flowers ("diverses figures allégoriques, les unes dans des attitudes reposées, les autres courant ou voltigeant. Au-dessus d'elles, quelques oiseaux brillants et des fleurs"). Behind these figures a simulated trellis follows the curve where the walls and the ceiling meet. The room's shape and the ornate gold leaf that covers much of it lend it the air of a distinguished cage for a very large bird. Lying in the center of this space, the intoxicated woman is fascinated by the moonlight on the boudoir's vivid colors, golden

"embroidery" and mirrors ("les lueurs s'accrochaient à toute cette broderie d'or, de miroirs et de couleurs bariolées"). The decor has the magical quality of a fairy kingdom ("ces paysages féeriques . . . ces horizons merveilleux"), and the woman enters fully into the experience of the marvelous, as if she were truly living in an eighteenth-century world.

Her intoxicated state, however, belies this time-travel. The woman is a thoroughly modern inhabitant of nineteenth-century France, whose singular vision is a sign of her participation in the avant-garde world of experimentation with drugs. Drug-taking was decidedly an activity of the artistic elite in mid-nineteenth-century Paris and had no counterpart in the previous century's literature or mores.[1] The confrontation of this woman's modern proclivities and the charmingly outdated aesthetics of her surroundings (their "vieux style" and "vieilles décorations") might be jarring, in fact, if the two worlds were not so seamlessly enmeshed in her hashish high. Instead, the fantasy world elaborated in the rich decor becomes the perfect foil for the fantastic troping of her intoxicated mind. The illusion is so overpowering that, although the woman is first tempted to laugh, she soon finds the "magic" taking on a certain "despotic reality." ("Je riais d'abord de mon illusion; mais plus je regardais, plus la magie augmentait, plus elle prenait de vie, de transparence et de despotique réalité.") No longer just a spectator, she comes to believe that she is at the center of a fantastic drama—Sleeping Beauty herself.[2]

This remarkable narrative stands out among the examples of drug highs that illuminate "Le Poème du hachisch" ("The Poem of Hashish"), the first part of Baudelaire's poetic essay on drugs, *Les Paradis artificiels* (1860).[3] Baudelaire is wonderfully adept at capturing the hallucinations of ordinary men and women under the influence. Like a ravishing decor or a brilliant stage set, the strange and beautiful stories of their drug-induced dreams attract our attention and remain in our minds, leaving the more serious aspects of the essay in the shadows. The extraordinary visual richness of these tales is so captivating that it tends to distract the reader from attending to the moral and aesthetic import of the work as a whole. But the visions are not as ornamental as they seem. In "Le Poème du hachisch," intoxication is a figure for the vertiginous experience of modern poetry, and the visions have much to tell us about Baudelaire's ideas of poetic production and reception in the last decade of his life, the period during which he undertook his most modern poetic project, the *Petits Poèmes en prose*. If the new genre of the prose poem emerged "out of precisely those elements of narrative prose which are . . . often construed as superfluous or merely ornamental digressions,"[4] these dazzling visions constitute

Typical elements of rococo decor: a trellis motif and a gilded cage framing a lady. Painted and sculpted panel from the hôtel Peyrenc de Moras, Paris (detail). Claude III Audran and Nicolas Lancret, 1724.

little prose poems in themselves—prose poems that both reflect on and embody Baudelaire's ideas of modernity.

Viewed in this light, as an early example of Baudelaire's modernist project, the story of the woman in the rococo boudoir is particularly curious. Why does the modern woman's poetic hallucination fuse so easily with the "old style" of the room in which she finds herself? What could be the point of situating a revolutionary new project, a project resolutely positioned in the present, against the backdrop of the rococo aesthetic of the eighteenth century? What do this exemplary anecdote, and the "Poème" that includes it, have to tell us about the temporal basis of modernity and about its supposedly radical innovations? The anecdote points to the conjunction of two seemingly opposite approaches to art—the exciting new ideas of modernity and the dusty remnants of the baroque. It also paves the way for the appearance, in the last chapters of the "Poème," of another eighteenth-century relic, "Jean-Jacques Rousseau," who surfaces as a figure for the "sensitive modern man" under the influence of hashish. Between the description of the rococo decor and this representation of a famous Enlightenment author, the eighteenth century assumes an unexpectedly high profile in one of modernity's founding texts.

The intertwining of these figures of the past with the most modern of all subjects—the recreational use of drugs—is intriguing, partly because Baudelaire seldom alludes to the rococo aesthetic or enlists it as an illustration of his own poetics,[5] but also because contemporary criticism has largely ignored the connection between Baudelaire and his eighteenth-century antecedents.[6] The insistence on Baudelaire's modernity, the literary historical assumption that Baudelaire founded a new kind of poetry around a new worldview, has of course been largely responsible for the discontinuity we perceive. A well-entrenched disdain for the rococo may also account for the scant attention critics have paid to the role of this art in Baudelaire's poetics. Often scorned as mere "decorative allegorism," the rococo is known as the "archaic," "strange," and even "demented" style of France's Ancien Régime.[7] Yet to dismiss Baudelaire's description of the rococo boudoir as mere "decorative allegorism" would be to overlook the crucial analogy between poetry and interior decor of which it is the vehicle. As our reading of the "Poème" will show, this unusual piece on the rococo dramatizes Baudelaire's ideas about poetry's effects. It thus raises many of the questions about modernity and cultural memory that this book attempts to address.

Pictorial Poetics: The Arabesque and the Grotesque in the Eighteenth Century

"Le Poème du hachisch" presents the rococo first and foremost as a visual style, synonymous with the "grotesque" or "arabesque" in art. Baudelaire's interest in the grotesque is well known, and his essay on it, "De l'essence du rire," has entered modern criticism as a seminal text for understanding literary irony.[8] However, like Théophile Gautier and E. T. A. Hoffmann, whose works on the rococo and the grotesque he greatly admired, Baudelaire was especially taken with the grotesque in the *plastic* arts, and this artistic aspect of his grotesque has never really been explored.[9] In "De l'essence du rire," he evokes visual objects from antiquity (masks, bronze figurines, muscular statues of Hercules, pointy-eared little Priapuses with their tongues stuck out)[10] and utilizes examples drawn from the theater to make his point; and even talking about a Hoffmann tale, he calls it "beautiful to see" ("beau à voir").[11] Baudelaire clearly recognizes a connection between visual art (especially the "old style" and "old decoration" of the rococo) and the poetics of modernity, and it therefore seems appropriate to begin this study with a review of the key elements of the pictorial grotesque in the eighteenth century. We shall then be in a position to ask how "Le Poème du hachisch" positions itself relative to this "outmoded" aesthetic. At this point, it may be sufficient to say that both turn around the key concepts of allegory and personification.

The artistic genre known alternately as grotesque or arabesque (or, less often, as Moor-esque, or *moresque*) was practiced in France from the Renaissance to the French Revolution.[12] Because it first proliferated in the sixteenth century, it is sometimes assimilated to the baroque in art. However, new French interpretations of the grotesque, as well as the "new arabesque"'s widespread adoption throughout Europe at the end of the seventeenth and the beginning of the eighteenth century, made this later period the genre's high point.[13]

The eighteenth-century grotesque, like earlier versions, took much of its vocabulary and grammar from the designs written about by the Roman architect Vitruvius and subsequently discovered in the ruins of Nero's palace (the Domus Aurea) and houses at Pompeii. Vitruvius, who disliked what came to be called the "grottesque," thought of it as an "unreal" style. He described it as having no "fixed or regular model. It's all only monsters now; they substitute reeds for columns . . . we see candelabras holding up little temples, from the roofs of which extend delicate, flexible leaves that, against all verisimilitude, bear little figures, some with animal heads, others with human faces, all things

that do not exist, did not exist, and cannot exist."[14] This "free, funny and un-settling painting" ("peinture libre et cocasse"), this "ornament without a name" ("ornement sans nom"),[15] was revived during the Renaissance in France and used extensively in the decoration of François I's palace at Fontainebleau. The fashion grew from there.

André Chastel has pointed out that the grotesque owes its originality to the two laws that govern it: the negation of gravity and the fusion of species ("l'*apesanteur* des formes et la prolifération insolente des *hybrides*"). In a world entirely defined by graphic play ("le jeu graphique"), unnamable figures that are half-vegetable, half-animal spiral into and around each other creating the gracious or tormented curves of the ornament. The play of these figures, unimpeded by any sense of concrete space and unconscious of any distinction or hierarchy of being, gives rise to a feeling of liberation and prompts analogies with the dream-state.[16] Indeed, one sixteenth-century synonym for the grotesque was *sogni dei pittori* (painters' dreams), designating a world characterized by "the dissolution of reality and . . . a different kind of existence."[17] The grotesque refused the demand for verisimilitude (*vraisemblance*), eschewed any regular order or rules, and thus exactly inverted the classical aesthetic that was beginning to take shape in France at the same time.

Although the eighteenth-century arabesques tamed some of this profusion of animal and vegetable life and promoted a more ordered composition, often focused around a single allegorical figure or scene, the genre continued to defy the hegemony of classicism.[18] In designs of the later period, thin stalks of elongated plants still support architectural structures, heads detached from bodies still swing suspended from branches, and fairies, chimeras, and other imaginary fauna still caper playfully throughout. The theatrical traits that Chastel identifies with the older versions of the grotesque also continue to have a prominent part in the interior decors of Claude III Audran (1658–1734), Claude Gillot (1673–1722), Antoine Watteau (1684–1721), and Christophe Huet (1700–1759). Characters from the commedia dell'arte and acrobatic monkeys drawn from the *parades* at the Foire St. Laurent or the Foire St. Germain are regular features of these wall paintings, rendering explicit the grotesque's affiliation with the arts of the spectacle:

> Two models (*patterns*) intervene with a rather striking insistence: acrobatics and the triumph, which introduces [the grottesque] effortlessly into the domain of circus games and buffoonery. The figures lend themselves to contorsions that may make us think of gymnasts elaborating with their bodies

The "theater" of the grotesque, featuring acrobats on a platform or stage. *Grotesques.* Engraving. Jean Berain, ca. 1690–1710.

who knows what decorative curves; and, on the other hand, we see appearing some sort of falsely solemn parades or extravagant processions . . . a rather obvious mockery of the usual street festivals.

The "poetics" of the decor thus became completely explicit. . . . what we might call the *theatrum,* the theatrical play, of the grotesque: a podium, a filiform structure with more than one floor, crowned by an elegant cornice, composes a kind of box for marionnettes where silhouettes are deployed. . . . A miniature spectacle is instituted. . . . An enduring affinity with the "Italian" comedy thus becomes apparent. The grotesque can draw to itself all the visual aspects of buffoonery.[19]

Undergirding this relationship between acrobats, marionettes, theater and the grotesque is the primary concept of the genre: metamorphosis or shape-changing.[20] Mutant vines and hybrid beings lead easily to scenes from Ovid or depictions of Momus and Bacchus, whose names evoke the mind-bending effects of irony and intoxication. Bruno Pons notes: "The arabesque is often associated . . . with drunkenness, if not with artificial paradises; one of the favorite themes is the bacchanalia where goat-footed worshipers and bacchantes get drunk and draw others into their pleasure."[21]

Bacchus, represented under the title *Le Faune*. Wall panel. Antoine Watteau, ca. 1707–8.

Smoke as a form of arabesque. Pierre Bourdon, *Livre premier des essais de gravure* (1703), plate 2. Courtesy, The Winterthur Library: Printed Book and Periodical Collection.

The connection between these ornaments and the human activities with which they were associated is not hard to divine. In the eighteenth century, grotesques formed the backdrop for theatrical performances and costumed balls held in the homes of wealthy aristocrats; they adorned beds and presided over lavish banquets where the wine flowed freely.[22] The style extended to personal objects such as tobacco boxes as well, for the arabesque was often associated with smoking: "In the *Livre premier des essais de gravure* by Pierre Bourdon, we see associated precisely with different ornaments—of which some are destined to decorate tobacco boxes—a man smoking a pipe. The curlicues of smoke are beautiful examples of changing forms that we can associate with an agreeable stupor."[23]

In their *Dictionnaire des arts de peinture, sculpture et gravure* (1792), Claude Watelet and Pierre Lévesque confirm this association between the arabesque and drug-induced lethargy. Reviving the old term for the grotesque, *sogni dei pittori,* they extend the dream analogy to include—apparently for the first time—the effects of opium:

[O]ne can only find probable models in the chimeras produced by sleep.
Arabesques can thus be called the dreams of Painting.

Reason and taste require that they not be the dreams of sick people, but
reveries similar to those that opium, in artistic doses, procures for voluptuous Orientals, who prefer them sometimes to less chimerical errors.[24]

From role-playing and dreams to drinking and drug-taking, the arabesque's
themes have in common the elements of illusion and illogic, the escape from
the world of the here-and-now to a world no longer governed by nature's laws
and man's conscious control. It is not surprising that critics have also linked
the genre to madness. As Pons argues, the arabesque brings together strange
apparitions and fleeting impressions that the mind and memory can scarcely
seize hold of, for the apparent logic we think we perceive in these works takes
a crazy turn when we try to understand it.[25] This is why critics like Vitruvius,
Watelet, and more recently Wolfgang Kayser, have found the genre more than
a little unsettling.[26] The grotesque can "make us feel as if the ground beneath
our feet were about to give way; . . . order is destroyed and an abyss opened
where we thought to rest on firm ground."[27]

The Grotesque in "Le Poème du hachisch"

The themes and forms that distinguish the eighteenth-century grotesque
find many an echo in Baudelaire's *Paradis artificiels,* especially in the work's
first part, the "Poème du hachisch" (the only part Baudelaire created in toto).
As I have already begun to suggest, the themes of the painterly grotesque (intoxication, theatricality, metamorphosis, the dream state, fusion of worlds, and
the absence of clear hierarchies) are also the themes of the "Poème," and even
its shape is reminiscent of the pictorial style.

Just as a rococo wall painting typically encloses an allegorical figure or
tableau within a proscenium arch or an overarching bower, the "Poème" too
proclaims its own circular, self-contained structure, framing a central motif.
The last paragraph of the text (in chapter 5 of the "Poème") explicitly refers
back to the beginning of the work, with the narrator's statement that "Con-
clure, c'est fermer un cercle" ("To conclude is to close a circle"). The narrator
then reprises some of the statements with which he opened the "Poème."
These retrospective remarks encourage the reader to compare the first and last
chapters, where the narrator sets out two different visions of poetry and poetic
creation. Taken together, these chapters make it clear that, although "Le

Poème du hachisch" is ostensibly a straightforward meditation on the physical properties, delusional effects, and moral connotations of hashish, it is also an exploration of poetry, its creation and its effects. (The title itself suggests as much. If the poem "about" (*du*) hashish is also a poem "engendered by" (*du*) hashish, then reflections about the drug are simultaneously reflections about poetic production.)

In its first and last chapters, the "Poème" posits a poetic ideal, a "paradise," a "garden of true beauty," the only "miracle" over which man has God-given power.[28] This miracle is a creation in which the poet's moral judgment (*sens moral*) balances or checks his powerful imagination and in which his intended meaning (*sens moral*) is transparent or clear.[29] The ideal poem bears the stamp of Christian values, such as hierarchy (subservience to God's will and creation), order or balance (especially the control of the imagination and the senses), and clarity (of meaning and purpose). It conforms to conservative, or classical, norms. The first and last chapters also point up the opposite of this Christian ideal: that is, the dubious, demonic pursuit of an *artificial* "paradise." A shortcut approach to creation, this involves the use of intoxicating substances to avoid the hard work and effort of will that should ideally undergird creativity, and the narrator assimilates it to the folly of replacing "solid furniture and real gardens with decors painted on canvas and mounted on [moveable] frames [*des décors peints sur toile et montés sur châssis*]." We recognize it as the illusory, theatrical ideal associated with the woman in the rococo boudoir. This opposition between the two "paradises" structures the "Poème," and in presenting it, the first and last chapters "Le Goût de l'infini" ("The Taste for the Infinite") and "Morale" ("Moral") frame the middle three.[30]

Within this outer frame, chapters 2 and 4 also form a pair, sharing a "scientific" bias, as well as an emphasis on definition and analysis. The title of the second chapter, "Qu'est-ce que le hachisch?" ("What Is Hashish?"), calls for a definition, which the chapter duly gives; and the narrator explicitly states that his objective in the fourth chapter, "L'Homme-Dieu" ("The Man-God"), is to "define and analyze" the psychological and moral effects of drugs on a carefully chosen scientific subject. Only the doubly framed central chapter, "Le Théâtre du Séraphin," stands apart. Not only is it not paired with another chapter, but in the exemplary story of the woman in the rococo boudoir, it develops an elaborate allegory for the experience of poetry. Although the woman explicitly wonders whether her hallucinations resemble "the enthusiasm of poets,"[31] her reaction to the golden "embroidery" and allegorical figures around her—her progressive surrender to the "despotic reality" of the ornate decor—is simul-

Doubly framed scenes of metamorphosis. Painted panels, Montagu House, London. Charles de Lafosse, Jacques Rousseau, Jean-Baptiste Monnoyer, and Jacques Parmentier, from a design by Daniel Marot, ca. 1690. Courtesy, Boughton House, The Duke of Buccleuch and Queensbury.

taneously an extended metaphor (or allegory) for the reader's own relationship to this text. The woman may assimilate her "poetic delirium" to the poet's creative high, but she is also experiencing the poetic effects of the ornate decor as she enters into the artful realm of the rococo, where rhetoric is rewritten as visual ornament and tropes are disguised as tropical birds (*les oiseaux brillants des tropiques*). With its thoroughly allegorical character and its emphasis on theater (including the reference in its title to a popular marionette theater founded in the eighteenth century),[32] this chapter resembles the theatrically staged and framed allegories of metamorphosis so common in the eighteenth century's painted grotesques.[33]

Given these arabesque features—the circular structure of the "Poème" and its double frame surrounding a central allegory—it is reasonable to wonder whether Baudelaire deliberately chose the subject, hashish, for its associations with the Arab world. When the narrator of the "Poème" repeatedly cites hashish's Arab origins in discussing the drug's provenance and uses (in chapter 2), the connection hardly seems coincidental.[34] Under the cover of a factual presentation (including dosages in grams and centigrams), the narrator manages to assert the "Arab-esque" filiation so often that it becomes one of the chapter's primary themes. We are reminded that, although French eighteenth-century grotesque paintings do not often evoke comparison with Arab art, some commentators of the period considered *grotesque*, *arabesque*, and *Mooresque* (or *moresque*) to be synonymous terms.[35]

But this pictorial resemblance is neither the only nor the most important link of the "Poème" to the painted grotesque. Judging from its reception history, the "Poème" is a text that confounds its readers, who find it maddening, if not rather mad. Their comments point to the problem of distinguishing figure from ground in the "Poème"—that is, ascertaining whether there is any ground at all on which to base an interpretation. For example, as critics regularly note, the text puts forward two divergent attitudes toward drugs, hesitating between the moral condemnation of hashish as inimical to the production of poetry and the seductive portrayal of the drug's poetic effects. Alexandra Wettlaufer cogently sums up the problem: "While ostensibly preaching the evils of opium and hashish, the author presents and even reproduces these states of intoxication in vivid and evocative detail, and while adamantly denying any points of intersection between the supernatural experiences of drugs and of art, his text creates a striking set of parallels between the two states."[36]

On a first reading, however, the problem may not be particularly apparent. The poet presents himself as a stable authority figure, an analyst and a moral-

ist (or ironist), who guides the reader firmly through the alternating "artistic" and "scientific" chapters of the "Poème." Although he presents numerous poetic anecdotes of drug hallucinations, he retains his position as a distant observer and wise commentator throughout, and there is little positive evidence to suggest that he has himself experienced any of the effects he describes. Furthermore, what I am calling the "scientific" chapters of the "Poème" seem to provide the very ground of which we speak. The second chapter, which matter-of-factly discusses the composition and typical doses of the drug and reviews the inconclusive experiments by the pharmacologists Smith, Gastinel, and Decourtive, provides a very literal basis against which to measure the figural excursions that make up "Le Théâtre du Séraphin," for example. And the fourth chapter, which proposes a pseudo-scientific experiment of its own, analyzing a fictional drug-taker's reactions to hashish, concludes with the narrator's very ironic description of the intoxicated subject's "monomania," and thus further reinforces his stable—negative—point of view. Firmly grounded by these reference points, a first reading of the "Poème" might well suggest that this is nothing more or less than a text condemning drug use. And yet, as critics repeatedly emphasize, the poetic, or figural, dimension of the work tends to overwhelm the rest.

As we have already seen, the "Poème" has an allegorical dimension, in which drugs and the experience of drugs serve as an extended metaphor for poetic production and reception. Once the topos of drug-taking is understood as a pretext for a discussion of poetics, the whole "Poème" becomes allegorical, and even its most literal chapters take on a new figural meaning. Furthermore, the circular structure of the "Poème" urges us to return to the beginning and reread, and this second reading, coming after the discovery of the central allegory, transforms our comprehension of the text.[37] In order to understand the "Poème" at this figural level, we must first analyze how allegory functions here—how it comes to overrun its frame and play such a dominant role.

Allegory, or the Indistinction of Figure and Ground

Allegory is the feature that most closely connects the visual and the literary forms of the grotesque—and in the "Poème," as we shall see, it logically leads to Rousseau. Because it sets into motion the dizzying indistinction of figure and ground, allegory is responsible for the difficulty of reading this text. It is therefore appropriate that the role and operations of allegory are primarily conveyed through two important figures for the reader: the woman in the rococo

boudoir and the "sensitive modern man" whom the narrator-poet ultimately conflates with "Rousseau."

The woman's positioning as a figure for the reader is the culmination of a process at work throughout the central chapter of the "Poème," "Le Théâtre du Séraphin." Reading is an important theme in the chapter, which opens with the naïve fictional reader of the "Poème" plying urbane consumers of hashish with questions. To quiet this impatient fellow and tame his fantasies, the narrator proposes to take him on a trip of his own—not a literal drug high, but a vicarious drug trip made possible by the stories the narrator recounts. The narrator positions the fictional reader before his narrative as if the reader (and, by extension, we) were about to take a drug:

> Voici la drogue [ou le "Poème"] sous vos yeux. . . . Vous pouvez avaler sans crainte; on n'en meurt pas. Vos organes physiques n'en recevront aucune atteinte. Plus tard peut-être un trop fréquent appel au sortilège diminuera-t-il la force de votre volonté, peut-être serez-vous moins homme que vous ne l'êtes aujourd'hui; mais le châtiment est si lointain, et le désastre futur d'une nature si difficile à définir! Que risquez-vous? . . . Ainsi c'est dit. . . . Vous êtes maintenant suffisamment lesté pour un long et singulier voyage. La vapeur a sifflé, la voilure est orientée, et vous avez sur les voyageurs ordinaires ce curieux privilège d'ignorer où vous allez. Vous l'avez voulu; vive la fatalité! (Baud., *OC*, 1: 409–10)

> Here is the drug [or the "Poème"] before your eyes. . . . You can swallow without fear; you won't die from it. Your physical organs will not receive any damage. Later on perhaps a too frequent recourse to the magic may diminish the force of your will, perhaps you will be less of a man than you are today; but the punishment is so far off, and the future disaster so difficult to define! What do you risk? . . . So the word is said. . . . You are now sufficiently ballasted for a long and singular voyage. The whistle has blown, the sails are hoisted, and you have the curious advantage over ordinary travellers of not knowing where you are going. You have desired it; long live fate![38]

If the experience of the stories is tantamount to a drug "trip," then the anecdotes of various drug highs that punctuate the text are so many *mises-en-abyme* of our reading. The narratives foster or enable our metaphorical voyage, just as the extraordinary decor—the tropical birds and allegorical figures of the rococo boudoir—prompts the woman's time-travel. Indeed, the narrator underscores the importance of the right "milieu" for our experience: "Si,

toutes ces conditions préalables observées, le temps est beau, si vous êtes situé dans un milieu favorable, comme un paysage pittoresque ou *un appartement poétiquement décoré,* si de plus vous pouvez espérer un peu de musique, alors tout est pour le mieux" ("If all these preliminary conditions having been observed, the weather is beautiful, if you are located in a favorable environment, such as a picturesque landscape or *a poetically decorated apartment,* if in addition you can hope for a little music, then all is for the best").[39] If the right decor—or text—promotes the best possible drug—or reading—high, then the woman's reaction to the rococo boudoir is a protracted metaphor for the reader's own "hallucinatory" experience of this text.[40]

Similarly, at the outset of chapter 4, the poet provides another figure for the reader, "a single fictional character" purposely created to serve as the subject of the poet's pseudo-scientific observations about hashish's effects.[41] He calls this fictional character a "sensitive modern man," someone "analogue à ce que le XVIIIe siècle appelait l'*homme sensible,* à ce que l'école romantique nommait l'*homme incompris,* et à ce que les familles et la masse bourgeoise flétrissent généralement de l'épithète d'*original*" ("analogous to what the eighteenth century called l'*homme sensible,* to what the romantic school named l'*homme incompris,* and to what families and the bourgeoisie generally damn with the epithet *original*")—and indeed he later assimilates him to "Jean-Jacques [Rousseau]." The poet then imagines how this man would react if pushed to an extreme by the drug. Before his study has progressed very far, however, the poet collapses his fictional character and the reader into one: "If you are one of these souls," he begins,[42] and throughout the rest of the paragraph, he addresses himself to "you." This brief apostrophe is sufficient to establish the connection between the reader and his surrogate. The sensitive man suffering from the effects of hashish takes his place alongside the intoxicated woman in "Le Théâtre du Séraphin" as a figure for the reader's experience.

As if to confirm this similarity, the poet begins his "scientific" experiment by placing his intoxicated man in a room that recalls the rococo boudoir: fleshy nymphs gaze out from the room's painted ceiling, characters from antiquity seem to exchange confidences with the viewer, and the sinuous lines of the room's arabesques constitute "a perfectly clear language in which you read the agitation and the desire of souls" ("la sinuosité des lignes est un langage définitivement clair où vous lisez l'agitation et le désir des âmes"). Making explicit the function of the rococo boudoir to which it is analogous, the poet forthrightly presents this room as a text, or more precisely, an allegory: "ce genre si *spirituel,* que les peintres maladroits nous ont accoutumés à mépriser,

mais qui est vraiment l'une des formes primitives et les plus naturelles de la poésie" ("that ever so *spiritual* genre, which awkward painters have accustomed us to regard with scorn, but which is truly one of the primitive and most natural forms of poetry"). In this allegorical setting, he goes on to explain the mechanics of allegory and so prepares us to understand the operation of his own "Poème."

According to the poet, allegory discovers its "rightful dominion" in the "intoxicated mind" ("l'allégorie . . . reprend sa domination légitime dans l'intelligence illuminée par l'ivresse"), where it enriches and enlivens whatever it touches. In the theater, for example, allegory allows dance, gesture or declamation to take on an unexpected "glory"; and through its mediation, music, "another language," becomes a meaningful poem for its listener. Thanks to allegorical personification, even the driest sentence in a book comes alive: "La grammaire, l'aride grammaire elle-même, devient quelque chose comme une sorcellerie évocatoire; les mots ressuscitent revêtus de chair et d'os, le substantif, dans sa majesté substantielle, l'adjectif, vêtement transparent qui l'habille et le colore comme un glacis, et le verbe, ange du mouvement, qui donne le branle à la phrase" ("Grammar, even arid grammar, becomes something like an evocative witchcraft; words resuscitate clothed in flesh and bone, the noun, in its substantial majesty, the adjective, transparent garment that clothes it and colors it like a glaze, and the verb, angel of movement, that sets the sentence in motion").

If allegory betokens a state of mind that disposes the reader to enter into the text and become one with it, this disposition is promoted by personification, which brings language to life—"les mots ressuscitent revêtus de chair et d'os . . . le poème entier [est] un dictionnaire doué de vie" ("words resuscitate clothed in flesh and bone . . . the entire poem [is] a dictionary endowed with life").[43] It is obviously this liveliness that the poet seeks to create by presenting allegorical figures like the woman in the rococo boudoir and the "modern sensitive man" to act as proxies for the reader. They bring the abstract or scientific discussion of drug effects down to a concrete level of personal experience with which the reader can identify. As figures of rhetoric, they transport the reader into their fictional world.

As elaborate allegories of poetic production and reception, based on the analogy between poetry and the rococo decor, the anecdotes of the intoxicated woman and her male counterpart are proof and explanation of allegory's central role in the "Poème." From these important passages, we understand that "hashish" and "intoxication" are code words for allegory, and that the "Poème

du hachisch" is an allegorical exposition of how allegory works—a theory and its practical demonstration rolled into one. By getting his allegory of the "sensitive man" off to a start with an explanation of allegory's operations, the poet gives the real readers of the "Poème" the tools we need to read (or reread) it. Although he claims that allegory finds its ideal home in the "intoxicated" mind, the narrator as poetic analyst or "scientist" apparently wants us to see and understand the "drug" we are taking before it has us under its spell. Once the drug has its way, we will be in no position to notice. Ignoring the difference between our everyday existence and the lives of fictional characters, just as the woman in the rococo boudoir believed that she was "the center of a fantastic drama," we too shall enter the realm of fiction. Intoxication or allegory effaces difference and bridges the abyss of time, allowing the reader (the nineteenth-century "drug-taker" or his twenty-first-century counterpart) to enter fully into an earlier life. Like a reverie or a painted grotesque, allegory correlates and fuses disparate states of being, entities, and eras into a single composition.[44]

In fact, the examples show that allegory has the tendency to draw everything into itself, as when the woman acknowledges that her vision "frequently absorbed all my other thoughts." Allegory is so pervasive that, even when the woman comes out of the drug high and feels a "prosaic satisfaction" ("une satisfaction prosaïque") at taking up her "real life" again ("je me suis enfin sentie chez moi, dans mon chez moi intellectuel, je veux dire dans la vie réelle"), she is still an allegorical figure. By virtue of the very idea that she has a "real life" outside the hallucinatory state of intoxication, she continues to function as a figure for the reader and thus blurs the boundary between fiction and reality, poetry and prose.

This tendency for allegory to spread itself out over all the parts of a narrative, even those that appear the most literal or real, accounts for the "monomania" that is the subject of this fourth chapter of the "Poème." Under the effects of the "drug," the "sensitive man"'s self-aggrandizement culminates in his taking himself for "God." This allegorical figure, the "modern sensitive man,"

se fait bientôt centre de l'univers . . . il devient l'expression vivante et outrée du proverbe qui dit que la passion rapporte tout à elle. . . . Tous les objets environnants sont autant de suggestions qui agitent en lui un monde de pensées, toutes plus colorées, plus vivantes, plus subtiles que jamais, et revêtues d'un vernis magique. (Baud., *OC,* 1: 436)

soon makes himself the center of the universe . . . he becomes the living and exaggerated expression of the proverb that says that passion relates every-

thing back to itself. . . . All the surrounding objects are so many suggestions that arouse in him a world of thoughts, all more colored, more living, more subtle than ever, and covered with a magic varnish.

The allegorical man has become the center of the textual universe. As the "living" and "exaggerated" expression of a proverb, he draws to himself all the rest of the textual material and infuses it with his allegorical "life." All the attributes, including the accoutrements and even the thoughts, of the personified figure are part of the allegory too.

Allegory expands in the manner of hyperbole until it encompasses the whole text. This is what the narrator means when he evokes the "monstrous growth of time and space," "that abnormal and tyrannical growth" ("accroissement monstrueux du temps et de l'espace," "cet accroissement anormal et tyrannique") that applies to all the "man-God's" feelings and all his ideas. This exposition of allegory's "monomania" prepares and explains what happens during the "second" reading of the "Poème," when the central allegory overruns its bounds to infuse the rest of the text with a new, figural meaning.[45] Allegory upsets the usual hierarchies and blurs the distinction between figure and ground.[46]

Errant Figures: "Le Thyrse"

Allegory's tyranny is such that it not only causes the reader to forget the reality of his life (transforming "man" into "God") but also threatens to overpower the poet as well, and this is another reason why it is blameworthy. Allegory has the propensity to exceed the poet's intentions and take away his control. Baudelaire's prose poem "Le Thyrse" ("The Thyrsus") gives a pointed example of the problem and underscores its relation to the arabesque. The poem describes the double composition of the Bacchic wand (the thyrsus), made up of a staff around which stems and flowers twine "in capricious meanderings" (my translation). The staff, the poet explains, is the artist's will, straight and sure; the sinuous flowers with their arabesque lines are the various rhetorical means at the artist's disposal for expressing his intention: "Ligne droite et ligne arabesque, intention et expression, roideur de la volonté, sinuosité du verbe, unité du but, variété des moyens, amalgame tout-puissant et indivisible du génie, quel analyste aura le détestable courage de vous diviser et de vous séparer?" ("Straight line and arabesque line, intention and expression, tautness of the will, sinuosity of the word, unity of goal, variety of means, allpowerful and indivisible amalgam of genius, what analyst would have the

hateful courage to divide and to separate you?").[47] "Le thyrse," as a metaphor for poetry, represents the fusion of the poem's elements into a single, indivisible whole.

But having asserted the unity of will and expression in art, the poet repeatedly raises questions that tend to undermine the indivisibility of this "all-powerful amalgam." What if the rhetorical arabesque is not subordinate to the will, does not dance around it in "mute adoration"? What if the decorative ornament proliferates on its own, independent of the poet's intention? The unanswered questions in the poem make us aware of the anxiety allegory can arouse. The questions point to the threat posed by allegory's proliferation and raise the moral issue implied in allegory's deviation from the straight and narrow course set out by the poet's will:

> Ne dirait-on pas que la ligne courbe et la spirale font leur cour à la ligne droite et dansent autour dans une muette adoration? Ne dirait-on pas que toutes ces corolles délicates, tous ces calices, explosions de senteurs et de couleurs, exécutent un mystique fandango autour du bâton hiératique? Et quel est, cependant, le mortel imprudent qui osera décider si les fleurs et les pampres ont été faits pour le bâton, ou si le bâton n'est que le prétexte pour montrer la beauté des pampres et des fleurs?

> Doesn't it seem that the curved and spiral lines are courting the straight line and dance around it in mute adoration? Doesn't it seem that all those delicate corollas, all those calices, explosions of odors and colors, are executing a mystical fandango around the hieratic staff? And yet what foolhardy mortal would dare decide if the flowers and vines were formed for the staff, or if the staff is but the pretext for highlighting the beauty of the vines and flowers?

The poet's fear of discovering his own impotence comes through clearly in his questions. Although he begins by assuming the subordination of rhetoric to meaning, he quickly loses his assurance. Evoking the "foolhardy mortal" who would try to impose a hierarchy on language, he seems to shrink from this risk.[48]

Yet, ultimately, the poet does unfold the meaning of his figure. Even as he suggests that it would be nearly impossible and certainly unseemly to do so, he takes the figure apart, in an act apparently intended to demonstrate his power over the rhetoric he puts into play. However, in the perverse fulfillment of his own subtle prophecy, his masterful analysis of the figure's many levels of meaning exposes the figure's tendency to spiral away from his control: The thyrsus is a "sacerdotal emblem" of the Bacchic priests and priestesses, who represent

the poet celebrating Beauty, incarnated here by the musician Liszt, who wields his "thyrsus" (or genius) with more "capriciousness" than any nymph and "improvises" songs in "the eternal city's splendors or the mists of the dreamy lands consoled by Cambrinus [the inventor of beer]." One can imagine the list of metaphors going on and on "capriciously." With every layer of figural meaning he exposes, the poet points up the figure's potential for endless meandering. By reinforcing the idea that the thyrsus is a "metaphor of metaphor," he contributes to the "peculiar vertigo" inherent in the figure's self-reflexiveness. As Richard Klein notes, "only when the figure has been elaborately extended, does it circle round and point obliquely to its own development. Which suggests that . . . all metaphor, if sufficiently extended [as in allegory], tends constantly to displace its center and to lose itself in the self-generating play of its spinning periphery."[49] The poem's references to Bacchus and Cambrinus prefigure these disorienting results.

In the "Poème du hachisch," the poet faces a similar threat. Describing how allegory's tendrils extend their grasp ever wider, in a tyrannical bid to encompass everything, he is careful to maintain a visible hold over his allegorical creation, reiterating that the intoxicated "sensitive man" is "mon homme supposé, l'esprit de mon choix" ("my man, the mind of my own choosing"), a fictional character he has created in order to "rendre mon analyse plus claire" ("make my analysis clearer"). He distinguishes himself from this specimen the way a lab technician might observe with detachment a culture that he has cultivated in a petrie dish: "J'assiste à son raisonnement comme au jeu d'un mécanisme sous une vitre transparente" ("I observe his reasoning as I would the play of a mechanism under a transparent glass")—a method in keeping with his objective to "définir et analyser le ravage moral causé par cette dangereuse et délicieuse gymnastique" ("define and analyze the psychological and moral damage caused by these dangerous and delicious gymnastics").

But the very emphasis on analysis, which suggests a poet in full control, becomes less convincing when his scientific object—the intoxicated "sensitive man"—begins to use the same language of analysis and judgment as his creator. The poet imagines his "man" converting feelings of remorse into one more source of narcissistic self-satisfaction and quotes him as saying:

Cette action ridicule, lâche ou vile, dont le souvenir m'a un moment agité, est en complète contradiction avec ma vraie nature, ma nature actuelle, et l'énergie même avec laquelle je la condamne, le soin inquisitorial avec lequel *je l'analyse et je la juge,* prouvent mes hautes et divines aptitudes pour la

vertu. Combien trouverait-on dans le monde d'hommes aussi habiles pour se juger, aussi sévères pour se condamner? (Baud., *OC*, 1: 435; my emphasis)

This ridiculous, cowardly or vile action, the memory of which made me momentarily agitated, is in complete contradiction with my true nature, my real nature, and the very energy with which I condemn it, the inquisitorial care with which *I analyze and judge it,* prove my lofty and divine aptitude for virtue. How many men would you find in the world as capable of judging themselves, as severe in condemning themselves?

When the scrutinized object speaks the same language as the observer-creator, the sanitary distance between them begins to vanish. As we have seen, the poet, too, wants to suggest that his "true nature" is "inquisitorial," that he judges, condemns, and thus separates himself from the drug-takers whose examples he puts before us. He is an ironist, capable of self-knowledge in a way he believes his "sensitive man" is not. But despite the poet's precautions, the difference he seeks to establish proves elusive. When the "sensitive man" shows that analysis can be a tool of narcissistic self-aggrandizement and is not confined to the practice of scientific detachment and objectivity, the clear demarcation between the poet's rational analysis and the sensitive man's delirium begins to blur. In the end, the poet's ironic condemnation of the "man-God" comes to apply to him too, as we shall see.

"Morale"

At the end of chapter 4, the poet conflates his sensitive man with "Jean-Jacques" and lambastes him for confusing dreams and action, mistaking ideas of virtue for virtue itself, and decreeing his own apotheosis:

[L'homme sensible] confond complètement le rêve avec l'action, et son imagination s'échauffant de plus en plus devant le spectacle enchanteur de sa propre nature corrigée et idéalisée, substituant cette image fascinatrice de lui-même à son réel individu, si pauvre en volonté, si riche en vanité, il finit par décréter son apothéose en ces termes nets et simples, qui contiennent pour lui tout un monde d'abominables jouissances: *"Je suis le plus vertueux de tous les hommes!"*

Cela ne vous fait-il pas souvenir de Jean-Jacques, qui, lui aussi, après s'être confessé à l'univers, non sans une certaine volupté, a osé pousser le même cri de triomphe . . . avec la même sincérité et la même conviction? L'enthousiasme avec lequel il admirait la vertu, l'attendrissement nerveux

qui remplissait ses yeux de larmes, à la vue d'une belle action ou à la pensée de toutes les belles actions qu'il aurait voulu accomplir, suffisaient pour lui donner une idée superlative de sa valeur morale. Jean-Jacques s'était enivré sans hachisch. (Baud., *OC*, 1: 436)

[The sensitive man] completely confuses dreams with action, and his imagination warming more and more before the enchanting spectacle of his own corrected and idealized nature, substituting this fascinating image of himself for his real self, so poor in willpower, so rich in vanity, he ultimately decrees his own apotheosis in these clear and simple terms, which contain for him a whole world of abominable pleasures: "*I am the most virtuous of men!*"

Doesn't that remind you of Jean-Jacques, who also, after having confessed to the universe, not without a certain voluptuousness, dared to give the same triumphal cry . . . with the same sincerity and the same conviction? The enthusiasm with which he admired virtue, the nervous tenderness that filled his eyes with tears at the sight of a beautiful action or at the thought of all the beautiful actions he would have liked to perform, was sufficient to give him a superlative idea of his moral worth. Jean-Jacques got high without hashish.

The sensitive man's (or "Jean-Jacques"'s) narcissism, with its blasphemous connotations, provokes the narrator's sarcasm. Damning his "man"'s deluded belief that he has "become God," the narrator charges that this "deplorable" creature would never be susceptible to the inference that there's "another God" and would certainly not defer to Him. These scathing attacks lay the basis for the "Morale" of the last chapter, where the poet-analyst explains at length the moral basis for his critique.

Chapter 5 brings out the moral dichotomy that subtends the opposition of the "artificial" and "real" poetic paradises. The poet-analyst condemns the passive, voluptuous enjoyment of "drugs" and praises the hard work and willpower involved in genuine poetic creation. According to the narrator, the drug-taker's egocentrism and the passivity it entails cause him to lose his freedom. "Hashish" vitiates the will, "de toutes les facultés la plus précieuse" ("the most precious of all the faculties"). Under the drug's spell, the man is caught up in his dreams and unable to take action in the world; the poet cannot summon the determination to write. Like "magic and witchcraft," allegory, the "drug," interferes with God's intentions;[50] it obliterates "the harsh accent of reality and the disorder of external life."[51] As long as it operates, the real world that requires us to make decisions, invoke our will, and confess our sins does not exist. This is its danger. The irony of allegory is that it builds upon but

completely ignores the disproportion between itself and the environment that surrounds it.[52] Allegory masquerades as a totality capable of taking over the world, while the world it seeks to control is in ruins. Only when time intervenes, "the next day" ("le lendemain! le terrible lendemain!"), when the intoxicated individual wakes up after the orgy, can she or he assess "hideous nature, stripped of its illumination of the night before" and see the "melancholy debris of [the] party."[53] For these moral reasons, the "Poème" ends with the narrator extolling the values of willpower, hard work ("l'exercice assidu de la volonté"), and intentionality ("la noblesse permanente de l'intention") as the only legitimate, moral means to achieve the poetic ideal, the "garden of true beauty."

The "Poème" appears to end where it begins—with the poet's praise of the true poetic paradise, the classical ideal. The apparent decisiveness and authority of this conclusion are opened to question, however, by the figures and style the poet puts into play. Although he propounds a work of art in which imagination, moral judgment ("sens moral"), and meaning ("sens moral") are well balanced, in the last paragraph of the "Poème," he reverts to a vocabulary and a stance familiar to the reader from the chapters on allegory.

After rejecting the recourse to "la pharmacie et la sorcellerie" as an aid to genius, the poet paints a picture of artistic success that could serve as an allegorical frontispiece to *Les Paradis artificiels* itself. In this tableau "a man (a brahman, a poet or a Christian philosopher)" stands on Mount Olympus, gazing down on the mass of humanity in the mud and brush below. This "man" represents the superiority of the sagacious artist who has preferred hard work to "black magic" as a means of attaining paradise. Muses dance around him, looking at him with loving eyes and brilliant smiles, while Apollo plays his lyre in accompaniment: "un homme (dirai-je un brahmane, un poète, ou un philosophe chrétien?) placé sur l'Olympe . . . ; autour de lui les Muses . . . le regardent avec leurs plus doux yeux et leurs sourires les plus éclatants; le divin Apollon . . . caresse de son archet ses cordes les plus vibrantes." Except for the boudoir setting, which is missing here, the scene is reminiscent of the woman's intoxicated vision, in which "toutes les divinités mythologiques me regardaient avec un charmant sourire, comme pour m'encourager à supporter patiemment le sortilège" ("all the mythological gods looked at me with a charming smile, as if to encourage me to bear up patiently under this magic spell"). Both the poet and the woman fantasize that they are at the center of a world of delights, in which the gods look upon them approvingly. Despite the Christian frame of this last chapter, the poet's mythological tableau does not represent the

Christian world in which hard work (or its opposite) may be rewarded by election or damnation; rather, it is an ego-gratifying image, a narcissistic ideal.

This is the type of vision that the poet excoriated in his ironic remarks on the "man-God," and that he found lacking in moral depth in the intoxicated woman's story: "le tempérament féminin, qui est peu propre à l'analyse, ne lui a pas permis de noter le singulier caractère optimiste de ladite hallucination. Le regard bienveillant des divinités de l'Olympe est poétisé par un vernis essentiellement hachischin" ("the feminine temperament, which is not well suited to analysis, did not allow her to notice the singularly optimistic character of [her] hallucination. The benevolent gaze of the gods of Olympus is poeticized by an essentially hashish-induced veneer"). In this last chapter of the "Poème," however, the poet is indulging in the same kind of optimistic fantasy. Significantly, he gives up all use of the vocabulary of analysis in these last pages, in favor of an emphasis on figuration. (The verb *se figurer* recurs here with the frequency of a refrain.)[54] His imagination is getting the better of his rational—and moral—judgment.

Despite the poet's multiple references in chapter 5 to the authority of religion and the postulation of a unique truth that will anchor language and stabilize values, the last page of the "Poème" is equivocal, as Michel Jeanneret points out:

> Into the very midst of this edifying line of argument is insinuated the reference to another paradise, which is not that of religion, but of poetry. As the antithesis of the hashish user, the narrator imagines *an allegorical character*—"a man (shall I say a brahman? a poet, or a Christian philosopher?)"—a strangely composite figure, where the spiritual vocation and the practice of art appear interchangeable. . . . A significant slippage: religion is no longer vigorous enough to place an absolute norm in opposition to the wanderings of the subject, and it is another ideal that, surreptitiously, takes over: writing.[55]

Jeanneret's perceptive comments highlight the reintroduction, at the moment when drugs are vehemently condemned, of the very rhetorical figure so prominently associated with drugs in "Le Théâtre du Séraphin" and "L'Homme-Dieu." In this poem, allegory is the trope of hallucination and narcissism; it's the "magic" or "witchcraft" that transforms the subject into a "god." Bound up as it is with the drugs the narrator now condemns, it should by rights be dismissed, together with the drug experience. Therefore its persistence in the last paragraph of the "Poème," with its florid style and overt

rhetoricity, leaves the moral and aesthetic lesson of the "Poème" oddly in doubt. As Jeanneret convincingly argues, "the poet does not reject the fantastic visions of the drug; he integrates them and goes beyond them. Neither does he line up on the side of univocal systems; we remain, with him, in immanence and in the sphere of subjective values. For these reasons, we shall refrain from concluding that the narcissistic temptation is an evil and that it has been truly controlled."[56] The flamboyantly allegorical ending of the "Poème" is thus quite ironic. Deploying a panoply of mythological deities, spiritual topographies, and rhetorical questions, the narrator raises the poet to the status of a "God" dominating mere mortals from the heights of Olympus (albeit the "Olympus of spirituality"), even as he evokes the poet's submissiveness to God's will. Under the guise of the Christian ethic, the poet glories in his own supremacy, in the manner of the "man-God" he was at such pains to revile.

Through its imagery and its wording, the end of the "Poème" echoes the end of chapter 4, which pokes fun at Rousseau, the sensitive man-God, for his hubris:

> Si par hasard un vague souvenir se glisse dans l'âme de ce déplorable bienheureux: N'y aurait-il pas un autre Dieu? croyez qu'il se redressera devant celui-là, qu'il discutera ses volontés et qu'il l'affrontera sans terreur. Quel est le philosophe français qui, pour railler les doctrines allemandes modernes, disait: "Je suis un dieu qui ai mal dîné"? Cette ironie ne mordrait pas sur un esprit enlevé par le hachisch; il répondrait tranquillement: "Il est possible que j'aie mal dîné, mais je suis un Dieu." (Baud., *OC,* 1: 437)

> If by chance a vague memory slips into the soul of this deplorably happy man: Mightn't there be another God? believe that he will stand up before that one, that he will discuss his will and that he will confront him without terror. Which French philosopher, to make fun of the modern German doctrines, said: "I am a god who has dined badly"? That irony would not have any effect on a mind carried away by hashish; he would reply calmly: "It may be that I have dined badly, but I am a God."

By concluding his "Poème" with a paean to "a poet . . . placed on the arduous Olympus of spirituality," looking down on the unfortunate mortals who have not been as abstemious as he, the poet assumes the stance of the superior, virtuous man and recapitulates the very posture of the man-God he despises. After mocking the sophistry of Jean-Jacques's reasoning, the poet's own speech becomes contaminated with the same sense of self-congratulation. The poet's irony does not prevent him from falling victim to the allegorical mechanism

he intends to decry.[57] At the end of the "Poème," the poet, like the man-God he reviles, "se livre candidement à sa triomphante orgie spirituelle" ("indulges candidly in a triumphant spiritual orgy").[58]

The apparent convergence of the detached poet-ironist and his polar opposite, the allegorical man-God, in the final pages of the "Poème" casts doubt on the oppositional structure of the "Poème" as a whole. On the one hand, "Le Poème du hachisch" seems to take a cue from one of Baudelaire's most admired authors, E. T. A. Hoffmann, of whom Baudelaire writes: "Ses conceptions comiques les plus supra-naturelles, les plus fugitives, et qui ressemblent souvent à des visions de l'ivresse, ont un sens moral très visible: c'est à croire qu'on a affaire à un physiologiste ou à un médecin de fous des plus profonds, et qui s'amuserait à revêtir cette profonde science de formes poétiques, comme un savant qui parlerait par apologues et paraboles" ("His most supranatural, most evanescent comic conceptions, which often resemble intoxicated visions, have a very visible moral aspect: you would think you were dealing with one of the most profound physiologists or alienists, who took pleasure in clothing this profound science in poetic forms, like a scientist who spoke in fables and parables") (Baud., *OC*, 2: 542). But which is the "science" in "Le Poème du hachisch": the science of drugs or the science of allegory? Whether or not it was the poet's intent, the "folie" that the poet alternately condemns and inhabits is the madness of rhetoric, not the lunacy induced by drugs. In the manner of the spiraling vines described in "Le Thyrse," the tyrannical "flowers" of allegory overrun and transform the poet's clinical and moral analysis of the drug, the "scientific" premise of the "Poème" (the thyrsus's "staff"). As one long allegory, the "Poème" develops the two aspects or *faces* of its central figure. It shows itself to be a hybrid text, which joins together extraordinary poetic exuberance and sober clarity as different attributes of the allegorical.

The Poet and "Jean-Jacques"

Allegory sweeps over the "Poème," embracing even the most literal elements of the text. The poet, who positioned himself as an analyst rather than a victim of its operation, is caught up in it, and in that sense is no different than his own creation, the "modern sensitive man" (or "Jean-Jacques"). Like the painted grotesque to which it is compared in the "Poème," allegory rides roughshod over rational judgment, intentionality, and will and nullifies the hierarchical order of beings that reason (or virtue) erects. This leveling effect brings the poet and Jean-Jacques into close proximity. But can we say that the

allegorical Jean-Jacques is the poet-ironist's other? The answer, I think, is both yes and no.

Baudelaire scholars like Jean Starobinski and Marc Eigeldinger have argued that Baudelaire detested Rousseau and only mentioned him in order to take his distance from him.[59] In "Le Poème du hachisch," the ironic and analytical poet who introduces Jean-Jacques certainly heaps scorn upon the eighteenth-century author for his narcissism, his deluded belief in his own virtue, and his vain idea of his own superiority and innocence. The poet accuses Jean-Jacques of confusing sentimental ideas with virtuous actions and proclaiming his own moral superiority on the basis of enthusiasm alone. Jean-Jacques, who got high just by imagining his virtue, plays the part of the moral monster. These critiques go to the heart of Rousseau's thinking, not only in his autobiographies (for instance his *Rêveries,* where Rousseau does proclaim his virtue, while blaming others for preventing him from putting that virtue into practice), but ultimately in those works where he envisions the natural goodness of man. The poet of the "Poème" accuses Jean-Jacques of being so delusional that he mistakes himself—a mere man—for a God.

However, read as an allegory, the "Poème" also shows how inescapable this posture is. And in demonstrating the ineluctability of this attitude, it erects Jean-Jacques—the prototype of the modern sensitive man—as the perfect type to embody the dilemma shared by modern man, who glimpses but fails to attain the real paradise, and modern poetry. Aware of the classical ideal that calls for the careful balancing of imagination and judgment, sensory appeal and moral clarity, but fully in the grip of allegory's hedonism, the modern poem—like this "Poème"—is unbalanced and demonic. "[M]odern art has an essentially demonic tendency," Baudelaire wrote in his essay on the contemporary poet Théodore de Banville (1861).[60] "And it seems that this infernal part of man, which man takes pleasure in explaining to himself, increases daily, as if the Devil was having fun fattening it up by artificial means" (Baud., *OC,* 2: 168).[61] Thus, whereas the poet seemed to be the guiding light of the "Poème," he ultimately cedes his place as its most important figure to "Rousseau." Taking over from the intoxicated woman, whose story is explained by his own, Jean-Jacques becomes the principal allegorical figure—or "god"—of this "Poème."

In this discussion of the poet and "Jean-Jacques," it is crucial to recognize, however, that the poet in the poem is not fully congruent with Baudelaire. Within the "Poème," both the poet and Jean-Jacques, each in his own way, are benighted. Jean-Jacques is blind to the ironic implications of his narcissism,

whereas the poet fails to acknowledge the impotence of his irony to contain this negative force. Baudelaire, on the other hand, writes out with great perspicacity the impossible tourniquet in which these two protagonists are caught.[62] It is Baudelaire, rather than his two allegorical figures, who recognizes the "permanent duality" of man. By writing out this duality ("the capacity to be simultaneously oneself and another") as personified by two separate figures, Baudelaire is able to convey the way they converge without cohering. In the final analysis, Baudelaire demonstrates his own superior understanding and lives up to the definition of the artist with which he concludes "De l'essence du rire": "l'artiste n'est artiste qu'à la condition d'être double et de n'ignorer aucun phénomène de sa double nature" ("the artist is only an artist if he is double and ignores no phenomenon of his double nature") (*Baud., OC,* 2: 543). If anything, Jean-Jacques ("l'homme incompris") and the poet (the disdainful moralist) are united but distinct projections of the author himself.

In this roundabout and ambiguous way, Baudelaire seems to be hinting at a complex relationship between himself and his eighteenth-century predecessor, which does not reduce to a simple opposition. Although Baudelaire had long been familiar with Rousseau's ideas and with contemporary myths about Rousseau (he first mentions Rousseau in connection with suicide in 1846), he turned to Rousseau often as he put his ideas about the grotesque into practice in "Le Poème du hachisch" and the *Petits Poèmes en prose.*[63] Just as he openly cited and rewrote Thomas de Quincey's *Confessions of an English Opium-eater* (1822) in the second part of *Les Paradis artificiels,* Baudelaire took up and reworked (albeit much more covertly) important sections of Rousseau's autobiographies and other writings in his prose poems. Baudelaire's poet acknowledges this way of working with others' texts when he announces at the end of chapter 1:

> Aujourd'hui, je ne parlerai que du hachisch, et j'en parlerai suivant des renseignements nombreux et minutieux, extraits des notes ou des confidences d'hommes intelligents qui s'y étaient adonnés longtemps. Seulement, je fondrai ces documents variés en une sorte de monographie, choisissant une âme, facile d'ailleurs à expliquer et à définir, comme type propre aux expériences de cette nature. (Baud., *OC,* 1: 404)

> Today, I shall speak only about hashish, and I shall speak about it following numerous minutely detailed pieces of information, extracted from the notes and confidences of intelligent men who had long been addicted to it. Only I shall fuse these various documents into a kind of

monograph, choosing a soul, moreover one that is easy to explain and define, as a type proper to experiments of this nature.

Later, when he presented *Les Paradis artificiels* in 1864 at a conference in Brussels, Baudelaire called the work (particularly the section derived from de Quincey) "un tel amalgame que je ne saurais y reconnaître la part qui vient de moi, laquelle, d'ailleurs, ne peut être que fort petite" ("such an amalgam that I wouldn't be able to recognize the part that comes from me, which, furthermore, must only be very small") (Baud., *OC,* 1: 519). By giving an important role to "Jean-Jacques" in a text that proclaims itself very much beholden to the work of others, Baudelaire is already making an oblique and displaced assertion of his indebtedness to Rousseau.

The "Man-God"

In several key texts (which Baudelaire knew well and indeed reworked as prose poems, as we shall see in later chapters), Rousseau took up the question of allegory, particularly on the opera stage. By the middle of the eighteenth century, the rococo aesthetic in France was rapidly being overtaken by a new emphasis on nature as the primary referent of art, and the grotesque was on the wane. The Paris Opéra was the one major institution in the country that clung to the aging aesthetic and perpetuated its values. In the dispute called the Querelle des Bouffons (1752–54), the Opéra became the target of the insurrectionist philosophes, who wanted to do away with this manifestation of royal power, luxury, and bad taste. Rousseau, as the central figure in the Querelle, spearheaded the drive to reform the lyric stage.[64] Much of his venom was directed at the disagreeable qualities of French operatic music and at the wrong-headed theories of the preeminent French composer of the time, Jean-Philippe Rameau. But Rousseau also addressed the insufficiencies of the drama itself. He wanted to replace the bizarre, heterogeneous, machine-driven spectacles, featuring pagan gods and mythological figures, with simpler dramas focused on mortal man.[65] Rousseau attacked the grotesque aesthetic of the Opéra for its failure to create a "reasonable illusion," singling out for criticism its exaggerated rhetoric (the unwarranted disparity between the trivial plot and its extravagant staging) and particularly its use of allegory. Rousseau regarded allegory as an intellectual exercise that prevented the spectator from becoming immersed in the action on stage, and thus as an obstacle to the creation of the reasonable illusion he wanted to achieve.[66]

Clearly, there is disagreement between Baudelaire and Rousseau where the theory and evaluation of allegory are concerned. Baudelaire praised allegory as "ce genre si *spirituel* . . . qui est vraiment l'une des formes primitives et les plus naturelles de la poésie" ("this genre, which is so *spiritual* [and which . . .] is truly one of the primitive and most natural forms of poetry").[67] Rousseau railed against it. But despite his vociferations, Rousseau used allegory to an impressive extent, in works ranging from *Julie, ou la Nouvelle Héloïse* to his autobiographies. It is not surprising that critics have singled him out as the founder of modern allegory.[68] Indeed, as we shall see in Chapter 5, Rousseau's "man" is as much an allegorical figure as Baudelaire's. Replacing the gods of the rococo, Rousseau substituted another—more convincing and less obvious—allegorical figure in their place. "Man" became Rousseau's new "god."

Thus when Baudelaire identifies "Jean-Jacques" as the quintessential allegorical figure, "l'homme-Dieu," he is both poking fun at Rousseau's sleight of hand and making an important point. Like Rousseau, Baudelaire took allegory seriously and pondered its role in art. Like Rousseau, he utilized it to structure his prose narratives, both "Le Poème du hachisch" and the *Petits Poèmes en prose.* But unlike Rousseau, who rejected the marvelous aesthetic with its showy allegories and elaborate machines in favor of a more subdued and subtle version of the figure, Baudelaire adopted the splashy rococo and utilized it *together with* the "modern" form of allegory he learned from his eighteenth-century predecessor. Whereas Rousseau made a great pretense of rejecting the hybridity and phantasmagoria of the rococo, while smuggling allegory back into his work under the cover of human forms, Baudelaire joyfully accepted the hybrid, using it in the hybrid genre of the prose poem and the hybrid text of "Le Poème du hachisch," while appearing to ridicule the hybrid "man-God"—Rousseau.

Rousseau is obviously an overdetermined figure for Baudelaire. Beyond his ambivalent personal feelings about this fallible man and literary god, Baudelaire also found in "Rousseau" a representation of the political turmoil of contemporary France and an emblem for the temporal and political dilemma of his own art. As a historical figure—the author deemed most responsible for the French Revolution—Rousseau was bound up with the chaos and anxiety created by that great upheaval, a link both to the Ancien Régime and to the emerging national consciousness that followed in the Revolution's wake. In the two decades between 1845 and 1865, when the past of the French Revolution intruded obsessively into the urgent debate over the future of France, the desire to recover the classicism and stability of pre-Revolutionary, indeed pre-

eighteenth-century France became the driving force in the interpretation of the legacy of Rousseau. As a much-disputed icon, "Rousseau" was thus a kind of ongoing and impossible "representation of the present" for the French intellectuals and politicians of Baudelaire's day. As we shall see in the next chapter, the name "Rousseau" captured the temporal conundrum of a past that haunted the present, preventing it from coming fully and uniquely into its own.

3

Identity Politics

"Rousseau" and "France" in the
Mid-Nineteenth Century

In 1861, a year after Rousseau appeared as the type of the "sensitive modern man" in "Le Poème du hachisch,"[1] Baudelaire proposed two possible titles for the new collection of prose poems he was readying for publication—titles that suggest that he again planned to adopt "Rousseau" as a distinctive and recurrent type in his last poetic work.

Over the years, the poet had considered and discarded various collective titles for the prose poems he began writing in 1855—titles such as "Poëmes nocturnes" (Nocturnal poems) or "Petits Poëmes lycanthropes" (Little were-wolf poems), which appeared only once, as well as some, like "La Lueur et la fumée" (Light and smoke), that were never used. But in a letter dated "Noël 1861," Baudelaire suggested two more concrete titles to his editor, Arsène Houssaye.[2] Both "Le Rôdeur parisien" (The Parisian stroller) and "Le Promeneur solitaire" (The solitary walker) painted a picture of an errant and isolated man, an overarching figure who would preside over the collected poems, presumably bringing them together as reflections of an individual experience. While both titles have a similar meaning, one of them, "Le Promeneur solitaire," specifically calls to mind Rousseau's unfinished autobiography, *Les Rêveries du promeneur solitaire* (*The Reveries of the Solitary Walker*), published almost a century earlier.[3]

However, Baudelaire's proposed titles were never adopted (the poems instead appeared under the generic heading "Petits Poèmes en prose," which is still used today),[4] and in the published dedication to the collection Baudelaire claims to have been inspired by Aloysius Bertrand and by Houssaye himself.

The provocative reference to Rousseau was erased, relegated to the margins of Baudelaire's work, where it tantalizes the curious critic and raises questions that have never received a satisfactory answer: Why would Baudelaire tip his hat to Rousseau? Did he intend this salute as an homage? Is there a substantial connection to Rousseau in these poems, or is the allusion ironic? Did the editor veto the title or did Baudelaire change his mind? And if he did have second thoughts, why? The title's meaning and the reasons for its disappearance remain uncertain.

Critics who have taken note of the discarded title have dismissed it as a put-down of an author Baudelaire abhorred. Jean Starobinski, the touchstone for recent readings of Rousseau's influence on Baudelaire, sums up the prevailing attitude:

> Baudelaire, who knew Rousseau and did not like him, had thought for a moment of giving the collection of his prose poems a Rousseauist title: Le Promeneur solitaire. It would have manifestly attached a work in which so many pages are inspired by urban strolling [*flânerie*] to an antecedent that evoked, in numerous pages, the encounters and the train of thoughts engendered by a walk outside the city walls. With such a title the prose poems would have been read as an echo of Rousseau, or as a response to Rousseau. There is no doubt that that is not the proper light in which to view the whole collection: but certain poems should be approached (and have been) with reference to Rousseau.[5]

Despite the numerous links between the two authors to which Starobinski alludes, there is surprising agreement among the critics that Baudelaire simply detested Jean-Jacques, and that "he set the title aside as an homage deemed illegitimate."[6]

But many other reasons not having to do with Baudelaire's attitude toward Rousseau could have intervened to make the title both appealing and unusable. Baudelaire might well have thought of this title, not only because of what his prose poems owe to the work of Rousseau, or because it evoked a characteristic of the best modern artists, but because the sign "Rousseau" encapsulated the political foment and the high anxiety of several key moments before and during the Second Empire. Precisely because of its allusion to the past, "Le Promeneur solitaire" was a reference to highly visible political debates that marked contemporary French life in the middle of the nineteenth century.

"Rousseau" was not a transparent name or essence in mid-nineteenth-century France but a cluster of aggressively contested meanings, which do not

settle into any uniformly shared understanding. In the years in question (roughly 1845 to 1865), Rousseau was represented either in the most glowing of terms, as a literary genius unsurpassed by contemporary authors, and even as the father of modern France, or else with revulsion, as a utopianist and hypocrite responsible for the worst excesses of the French Revolution and the nineteenth-century revolutions that followed it. Both sides made available many clichéd portraits or caricatures of Rousseau, on which I believe the prose poems ultimately drew.

Modernity and the Memory Crisis

As Richard Terdiman has argued, the traumatic upheaval of the French Revolution caused a "memory crisis" in France in the nineteenth century by disrupting the link between the French and their cultural past.[7] Pierre Nora describes this crisis as the loss of "memory" and the turn to "history." If ever there was a golden age in France when memory was a collective, unselfconscious, "perpetually actual phenomenon," it definitely did not survive the French Revolution.[8] In the absence of such a "living" memory, the nineteenth century called upon history instead to provide a "national definition of the present," a new basis for national unity. This far from simple task involved, not only "reevaluat[ing] the monarchical past,"[9] but determining the meaning and effects of the French Revolution for the present day. Although not an actor in the great Revolution himself, Rousseau was considered its principal author, and as such he figured prominently in the nineteenth century's efforts to define "the spirit of France."

Throughout the nineteenth century, but particularly between 1845 and 1865, Rousseau was the subject of intense debate among various segments of the intellectual elite—the members of the Académie française, professors at the Ecole normale and the Collège de France, and literary critics, as well as political philosophers and politicians. "Between 1830 and 1878, the debate about Rousseau lost none of its pertinence and its virulence," observes Raymond Trousson, who has inventoried Rousseau's reception from the Revolution through the first half of the twentieth century. "Pulled to one side and another by the right and the left, venerated by Georges Sand or Michelet, abominated simultaneously by Lamartine, the Catholics and Proudhon, he never ceases to be present in the political and religious conscience [of France]."[10] The competition to elevate or debase Rousseau was coterminous with the struggle to seize or maintain power over the dominant discourse (that is, to determine which

past would underpin the national identity of France), and this conflict inevitably came to inhabit his name. "Rousseau" is a classic example of the "ideological sign" identified by V. N. Volosinov, in which "differently oriented accents intersect. . . . The sign becomes an arena of the class [or, in this case, intraclass] struggle."[11] Any attempt to understand what Rousseau represented for Baudelaire must therefore address the difficult issue of what "Rousseau" (i.e., the name Rousseau) stood for in the mid-nineteenth century generally.[12]

A detour through a few works of history and literary commentary dating from shortly before and just after the Revolution of 1848 and from 1861 (when the Risorgimento in Italy brought revolution to France's door) will help us comprehend the dramatically different ideas and the extraordinary passions that were attached to the name "Rousseau." Even this brief and far from exhaustive survey will provide a compendium of images of Jean-Jacques, both damning and dithyrambic, on which Baudelaire evidently drew; and it will point up his dilemma. Like other artists of the time, Baudelaire was unavoidably positioned by the ongoing struggle over national self-definition raging around him, both the overt political battles and armed skirmishes of the February Revolution and the more diffuse discursive struggle of the later years. These ideological conflicts opened to criticism all but the most innocuous or veiled use of Rousseau's name and works. The purpose of the following review is therefore twofold: to take note of some important contemporary ideas about Rousseau and the ideological tensions informing them; and to show how these ideological forces impinged upon Baudelaire's writing, resulting in the caricatured images of Rousseau that punctuate the *Petits Poèmes en prose*. Baudelaire hid his debt to Rousseau under the appearance of mockery, and his duplicitous treatment of Rousseau is a particularly apt sign of his poems' modernity.[13]

"Rousseau" and "the Spirit of France"

Jules Michelet's ambitious *Histoire de la Révolution française* (1847–53) tackles only the history of the French Revolution, and Désiré Nisard's *Histoire de la littérature française* (1844–61) completely skirts it, but both have as a more or less explicit subtext the work of "social bonding and reconstitution" that was the Revolution's legacy.[14] Writing in a post-Revolutionary era that was still subject to revolutionary upheaval, both Michelet and Nisard were concerned to create an image of "l'esprit français" or "l'esprit de la France" with which their readers could identify. In other words, they wanted to represent "France" to herself, endowing her with a history or a past that would give the nation a

"sacred foundation."[15] Because they came at this common project from very different spots on the political spectrum (Michelet was a republican, Nisard a conservative), the representation of this "spirit" and the appropriate mode of its reception or recognition is quite different in each; and these differences are readily apparent in their treatment of "Rousseau." Read together, these two authors give us a picture of the politics of representation in the mid-nineteenth century.[16]

In the 1847 preface to *L'Histoire de la Révolution française,* Michelet makes explicit the link between "the spirit of the Revolution" and "the spirit of France":

> Only in [the spirit of the Revolution] did France become aware of herself. In every moment of weakness when we seem to forget ourselves, it is there that we must search for ourselves, seize hold of ourselves again. . . . The Revolution is in us, in our souls. . . . Living spirit of France, where would I grasp you, if not in myself?[17]

Believing that recent generations of Frenchmen had lost touch with this powerful living spirit, however, Michelet conceives it as his mission to recall the spirit and place it before them. At the same time, he reminds his contemporaries of their debt to their "father," the eighteenth century:

> [T]hat century founded liberty by freeing the spirit [*l'esprit*], until then bound by flesh, bound by the material principle of the double—theological and political, priestly and royal—incarnation. That century, the century of the spirit [*l'esprit*], abolished the gods of flesh, in the state, in religion, so that there were no longer any idols, and the only God was God.[18]

In Michelet's narrative, the Revolution begins not in 1789, but forty years earlier. In the mid-eighteenth century, the writings of the philosophes freed the nascent French spirit from its unhealthy ties to earthly institutions and thus founded the true France, creating individual rights and constituting man. Partly as a result of their work, the king became an object of horror. The "dogma of the royal incarnation" perished forever, to be replaced by "the royalty of the mind."[19] But Michelet makes it plain that the all-important marriage of feeling and ideas, the basis of a new national unity, was the unique contribution of Rousseau. It was Rousseau who had given birth to the "living spirit of France" that Michelet now resurrects in his history.

Not only is Rousseau the father of the new French spirit, but Michelet's narrative makes him its pure embodiment. Although Michelet rejoices in the

release of the spirit from the flesh, in the crisis of faith that caused France to turn away from the divine right monarchy, he needs to give a life to this liberated spirit in order to show it at work. There must be men imbued with the new spirit if there is to be a French Revolution. Michelet thus turns to Rousseau in order to give a name and an existence to the "spirit of Revolution," the true "spirit of France."[20]

Rousseau fills the void in Michelet's version of history between the death of the monarchy in midcentury and the birth of the people during the Revolution. Therefore it is fitting that the story Michelet tells about him interweaves the ideas of death and rebirth. According to Michelet, Rousseau speaks of renascence to a dying society and carries it off, because he delves into his own heart to anchor his philosophy there. Rousseau speaks to an enslaved world and makes the people into gods. The new spirit of France that passes through Rousseau is pure Logos: it sings more than speaks, it is a warm breath of youth and love, a melody from the heart. The essence of "France" is not encapsulated in the philosophical phrases that create the new world. Instead, it is the "young and moving voice" that sings out in the *Confessions* and the *Rêveries* and touches everyone: "The Confessions, which appear after the death of Rousseau, seem like a sigh from the tomb. [Rousseau] comes back, he resuscitates, more powerful, more admired, more adored than ever."[21] Rising from the dead, Rousseau raises France with him. Resurrected, he becomes the material for a new foundation legend, which, thanks to Michelet, will give the people of France a new national tradition, a new life.

Rousseau gives his name to the new spirit of France, and with it a kind of body. But unlike the stifling body of the king, this body is acceptable because it is imprecise: at once decaying flesh and youthful passion, it is neither precisely young nor precisely old. As a figure of transition, according to which the old (institutional) bodies die, leaving the spirit of Revolution to flourish in a new age, Rousseau balances the best of the past with hope for the future. More heart than mind, more melody than thought, Rousseau allows the French spirit to come to life in its least encumbered form.

Well before Baudelaire, Michelet chose Rousseau as the personification of the modern era, a kind of "man-God" for modern France. By evoking Rousseau in the title of his prose poems, Baudelaire would have linked up with a republican current that wanted to make "Rousseau" the allegorical figure of the *new* France. But this was not the only resonance of the name at the time. Rousseau was considered in other quarters to be a despicable figure tying France to its unwanted revolutionary *past.* Rousseau was treated with con-

tempt by the conservatives like Désiré Nisard, who yearned to put the past upheavals as far away as possible from the new, stable nation they hoped to create.

Nisard, an educator and critic, published the first volume of his *Histoire de la littérature française* in 1844. Like Michelet, he prefaced his work with an evocation of "l'esprit français," which he identifies as "the most complete and purest image of the human mind."[22] Nisard, too, aims to be the medium through which this "spirit" will come alive for a new generation. By transmitting to younger readers only the essential, "permanent" works of French literature, the works of the "beloved masters," he intends to settle France's future on the best examples of its cultural past. Given the prevailing doubts about the social and political order, Nisard asserts, there is clear value in knowing "the very nature of the spirit (or mind) of our country" ("la nature même de l'esprit de notre pays").[23]

Nisard wants to show the French "spirit" in the healthiest, most vigorous expression of the French intellect. But in order to produce his "portraits" of "l'esprit de la France," he also had to identify what the French spirit (or mind) was not. "We must distinguish its healthy state from its illnesses; its eras of vigor from its eras of weakness," he writes. So that the reader may learn to guard against them, Nisard adds a few examples of the weakness or disease he has in mind—and Rousseau is foremost among them.[24]

Nisard makes this point with particular force in the preface to the fourth volume of his *Histoire,* which came out in 1861, although parts of it were written earlier (presumably in the late 1840s). Publication of this last volume, devoted to the eighteenth and nineteenth centuries, was suspended as a direct result of the revolutionary events of 1848. Explaining this interruption, Nisard says only that he did not wish to engage in polemics by taking a position completely opposed to the prevailing view, which favored "the most dangerous doctrines of the eighteenth century." By the time he finally brought out the fourth volume, Nisard was quite serene about the past, but on the subject of Rousseau he had lost none of his vehemence: "However, regarding J.-J. Rousseau in particular, I sense that the calm that has taken hold in me has hardly modified my feelings, and I had to change very little as to the substance in the chapter that is devoted to him, the oldest one in this volume," he writes. "Rousseau has two defects of which I am not about to become tolerant: a chimerical mind [*l'esprit de chimère*] and bombast [*la déclamation*]."[25] Nisard locates the essence of the French spirit in the love of order and discipline and believes that its natural expression is the logical order of the French language.

For him the high point of French literature is the seventeenth century, and the exemplary text is Descartes's *Discours de la méthode*.[26] Nothing could be more unlike this natural order of the mind than the "spirit of anarchy" or the equivalent "chimerical spirit" that he attributes to Rousseau. The Revolution of 1848 may have prevented Nisard from articulating this view publicly, but there is nothing about it that isn't already implicit in his concept of French history. For Nisard, the eighteenth century—Michelet's "heroic age of the spirit"—is an era of decline or decay, when the great French spirit of order and discipline was dangerously weakened.

If Michelet resurrects Rousseau as the personification of "France," Nisard would rather consign Rousseau to the grave. For him, Rousseau is the very type of the diseased mind. Rousseau represents everything Nisard detests, and he hates the bloodshed Rousseau's ideas have provoked. Although he does not conceal his loathing for the ideas he finds in Rousseau's political writing, Nisard reserves his harshest judgment for the *Confessions*. Rousseau's personal narrative obviously departs from the standard set by Nisard's ideal model, the seventeenth-century poet, who only reveals in his work those aspects of himself which he has in common with all men. (The seventeenth-century artist, conforming to strict poetic rules, was most apt to represent the French mind— and spirit—because he did not represent himself.) Nisard is particularly repelled by the discontinuity between Rousseau's life and his writing, which the autobiography reveals. Far from building his philosophy on his own suffering (as Michelet asserts), Nisard's Rousseau is only a dreamer, a "speculator," who cares little about the practical application or implications of his work. He is a utopianist—a hypocrite, a "charlatan." In support of his claims, Nisard repeatedly cites Rousseau's abandonment of his children. Rousseau was a bad father who had no right to counsel others on how to raise their own offspring. He was even the father of bad (i.e., utopian) works. Rousseau was thus not properly a father at all; certainly, he could not be the "father" of modern France.[27]

For Nisard, "l'esprit français" is synonymous with the superior mind of the great French authors, and Rousseau's "esprit de chimère" is its antithesis. Far from representing the "spirit of France," Rousseau represents instead the mental illness ("la folie") that threatens to sap France's strength, the health of its great minds. "[I]n the seventeenth century," Nisard exclaims, "[the mind] believed that it was made only to serve truth; in the eighteenth century, it began to take pleasure in itself; in the nineteenth, thanks to the example of Rousseau, it values itself more than the truth and less than its reputation [literally, the

noise that it makes]."[28] If Michelet's Rousseau is a man-God, Nisard's Rousseau resembles a devil, responsible for the evils that beset France.

Nisard never mentions Michelet at any point in his *Histoire,* but he implicitly attacks him throughout his chapter on Rousseau. In what is clearly a calculated, almost point-for-point rebuttal, he turns Michelet's Rousseau on his head. As these dueling histories attest, the content of France's national memory was very much at issue not only during Baudelaire's formative years but also in the last decade of his working life. Versions of the past played themselves out in the collective consciousness of French society, not just in Baudelaire's personal iconography, and in 1861, Baudelaire's allusion to Rousseau was overdetermined. In proposing to give his new collection of prose poems the title of Rousseau's last autobiographical work, he was toying with a reference that had immense political implications.

The Year 1861

Broadly stated, in mid-nineteenth-century France, the name "Rousseau" had come to represent the French Revolution's excesses for the champions of stability and order, whereas it represented the sovereignty of the people to those who sought social and political reform. The debate raged for years, with first one side, then the other gaining dominance. Depending on whether sympathies lay with the restoration of the monarchy or with the republic, Rousseau was alternately revered as the divine inspiration of "a generous and liberating Revolution" or—more often—vilified as the abhorrent instigator of France's worst troubles, "purveyor of the guillotine, responsible for bloody excesses."[29] In January 1848, the July Monarchy suspended Michelet's popular course on the Revolution and Rousseau at the Collège de France—the authorities clearly believed that Michelet's passionate retelling of France's history was igniting the emotions that would soon explode in fighting at the barricades.[30] Then, in February, the monarchy collapsed, and the tables were turned. Michelet's course was reinstated, opponents of the new republic kept mum about their views, and arguments about Rousseau temporarily subsided. Finally, with the creation of the Second Empire, harsh new laws ushered in an era of government censorship, and the renascent republican fervor was quelled. The repressive regime sent Michelet into exile and restored Rousseau's detractors to power.[31] However, the capacity of the name "Rousseau" to arouse political passions did not dissipate so quickly. When the regime relaxed some of its most draconian laws in the early 1860s, and liberals and republicans be-

gan again to agitate for reform, even the Académie française found itself embroiled in political debate, and Rousseau became once more the focus of attack.[32]

Baudelaire, in his twenties in 1848, took to the streets with many other young men and lived out the February Revolution with enthusiasm for the new socialist or *democ-soc* ideals.[33] But, like others of his generation, he was quickly disillusioned by the subsequent election and coup d'état of Louis-Napoléon, and he pronounced himself "physiquement dépolitiqué."[34] Critics generally agree that in his later life and work, Baudelaire was either apolitical or downright reactionary. If, in his early years, he took the side most often associated with Rousseau, in his later life, he apparently turned against his utopian impulses. However, in a letter to Nadar in May 1859, Baudelaire devoted several paragraphs to commentary on the political events of the day, noting that although he had tried, he hadn't been able to give up his interest in the subject: "Je me suis vingt fois persuadé que je ne m'intéressais plus à la politique, et à chaque question grave, je suis repris de curiosité et de passion" ("I have persuaded myself twenty times that I was no longer interested in politics, and each serious question stirs up my curiosity and passion");[35] and as late as 1862, in a letter to Sainte-Beuve, he intimated that he still felt the occasional effects of "un vieux fonds d'esprit révolutionnaire" ("an old reserve of revolutionary spirit").[36] Baudelaire may have aligned himself at times with the dominant reactionary discourse, but when the conservatives launched their most scathing attacks against the "utopian Rousseau" in 1861, he did not follow suit. On the contrary, Baudelaire's old utopianism seems to have resurfaced just as he was readying the first twenty-six prose poems for publication in *La Presse*.

The early 1860s were a period of liberalization, when the Senate and the Assembly won the right to address the government (*décret* of November 24, 1860), to publish their debates in *Le Moniteur* (*sénatus-consulte* of February 1, 1861), and to vote on specific items of the budget (*sénatus-consulte* of December 31, 1861). A few legislators took advantage of the new openness to call for freedom of the press, and the government did soften its repressive measures slightly. As a result, the daily newspaper *Le Temps,* founded in April 1861, quickly became the *porte-parole* of liberal thought.[37]

The government's perceived opening to the left was compounded during these years by Napoléon III's controversial war in Italy, which turned many former supporters against him. Catholics who feared the war's effects on the papacy, bankers and businessmen who worried about the state of the nation's finances (and their own), and moderates repelled by the idea of revolutionary

contagion and the revival of socialist thought, all saw the Italian campaign as a major crisis for France. In the Assembly, Emile Keller, a deputy from the Haut-Rhin, openly protested the emperor's policies (January 13, 1861) and called on the regime to choose between conservatism and revolution.[38]

In the midst of this ferment, the dominant conservative discourse became even more extreme—and, as we might expect, its violence was particularly evident in its virulent attacks on Rousseau. Texts by influential authors at different places on the conservative spectrum paint strikingly similar pictures of Rousseau's "utopianism" and its disastrous effects on the nineteenth century's troubles. For the increasingly conservative Lamartine, the revolutionary activities of the Risorgimento were a warning at France's door of things to come.[39] Writing to a correspondent in February 1861, Lamartine evoked his fear of a return to chaos:

> Literary business [*Les affaires littéraires*], so good for me last year, is suffering terribly from the awful enigma into which the inexplicable Italian adventure is plunging Europe. *France, internally, is on the eve of an 1848.* I don't see any way out of the situation if we continue to let ourselves be led by that blind dog the king of Piedmont.[40]

And two months later, he went further still:

> There is no more salvation. Those people, possessed by the Satan of ruins, think that they can wage [17]93 externally without having [17]93 at home. They are wrong. We should expect everything and anything. The emperor doesn't seem to be his own man. His evil genius is leading him who knows where. *There is great demagogical agitation; upright people of every stripe are very intimidated.*[41]

In this fearful political mood, Lamartine attacked the "utopian" Rousseau in the 65th *entretien* of his *Cours familier de littérature*:

> After Fénélon, J.-J. Rousseau was the great, the fatal utopianist of society. He was obviously inspired by Fénélon, who was inspired by Plato. Thus errors are seductive, just as truths are: going back through the centuries to the origin of the world, sophists engender themselves and perpetuate themselves through the generation of smooth orators [*en génération de rhéteurs*].
>   When there occurs among these masters of social rhetoric a writer who is more inspired, more contagious than the others, and when the birth of this author, the sovereign of error, coincides with a moral upheaval or a po-

litical cataclysm of his country's institutions, then, instead of simply finding some readers who are pleased to have their imagination cradled by his dreams, this utopian writer has followers to propagate his chimeras, and arms to execute his ideas.

Such was, on the eve of the French Revolution, J.-J. Rousseau.[42]

Threatened by the specter of revolution and worried about his own finances and the financial state of the country, Lamartine accuses Rousseau of sophistry, impossible dreams, or chimeras, and overblown language. These are typical features of the conservative, anti-utopian discourse aimed at discrediting Rousseau—and the socialists—once and for all.

From within the ranks of Napoléon III's most loyal supporters came equally vitriolic outcries against Rousseau. Indebted to the emperor, under whom his career had flourished, Nisard shared Lamartine's fear of revolutionary activity. As we have seen, the Revolution of 1848 had interrupted his ascent in the bureaucratic ranks and caused him to suspend publication of his *Histoire* after the third volume. The new revolutionary stirrings might have the same effect. The political circumstances in 1861 explain why Nisard unleashed all his vehemence against his archenemy in the preface to the fourth and last volume of his literary history. "Of all the utopias of J.-J. Rousseau, the most vain and the most dangerous is the one of which he is the hero," Nisard states, referring to the *Confessions*.[43] Rousseau's "honnêteté" (his moral uprightness) is only in his head, like a kind of "intoxication, in which he forgets what morality commands in those people whose virtue comes from the heart."[44] Rousseau's utopian political philosophy is, therefore, nothing more than an attempt to redeem his scandalous personal behavior—the fact that he abandoned his children to foundling homes (les Enfants trouvés):

> To desire the union of a people in a single family, the union of nations in a single people, to make the state a father and all the citizens children among whom his hand divides equally the fruits of a common labor; all that calms the utopianist about what he has neglected to do to spread a little happiness around himself. His chimera takes the place of his conscience.[45]

Nisard obviously feels it his duty to warn his readers against the evil that once again threatens France by showing them its source:

> [I]f the primary cause of this utopia is a fault against nature and honor, we must not be afraid to discredit it by pointing out its cause. *We live in a time*

> *when it is of great interest to French society to know that all the anarchical ideas of the past sixty years were born from this utopia,* born itself of a fault so great that one is tempted to look for an excuse for it in the beginning of madness [*dans un commencement de folie*].[46]

To Nisard, this warning against the (socialist) anarchy and madness stemming from "Rousseau" is just as urgently needed in 1861 as it was thirteen years earlier.

Baudelaire's Double-bind

The fear and loathing expressed by Lamartine and Nisard in the face of a new revolutionary "utopianism" is worlds away from the rekindled enthusiasm Baudelaire was experiencing at the same moment.[47] Baudelaire was clearly moved by the new relaxation of censorship and the ensuing political foment. It must have seemed to him that he was reliving some of his "utopian" past. Around 1858, after a hiatus of many years, he took to reading Proudhon again, and he may have been aware of Proudhon's book *Du principe fédératif et de la nécessité de reconstituer le parti de la Révolution* (1860), which undoubtedly contributed to the conservatives' unease by encouraging the reestablishment of a revolutionary party.[48] It was in the spring of 1859, barely a month before Napoléon III's victories at Magenta and Solferino in Italy, that Baudelaire confessed his ongoing interest in politics to Nadar. And the "old reserve of revolutionary spirit" that he later mentioned to Sainte-Beuve was almost certainly behind his decision to apply for a seat in the Académie française in 1861. This event, which has baffled so many commentators, is consonant with the resurgence of Baudelaire's "utopianism" during this key period and illuminates the nature and place of that utopianism at this time in the poet's life.

Baudelaire did not run for just any seat in the Academy. Rather, he chose specifically to replace Lacordaire, the passionate priest whose sermons and lectures in the cathedral of Notre-Dame had galvanized the Parisian public in the 1830s and 1840s, and who had been one of the idols of Baudelaire's republican youth.[49] Lacordaire had only been elected to the French Academy in 1860 and had died shortly after his reception the following year; the brouhaha surrounding his candidacy was still very much alive. In light of his well-known republican sympathies, the prelate's election had been an obvious polemical move by the Académie and a clear sign of its opposition to the emperor. Lacordaire's republican past, his brief role as a representative in the Assemblée constituante in 1848, and his notorious last sermon at the Eglise Saint-Roch in

1853,[50] made his election in 1860 a political scandal.[51] No one, least of all Baudelaire, could have mistaken the meaning of the Académie's actions, its will to mount a worldly revolt (a "fronde mondaine") against the regime.[52]

Although Baudelaire did not say so directly, he must have had this background in mind when he campaigned to replace the priest. In a letter addressed to the Academy's secretary, Villemain, but sent in the form of a draft to Sainte-Beuve and another Academician, the poet Alfred de Vigny, Baudelaire explained why he had chosen to apply for Lacordaire's seat:

> Que, le père Lacordaire excitant en moi cette sympathie, non seulement par la valeur des choses qu'il a dites, mais aussi par la beauté dont il les a revêtues, et se présentant à l'imagination non seulement avec le caractère chrétien, mais aussi avec la couleur romantique . . . , je prie M. Villemain d'instruire ses collègues que j'opte pour le fauteuil du père Lacordaire.[53]

> That, Father Lacordaire exciting in me this sympathy, not only because of the value of the things he said, but also because of the beauty in which he clothed them, and presenting himself to my imagination not only with a Christian character but also with a romantic color . . . , I beg Mr. Villemain to instruct his colleagues that I am opting for the seat of Father Lacordaire.

Sainte-Beuve, who supported the emperor and hoped to add some like-minded thinkers to the Academy's rosters, was quick to reproach Baudelaire for this decision: "This express choice of Father Lacordaire, the *Catholic/romantic,* appears excessive and shocking, which your good taste as a candidate does not want to do."[54] Sainte-Beuve, himself a former romantic, does not emphasize the real reason why Lacordaire was an "excessive and shocking" choice, and Baudelaire too slides over the political point. But his vague allusion to "la valeur des choses que [Lacordaire] a dites" is undoubtedly a reference to the priest's oppositional rhetoric in the 1830s and 1840s and his overt republicanism in 1848. And in Baudelaire's letter to Vigny, he more or less admits as much: "le sentiment et l'instinct me persuadent qu'il faut toujours se conduire *utopiquement,*" he states, before adding, "c'est-à-dire comme si on était sûr d'être élu, quand même on est certain de ne pas l'être" ("feeling and instinct persuade me that one should always conduct oneself *utopically,* that is as if one were sure of being elected, even when one is certain of the opposite").[55]

Baudelaire had good reason to suspect that he would not be successful, but the upwelling of his utopian sympathies continued even as his candidacy foundered. In a letter addressed to Sainte-Beuve in January 1862, for example,

he exclaims over an article by his friend on the upcoming elections, which he saw as supportive of his own bid. Baudelaire, who had been coolly received by most of the Academicians he visited, was impressed by Sainte-Beuve's proposal for a structural reform of the Academy and comments enthusiastically:

> Ah! et votre utopie! Le grand moyen de chasser des élections le *vague, si cher aux grands seigneurs!* Votre utopie m'a donné un nouvel orgueil. Moi aussi, je l'avais faite, l'utopie, la réforme. . . . Il y a cette grande différence que la vôtre est tout à fait viable, et que peut-être le jour n'est pas loin où elle sera adoptée.[56]

> Ah! and your utopia! A great way to banish from the elections the *vagueness, so dear to the great lords!* Your utopia gave me a new pride. I too had come up with it, utopia, reform. . . . There is this big difference that yours is entirely viable, and that perhaps the day is not far off when it will be adopted.

Baudelaire's reaction, contradictory and ironic though it may seem, sheds light on the nature of his "utopian" thought at the time. Sainte-Beuve's open dislike of the Academy's self-perpetuating monarchist traditions obviously impressed Baudelaire. In an odd way, Sainte-Beuve's opposition to the Academy's old guard put him in a position roughly analogous to that of the "utopian" socialists and radical republicans who had fought against the monarchists in 1848 (notwithstanding that Sainte-Beuve was a loyal Bonapartist when he wrote this critique); and it is this analogy that Baudelaire picks up and applauds. Quoting the reference to "les grands seigneurs" whom Sainte-Beuve wishes to maneuver out of power, Baudelaire marks the social character of his mentor's reform.

As a writer wholly outside the precinct of the Academy and one of the Bohemians who stood to benefit from Sainte-Beuve's projected changes, Baudelaire quickly fell in with his mentor's plans. He even published his approval of Sainte-Beuve's ideas in an article in the *Revue anecdotique,* where he again underscored the positive "utopian" character of Sainte-Beuve's proposal ("la très raisonnable utopie de M. Sainte-Beuve").[57] Nonetheless, Baudelaire thought it prudent to publish this article anonymously, which points up his difficult double-bind: a "utopianist" whose *democ-soc* past linked him more closely to Lacordaire and the "frondeurs," Baudelaire also sought the support of the influential critic who wanted to eliminate oppositional politics from the Academy. Yet Baudelaire could scarcely afford to take credit for his piece in support of Sainte-Beuve, because to do so would have put an immediate end to his

hopes for membership in the Académie. His intricate dance between the two opposing camps testifies poignantly to the difficulty of surviving in the highly charged political atmosphere of the early 1860s.

Baudelaire's covert activism is one example of the artist's need to be duplicitous and double-dealing during this period. Although Baudelaire could not risk proclaiming his enthusiasm for the old-style "utopianism" of his past, he reasserted it obliquely and in distorted ways—to the very people who would be least receptive. In 1861 and 1862, it is this twisted oppositional or counter-discursive position that constitutes what he proudly names his "utopia."

Baudelaire was patently not a reactionary in the common mold. When Baudelaire talked about "utopias," it was with reference to both a period of his own life that he had not entirely abjured and an oppositional stance that was still in his mind. While he no longer believed in "the intrinsic goodness of man and nature," he had not completely foresworn "l'amour de l'utopie, des idylles révolutionnaires" ("the love of utopia, of revolutionary idylls").[58] In the 1860s, Baudelaire was more utopian than critics have generally allowed, and this lingering sympathy makes itself felt in the polemical title he proposed to Houssaye in December 1861—"Le Promeneur solitaire." In taking up and incorporating Rousseau's work in his own and especially in invoking Rousseau in the title of his collected poems, Baudelaire had to be aware of the subversive political implications of his poetic activity.[59]

Flaunting a reference to Rousseau's work at a time when Rousseau's name was anathema to some of the most prominent men in French literary and political circles was a sure way to be noticed. As Starobinski remarks, such a gesture would have been read as a sympathetic echo of the controversial author or at least a response to his work. In either case, the title would have encouraged pointed attacks. Perhaps Baudelaire backed off his overt oppositional stance after his decision to seek election to the Académie française provoked such negative comment. Whether he himself withdrew the title or Arsène Houssaye refused it,[60] the political circumstances at the time leave little doubt that the decision was the prudent one. Baudelaire's title was probably intended as an homage to Rousseau, and whether or not it was "illegitimate"—that is, based on insufficient common ground—is one question that subtends this book. However, by one standard, that of the dominant conservative discourse, the answer is unequivocal: the homage did not conform to the "legitimate" point of view and therefore was best set aside.

Baudelaire's involvement with Rousseau and Rousseau's texts occurred at a time when he was revisiting his socialist past and may well partake of Baude-

laire's positive disposition toward the utopian. But Baudelaire's utopianism is not to be understood as a pure socialism à la Proudhon or Fourier. Rather, it is both a general dissidence—a critical energy and anger unleashed against the dominant discourses of Napoléon III's regime—and a kind of idiosyncratic fantasy. Reflecting back on 1848 in a series of journal entries about his state of mind at the time, Baudelaire wrote:

> 1848 ne fut amusant que parce que chacun y faisait des utopies comme des châteaux en Espagne.
>
> 1848 ne fut charmant que par l'excès même du Ridicule. (Baud., *OC,* 1: 680)

> 1848 was only amusing because everyone built utopias like castles in Spain.
>
> 1848 was only charming because of the very excess of Ridiculousness.

"Utopia," for Baudelaire, designated an aesthetic category (of whimsy and excess) as much as a political one. And it was on the basis of aesthetics, as much as by his power to connote political opposition, that Baudelaire was attracted to Rousseau.

4 | *Baudelaire's* Physiologie

Rousseau as Caricature and Type in the
Prose Poems

By reducing complex arguments and rich narratives to single epithets or isolated images, Rousseau's enemies used his own words and self-portraits against him. Projecting their anxiety about their ability to determine and police the boundaries of "France" (both the literal boundaries they saw threatened by outside revolutionary movements and the identity of the "France" that they were discursively constructing at home), conservative French intellectuals in the mid-nineteenth century seized upon Rousseau as the nation's Other and wasted no opportunity to stereotype him as such. Baudelaire, in his own convoluted way, takes part in this "other"-ing process. By adopting in his prose poems the verbal caricatures available to him in the dominant discourse, he perpetuates the stereotypes and reinforces the oppositions put into play by his conservative compatriots. At times, he even seems to share their immense hatred of Rousseau. But Rousseau is a complex figure in *Le Spleen de Paris*. I believe that his widespread image and discursive function as "outcast" underlie many of Baudelaire's most affecting poems—those that elevate the marginal individual to "the status of modern hero" and thereby "unmask the arrogance and materialism of the Second Empire."[1] As the prototype of the outcast, "Rousseau" generates most of the compelling social types that suggest Baudelaire's resistance to the conservative economic and political practices of his day.

The type is a nexus of various aesthetic and sociohistorical currents that interested Baudelaire. Derived from ancient classical theater, mediated and relayed by medieval farce and the commedia dell'arte, linked to the nineteenth-century fascination with physiognomy and its social implications, wellspring

of caricature and key tool of allegory, the type is a locus of extreme density in Baudelaire's poetry. Although in our day and age, types appear to be synonymous with stereotypes—a reductive and dismissive approach to human character and experience,[2] they were at the heart of some of Baudelaire's most far-reaching works. Through his use of types—and especially his use of Rousseau as stereotype, social type, and personification in *Le Spleen de Paris*—Baudelaire reached back to those currents of Western art that we call "grotesque" and simultaneously participated in the contemporary sociohistorical debates of his day.

The Grotesque and Caricature

In the nineteenth century, the grotesque visual art associated with the rococo gave way to another fanciful and free artistic style, caricature. In eighteenth-century France, caricature was a newly emerging art form;[3] but with the proliferation of newspapers in the nineteenth century, it acquired particular cultural and political importance and took over where the grotesque left off: "Where did the playful spirit go, the equivalent of verbal pranks, that type of 'laughter' that took hold in the 'variety and strangeness' of ornament? Probably, looking at it closely, [it went] into caricature, that invention of disrespectful humor, which crossed the eighteenth century and would blossom with the press."[4] The German critic Friedrich Schlegel thought of caricature as "a passive connection of the naïve and the grotesque" and, taking his cue from Schlegel, Wolfgang Kayser concludes that "the grotesque is caricature without naïveté."[5] Baudelaire, too, associates the genres. Werner Hofmann observes: "For Baudelaire, caricature is inscribed in that family of forms that he characterizes in his notes on art in Belgium: 'Permanent state of transition.' . . . Well before art historians, Baudelaire delimits the different manifestations of a morphology of transitions: the gothic, the baroque, the rococo—and caricature, in other words, an anticlassical morphology."[6] Baudelaire equated some of the best caricature with the grotesque and, as we shall see, he put both to work in his poems in prose.[7]

The pictorial grotesque, with its curvilinear forms, fanciful creatures, and pervasive theatricality, may seem remote from the worldly subjects and satirical intent of caricature, until we begin to acknowledge their common ancestors (Callot's etchings of oddly human creatures, for example, or Arcimboldo's extraordinary reduction and transformation of forms)[8] and the way both the grotesque and caricature heighten our awareness of "the strangeness, oddity,

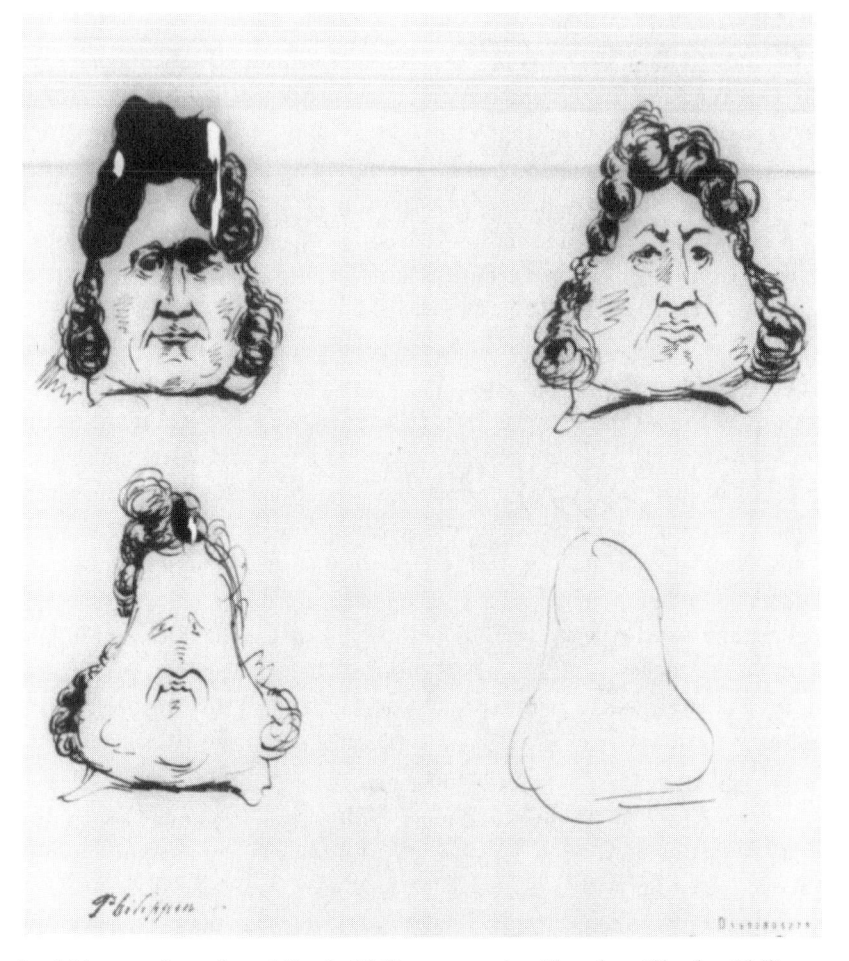

La Métamorphose du roi Louis-Philippe en poire. Sketches Charles Philipon drew in court in 1831 to defend himself against charges of defaming the king. Courtesy, Bibliothèque nationale de France.

and chaos of ordinary experience."[9] The visual grotesque and caricature have in common a freedom of invention, a light-heartedness (or a certain "excess of ridiculousness"),[10] and a predilection for metamorphosis. Both are fascinated with "the uncanny element when objects suddenly twist themselves into other shapes" or stand "on the threshold of two meanings."[11] Just as the grotesque showcases Phaeton's sisters being changed into trees or Actaeon becoming a stag, caricature turns an envious man into an owl or a king into a pear.[12]

What interests me particularly, however, is the focus on personification common to both. Obviously, personification presents itself very differently in the two genres. Whereas the grotesque art of the rococo period features mythological gods representing Beauty, Poetry, and other abstract ideas, caricature is allegorical insofar as it makes use of human figures or types to represent an attitude, a situation, or a social category.[13] In caricature, recognizable men and women replace the gods, who have lost their credibility. Nineteenth-century caricature benefited from the interest in physiognomic types promoted by Johann Lavater in the last years of the 1700s and from the subsequent vogue for representations of social types in books like the *Physiologies,* which proliferated in the 1840s, or the multivolume compendium, *Les Français peints par eux-mêmes.*[14] In these series, a wide range of middle-class life was categorized "according to profession, trade and avocation, [and] diagnosed by habits, customs and manners."[15] Illustrations accompanied the verbal descriptions, and the types thus crossed easily into caricature. Indeed, well-known caricaturists such as Joseph Traviès, Gavarni (Sulpice Guillaume Chevalier), and Honoré Daumier contributed illustrations to the *Physiologies.*

But caricatured types and traditional allegory have more in common than appearances might suggest. Just as traditional allegory associates personified ideas with emblems that allow them to be readily identified (the scales with Justice, the torch with Liberty, and so on), social types have their own physical tics and emblems (the paunch and wallet of the Banker, the stooped posture, broad-brimmed hat and crutches of the Beggar, the stick and sack of the Ragpicker).[16] Ernst Kris and E. H. Gombrich argue that even a topical caricature, representing actual, historical persons, reshapes these individuals as types;[17] treating them in a reductive and formulaic manner, caricature effectively turns these real persons into personifications or "walking Ideas."[18] Angus Fletcher, too, assimilates personification to caricature. Personification, he argues, exerts strong control over the message of an allegorical work, a control that

> may be thought of as a narrowing, a constriction, a compartmentalizing of meaning. Even when the allegory is more naturalistic, when it appropriates the language of documentary journalism, it bottles up concepts in the form of caricatures. . . . Even supposing that caricature evinces a delight in exaggeration of real characteristics, it still transforms what is purportedly real into an abstraction. . . . I would argue that caricature, as I have described it, is allegorical in essence, since it strives for the simplification of character in terms of single, predominant traits. The traits thus isolated are the iconographic "meanings" of each agent.[19]

Removed from their context, isolated as individual fragments, and set off by "a fixed frame," caricatured types, like personifications in traditional allegory, "appear as exemplary, as models, as significant, and [they] leave all 'the rest' in abeyance."[20]

Types provide a glimpse into an event or an era by isolating its most characteristic—and most easily characterized—features. Capturing the most telling attitudes or social categories of an epoch, types acquire such power that they assume "the stature of a moral model."[21] For their pictorial shorthand, their density of meaning and their moral value, Baudelaire viewed human types as the allegorical figures of choice for modern times.[22] If nothing else, we can infer this from Baudelaire's ample use of caricatured types in the *Petits Poèmes en prose*.

The Prose Poems as Caricature

Baudelaire was fascinated by caricature and wrote two essays on French and foreign caricaturists, which are usually read in conjunction with his essay on laughter, "De l'essence du rire." (In fact, Baudelaire originally intended to take caricature as his subject in the essay on laughter, which suggests the proximity of caricature and the grotesque in his mind.) Baudelaire admired caricature as a "fugitive" art capable of recording the events of modern life,[23] and his prose poems, too, have been described as "essentially fugitive," "fortuitous encounters of a dispersed, vaporized thought, catching hold of each object during its stroll in the modern capital," "fragments of an experience that is never successfully synthesized."[24]

By virtue of their autonomy and their diversity, the prose poems present themselves as a loose collection of vignettes and images that resemble the individually published and disseminated work of the caricaturists so popular in Baudelaire's day. Many of the poems have titles, such as "Chacun sa chimère" ("To Each His Chimera"), "Un Plaisant" ("A Joker"), "Le Joujou du pauvre" ("The Pauper's Toy"), "Les Yeux des pauvres" ("The Eyes of the Poor"), "Laquelle est la vraie?" ("Which Is the True One?"), "La Fausse Monnaie" ("The Counterfeit Coin"), "Un Cheval de race" ("A Thoroughbred"), "Le Galant Tireur" ("The Gallant Marksman"), and "Assommons les pauvres!" ("Let's Beat Up the Poor!"), that call to mind cartoon subjects or legends.[25] Furthermore, many of the poems have an evident visual quality.[26] The scene of the bourgeois saluting the donkey in the slush-covered street in "Un Plaisant," the decrepit acrobat shunned by the crowd in "Le Vieux Saltim-

banque" ("The Old Acrobat"), and the poor "family of eyes" marveling together at the extraordinary luxury of the new café in "Les Yeux des pauvres"
are just three of the vivid images that the prose poems inscribe indelibly in our
minds.[27] Finally, the poems make poignant use of the juxtaposition of opposites—the opposition of a type to its other (rich to poor, beautiful to ugly,
young to old) or the creation of situational contrasts,[28] a device frequently
used to focus and enliven caricature. When Baudelaire depicts the chagrin of
the old woman rejected by a newborn baby in "Le Désespoir de la vieille"
("The Old Woman's Despair"), the exquisite sensitivity of the fool or madman
and the cold disdain of the statue he loves in "Le Fou et la Vénus" ("The Fool
and the Venus"), or the radically dissimilar women each calling herself Bene-
dicta in "Laquelle est la vraie?" he draws on this caricatural approach.[29]

If a number of the poems in *Les Fleurs du mal* reveal Baudelaire's efforts to
create a "pictorialist poetics" by transposing works of painting or sculpture
into verse,[30] the prose poems represent Baudelaire's attempt to create a literary
genre that would emulate caricature's modernity.[31] Baudelaire wants to capture
his era by presenting its types. Although a few rich bourgeois—the speculator
of "La Fausse Monnaie," the fatuous partygoer of "Un Plaisant," and the
philanthropic journalist of "La Solitude"—anchor the analogy between the
Petits Poèmes en prose and the popular physiognomies of the day, Baudelaire is
especially taken with his society's marginal figures and outcasts. Beggars, fair
performers, itinerant peddlers, desperately poor families, street urchins, artists'
models, little old ladies, and widows traverse *Le Spleen de Paris,* evoking the
Parisian underclass of the mid-nineteenth century. These types attest to the
internal and external boundaries being drawn by the nationalist discourse of
the day, which discriminated between foreigners and Frenchmen, as well as
between marginalized social and economic groups and the vigorous, virile
bourgeoisie.

Presenting the oppressed with understanding and affection, Baudelaire
reinscribes the dichotomies imposed by the dominant discourse—with a difference. As Ainslie McLees argues, Baudelaire's poetic caricatures call forth such
empathy for the marginal types they depict that these figures often emerge as
"the heroes of modern life, the gods of ancient mythology."[32] Contrasting the
little old lady's joy as she dotes on a newborn child with the "eternal solitude"
she feels when the baby rejects her, the third-person narrator of "Le Désespoir
de la vieille" enters closely into the marginalized woman's thoughts. Similarly,
the immobile old acrobat deserted by the fairgoing crowd in "Le Vieux Saltimbanque" brings a lump to the narrator's throat and causes him to feel "sudden

pain." And the narrators of "Les Yeux des pauvres" and "La Fausse Monnaie" roundly criticize their friends who disregard the plight of the poor.[33] By calling sympathetic attention to those who are excluded by his society, Baudelaire takes a stand against the values and practices of the conservative majority.

In the same vein, the prose poems manifest Baudelaire's will to engage with current events and ideological debates.[34] "Chacun sa chimère," for example, makes subtle allusion to the Risorgimento, by associating "Roman foot soldiers" with the chimerical turn of mind usually deemed diagnostic of utopianism: "Chacun d'eux portait sur son dos une énorme Chimère, aussi lourde qu'un sac de farine ou de charbon, ou le fourniment d'un fantassin romain" ("Each one of them carried on his back an enormous Chimera, as heavy as a sack of flour or coal, or the equipment of a Roman foot soldier"). Tucked into a list of innocuous burdens born by laborers and peasants, the reference to the "fourniment d'un fantassin romain" might be a reminder of the long ago past (indeed, the very next paragraph alludes to "anciens guerriers"). But in a poem that foregrounds "chimeras," the buzzword so readily proffered by the conservatives in 1861 to attack the revolutionary movement at France's door and the sympathetic stirrings it caused at home, the allusion to the Roman army had very up-to-the-minute connotations. Despite the narrator's ultimate assertion of his indifference to chimerical ideals, the poem is, if anything, a sign of Baudelaire's renewed interest in utopian politics.[35]

Similarly, "Un Plaisant" goes beyond the expression of extreme annoyance at the self-satisfaction and condescension of the bourgeoisie. It conveys more than dismay at the violent contrasts between the newly minted leisure class, celebrating the New Year with excess, and the duty-bound workers who have no respite from their labor. When the narrator concludes that his protagonist (the "magnificent imbecile" who ceremoniously salutes a passing donkey and then seeks his friends' approval) concentrates in himself "all the spirit of France," he is setting out more than a satire of a single type or even a satire of social mores. His tongue-lashing takes unspoken aim at the fatuousness of the ongoing debates about the present and future identity of France; it has a distinct political edge. The backdrop of the vignette, the "official delirium" ("délire officiel") of the holiday, subtly prepares and supports this political meaning. The "spirit of France" surfaces as an issue in the context of—and actively promoted by—the officious government of Napoléon III, and the poem expresses "incommensurable rage" at this fact.

Baudelaire was not indifferent to the ideological issues of his day; and, as these two examples reveal, his caricatures often have an ideological content

that goes well beyond identification with the poor. Beyond this surface meaning, I submit, they contain "an element of riddle-guessing and of punning, involving the audience in the pleasures of deciphering a silent code," to use Judith Wechsler's words.[36] Such a code is at work in the caricatures of Rousseau that Baudelaire draws precisely from the contemporary debates over "l'esprit de la France." As I hope to demonstrate, Rousseau is the "enigmatic man" of *Le Spleen de Paris,* whose role in the collection the liminal poem "L'Etranger" ("The Foreigner" / "The Stranger" / "The Outsider") obliquely sets out.[37] He is the encoded figure whose shadowy presence Baudelaire's anonymous social types all but conceal.

In sum, in appearing to portray "types rather than individuals, and modest, often domestic, situations,"[38] Baudelaire plays a double game.[39] Social caricature, which "predominated during the periods of political censorship, from 1835 to 1848 and from 1852 to 1866,"[40] allows him to keep under wraps the primary object of his fascination—Rousseau.[41]

Rousseau as Social Type

When Baudelaire adopted the fallen idol of the French Revolution as the dominant figure in his prose poems, he took on a preexisting set of verbal caricatures and images that clustered around Rousseau's name. "Rousseau" as "outcast" had already generated a series of "secondary personalities" or "partial aspects" that Baudelaire could spin off into a wide variety of individual types for use in his poems.[42] Indeed, the Rousseau caricatures that are objects of scorn in the dominant discourse turn up in the prose poems among the marginal figures that Baudelaire sympathetically portrays.[43] To name but a few of the images that Baudelaire borrows from the contemporary political discourse, "Rousseau" is:

• The foreigner or stranger (*l'étranger*). As a Genevan, Rousseau was obviously a foreigner, and most critics mention this in passing, usually to make a negative point. Victor Cousin accuses Rousseau of taking art too far and having excessive scruples, "which have the whiff of a foreigner" ("qui sentent un peu l'étranger"). Similarly, the legitimist cleric Denis de Frayssinous charged that Jean-Jacques had spread "a profusion of brilliant and seductive lies; . . . and the century that called itself the century of light prostrate[d] itself before the foreign sophist [*le sophiste étranger*] who gravely spout[ed] the most savage theories." Clearly anticipating the counterrevolutionary

current of the middle years of the century, these authors suggest that Rousseau falsifies "the French spirit."[44] The characterization finds its clearest expression in Baudelaire's liminal poem "L'Etranger," which is in many ways a counterpart to Rousseau's own self-portrait in the first of his *Rêveries*.[45]

- The loner (*le solitaire*). Rousseau's solitude is a recurring theme in discussions of the author, including one of the earliest depictions Baudelaire would have encountered—the generally positive pages Abel-François Villemain devoted to Rousseau in the twenty-third, twenty-fourth, and twenty-fifth lessons of the *Cours de littérature française,* a book Baudelaire won as a school prize in 1838.[46] This solitude is underlined, of course, in Rousseau's own final venture into autobiography, *Les Rêveries du promeneur solitaire,* and throughout Baudelaire's poems.

- The mountebank (*le saltimbanque* or *le charlatan*). The accusation that Rousseau was a sophist or a hypocrite takes various forms. As we saw in Chapter 3, Nisard uses the word *charlatan* with all the virulence it can convey to dismiss "Jean-Jacques," and Proudhon attacks Rousseau as "le charlatan genevois." In fact, Proudhon concludes his scathing comments on the *Contrat social* by calling it Rousseau's "masterpiece of oratory juggling."[47] This negative stereotype, and especially Proudhon's association of it with "juggling," undoubtedly influenced Baudelaire's depiction of Rousseau as the immobile acrobat in "Le Vieux Saltimbanque," although Baudelaire borrows the physical traits of the old performer from various of Rousseau's self-portraits and the description of the fair from Rousseau's writing on the Paris Opéra.

- The beggar (*le mendiant*). Authors as ideologically diverse as Villemain (*Cours,* 2: 221), Louis Blanc, Michelet, and Sainte-Beuve evoked Rousseau's poverty. Louis Blanc depicts Rousseau as "a poor child from Geneva, who had been a vagabond, who had been a beggar and a lackey [*un mendiant et un laquais*]!"[48] Baudelaire uses the figure incidentally in several poems and gives the beggar a central role in "La Fausse Monnaie," which, I believe, builds upon an example in Rousseau's fourth *rêverie.*

- The madman (*le fou*). This trait is so frequently cited by both partisans and detractors as to be nearly universal in nineteenth-century depictions of Rousseau. Nisard, as we saw, uses it to undermine Rousseau, his works, and their effects on nineteenth-century politics. But in "Le Fou et la Vénus," Baudelaire may have been responding to Sainte-Beuve's assessment that Rousseau preferred abstract beauty to its earthly incarnation.[49]

- The creator of chimeras (*l'esprit de chimère*). In "Chacun sa chimère,"

Baudelaire both references the contemporary revolution in Italy and relates it to the current worries about the renascent utopianism that fueled it. In this connection, the topic of "chimeras" could hardly fail to evoke the violent attacks against Rousseau by conservatives such as Lamartine and Nisard.

• And even the old or masculinized woman (*le femmelin*). Rousseau's greatest admirer, Michelet, exclaims ("what a marvelous thing") that Rousseau had the forcefulness and rational vigor of the Port-Royal writers "in the heart of a woman."[50] From an opposite point of view, Proudhon puts down Rousseau, whom he holds partly responsible for the nineteenth-century's moral decay, calling him "the first of those *little women* of the mind ['ces *femmelins* de l'intelligence'], in whom, their ideas becoming clouded, passion or emotion takes over from reason, and who, despite their eminent, even virile qualities, make literature and society bend toward their decline."[51] In "Le Désespoir de la vieille," Baudelaire combines this caricature of Rousseau as a woman with Rousseau's own musings, in the ninth *rêverie*, about children's horror of his aging face.

The list is not exhaustive, as we shall see. Baudelaire, who thought that creating a cliché was the soul of genius ("Créer un poncif, c'est le génie. Je dois créer un poncif"),[52] did not have to put his creative ability to the test in this way. Instead, he found a series of ready-made images or "idées reçues" in the contemporary iconography of Rousseau, and he displayed his genius by expanding upon these received images in rhetorically and ideologically complex ways.

Psychoanalysts and art historians, basing their ideas on Freudian psychology, argue that the impetus for caricature is aggression, the will to diminish or debase the subject.[53] This is certainly true of the reductive images of Rousseau bandied about with relish by the likes of Désiré Nisard. In the heated disputes over the "spirit of France," Rousseau is more often than not the villain, and the aim of the caricature or stereotyping is to unmask, degrade, and disarm this eighteenth-century monster.[54] Baudelaire does engage in some Rousseau-bashing, and nowhere more joyfully than in "Le Mauvais Vitrier," as we shall see. But Baudelaire does not follow Nisard and his fellow travelers in their one-sided attacks on Rousseau. For one thing, in his critical remarks on the caricaturist Nicolas Charlet, Baudelaire makes it clear that he does not condone the use of caricature for the dissemination of "nationalist stupidities" and political slogans, and, furthermore, that he does not believe that such caricature has lasting value.[55] For Baudelaire, the effectiveness of cartoons derives

from the disinterested depiction of moral ugliness,[56] not from simplistic adherence to one ideological position or another. Baudelaire's ideas about caricature's function seem to preclude any dogmatic position-taking.

Instead, Baudelaire practices what Richard Terdiman calls "re/citation." By knowingly repeating the conservatives' seemingly endless clichés about Rousseau, Baudelaire "attempts to introduce difference" within the dominant discourse's hackneyed slogans.[57] In so doing, he distances himself from the mindless nationalism so prevalent at the time and reveals his desire to assert his own independent ideas about Rousseau over against the mind-numbing rhetoric of others.

"Le Promeneur solitaire"

Baudelaire's will to do something different with "Rousseau" comes through in his choice of "Le Promeneur solitaire" as a possible title for his poems. We know that Baudelaire had the eighteenth-century author in mind as he searched for a title for his collection. The indirect references to Rousseau's *Rêveries du promeneur solitaire* in Baudelaire's letters in the early 1860s testify to the impact this work had on him when he was composing the poems in prose. In February 1860, Baudelaire wrote to his friend Auguste Poulet-Malassis about the "rêveries" he thought of writing to accompany Charles Meryon's engravings of Paris: "voilà une occasion d'écrire des rêveries de dix lignes, de vingt ou de trente lignes, sur de belles gravures, les *rêveries philosophiques d'un flâneur parisien*" ("there's an opportunity to write some reveries of ten, twenty, or thirty lines, on some beautiful engravings, the *philosophical reveries of a Parisian stroller*").[58] And in February 1862, between the letter to Houssaye in which he suggested "Le Promeneur solitaire" as a title and the publication of the prose poems, he made a similar reference, promising to send Sainte-Beuve "plusieurs paquets de *Rêvasseries* en prose" ("several packets of *ungainly Reveries* in prose").[59] Between the demise of the Meryon project and the collective publication of the poems by Houssaye, the plan to write the "reveries of a Parisian stroller" became the basis for the *Petits Poèmes en prose.*[60]

However, I submit that "Le Promeneur solitaire" was suggested to Baudelaire as a possible title for his work not only by Rousseau's *Rêveries* but also by the nineteenth-century's infatuation with the *Physiologies,* which depicted a given social type—"the Englishman in Paris," "the cuckold," "the salesgirl," "the deputy," "the drinker"—in multiple versions and poses.[61] Indeed, the other title Baudelaire proposed to Arsène Houssaye, as an alternative to "Le

Promeneur solitaire," was "Le Rôdeur parisien," which imitates the title of Balisson de Rougemont's six-volume *Le Rôdeur français; ou, Les Moeurs du jour* (1816–27), a forerunner of the *Physiologies*. The possibility that Baudelaire had in mind the fashionable books of his time as he developed his prose poem collection is reinforced in his letter-preface to Houssaye. Baudelaire's famous statement that he has created a work with no connecting narrative or thread—"Nous pouvons couper où nous voulons, moi ma rêverie, vous le manuscrit, le lecteur sa lecture" ("We can cut where we want, I my reverie, you the manuscript, the reader his reading")—and his reference to his collection as a "tortueuse fantaisie," or tortuous fantasy (like a serpent), seem to echo a humorous remark by Charles Philipon in his *Physiologie du floueur*. There, Philipon, the publisher of many of the nineteenth century's most famous caricaturists, teases his own editor about the kind of cookie-cutter production in which they are engaged: "Here, Aubert, here is a chapter that we shall lengthen by a league, if that is necessary,—a chapter that you will cut, like a thread, just at the place where your one hundred and twenty-one pages come to an end." Accompanying this needling dialogue is a drawing of a man in a landscape "holding an enormous ribbon of paper covered with various hieroglyphic images" and shaped like a slithering snake.[62] Taking up, tongue in cheek, Philipon's humorous critique, Baudelaire displays his awareness of the formulaic conditions governing the new mass production of books and links his own work to this ephemeral new genre.[63]

According to Richard Sieburth, who has thoughtfully analyzed the *Physiologies,* these topical books transformed the radical anonymity of the Parisian crowd "into a lexicon of nameable stereotypes, thereby providing their readers with the comforting illusion that the faceless conglomerations of the modern city could after all be read—and hence mastered—as a legible system of differences." Baudelaire, too, may have wanted to defuse the "genuine social antagonisms or class conflicts which might otherwise imperil the nervous complacency" of his readers, when he offered "Rousseau" back to the conservative public as a mirror of its own preoccupations.[64] Or, more likely, he may have intended to trade on Rousseau by turning him into a marketable commod-

(*On pages 87–89*) Types drawn from the *Physiologies: Boulanger* and *Charretier* by Gavarni, in Rittner and Goupil, *Physionomie de la population de Paris* (1831); *Le Chiffonnier* by Joseph Traviès, in *Physionomie de Paris* (1840). Courtesy, Bibliothèque nationale de France.

Gavarni

Lith. de Kony.

BOULANGER.

Baker.

à Paris chez Aubert et Compd. Grand Montmartre 1842.   London Published by Tilt & Bogue, Fleet Street.

CHARRETIER.

Carter.

A Paris chez Hallare et Gouget, Rue Montmartre 11. London Pub.d Sep.t 1831. Tilt, &c. Fleet Str.t 86.

LE CHIFFONNIER.

Je n'aime pas l'Auteur qui a dit « Il est défendu de déposer des ordures le long des murs. »

ity—producing a whole gallery of Rousseau caricatures, in the manner of the *Physiologies.*

Yet, despite this obvious inspiration, "Le Promeneur solitaire" is not a mere work of mechanical reproduction, featuring clichés of Rousseau. Reading through the collection of prose poems, it becomes clear that the eponymous walker is also the poetic "I" who gathers these vignettes into a loose relationship based on his experience of the city. The themes of solitude and walking are a leitmotif of the *Petits Poèmes en prose,* and "le promeneur solitaire et pensif" is a recurrent figure, a shadow of the poet, who traverses and provides a tenuous link between the poems.[65] In his journal, for instance, Baudelaire refers to the man of genius as "un, donc solitaire" ("one, therefore solitary"), and he clearly approves and partakes of this difficult solitude.[66]

Baudelaire also uses the epithet to refer to other artists and poets with whom he identifies. The solitary walker is not just an apt image of the narrator or the principal protagonist of the poems but a collective name Baudelaire gives to the artists he admires—those who, as Benjamin puts it, "crossed the city . . . lost in their thoughts or their worries."[67] The watercolorist and illustrator Constantin Guys, whose work Baudelaire extols in "Le Peintre de la vie moderne" ("The Painter of Modern Life"), is one such "solitary man" who moves in the crowds;[68] Thomas de Quincey is another. Baudelaire paints a picture of the Englishman, whose story he retells in part 2 of the *Paradis artificiels,* as "un promeneur sombre et solitaire, plongé dans le flot mouvant des multitudes" ("a somber and solitary walker, plunged into the moving flow of the multitudes"); and he identifies his own nightmares with de Quincey's melancholy and pain. Rousseau, who first identified himself as a marginal figure cast out by his society and expressed the pain entailed in that situation, is thus the prototype of many others.[69] Just as "Jean-Jacques" in the "Poème du hachisch" is the "modern man with his acute and vibrant senses, his painfully subtle spirit," Rousseau is once again "a type, a hero" in the *Petits Poèmes en prose.*[70] Representing "modern man in his entirety, with his weaknesses, his aspirations and his despair,"[71] he succinctly attaches Baudelaire's idea of the modern artist to his modernist project, the poems in prose.

Baudelaire thought of *la modernité* as a "portrait" of the present, combining immutable beauty with the transitory, fugitive, or contingent aspects of social life, which give each period its distinctive character.[72] In the chapter on modernity in "Le Peintre de la vie moderne," he observes that "la plupart des beaux portraits qui nous restent des temps antérieurs sont revêtus des costumes de leur époque" ("most of the beautiful portraits that are left to us from

previous ages are wearing the dress of their period") and concludes that the artist of modernity must seek out for his portrait not only the fashions, but the professions and the characters that are metonymic signs of his time. Types incarnate "l'idiotisme de beauté particulier à chaque époque" ("the idiomatic language of beauty peculiar to each epoch").[73] They serve modernity as one effective means of capturing those ever-changing elements that make the present unique; they help the artist "vitalize" or "vivify" the present and defy the deadliness of time.[74] Like "le militaire," "le dandy," and "la femme galante," types painted by Guys, they capture the ethos of their day.[75] (For example, if dandyism is "the last flash of heroism in periods of decadence," if dandies appear at those times when democracy is not yet all-powerful and the aristocracy is only partially destabilized and defiled (Baud., *OC*, 2: 711), then the presence of dandies in Guys's sketches connotes the transitional, decadent, and unbalanced character of French society under the government of Napoléon III.)

Types, in Baudelaire's usage, are human figures whose character or style gives them a distinctive stamp, a singularity that is paradoxically emblematic of an era. Individuality and imperfection are essential,[76] for they are the key to recognizability, which in turn allows the figure to embody a social category or a way of being.[77] Charles Nodier, in his essay on types in literature (1830), argues that no fictional character or dramatic persona can be a type if it doesn't have "that original expression of individuality" that is so surprising and so indelible that it becomes familiar, across cultures and languages, to everyone.[78] Nodier has in mind those characters or proper names—such as Hamlet, Werther, or René—that are transformed over time into common nouns or household words. As "persons" or personifications, they bring life to abstract or general ideas. Thus "Achilles" is an expressive word for "hero" or "demigod"; "Hamlet" is a "complete prototype of the Middle Ages"; and Chateaubriand's "René" is "the mortal anxiety, the inexorable doubt, the inconsolable despair of a death without a future; he's the horrifying cry of social creation at the moment of its dissolution."[79]

Rousseau, the proper name behind "Le Promeneur solitaire," is just such a distinctive and familiar figure. Although he is the emblem of an earlier age, whose temperament he seemed so well suited to express,[80] he continues to have value for Baudelaire as the prototype of the alienated modern man or artist and as the refracted image of the French Revolution, whose effects were at least partly responsible for this alienated state. "Le Promeneur solitaire" is a character who is not necessarily prevalent but is nonetheless typical of the modern age—summing up in himself an attitude fostered by the unique so-

cial and political climate of the time.[81] He brings to mind the restlessness and melancholy of the individual confronted with the extraordinary flux of the modern city, or the artist's isolation as he tries to seize and translate into words the distinctiveness of his ever-changing surroundings. As Benjamin argues, "The allegorist's gaze that falls upon the city is . . . the gaze of alienated man."[82]

"Rousseau" as Baudelaire's Standard-bearer

Baudelaire's choice of a familiar and historically rooted type as the over-arching figure for his poetry collection helps elucidate his project in the prose poems and its relationship to caricature. In choosing Rousseau, the prototypical "solitary walker," as his quintessential type, I submit, Baudelaire was emulating two artists he admired, the poet Aloysius Bertrand and the popular French caricaturist Honoré Daumier. In the letter-preface to the *Petits Poèmes en prose,* Baudelaire specifically cites Bertrand's book as the inspiration for his own; and although critics have discounted this assertion, it is clear that Baudelaire shared Bertrand's interest in allegorical figures or types and was prone to using them in his work.[83] In his book of prose poems *Gaspard de la Nuit,* Bertrand literally envisages art "under [the] double personification" or the "two antithetical faces" of the real-life artists Rembrandt and Callot, conceived as artistic types.[84] Bertrand takes "Rembrandt" to represent the sublime philosopher absorbed in meditation and prayer, while his "Callot" is the boisterous soldier who enjoys the sensual pleasures of life. Thus reduced to simple figures or caricatured types, "Rembrandt" and "Callot" become the allegorical bearers of Bertrand's ideas about the doubleness of art in the same way that "Rousseau" is Baudelaire's (hidden) standard-bearer.

Daumier, too, whom Baudelaire lionized as "one of the most important men of modern art,"[85] makes extensive use of individualized types in his cartoons:

> One of Daumier's most effective satirical tricks is the use of type-figures, especially Ratapoil and Robert Macaire. Ratapoil was what Henry James . . . called "the ragged political bully, or hand-to-mouth demagogue," while Macaire, originally a character in a popular melodrama, epitomized the arch swindler who can turn his hand to anything. . . . These invented characters gave a narrative coherence to drawings published regularly but separately in the satirical journals, and encouraged a kind of complicity as readers followed their adventures week by week.[86]

Robert Macaire agent d'affaires. Honoré Daumier, 1836. *Caricaturana,* no. 13.
Courtesy, Bibliothèque nationale de France.

Like Ratapoil, Macaire was a fictional character, endowed with a proper name and a set of characteristics already well known from his role in the theater, who was "put through a variety of contemporary situations and stresses and given different professions" in Daumier's one hundred and one drawings of him.[87] Macaire took on various roles and incarnated a variety of social types compatible with his core characteristics, ranging from the self-reflexive "Robert Macaire congratulating Daumier on his series," to the speculator, to the ubiquitous Macaire ("Robert Macaire partout," as Jean Adhémar calls him) who turns up in almost every walk of life.[88] Macaire was "not merely a name, but also an image with the power to generate numerous associations."[89] Because his character was so pervasive—so recognizable among real Parisians of the 1830s, the editors of *Le Charivari,* the publication that commissioned Daumier's drawings, concluded that Macaire's "type persists as the most complete personification of the period."[90] As we have seen, evidence internal to the poems suggests that Baudelaire wanted "Rousseau" to function in the prose poems in much the same way.

Combining Bertrand's use of real historical figures as allegorical types with Daumier's use of a single type-figure to provide continuity among his separately published lithographs, Baudelaire's Rousseau would have given a narrative coherence, an artistic stamp, and a certain political flavor to the *Petits Poèmes en prose* had Baudelaire acknowledged his presence by retaining the title "Le Promeneur solitaire."[91] Once it was dropped, however, the frame of reference for the poems was erased, and the various characters Baudelaire based on Rousseau lost their topical punch. No longer linked to a proper name or recognizable figure, the poems became a series of seemingly generic social caricatures.[92]

Nonetheless, even without the title, Baudelaire uses his chosen type ("Rousseau") to full advantage. Masquerading as an anonymous outcast alternately representing a social class, a trade, a personality type or an activity, Rousseau's features run through the poems the way the familiar face and frame of Macaire dominated Daumier's cartoons between 1835 and 1838.[93] More important than his simple presence as a faintly ridiculous or pathetic figure, however, is the way he functions as the allegorical bearer of the poet's ideas about art and the artist. Rousseau was not only an alienated man and beleaguered artist in his own time, but also the principal theoretician and early practitioner of modern allegory, which Baudelaire studied carefully and puts into practice in his poems. Baudelaire's modernist aesthetic, built around the allegorical use of social types,[94] finds its form in the fugitive art of verbal caricature and its

prototype in the "person" of "Rousseau," as an analysis of "Le Mauvais Vitrier" ("The Bad Glazier") will show.

Rousseau in "Le Mauvais Vitrier"

What makes "Le Mauvais Vitrier" a particularly apt example is that it combines caricatures of Rousseau, written out as the deceptive story of a marginal social type (the glazier), with reflections on personification (the very rhetorical trope implicated in allegorical types); and it picks up this subject, together with its plot outline, from Rousseau's own eighth *rêverie*. Although scholars have linked "Le Mauvais Vitrier" to Arsène Houssaye's prose poem "La Chanson du Vitrier" and to Edgar Allan Poe's story "The Imp of the Perverse,"[95] Baudelaire's poem engages primarily in a complicated dialogue with Rousseau—an intertextual relation that has never been discussed. By conflating the caricatured type with recognizable clichés of Rousseau and a reflection on personification, "Le Mauvais Vitrier" brings out the connections that make caricature an allegorical art and demonstrates Rousseau's central role as a figure for this process. A close look at the poem and at the textual intertwinings will enable us to understand how and why Rousseau emerges as Baudelaire's figure of the grotesque.

"Le Mauvais Vitrier" is a poem in two parts. The first seven paragraphs develop the paradox that some "purely contemplative souls, completely unsuited for action" do nonetheless act at times "with a speed of which they would not have believed themselves capable." Along with several examples of the "absurd and dangerous" actions that these people commit, the narrator cites various attempts to comprehend this peculiar phenomenon, all of which yield the conclusion that such a double character or changeable behavior cannot be explained. Whatever prompts such people to deviate suddenly from their own natures and become different from themselves can only be "une impulsion mystérieuse et inconnue" ("a mysterious and unknown impulse") or "des Démons malicieux" ("malicious Demons").

In the second part of the poem, the narrator names himself as one of these strange individuals. He relates an incident in which he became suddenly and arbitrarily violent toward a poor glazier who was innocently peddling his wares on the streets of Paris. Tired of doing nothing and "pushed" to make some grand gesture, the narrator opened his garret window and heard the discordant cry of the peddler below. Instantly overtaken with a sudden and despotic hatred for this poor man, the narrator called him up to his sixth floor flat, where

he proceeded to excoriate the vendor for having no colored panes of glass. Instead of concluding a purchase, the narrator accused the man of impudence for daring to walk about the poor parts of town without offering its downtrodden inhabitants a brighter view of life ("la vie en beau"). As if in punishment, he then pushed the glazier down the stairs and promptly hurled a flowerpot from his balcony at the peddler's emerging back.[96] The results were catastrophic; the glazier lost his balance and fell backward, crushing his fragile merchandise: "[J]e laissai tomber perpendiculairement mon engin de guerre sur le rebord postérieur de ses crochets; et le choc le renversant, il acheva de briser sous son dos toute sa pauvre fortune ambulatoire, qui rendit le bruit éclatant d'un palais de cristal crevé par la foudre" ("I let my engine of war drop down perpendicularly on the back edge of [the] frame [that held his wares]. The blow [*le choc*] knocked him over, and he ended by breaking under his back all his poor ambulatory fortune, which made the clattering sound of a crystal palace smashed by lightning"). Looking back on the incident, the narrator acknowledges that he was "drunk with madness" ("ivre de ma folie"); but although he knows that he may have damned himself by his despicable actions, he is still unrepentant. For all its moral dubiousness, his "prank" gave him infinite pleasure.

On the strength of the gratuitous violence it depicts, "Le Mauvais Vitrier" is horrifying; and yet it outlines a situation familiar from Baudelaire's essay on laughter. The sudden mysterious and unwilled transformation of the narrator and the other "inoffensive dreamers" in the poem recalls the example of the commedia dell'arte troupe in "De l'essence du rire," who are magically transformed from ordinary people into comic types or masks when the "breath of the marvelous" ("le souffle merveilleux") floats over them.[97] The players are propelled by an unnamable energy into their new existence.[98] Before the public's eyes, they become different from themselves. As in "Le Mauvais Vitrier," there is no obvious explanation for the change that comes over the performers and therefore there are no proper terms with which to convey it. The subtle metamorphosis that overtakes these "persons" renders the moment when the grotesque takes hold of the sign and whirls the viewer or reader away into a new, irrational world. In just the same way, "Le Mauvais Vitrier" unfolds under the sign of the grotesque. Thus this poem, which combines politically motivated caricatures of Rousseau with a critical rewriting of Rousseau's eighth *rêverie,* is of no small interest for our understanding of Rousseau as the figure of the grotesque.

The caricature of Rousseau in this poem has a double (and contradictory) origin. It seems to stem from a comment made by Proudhon, who grudgingly admired Rousseau's capacity for rousing souls to action ("he set fire to the powder that had been accumulating among the literate French for two centuries"),[99] and especially from negative remarks by Baudelaire's sometime mentor, the influential literary critic Sainte-Beuve. In a column dated November 4, 1850, devoted to Rousseau's *Confessions,* Sainte-Beuve writes several paragraphs on the subject of Rousseau's character. Among other traits, he cites Rousseau's timidity and the spontaneous acting-out that was its counterpart: "[Rousseau] has these long periods of timidity that suddenly turn into the brazen acts of a *scamp* or a *good-for-nothing,* as he calls himself."[100] According to Sainte-Beuve, Rousseau has "a sick side, too much ardor mixed with inaction and idleness [*trop d'ardeur mêlée à l'inaction et au désoeuvrement*], a preponderant imagination and sensitivity that are inward-turning and self-consuming."[101] This thumbnail sketch of Jean-Jacques as "timide" and "désoeuvré" but also capable of sudden, ill-considered, and mean-spirited action gives rise to the lineup of indolent or timid men in Baudelaire's poem, who act without regard for the consequences of their behavior or, worse, out of deliberate malice.[102] The narrator's own "oisiveté" and his explanation that impulsive men like himself are motivated "par caprice, par désoeuvrement" bring him into line with this negative image of Rousseau.

On the basis of this analogy between the narrator and "Rousseau," the poem appears to be an ironic but savage indictment of Rousseau's irresponsibility and self-delusion. Because he is unable or unwilling to identify with the misfortunes of others, the narrator-"Rousseau" engages in a recklessly immoral act, which is likely to bring him eternal damnation. The poem concludes with a sarcastic remark that makes the moral point: "Mais qu'importe l'éternité de la damnation à qui a trouvé dans une seconde l'infini de la jouissance?" ("But what does an eternity of damnation matter to someone who has experienced for one second the infinity of delight?"). Insofar as the narrator is an avatar of Rousseau, the poem lambastes its model and his kin for selfishly indulging their own whims at the expense of others.[103]

But Baudelaire is not content to borrow the traits for his caricature of Rousseau from Sainte-Beuve and the contemporary political discourse; he also seeks out an example of Rousseau's self-involvement or "inward-turning" in Rousseau's last autobiography and reworks it in his poem. In the eighth *rêverie,* Rousseau depicts himself as an impulsive man, whose behavior

changes with the shocks or blows inflicted on him by others. Although he is naturally indolent, he can become passionate and enraged when affected from without. "C'est mon naturel ardent qui m'agite," Rousseau says, "c'est mon naturel indolent qui m'apaise" ("It's the ardour of my character that excites me and the nonchalance of my character that pacifies me").[104] If left to himself, however, he is stable and calm. He enjoys being alone and avoids contact with others. In this way, Rousseau claims, he achieves a certain contentedness and an indifference to the world at large. The self-portrait he paints coheres with Sainte-Beuve's assessment of Rousseau and with Baudelaire's poem, except for one particular: since Rousseau places the blame for his erratic behavior on others' malevolence and positions himself as the unwitting and passive victim of their actions, he carves out a role for himself that resembles not so much that of Baudelaire's narrator as that of the "vitrier." If Rousseau is the poor glazier who does nothing to merit the narrator's attacks, the poem's stance toward the eighteenth-century figure is much less clear. Is Baudelaire, then, attacking Rousseau on a whim? When the narrator throws his flowerpot at the glazier's "fortune ambulatoire," is he merely having fun destroying Rousseau's "ambulatory" work, *Les Rêveries du promeneur solitaire*? Or does the narrator's complaint about the glazier's lack of beautiful colored glass represent an attack on Rousseau for not being *enough* of a utopianist, for his failure to support the cause of the poor despite his own experience of poverty, or even for his supposed realism?[105] Reading the poem alongside the Rousseau work leaves open the question of where Baudelaire stands.

It might be enough to say that "Le Mauvais Vitrier" is a modernist poem by virtue of its duplicity. Putting into play a negative caricature of Rousseau that brings out the eighteenth-century author's bad character, it overtly takes the side of the dominant conservative discourse that scorns or even vilifies Rousseau (although, admittedly, no one has ever taken note of this "overt" stand). Beneath this surface negativity, however, is what appears to be more of the same. However we look at it, the underlying allegorical meaning seems thoroughly damning. But—as we have come to expect from Baudelaire's allegories—the poem is more than double; the extensive attack on Rousseau is balanced by the poem's pervasive rhetorical and textual use of the same *rêverie* on which its plot relies. In addition to being an exculpatory explanation of Rousseau's character, the eighth *rêverie* is an exploration of the operation and value of personification, and Baudelaire trades heavily on this fact. If the plot of "Le Mauvais Vitrier" leads us to believe that Baudelaire hates Rousseau, Baudelaire's admiration for Rousseau comes out in the poem's rhetorical subtext.

Personification in the Eighth Rêverie and "Le Mauvais Vitrier"

Rousseau's eighth *rêverie* takes up a philosophical question that has rhetorical ramifications. The subject of the *rêverie*—whether events in life are best viewed as random and mechanical or as personally willed—can also be read as an inquiry into rhetoric's mechanical operation and "personal" effects.[106] Rousseau's ostensible purpose in this *rêverie* is to understand why he is hated and shunned by other men, so that he can harden himself against them. Scrutinizing his enemies' behavior, however, Rousseau quickly comes to the realization that he will never be able to understand them. Because their actions have no relation to logic, because they do not reflect any principled judgment, they must be the effect of chance ("l'effet du hazard"). Determining that their actions are devoid of content, Rousseau decides that the men themselves are merely "des êtres méchaniques qui n'agiss[ent] que par impulsion et dont je ne [peux] calculer l'action que par les loix du mouvement" ("mechanical beings, entirely governed by external impulses [impulsion], whose behavior I [can] only calculate according to the laws of motion").[107] This accomplishes two goals: once the enemies are depersonalized and viewed as machines, their intentions or the meaning of their actions no longer matter; the men are simply "des masses différemment mues, depourvues à mon égard de toute moralité" ("bodies moved in different ways, devoid of any moral relation to me").[108] And yet, devoid as they are of any meaning, they immediately return within the reach of understanding, converted from illogical events to necessary and measurable physical laws.

On the basis of these initial observations about his own fate, Rousseau recommends against personification. Because personal insult is so much more damaging than mere physical destruction, he argues that the best way to keep sanguine about misfortune is not to attribute it to other people's malice—not to personify it:

Dans tous les maux qui nous arrivent, nous regardons plus à l'intention qu'à l'effet. Une tuile qui tombe d'un toit peut nous blesser davantage mais ne nous navre pas tant qu'une pierre lancée à dessein par une main malveillante.[109] Le coup porte à faux quelquefois mais l'intention ne manque jamais son atteinte. La douleur matérielle est ce qu'on sent le moins dans les atteintes de la fortune, et quand les infortunés ne savent à qui s'en prendre de leurs malheurs ils s'en prennent à la destinée qu'ils personnifient et à laquelle ils prètent des yeux et une intelligence pour les tourmenter à dessein. C'est ainsi qu'un joueur dépité par ses pertes se met en fureur sans

savoir contre qui. Il imagine un sort qui s'acharne à dessein sur lui pour le tourmenter et trouvant un aliment à sa colère il s'anime et s'enflamme contre l'ennemi qu'il s'est créé. L'homme sage qui ne voit dans tous les malheurs qui lui arrive[nt] que les coups de l'aveugle necessité n'a point ces agitations insensées . . . il ne sent du mal dont il est la proye que l'atteinte materielle et les coups qu'il reçoit ont beau blesser sa personne pas un n'arrive jusqu'à son coeur.

In all the ills that befall us, we are more concerned by the intention than the result. A tile that falls off a roof may injure us more seriously, but it will not wound us so deeply as a stone thrown deliberately by a malevolent hand. The blow may miss, but the intention always strikes home. The physical pain is what we feel least of all when fortune assails us, and when suffering people do not know whom to blame for their misfortunes, they attribute them to a destiny and personify this destiny, lending it eyes and a mind that purposely torments them. In the same way a gambler who is angered by his losses will fly into a fury against some unknown enemy; he imagines a fate that deliberately persists in torturing him, and having found something to feed his anger on, he storms and rages against the enemy that he has himself created. The wise man sees in all his misfortunes no more than the blows of blind necessity and feels none of this senseless agitation . . . he feels only the physical impact of the evil that besets him, and though the blows may hurt his body, not one of them can touch his heart.[110]

"Persons" have innerness, logic, and ethical responsibility; machines do not. Thus the unlucky gambler who personifies fortune, endowing "her" with eyes, intelligence, and the intent to do him deliberate harm, makes himself even more unhappy; whereas the wise man who views his reverses only as "les coups de l'aveugle nécessité" ("the blows of blind necessity") is not prey to such unnecessary misery. Persons have intentions, which can be very hurtful; therefore it's better to view life as a series of random mechanical events.

This passage on personification is quirky and dense. In the example of the gambler Rousseau explicitly names chance (and loss) as the impetus behind personification, while personification works to oppose chance by attributing deliberate intent to others. Chance is the irrational problem that personification is called on to overcome. But in the example of the wise man and in Rousseau's own situation, chance is the remedy for the irrational behavior that personification promotes. Chance is alternately a problem and a cure—and so is personification. This short passage raises many questions about the value, effects, and function of personification, especially in a work that makes such frequent use of it. Rousseau presents personification as a choice he makes de-

liberately. He claims that a wise man is able to remain calm in the face of adversity by deciding not to personify his fate. But in the examples that illustrate the wisdom of rejecting personification, personification persists, not only in the "persons" of the gambler and the wise man, but also in the figures of "[sighted] fate" and "blind necessity." Personification comes back by chance, it seems, just when Rousseau expresses the intention to eliminate it.

This is perhaps even more evident in Rousseau's attempt to construe his enemies' impulses as predictable laws of motion. Both playing on and attempting to erase the double meaning of "impulsion," Rousseau wants to convert a series of inexplicable events into a necessary fact of life, in order to lessen their hold on him. But language has its own laws and is not so easily controlled. Rousseau may deliberately stress the idea that "impulse" is a physical phenomenon that can be calculated or predicted, but the notion that "impulse" is an unpredictable urge impelling human behavior persists despite his efforts. The difference between "impulse" as physical law and "impulse" as random psychological event makes all the difference to Rousseau, who relies on this difference to guarantee his own indifference to events; yet he is unable to keep the two apart in his eighth *rêverie.* Simultaneously designating two very different types of phenomena, the word "impulse" has an uncontrollable tendency toward personification.

As the persistence of the personal meaning of "impulse" shows, personification is not a technique systematically chosen or willed by the author; it is part of language's incontrovertible "mechanics." The referential shift from one idea of "impulse" to another is not subject to individual control. Necessary and unavoidable, it can be set in motion by an arbitrary "impulse" of language, acting without a cause. When Rousseau uses the example of the gambler personifying fate, he hints at this fact. The personification of chance imputes inscrutable and arbitrary intentions to a human figure and thus carries forward the theme of the impulsivity of human subjects; but, conversely, it also endows fate (or linguistic necessity) with the potential to control personification itself. The example raises the possibility that "persons" are created randomly or mechanically, as a necessary and unwilled effect of language; and this intuition is borne out by the remainder of the eighth *rêverie,* where the mechanics of personification ultimately benefit the autobiographical hero.[111]

In the second half of the *rêverie* Rousseau explains how the blows of fate (or the actions of others) set off his "mouvements involontaires." If his eyes flash or his limbs tremble, he asserts, that is beyond his control: "cela tient au seul physique"; it is "all purely physical" (1: 1083, 76). Reason and will can neither

cause nor govern these movements. Rousseau's passions are the necessary—unwilled and ungovernable—effect of the impact ("choc") of an external stimulus on his senses. But this reaction also has an end:

> Tout vient également d'un tempérament versatile qu'un vent impetueux agite mais qui rentre dans le calme à l'instant que le vent ne souffle plus. . . . Je cede à toutes les impulsions présentes, tout choc me donne un mouvement vif et court, sitot qu'il n'y a plus de choc le mouvement cesse, rien de communiqué ne peut se prolonger en moi. (1084)

> [A]ll my behaviour is equally the work of a volatile temperament which is stirred up by violent winds but calms down as soon as the winds stop blowing. . . . I give way to the impulse of the moment; every shock sets up a vigorous and short-lived motion in me, but as soon as the shock is over, the motion vanishes, and nothing that comes from outside can be prolonged within me. (134)

His state of being depends on the presence or absence of an outside motor force (a "shock," or an impetuous "wind"). Like his enemies, Rousseau may act impulsively, but only when he is externally and randomly driven (or pushed) to do so.

Under the circumstances, the only way to gain control is to give it up. Here again reason and will have no part; there is no countervailing personal, moral force that can stand against natural law. The initial "explosion" simply runs its course until the body, no longer impelled to act, naturally comes to rest. Outside forces eventually cease and Rousseau then finds "himself"—at rest, unmoved by the impulses of other men, indifferent. Rousseau's excitable and impulsive side may be problematic in that it allows others to control him, but it is also the necessary means by which motion carries him to a "constant" state. Arriving at stasis in the world of motion is the equivalent of attributing stable properties or a proper self to the hero of this narrative. In an unexpected turnabout, personhood is the end result of "impulsion." The autobiographical hero, "Rousseau," is the rare "person" who exhibits no will, exercises no ethical responsibility, and is moved by the random laws of motion. Indeed, "Rousseau" personifies the *mechanics* of personification. Personification and mechanics are not so easily sorted out.

Baudelaire is well aware of this conundrum in Rousseau's text. His poem investigates the contradictory claims of the eighth *rêverie* by imagining a concrete incident to illustrate Rousseau's abstract theorizing. It seems that Baude-

laire is taking Rousseau to task for his convoluted position by giving dramatic examples that call Rousseau's reasoning and his ethics into question. But Baudelaire's personification of Rousseau's metaphysical notions is not added onto the Rousseau text as a critique; it follows from the statements about personification in the eighth *rêverie* itself. Nonetheless, where the *rêverie* only hints at the relationship of ethics and rhetoric, Baudelaire's poem brings rhetoric's ethical dimension into the open.

The moral lesson of both the *rêverie* and the poem depends on how we interpret the "impulse" (or "choc") that propels Jean-Jacques, Baudelaire's narrator, and the "vitrier." How we judge their actions hinges on whether we understand "impulse" as the mechanical law of bodies in motion—like the fall of the apple from the tree that supposedly led to Newton's theory of gravity—or as the unchecked "impulse" of combustible emotions and the "pushing" of others that may result. In other words, the interpretation of both the *rêverie* and the poem turns upon the multiple meanings of the word "impulsion." Baudelaire appears to give a particular spin to this ambiguous word when he represents the narrator's impulsive hatred at work against the "vitrier." He seems to leave little room for the mechanical interpretation of "impulse" when he lays emphasis on the narrator's deliberate and malicious actions—although he does call the flowerpot an "*engin* de guerre" (an "*engine* of war").[112] But by dramatizing the debate about "impulsion" as an encounter between two people, Baudelaire in fact investigates both the mechanical impact of "blows" and the moral impact of personification.

Reading the poem in the most objective or mechanistic way, it is safe to say that the peddler, who is suddenly knocked over by the blow (the "choc renversant") of the flowerpot hitting the windowpanes on his back, represents the mechanical meaning of "impulsion." An object falling perpendicularly with the weight of gravity hits the heavy frame strapped to his back, causing him to fall down in turn, which brings about the ultimate misfortune, the physical destruction of his livelihood (his "fortune ambulatoire"). It is also clear, from the mechanistic point of view, that the "I" incarnates the propulsion of the blow, that is, the mechanical force (or "engine") that sets it in motion. From this perspective, "je" and "le vitrier" represent two sequential moments of the same movement, or the difference between the active and reactive phases of a body being set in motion. Personifying the idea of "impulse" as the dissimilar motions of two individuals, the narrator and the glazier bring to light the slight but operative difference within the mechanical meaning of the word.

Of course, this reading would be incomplete if it did not take into account

the psychological meaning of "impulsion" as well, the idea of unchecked emotional impulse that precipitates the narrator's action. Like the men he describes in the first part of the poem, who set fires for no real reason, "pour tenter la destinée" ("to tempt fate"), the narrator acts because he has nothing better to do ("par désoeuvrement"); he's "out of work." His impulse is just as capricious and meaningless as his gesture when he intentionally hurls the pot toward the glazier's back. This *deliberate* move, which is a perfect example of a *random* act, confirms Rousseau's intuition about how personification works. Personification makes the random appear deliberate. Thus when Baudelaire's narrator accuses the "bad" peddler of having no colored panes of glass to sell and pushes him down the stairs, his speech converts a chance encounter into a deliberate one and a meaningless, random act into a (supposedly) moral punishment.

"Le Mauvais Vitrier" makes obvious the advantages and the dangers of personification that Rousseau only hinted at. Personification can enliven an abstract idea like "impulsion" or "choc" and, in so doing, give color to a philosophical (or rhetorical) inquiry. But in replacing the lifeless idea or random act with a "living person," personification also brings moral judgment to bear on the effects of mere chance. As Rousseau intimated, it is impossible to avoid attributing innerness (in the form of intelligence, deliberation, or purpose) to a "person" one has invented. Once it is put to work ("mise en oeuvre") in a narrative, personification automatically raises the issues of will or intention and morality—even in an expression that *negates* intent, like "blind necessity."[113] To borrow a phrase from Baudelaire's poem, personification "opens a window" that cannot be easily shut. By its very nature, personification brings together the inanimate and the animate, the random and the intentional in a tense encounter, and sets off a spark that nothing can arrest. It is an impersonal or mechanical force that causes conflagrations of emotion and paroxysms of moral judgment. If there is any "engin de guerre" in this poem, it is the device of personification itself.

The Allegorical Meaning of "Le Mauvais Vitrier"

It is tempting to read "Le Mauvais Vitrier" as a virulent attack on Rousseau's moral opacity. Rousseau leaves himself open to blame when he relies on the same impersonal laws of motion that account for his enemies' "mechanical" behavior to undergird his own self-portrait. Whereas it may be logical for him to assert that his enemies are "machines" because their actions are baseless

and their intentions inscrutable, he is not so convincing when he claims that his own actions are acceptable because outside shocks set off his uncontrollable impulses. In order to assert that events are entirely out of his control, Rousseau has to give up his will, his reason, and his judgment; yet he still insists that, unlike his "mechanical" enemies, he is a "man."[114]

However, personalizing the poem as a statement exclusively about Rousseau would be falling into the very rhetorical trap that the poem explores. Any reading of "Le Mauvais Vitrier" must balance the moral effects of personification against rhetoric's "blindly" necessary acts. The poem is and is not an attack on Rousseau. Elaborating on contemporary caricatures of Rousseau, Baudelaire unfolds the consequences of these images in a dramatic narrative with a severe moral point. Yet the poem, which at first seems to flirt with the contemporary hostility toward the eighteenth-century author by repeating and illustrating the politically motivated caricatures in circulation at the time, reads in the end like Baudelaire's private joke. Baudelaire has fun attacking Rousseau in the outlines of his story—throwing rhetorical flowers at Rousseau's colorless wares. In a demonstration of his own brilliance, Baudelaire writes out as a story of destruction his own ability to "crack" Rousseau's rhetoric and unsettle his literary "fortunes." But this braggadocious stance is itself phony (or hypocritical). For the rhetorical principle that Baudelaire criticizes in Rousseau is the very same force that generates the poet's own grotesque texts. Reading Rousseau's self-portrait as an elaborate example (or allegory) of personification, Baudelaire *repeats* this allegory through his own figure of Rousseau.[115] "Rousseau" in this poem is at once a caricatured portrait drawn from the political discourse of the day and the personification of personification. For Baudelaire, "Rousseau" is not just a type or a stereotype, he is the very figure of allegory itself.

Baudelaire's choice of "Rousseau" as his ready-made cliché is a stroke of genius. As an author who himself understood the mechanical workings of personification and displayed them in his own self-portrait, Rousseau is the perfect "poncif." Literally a stencil, a tool for reproducing an image by tracing it onto another surface, a "poncif" is a technique for obtaining multiple figures from a single template—an appropriate metaphor for the grotesque's generative effects. Baudelaire was perfectly aware of personification as an ungovernable force or immutable law randomly producing "persons" as morally ambiguous signs. This is clear from the way he explains the incomprehensible behavior of the timid individuals whose daring acts he describes. When he

refers to the unknown cause of their sudden metamorphosis as either "a mysterious and unknown impulse" or "malicious Demons," and later calls the instrument of the action (that is, the flowerpot) an "engin de guerre," Baudelaire deliberately takes up the eighteenth-century metaphors for allegory.[116] In the next chapter, we shall see just how "demons" and "machines" figure in the eighteenth-century's ideas of rhetoric, and how they shape Baudelaire's modern grotesque.

5 ▮ *Machines, Monsters, and Men*
Realism and the Modern Grotesque

When Baudelaire puts into play, in "Le Mauvais Vitrier," the perennial code words for allegory—words like *engin* and *démon,* which refer to the trope's machinelike or demonic agency—he points obliquely to his project in that poem and others. In the *Petits Poèmes en prose,* Baudelaire writes out the eternal structure of allegory as the ephemeral story of a nineteenth social type or the topical story of the contemporary politicization of Rousseau. Combining timeless rhetorical structures with time-bound elements relative to the era of their creation, the prose poems serve as so many examples of Baudelaire's idea of beauty, as he defines it in "Le Peintre de la vie moderne":

> Le beau est fait d'un élément éternel, invariable, dont la quantité est excessivement difficile à déterminer, et d'un élément relatif, circonstanciel, qui sera, si l'on veut, tour à tour ou tout ensemble, l'époque, la mode, la morale, la passion. Sans ce second élément, qui est comme l'enveloppe amusante, titillante, apéritive, du divin gâteau, le premier élément serait indigestible, inappréciable, non adapté et non approprié à la nature humaine. Je défie qu'on découvre un échantillon quelconque de beauté qui ne contienne pas ces deux éléments.[1]

> The beautiful is made up of an eternal, invariable element, the quantity of which is excessively difficult to determine, and of a relative, circumstantial element, which will be, if you will, alternately or all at once, the era, fashion, psychology or mores, passion. Without this second element, which is like the amusing, titillating, stimulating envelope of the divine cake, the first

element would be indigestible, unappealing, poorly adapted and inappropriate to human nature. I defy anyone to discover any example of beauty that does not contain these two elements.

Baudelaire was obviously fascinated by his contemporaries' caricatures of Rousseau, their political connotations, and the implications of this ongoing obsession with the traumatic past (represented by Rousseau) for any delineation of the present. What we might call the Rousseau phenomenon was a key characteristic of the society and times in which Baudelaire lived, and by foregrounding it in the poems, Baudelaire provides an amusing, provocative, and digestible surface for his little "cakes." But as our reading of "Le Mauvais Vitrier" demonstrates, the poet was also fascinated by Rousseau's own analysis—and use—of rhetoric. Baudelaire was a perceptive student of Rousseau's rhetorical practices, who saw through even Rousseau's most persuasive autobiographical texts to the core rhetorical devices at work there. Very much like the poet in "Le Poème du hachisch" observing his "man" as if he were a mechanism under glass,[2] Baudelaire scrutinized Rousseau's autobiographical narratives (and other writings) and observed the rhetorical machinery operating in them. Indeed, I believe Baudelaire learned from Rousseau how a rhetorical figure that was dismissed as dry, hackneyed, and mechanical in the late eighteenth century could mechanically generate stories that were lively, titillating, and new. Thus Rousseau's influence over the prose poems extends far beyond the surface manifestations of the "Rousseau" caricatures. Even where "Rousseau" is absent as a type or a caricature, Rousseau's work is frequently present as an intertext. Rousseau's talents as a storyteller and a rhetorician had a tremendous impact on Baudelaire, and we cannot calculate their effects solely on the basis of the presence of Rousseau types in some of the poems.

In order to better grasp the fresh ideas that Baudelaire derived from his reading of Rousseau, therefore, we must look back at Rousseau's rhetorical theory and practice and his role in the Enlightenment attack on the rococo. This necessary step back in time will allow us to understand the eighteenth century's increasingly negative concept of the grotesque, which Baudelaire knew well and against which he defined his own theory and practice. It will also give us the opportunity to test the assertion of Sainte-Beuve, Baudelaire's sometime mentor, that Rousseau's artistic legacy lies in his realism. This evaluation of Rousseau's contribution to modern aesthetics, although controversial, goes some way toward explaining the convergence of the grotesque and the real, or the eternal and the topical, in Baudelaire's poems.

This chapter, then, falls loosely into three sections. First, drawing on Sainte-Beuve, it examines the claim that Rousseau was a realist. Then, in order to provide an explanatory context for the tension between the grotesque and the real in Rousseau's work, it briefly reviews the debate surrounding the grotesque in the mid-eighteenth century. Finally, an analysis of Rousseau's satirical letter on the Paris Opéra in his epistolary novel *Julie; ou, La Nouvelle Héloïse,* where the struggle between grotesque and real asserts itself with comic vigor, sets up a reading of four Baudelaire poems that incorporate key elements of Rousseau's text: "Le Vieux Saltimbanque," "Le Crépuscule du soir," "Une Mort héroïque," and "La Corde." In the *Petits Poèmes en prose,* as we shall see, Baudelaire enters into a complex dialogue with Rousseau regarding the real and the grotesque; and in the process, he reinvigorates a rhetorical genre that had been given up for dead.

Sainte-Beuve on Rousseau's Realism

It is often alleged that Baudelaire got his ideas about Rousseau from the arch-conservative Joseph de Maistre, whom he read in or after 1851.[3] However, although Baudelaire openly credited de Maistre with teaching him "how to think,"[4] the notion that de Maistre taught the poet *what* to think about Rousseau, in particular, has always seemed needlessly reductive to me. Given the widespread discussion of "Jean-Jacques" throughout the first half of the nineteenth century, it is more than likely that Baudelaire had imbibed ideas and images of Rousseau from other sources long before he read de Maistre.[5] Furthermore, I submit that if anyone was Baudelaire's "maître à penser" when it came to Rousseau, it was not de Maistre but Sainte-Beuve, whom Baudelaire also considered an intellectual "midwife."[6] Baudelaire had admired Sainte-Beuve even as a young man,[7] and he turned to him on many occasions for advice and help in the pursuit of his literary objectives. Baudelaire's correspondance shows that he kept up to date with Sainte-Beuve's work as an influential critic, and his prose poems bear important traces of that reading.[8]

Sainte-Beuve differed from most essayists writing on Rousseau in his detailed analysis of Rousseau's originality, and his praise of Rousseau seems to have inspired Baudelaire. Where other critics paid only lip-service to Rousseau's eloquence, Sainte-Beuve interspersed his commentary on Rousseau's life and morals with perceptive asides about Rousseau's aesthetic achievement. Sainte-Beuve extols Rousseau, not as the author most often deemed responsible for the French Revolution, but as a revolutionary talent whose

genius was unsurpassed even in the nineteenth century. His columns bring into focus the artistic side of Rousseau at a time when this aspect was overshadowed by the political impact of his thought,[9] and in these columns the critic lays down a challenge and some guiding principles, which I believe the younger poet took up.

Of the three articles that Sainte-Beuve devoted to Rousseau during the period that concerns us (in April and November 1850 and in July 1861), the first two left discernable marks on Baudelaire's work.[10] In the first essay ("Madame de la Tour-Franqueville et Jean-Jacques Rousseau," April 29, 1850), the critic sets out to explain Rousseau's rude behavior toward an eager female correspondent. Madame de la Tour-Franqueville was an admirer of Rousseau's novel *Julie* and considered herself to be the living incarnation of Rousseau's fictional heroine. In a passage that was very likely the origin of Baudelaire's poem "Laquelle est la vraie?" Sainte-Beuve concludes that Rousseau was too enamored of his fictional ideal to accept the existence of a real-life Julie:

> [L]'amour de Rousseau n'était pour aucune femme vivante, ni pour une de ces beautés d'autrefois, que ressuscitent les rêves du poëte. Son amour était celui de l'idéale beauté, du fantôme auquel lui-même prêtait vie et flamme: c'était ce fantôme seul, tiré de son sein, et formé d'un ardent nuage, qu'il aimait, qu'il embrassait sans cesse, à qui il donnait chaque matin ses baisers de feu . . . et quand il se présenta une femme réelle qui eut l'orgueil de lui montrer l'objet terrestre de son idéal et de lui dire: *Je suis Julie,* il ne daigna point la reconnaître; il lui en voulut presque d'avoir espéré se substituer à l'objet du divin songe.

> Rousseau's love was neither for any living woman nor for one of those beauties of yesteryear that the poet's dreams recall to life. His love was for ideal beauty, for the phantom to which he himself gave life and passion: it was that phantom alone, drawn from his breast and formed of an ardent cloud, that he loved, that he endlessly embraced, that he kissed with passion each morning . . . and when a real woman presented herself who had the proud daring to show him the earthly object of his ideal and to say to him: *"I am Julie,"* he did not deign to recognize her; he was almost angry with her for having hoped to substitute herself for the object of his divine dream.[11]

Drawing as it does on Rousseau's letters and extracting from them psychological insights such as these, Sainte-Beuve's analysis is unparalleled: he is a master at singling out character traits that pin "Rousseau" to the page for our scrutiny.

But the critic's most important contribution to Rousseau reception is his November column, where he goes beyond the stereotype of Rousseau as a dreamer or a mawkish sentimentalist to focus instead on Rousseau's originality as a writer and a *realist.* From Sainte-Beuve's point of view, Rousseau had revolutionized the French language more than any author since Pascal, and despite his many imitators, Sainte-Beuve argued, Rousseau remained unique.[12]

For Sainte-Beuve, the singular difference between the eighteenth-century genius and his nineteenth-century look-alikes is Rousseau's class background—his lower-class origins and his experiences as a servant. These roots give Rousseau his distinctive language, full of "rough accents" and "raw earthiness" (82), "details in bad taste in which he speaks of theft and of *grub*"[13]—in sum, "certain ignoble, disgusting, cynical expressions, which the upstanding man wouldn't use and doesn't know."[14] Rousseau is not "a man of the proud aristocratic race" like Chateaubriand, and his language sometimes reveals his poor breeding, but Sainte-Beuve concludes that his inferior background is ultimately Rousseau's strength. Lacking an aristocratic sense of honor, Rousseau dares to speak of subjects that others deem insignificant. He is willing to show his love of simple things, simply expressed. Sainte-Beuve considers him better than his closest disciple; "at bottom he is truer, more real, more alive" than Chateaubriand (87). It is this realism, discernible especially in Rousseau's use of detail, that attracts the astute critic.

Sainte-Beuve gives several examples. First, Rousseau knows how to capture the essential element that will anchor his fictional characters in a recognizable and unforgettable place. Like a painter, he makes sure that nothing is missing in his "dessin" (92) or "tableau" (93).

> En tout, comme peintre, Rousseau a le sentiment de la *réalité.* Il l'a toutes les fois qu'il nous parle de la beauté, laquelle, même lorsqu'elle est imaginaire comme sa *Julie,* prend avec lui un corps et des formes bien visibles, et n'est pas du tout une Iris en l'air et insaisissable. Il a le sentiment de cette réalité en ce qu'il veut que chaque scène dont il se souvient ou qu'il invente, que chaque personnage qu'il introduit, s'encadre et se meuve dans un lieu bien déterminé, dont les moindres détails se puissent graver et retenir.

> In everything, like a painter, Rousseau has the feeling of *reality.* He has it every time he speaks to us of beauty, which, even when it is imaginary like his *Julie,* takes on a body and very visible forms, and is not at all an ungraspable rainbow in the air. He has the feeling of this reality in that he wants every scene he remembers or invents, every character he introduces, to be

framed and to move in a well-delineated place, the smallest details of which can be engraved and remembered.[15]

Second, Rousseau even includes realistic details about meals and food in his fiction. Rousseau has been hungry, Sainte-Beuve notes; and his difficult life, his experiences as an "homme du peuple" (92), lend "guts" to even his most ideal scenes: "Therefore he will never forget, even in the ideal picture he later gives of his happiness, to include those things from real life and from common humanity, those things from the *guts* [ces choses des *entrailles*]. It's through all these true aspects, combined with his eloquence, that he grabs hold of us" (92).

Sainte-Beuve insists particularly on a passage in which Rousseau describes how hunger overtakes him after he's had a nap in a beautiful country spot. He walks to the city, "resolved to spend two pieces of 'six whites' that I still had on a good lunch" ("résolu de mettre à un bon déjeuner deux pièces de six blancs qui me restaient encore").[16] Sainte-Beuve comments:

> Tout le Rousseau naturel est là avec sa rêverie, son idéal, sa réalité; et cette pièce de *six blancs* elle-même, qui vient après le rossignol, n'est pas de trop pour nous ramener à la terre et nous faire sentir toute l'humble jouissance que la pauvreté recèle en soi quand elle est jointe avec la poésie et la jeunesse. J'ai voulu pousser la citation jusqu'à cette pièce de six blancs pour montrer qu'avec Rousseau nous ne sommes pas uniquement dans le *René* et dans le *Jocelyn*.

> All the natural Rousseau is there, with his reverie, his ideal, his reality; and this *six blancs* coin itself, which comes after the nightingale, is enough to bring us back to earth and to make us feel all the humble pleasure that poverty harbors when it is joined with poetry and youth. I wanted to extend the quotation as far as this coin to show that with Rousseau we are not only in the world or the style of [Chateaubriand's] *René* and [Lamartine's] *Jocelyn*.[17]

By emphasizing the differences between Rousseau and his romantic disciples, Sainte-Beuve's analysis goes to the heart of what is unique about Rousseau and what Baudelaire himself will emulate.

Sainte-Beuve issues a kind of challenge in his commentary on the *Confessions*—a challenge to those who themselves want to be "nouveaux." No one has yet gone beyond Rousseau, he claims. He is "still superior to his descendants" (97); "Rousseau's style still remains the surest and most solid example one can offer of modern innovation" (96).[18] It is not difficult to imagine

Baudelaire picking up the glove and focusing on this high standard as he worked on his "second poetic revolution."

Elements in the prose poems suggest that Baudelaire took note of all the realistic traits singled out for comment by his friend: the desire to paint a scene, evoked in "Le *Confiteor* de l'artiste" and in the title of "Le Désir de peindre"; the frame and setting that anchor a description so it can be visualized and fixed in the mind, characteristic of most of the prose poems; the tension between "la vie réelle" and "le tableau idéal" that structures "La Chambre double," "Laquelle est la vraie?" and others; the use of realistic details such as money and food in poems like "La Fausse Monnaie" and "Les Yeux des pauvres"; a language throughout the poems that is often less than seemly or poetic;[19] and the class-consciousness of so many of the texts.[20] Ambitious to become the modern innovator whose work would be the new benchmark for successive generations, replacing that of Rousseau,[21] Baudelaire must have found useful guidelines for his own undertaking in Sainte-Beuve's acute analysis of Rousseau's unmatched contributions to literature. By accepting the challenge of excelling in the very areas where Rousseau remained uncontested, Baudelaire staked out for himself a terrain where no one else had succeeded—a terrain, that is, among the fertile fields already delimited by Rousseau.

The Enlightenment against the Rococo: La Querelle des Bouffons

It is clear that Baudelaire carefully parsed the works taken up by Sainte-Beuve; but although he incorporated many of the traits that the critic underscored, it was not exactly in the service of realism. Baudelaire detested this relatively new literary trend and had no desire to adopt it.[22] In his notes for an article now entitled "Puisque réalisme il y a," he admits that people had tried to pin the "realist" label on him, "although I have always worked hard not to deserve it" ("bien que je me sois toujours appliqué à le démériter").[23] His reading of Rousseau led him, instead, to the intersection of the real and the grotesque.

There is no doubt that Rousseau was a proponent of a certain realism, but whether his work can be called "realist" is another matter. Like the beautiful Bénédicta in Baudelaire's "Laquelle est la Vraie?" Rousseau's realism has an ugly double. The grotesque haunts the real and divides the texts on style that Baudelaire read, copied, and rewrote. Rousseau frequently says one thing and does another; his aesthetic theory and his own style are often at odds. Rousseau's writing on style calls realism into question, while it brings out its political consequences; and Baudelaire was well aware of these implications.

Rousseau's work can help us recognize and understand the aesthetic values and political subtext of Baudelaire's prose poems.

This chapter and the next focus on two texts about opera, composed between 1758 and 1761, when Rousseau was thinking about language, music, and the theater in relation to the state—texts that Baudelaire knew in detail and rewrote.[24] The famous satirical letter on the Paris Opéra in Rousseau's *Julie* and the entry "Opéra" in his *Dictionnaire de musique* reflect and extend the campaign against the Paris Opéra, known as the Querelle des Bouffons, waged by Rousseau, Grimm, Diderot, and other contributors to the *Encyclopédie,* beginning in 1752.[25] This quarrel, which weighed the relative merits of the Italian and French operatic styles, ostensibly focused on the weaknesses of the French lyric drama and the unsuitability of harmony (as opposed to melody) for expressing human emotions. But, in fact, the Querelle was far more than a critique of the French musical practices of the day. As Rémy Saisselin observes, it "signal[ed] the end of the baroque world" and its "aesthetics of pleasure" and marked the beginning of "the Enlightenment as a philosophical movement. . . . The attack on French opera was thus also an attack on the entire Rococo."[26] What Baudelaire found in Rousseau's satirical letter on the Paris Opéra and the entry in the music dictionary, then, was a critique of rococo aesthetics and particularly of the marvelous, machines, and allegory (three almost interchangeable terms in the mid-eighteenth century).

Although Rousseau and the other participants in the Querelle typically refer to the marvelous and do not use the term *grotesque* per se, it is important to realize that the same grotesque principles inform both painting and the visual spectacle of the opera in the rococo period. As we saw in Chapter 2, the painted grotesque borrowed some of its vocabulary—its acrobatic performers, stagelike platforms, and "proscenium" arches—from the popular Parisian fair theaters (heirs to the commedia dell'arte)[27] and is thus visibly tied to the dramatic arts. Furthermore, if the grotesque in painting is the product of an extraordinary liberty of thought, evidenced by the "fictive beings, and even [composite] creatures" it puts into play,[28] the marvelous in the theater is similarly associated with freedom of invention or the imagination run riot. The marvelous, like the grotesque, eschews the usual hierarchy of beings and defies the laws of nature. This is precisely the aspect of the opera that Friedrich Melchior Grimm derides as ridiculous in his *Encyclopédie* article "Poëme lyrique":

> Thus the visible marvelous is the soul of French opera; the gods, the goddesses, the demigods; shades, genies, fairies, magicians, virtues, passions, ab-

stract ideas, and personified moral beings are the actors. The visible marvelous has appeared to be so essential to this drama that the poet cannot conceive of treating a historical subject without mixing in some supernatural incidents and imaginary beings of his own creation.[29]

Operas might include "an aerial genie, a game, a laugh, a pleasure, an hour, a constellation, all these bizarre allegorical beings, whose names we read with astonishment in the programs."[30]

As the above quotations from Grimm's article suggest, the obvious artificiality of the marvelous spectacle bore the brunt of the philosophes' attack. In particular, they disliked the use of what they called "machines," which were found in both epic poetry and on the stage. The term apparently originated in the theater, where it designated the real machinery used to bring the supernatural characters on and off the set "in a manner that imitates the marvelous."[31] In poetry, by analogy, "machines" designated the often crude or mechanistic interventions of gods, genies, or other supernatural creatures to solve problems the poet (or the mortals in the poem) couldn't handle in any other way.[32] In this poetic context, a "machine" (also referred to as an *engin*) was synonymous with allegory.[33] Often "machines" crossed over from one genre to another when an epic poem, such as Tasso's *Gerusalemme liberata,* became the basis for an opera.[34] Thus, the term "marvelous" encompassed the creation of various allegorical characters, ranging from pagan gods embodying distinct ideas to fictional creatures sprung from the poet's imagination, brought into play through the use of literal or rhetorical "machines." The marvelous, machines, and allegory are so bound up with one another in the philosophes' discourse on the opera as to become almost indistinguishable.

Clearly, the rococo aesthetic permeated and united the visual, poetic, and dramatic arts (whether "grotesque" or "marvelous") in the period leading up to the 1750s.[35] By the mid-eighteenth century, however, a portion of the theater-going public was no longer impressed with these extravagant effects. This shift away from "le merveilleux" is clearly in evidence in an influential treatise by the abbé Charles Batteux, *Les Beaux-Arts réduits à un même principe,* originally published in 1746,[36] which lays out many of the issues involved in the Encyclopedists' critique. Batteux declares that the underlying principle uniting the arts should be the imitation of "beautiful nature." He decries anything that transgresses this rule—and he is therefore adamantly opposed to the "monsters" so rampant in recent (grotesque) art. His second chapter begins with a crisp statement of his position:

Les monstres mêmes, qu'une imagination déréglée se figure dans ses délires, ne peuvent être composés que de parties prises dans la nature: et si le génie, par caprice, fait de ces parties un assemblage contraire aux lois naturelles, en dégradant la nature, il se dégrade lui-même, et se change en une espèce de folie. Les limites sont marquées: dès qu'on les passe, on se perd; on fait un chaos plutôt qu'un monde, et on cause du désagrément plutôt que du plaisir.[37]

Even monsters, which an unregulated imagination pictures in its delirium, can only be composed of parts taken from nature: and if genius capriciously makes of these parts an assemblage contrary to natural laws, by degrading nature it degrades itself and becomes a kind of madness. The limits are set out: as soon as a person crosses them, he is lost; he creates chaos rather than a world, and he causes displeasure rather than pleasure.

Batteux's fear of the unruly imagination, its "delirium," its "madness," and the "chaos" it can cause, leads him to police the productions of genius. He knows nature's laws and patrols the limits of the natural. "Qu'ai-je à faire de cette Forêt enchantée du Tasse, des Hippogriffes de l'Arioste, de la Génération du Péché mortel dans Milton? Tout ce qu'on me présente avec ces traits outrés et hors de la nature, mon esprit le rejette: *incredulus odi*." ["Je n'en crois rien, et je m'indigne."] ("What do I care about that enchanted forest in Tasso, the hippogriffs in Ariosto, the generation of mortal sin in Milton? Everything that is presented with these outlandish and exaggerated attributes, my mind rejects: *incredulus odi*." ["I don't believe a word, and I am indignant."]).[38]

The grotesque results, Batteux believes, when the basic rule of harmony of style is flaunted. This is the rule that requires the style to agree with the content and that looks for a proper balance or proportion between them. As Batteux explains, "Les arts forment une espèce de république, où chacun doit figurer selon son état" ("The arts form a sort of republic, where each one should appear in proportion to its status"). When the poet fails to achieve the appropriate balance—when he doesn't adopt the right tone for the genre he has chosen, or when he has commingled two or more genres—then the harmony of the whole is missing and the poem becomes "une mascarade: c'est une sorte de grotesque qui tient de la parodie" ("a masquerade: it's a kind of grotesque that is close to parody").[39]

By applying this rule of proportion between form and content or appearance and being, Batteux wants to rescue the arts from collapsing irremediably into the grotesque. But when it comes to the opera, which surpasses the usual laws of verisimilitude, Batteux relents. Opera concerns itself with extraordi-

nary actions and can accommodate the old-style "merveilleux" with its magical, fairytale events: "C'est le ciel qui s'ouvre, une nue lumineuse qui apporte un être céleste; c'est un palais enchanté, qui disparaît au moindre signe, et se transforme en désert, etc." ("It's the sky that opens, a luminous cloud that bears a celestial being; it's an enchanted palace, which disappears at the least signal and transforms itself into a desert, etc.").[40] With Batteux, at midcentury, we find ourselves at a turning point, where the standard of the reasonable imitation of the best in nature imposes itself with vigor but has not yet completely eradicated the old aesthetic principles and styles.

When the philosophes took up the cause of operatic reform in 1752, they espoused some of the same ideals Batteux expressed but applied them with greater uniformity. Their thinking about the Paris Opéra reflects not only their desire for verisimilitude in art but their rejection of the luxury and magnificence long associated with the monarchy. The Paris Opéra, which had its roots in Louis XIV's love of spectacle and dance, had changed remarkably little since its creation.[41] As an extension of the royal "fêtes" that exalted the Sun King, his grandeur and his glory, the standard repertory operas of Lully and Quinault bore the mark of the great monarch, who was often both the principal organizer or "machinist" of these events and a featured player, disguised as a pagan deity or other allegorical figure.[42] Everything about the Opéra bespoke its royal heritage long after its famous patron's demise.[43] Thus, the philosophes' campaign for operatic reform had political overtones; it marked the development of a new link between republican views and aesthetic theory. As William Weber observes, "Through the use of code words—*la musique française,* to mean the court musical tradition—the *Encyclopédistes* made their political point on a relatively safe ground."[44]

This political point involved the need for greater freedom of thought and speech; a new emphasis on the common man or the bourgeoisie instead of the social elite (or the gods); the closure of the breach between reality and appearance in language, art, and social interaction; and the creation of a theater that would truly reflect (or promote) a more egalitarian idea of the public and the nation.[45] Beginning with his *Lettre sur la musique française,* Rousseau became the "most eloquent spokesman" for these ideals—and the symbol of revolution.[46] His satirical letter on the Paris Opéra in *Julie* and his *Dictionnaire de musique* article "Opéra" follow this line.

The Letter on the Paris Opéra: The Grotesque

Letter 2.23 in Rousseau's *Julie,* written by the protagonist St. Preux to his friend Claire d'Orbe, is one of several letters in the novel that describe life in Paris, contrasting its decadent pleasures with the gentler and far more satisfying recreations in the pays de Vaud. But letter 2.23 is not about the perils of the city per se, even though it takes aim at the Paris Opéra. The letter's real subjects are aesthetics and representation, and beyond the uproarious descriptions of French operatic practice lie several important issues for both novelists and poets: the ability of language to convey meaning and truth, the proper use of figural versus literal language, the politics of rhetoric, and the creation and place of illusion in the world.

References near the beginning of the letter place it under the sign of Momus: St. Preux makes it clear that right-thinking visitors to the Paris Opéra would make fun of it if they could, but government censorship makes it impossible to laugh in public at this supposedly august institution. Pope is evoked, and Macrobius's *Saturnalia* is the subject of a long editorial note—two deictic references designed to alert the reader to the letter's thoroughly satirical intent. The object of all this aggressive humor is the grotesque aesthetic that still dominates the lyric theater. St. Preux contests both the Opéra's subject matter (its bizarre melange of "Gods, leprechauns, monsters, Kings, shepherds, fairies, fury, joy, a fire, a jig, a battle and a ball")[47] and its means of production, which are so inept and ill-adapted that they destroy any illusion of reality. The elaborate machinery set up to depict both natural and supernatural objects is so ungainly that it calls attention to its artifice and interferes with the verisimilitude that supposedly governs theatrical representations. The Paris Opéra exactly inverts the proper order of priorities; instead of representing great men of history in a simple and economical manner, "on fait de petites choses avec de grands efforts" ("small things are achieved with great efforts").[48] The means of production are out of proportion to the trivial subject of representation. The Paris Opéra is grotesque both because it puts "monsters" (and hybrid spectacles) on stage and because its staging is mechanical, obtrusive, and therefore excessive. And yet the public is happily taken in. St. Preux remarks sarcastically: "Cet assemblage si magnifique et si bien ordonné est regardé comme s'il contenoit en effet toutes les choses qu'il répresente" ("This most magnificent and well arranged ensemble is considered as if it indeed contained all the things it represents") (Rouss., *OC*, 2: 281; *CW*, 6: 231).

The public's willingness to accept the Opéra's "magnificent" admixture of

objects at face value, their belief that lavish appearance betokens abundant substance, is in turn the basis for the more general belief in the Paris Opéra's "majesty"—a belief propagated by the Académie royale de musique and supported by the monarchy's vigorous censorship. Noting that the Paris Opéra is said to be "le spectacle . . . le plus voluptueux, le plus admirable qu'inventa jamais l'art humain. . . . le plus superbe monument de la magnificence de Loüis quatorze" ("the most voluptuous, the most admirable spectacle that human art ever invented. . . . the most superb monument of the magnificence of Louis XIV" [trans. modified]),[49] St. Preux comments: "Voilà . . . comment, dans certains pays, l'essence des choses tient aux mots, et comment des noms honnêtes suffisent pour honorer ce qui l'est le moins" ("That . . . is how in certain countries the essence of things hangs on words, and how honest names suffice to exalt what is least honest").[50] The language applied to the theater suffers from the same grotesque disjunction between appearance and essence as the operatic productions themselves. The aesthetic problem of the proper choice and alignment of subject matter and means of representation applies not just to the drama but also to the relation between words and the essence of the things they designate. St. Preux's critique of the opera and the implicit values that underlie it can be read as a commentary on rhetoric and on representation in general, and certainly Baudelaire understood this.

St. Preux's satire is a frontal assault on blatant figures and particularly allegory, which is the most unbearable form of figuration, according to him, because it conveys "no feeling, no tableaux, no situations, no warmth, no interest, nothing that could give rise to music, flatter the emotions and nourish illusion." St. Preux's comments echo Rousseau's condemnation of allegory in his *Dictionary* entry on the ballet. Allegory is an intellectual exercise, Rousseau asserts; it presents metaphysical ideas in the form of sensory images and makes the spectator work hard at understanding the relationship between the two. Rather than facilitating the spectator's involvement with the performance or the text, allegory obscures meaning and constantly engages the mind in deciphering its figures and its "puns, allusions and epigrams." It is the obverse of compelling illusion.[51]

St. Preux's description of the opera's machines and special effects underscores the distracting discrepancy between the sensory sign and the idea it represents. For example, he describes the backdrop as:

un grand rideau [grossierement peint] et presque toujours percé ou déchiré, ce qui représente des gouffres dans la terre ou des trous dans le Ciel, selon la

perspective. Chaque personne qui passe derriere le théatre et touche le rideau, produit en l'ébranlant une sorte de tremblement de terre assés plaisant à voir. Le Ciel est réprésenté par certaines guenilles bleuâtres, suspendues à des bâtons ou à des cordes, comme l'étendage d'une blanchisseuse. Le soleil . . . est un flambeau dans une lanterne. (Rouss., *OC*, 2: 283)

a large curtain painted [sketchily], and almost always pierced or torn, which represents chasms in the earth or holes in the Sky, according to the perspective. Every person who passes behind the stage and touches the curtain, produces in shaking it a sort of earthquake that is rather amusing to see. The Sky is represented by certain bluish tatters, suspended on sticks or ropes, like a washerwoman's clothesline. The sun . . . is a torch in a lantern. (Rouss., *CW,* 6: 231–32)

The chariots of the gods and goddesses are four beams in a frame suspended from a rope and adorned with a roughly painted canvas, which serves as a cloud. And trapdoors opening in the stage are the sure sign that little "Demons are about to emerge from the cellar." In short, natural and supernatural phenomena occur on stage through the intervention of all-too-obvious contraptions, which destroy not only the illusion but also the uplifting connotations that might otherwise attach to the sun, the heavens, and the gods.

These same defects are immediately apparent in St. Preux's own style, which parallels the elaborate and ungainly productions he relates. Even as he describes how the stage is set and how the visual effects are created, his language displays the verbal counterpart of the Opéra's extravagance. St. Preux repeatedly names the relationship between two terms, stating in the most flat-footed manner that one thing "represents" or "is represented by" another. Or he uses similes that make pitifully clear the association of the noble and the base, as in the comparison of the sky to the washerwoman's laundry. Sometimes he makes bad jokes: speaking of the "dragons, lizards, tortoises, crocodiles [and] huge toads" that shuffle "menacingly" around the stage, he remarks, "Chacune de ces figures est animée par un lourdaut de Savoyard, qui n'a pas l'esprit de faire la bête" ("Each of these figures is animated by a dumb Savoyard, who hasn't enough presence of mind to horse around")![52] The very visibility of St. Preux's play on words, the amusing way his own rhetoric calls attention to itself, is part of the point Rousseau wants to make. St. Preux's poor figures are like the trapdoors in the Opéra stage or the ropes that hang down from on high; they call attention to their own operation and announce the lumbering transfer of meaning of which they are the vehicle. As we begin

to understand, these awkward attempts at figuration make emotional identification with the action almost unthinkable. One may be entertained, but it is hard to become emotionally engaged when confronted with such intrusive mechanical devices. That is undoubtedly why Rousseau elsewhere refers to the Opéra's machines as "those bad supplements" ("ces mauvais suppléments") and why he wants to exclude them from the Opéra stage.[53]

In this critique of allegory, Rousseau has much in common with the authors of the *Encyclopédie* articles on "Machine" and "Merveilleux," who make explicit the connection between machines, the marvelous, and overworked rhetorical figures. The anonymous author of the entry "Merveilleux" rejects the marvelous in literature and the opera on at least two grounds. First, references to Greek and Roman gods and goddesses have no reality, that is, no emotional meaning for the modern public;[54] and second, intermingling real and metaphysical beings destroys the unity of a work.[55] In short, the unwarranted and meaningless use of mythological figures or allegories is little more than an ornament covering over a void.[56] This is clearly what Rousseau wants to illustrate through the satire of the Paris Opéra. Empty signs, like so many "dragons, lizards, tortoises [and] huge toads" moved by mindless Savoyards, may amuse a childish public, but they do not make sense—they are meaningless in themselves and they detract from the sense of the whole.

St. Preux designates this same void when he cites the example of the tragic death, on stage, of the little chimney sweeps who sometimes play the part of devils. These youngsters are hoisted up to the "skies" on ropes, until they disappear "majestically" in the rags representing clouds. But sometimes the ropes break, and then "the infernal spirits and immortal Gods fall, are maimed, [and] sometimes killed" ("les esprits infernaux et les Dieux immortels tombent, s'estropient, se tuent quelquefois").[57] The blatant contrast between the spirits or gods and the mortals who portray them ceases to be funny at such a moment, and the full and tragic consequences of allegory are revealed. The connection between the sensory representation and the metaphysical idea it represents is so tenuous that it sometimes fails altogether, thus destroying any semblance of meaning or understanding. In some ways, allegory—the "demonic agency"—is tantamount to death.

The Letter on the Paris Opéra: The Real

Rousseau's goal is to communicate meaning without recourse to the type of detrimental figure or "mauvais supplément" exemplified by St. Preux's own de-

scriptions. At the very least, Rousseau wants to do away with the obvious link or middle term between the two elements of the figure—the "this represents that" style of representation. Nonetheless, if his objective is to achieve a kind of transparency, he is not proposing some immaterial ideal. Rousseau's aim is to produce a "reasonable illusion,"[58] by putting on stage a worthy subject (a man of noble character, for example), and establishing production values appropriate to this subject. He states these values clearly in his dictionary entry on "Opéra," but they are also implicit throughout the satirical letter; and they are dramatized in the subtle but telling story of Laberius, which St. Preux advances as a counterpoint to the French practices he scorns.[59] The example of Laberius gives us the opportunity to assess what Rousseau's realism might be.

Laberius was a popular playwright during the last days of the Roman republic, under Julius Caesar. As a writer of mime plays or satires, which frequently criticized the ruling powers, he offended Caesar with some of his attacks. Caesar's response, his challenge to Laberius to go on stage and show off his talents as an actor, was an insult and a humiliation, which changed the author's life.[60] An explanatory note by the novel's fictional editor recounts Laberius's plight:

> Forcé par le Tiran de monter sur le théatre, il déplora son sort par des vers très touchans, et très capables d'allumer l'indignation de tout honnête homme contre ce César si vanté. *Après avoir*, dit-il, *vécu soixante ans avec honneur, j'ai quitté ce matin mon foyer chevalier Romain, j'y rentrerai ce soir vil Histrion. Hélas, j'ai vécu trop d'un jour. O fortune! s'il falloit me deshonorer une fois, que ne m'y forçois-tu quand la jeunesse et la vigueur me laissoient au moins une figure agréable: mais maintenant quel triste objet viens-je exposer aux rebuts du peuple Romain? une voix éteinte, un corps infirme, un cadavre, un sepulcre animé, qui n'a plus rien de moi que mon nom.* Le prologue entier qu'il récita dans cette occasion, l'injustice que lui fit César piqué de la noble liberté avec laquelle il vengeoit son honneur flétri, l'affront qu'il reçut au cirque, la bassesse qu'eut Ciceron d'insulter à son opprobre, la réponse fine et piquante que lui fit Labérius; tout cela nous a été conservé par [Macrobe],[61] et c'est à mon gré le morceau le plus curieux et le plus intéressant de son fade recueil. (Rouss., *OC*, 2: 282)

Forced by the Tyrant to go on stage, [Laberius] deplored his fate in most touching verse, capable of provoking the indignation of any honorable man against this vaunted Caesar. After living sixty years with honor, he said, I left my home this morning a Roman knight only to return there this evening a vile Histrion. Alas! I lived one day too long. O fortune! If I had to be dishon-

ored one day, why did you not do it when youth and vigor at least left me with an agreeable figure? But now, what a sorry and repulsive object I put before the Roman people. A spent voice, a decrepit body, a corpse, a living sepulchre, which has nothing left of me but the name. The entire prologue that he recited on this occasion, the injustice that Caesar did him, annoyed by the noble freedom with which he avenged his tainted honor, the affront he received in the circus, the baseness of Cicero in jeering at his shame, and the shrewd and tart reply that Laberius made; all this has been preserved for us by [Macrobius]; and this is to me the most curious and interesting piece in [Macrobius's] insipid collection. (Rouss., *CW*, 6: 231; trans. modified)

The Laberius example teaches many stylistic and rhetorical lessons. First, the story restores the proper order of priorities, which is inverted by the Paris Opéra. Instead of creating "small things with a great effort," it represents, in a simple and economical manner, a great man of history. The dramatic intensity of Laberius's misfortunes, hinging on his plight as a man and a citizen of the endangered Roman republic, contrasts with the "false magnificence" of the French opera—and of the monarchy that sponsors it. Where the Opéra takes as its subject matter gods, devils, monsters, and other hybrid creatures, Laberius is on the side of the real. The pain he experiences, the lamentable condition of his body, and his unjust fate are altogether human and recognizable in the world.

Not only is Laberius a noble and dignified man, concerned with important matters like honor, freedom, and civic responsibility, but he goes on stage to represent himself and speak in his own name. He uses the opportunity to address his own fate. Laberius's performance is remarkably self-referential. He speaks to the moment, as it were, and his words exemplify an ideal coincidence of speech and event. Unlike the performances of the Opéra, where the means of representation and the entities represented are disparate and disjoined, Laberius shows himself on stage in a uniquely transparent moment.

But a closer look at Laberius's performance reveals the example's complexity. Laberius's speech captures the moment when he is suspended between two states, no longer simply the Roman knight and not yet fully the vile actor. When the performance is over, Laberius will no longer be able to take his seat with the other Roman gentlemen in the arena; however, while the performance lasts, the metamorphosis is incomplete. When Laberius says, "I left my home this morning a Roman knight, only to return there this evening a vile actor," he allows us to understand his time on stage to be the transition between the two. The present moment of his speech is the turning point in this

process of substitution and degradation, a liminal moment juxtaposing past and future, life and death. What Laberius gives his audience, then, is a hybrid or an oxymoron—"an animated tomb" ("un sépulcre animé").

Forced to make a public spectacle of his decimated body and feeling the shame of having his reputation reduced to his name alone, Laberius views himself as a kind of monster. He calls himself "a sorry and repulsive object" and laments his barely audible voice and his deformed body, saying they have "nothing left of me but the name." His situation—the discrepancy between his name and his condition—returns us to the problematic relation between words and things that St. Preux has been discussing all along. In fact, when Laberius takes to the stage, he has nothing to show but the process of degradation—or figuration—itself. Laberius gives face and form to the problem of allegory (as the liminal or hybrid state between life and death, meaning and the void), which is at the very heart of St. Preux's letter.

The story of Laberius's misfortunes may be more directly related to the life-and-death issues that affect the audience, and may therefore come across as more "real" (having more feeling, warmth, and interest) than the activities of the gods and goddesses that the marvelous puts on stage. But the example of Laberius is not a complete repudiation of allegory, nor a rejection of the material reality or sensory image on which allegory relies. If Rousseau objects to the mechanics of rhetoric as inimical to the creation of illusion, he nonetheless retains and makes powerful "realistic" use of allegory, that rhetorical "machine."

Without saying as much, Rousseau seems to come to the same conclusion as the author of the *Encyclopédie* article "Merveilleux," who remarks: "Ce n'est donc plus dans la poésie moderne qu'il faut chercher le merveilleux, il y serait déplacé, et celui seul qu'on y peut admettre réduit aux passions humaines personnifiées, est plutôt une allégorie qu'un merveilleux proprement dit" ("We should no longer look for the marvelous in modern poetry, for it would be out of place there, and the marvelous reduced to personified human passions, the only kind allowable today, is rather an allegory than the marvelous proper"). Rousseau's modern aesthetic detaches allegory from other marvelous traits, such as the representation of supernatural creatures and obvious rhetorical devices, but does not do away with it altogether. Allegory continues to be the foundation for representation, now disguised as the real.

Realism and the Grotesque in Baudelaire's Poems

St. Preux's comic letter dramatizes the vacuousness and obscurantism of rococo allegory, yet it presents, in its margins and interstices, the model of another allegorical mode, in which presence and meaning are apparently restored. Rousseau views allegory as having one of two forms (either blatantly
and comically improbable or serious and human), and he wants to replace the
one with the other. However, when Baudelaire takes up the satirical letter and
works it into at least four of his prose poems—"Le Vieux Saltimbanque," "Le
Crépuscule du soir," "Une Mort héroïque," and "La Corde"—he intermingles
the two. Baudelaire learns from Rousseau and borrows from him, but he does
not always adhere to his model. Baudelaire's prose poems are hybrids, not only
because they draw together poetry and prose, but also because they bring together the real and the grotesque in a radically new and unsettling way. Baudelaire turns the hybridity characteristic of the grotesque opera productions away
from the monsters they represent and the excessive machinery they use and
puts it to work in the rhetoric of his poems.

This is immediately obvious in "Le Vieux Saltimbanque" ("The Old Acrobat"), which sets the story of a poor, decrepit acrobat against the backdrop of
a popular fair, chock-full of activity and fun. The presence of "danseuses, belles
comme *des fées*," "un escamoteur éblouissant comme *un dieu*," and "les *Hercules,* fiers de l'énormité de leurs membres" puts the fair squarely on the side of
the grotesque, with its mythological and magical subjects;[62] and in fact, the
poem takes its setting from St. Preux's comparison of the Opéra and "la foire":
"je suis persuadé qu'on applaudit les cris d'une Actrice à l'Opéra comme les
tours de force d'un bâteleur à la foire" ("I am persuaded that they applaud an
Actress's cries at the Opéra as they do an acrobat's feats at the fair").[63] Baudelaire's lively description of the fair derives much of its imagery and vivacity
from St. Preux's physical description of the opera stage. St. Preux's long enu-
meration of odd devices used in the representation of both natural scenes and
mythological characters, combined with the juxtaposition of opposites: "les
Dieux immortels . . . se tuent quelquefois" ("the immortal Gods . . . sometimes are killed"); ironic word choice: "ce magnifique char" ("this magnificent
chariot"), "cette agréable musique" ("this agreeable music"); silly analogies: "le
Ciel est représenté par certaines guenilles . . . suspendues à des bâtons ou à des
cordes, comme l'étendage d'une blanchisseuse" ("the Sky is represented by certain . . . tatters, suspended on sticks or ropes, like a washerwoman's clothesline"); and outrageous puns: "chacune de ces figures [dragons, lézards, croco-

diles, et crapauds] est animée par un lourdaud de Savoyard qui n'a pas l'esprit de faire la bête" ("each of these figures [dragons, lizards, crocodiles, and toads] is animated by a dumb Savoyard, who hasn't enough presence of mind to horse around") make St. Preux's description a verbal playground. (Perhaps we need look no further for reasons why Baudelaire found it so appealing!)

The description is so outrageous that it sets the tone for the verbal extravagance and thematic gaiety of Baudelaire's fair, but it also provides images and expressions that Baudelaire uses almost verbatim to represent the excitement and the tragedy that unfold in that place. The "mélange de cris, de détonations de cuivre et d'explosions de fusées" ("blend of shouts, booms of brass, and explosions of rockets") that is the hallmark of the fair scene in the poem recalls the "pétard au bout d'une fusée" ("firecracker at the end of a squib") that stands in for lightning at the opera and mixes with the "cris affreux" ("awful whines") of the opera singers themselves. But the "deux ou trois chandelles puantes et mal mouchées" ("two or three stinking and ill-trimmed tallow candles") that St. Preux describes, whose smoke covers the "divinity" like incense as he swings above the stage, come to accent the tragic rather than the comic elements of Baudelaire's fair. The candles no longer shine on the movements of an actor crudely representing a god; instead, they illuminate the spent acrobat and his distress:

> [J]e vis un pauvre saltimbanque, voûté, caduc, décrépit, une ruine d'homme, adossé contre un des poteaux de sa cahute; une cahute plus misérable que celle du sauvage le plus abruti; et dont *deux bouts de chandelles, coulants et fumants,* éclairaient trop bien encore la détresse.

> I saw a pitiful acrobat, stooped, obsolete, decrepit, a human ruin, backed against one of the posts of his shack; a shack more wretched than that of the most mindless savage, and whose adversity was still illumined all too well by *two burned-down candles, dripping and smoking.* (Baudelaire, *Parisian Prowler,* trans. Kaplan, 29; my emphasis)

In place of a satirical piece making sport of the lyric theater, Baudelaire has written a tragedy set off against a background of lighthearted pleasure. His text juxtaposes the comic and the tragic, uniting them by placing them in a single theatrical setting and evoking the idea of change (or loss) over time: the ruined acrobat has "survived" the generation he used to amuse; he "no longer" attracts the forgetful world. These modifications relate back to the Laberius story, where time (the events of one day) also makes the difference between a robust

life and a kind of death. Baudelaire's poem takes Rousseau's anecdote from the margins (in the footnotes of St. Preux's letter) to the center of the text. By locating the "realistic" description of the impoverished actor's desperate plight *within* the extravagant setting of the fair, the poem directly raises the question of the relation between the grotesque and the real that underlies Rousseau's work.

But this question implies another; for before we can determine the relation between the two styles, we should be sure that we know which is which. If the grotesque is the name for a certain subject matter—supernatural gods, devils, monsters and fairies, for example, then the old acrobat is on the side of the real. His pain and his dire circumstances tie him to the world; it's the fair that represents a much-needed respite from this all-too-difficult reality: "un armistice conclu avec les puissances malfaisantes de la vie, un répit dans la contention et la lutte universelles" ("an armistice contracted with life's malevolent forces, a respite from universal disputes and struggles"). But if, on the other hand, the grotesque names the disproportion of means to ends, or the imbalance between the sign and what it designates, then doubt is shed on the realism of the old man's story. While the old "saltimbanque" is described in sober terms befitting his unhappy state, *he himself* is an empty sign. Only the narrator's retrospective interpretation of the acrobat as a "figure of the old poet" eventually fills this void.[64] The worn-out acrobat raises important questions about the nature of the grotesque and whether (or how) it differs from the real. The Baudelaire poems that borrow from Rousseau's letter all return to these issues.

The same dichotomous structure that "Le Vieux Saltimbanque" borrows from Rousseau is featured again in the early prose poem "Le Crépuscule du soir" ("Twilight"), which Baudelaire revised substantially in 1862. Evening (meaning both the twilight of life and the end of the day in this poem) is the moment that precipitates important changes of mood and behavior in men. The poem opens quietly. But the peaceful thoughts of tired laborers coming home for the evening are suddenly interrupted by the jarring cacophony that descends around them from the insane asylum above the city. "Cette sinistre ululation," "cette imitation des harmonies de l'enfer," "un grand hurlement, composé d'une foule de cris discordants, que l'espace transforme en une lugubre harmonie" ("This ominous ululation," "this imitation of hell's harmonies," "a great howling, composed of a multitude of discordant shouts . . . transformed by the space into a dismal harmony") sets the tone for the featured stories of two madmen whose illness is aggravated by the setting sun, as if dusk were for them "un signal de sabbat" ("a sign of witches' sabbath").

These analogies between madmen's cries and music at its worst, together with the references to "l'enfer" ("hell") and "[le] sabbat" ("[the] witches' sabbath"), tie the poem's theatrical frame (¶¶ 1–3, added in 1862) to St. Preux's assessment of the awful music at the Opéra:

> Mais ce dont vous ne sauriez avoir d'idée, ce sont les cris affreux, les longs mugissemens dont retentit le théatre durant la représentation. On voit les Actrices presque en convulsion, arracher avec violence ces glapissemens de leurs poumons, les poings fermés contre la poitrine, la tête en arriere, le visage enflammé, les vaisseaux gonflés, l'estomac pantelant: . . . leurs efforts font autant souffrir ceux qui les regardent, que leurs chants ceux qui les écoutent, et ce qu'il y a de plus inconcevable est que ces *hurlemens* sont presque la seule chose qu'applaudissent les spectateurs. . . . Imaginez les Muses, les Graces, les Amours, Vénus même s'exprimant avec cette délicatesse, et jugez de l'effet! Pour les Diables, passe encore, cette musique a *quelque chose d'infernal* qui ne leur messied pas. Aussi les magies, les évocations, et toutes les *fêtes du Sabat* sont elles toujours ce qu'on admire le plus à l'Opéra françois. (Rouss., *OC*, 2: 285; my emphasis)

> But you could have no idea of the awful whines, the long howls with which the theater reverberates during the performance. The Actresses are seen almost in convulsions, violently forcing these yelpings from their lungs, their fists clutched against their breasts, head thrown back, face inflamed, veins bulging, stomach throbbing; . . . their efforts cause as much suffering to those who are watching them as their singing does to those who are listening, and even more inconceivable is the fact that these *howlings* are almost the only thing the audience applauds. . . . Picture the Muses, the Graces, Cupids, Venus herself expressing themselves with such refinement, and imagine the effect! Where the devils are concerned, it is good enough, *something infernal* about this music is not unsuited to them. And so feats of magic, evocations of spirits, and all the *rites of Sabbath* are always the things most admired at the French Opéra. (Rouss., *CW*, 6: 233; my emphasis)

St. Preux rails against the disparity between actor and role and calls on us to imagine how awful it is when allegorical figures such as Grace, Love, or Beauty (Venus) are represented by ham-fisted performers. The singers make no attempt to hide their excruciating efforts and the result is a painful war between the real and the ideal. The singers' contortions so disfigure the idea they are meant to incarnate as to make the representation monstrous—hardly less grotesque than the excited behavior of the hospice's inhabitants. If Baudelaire has

transformed the context of Rousseau's description, in so doing, he has rendered the "madness" of Rousseau's artistic nightmare as literal lunacy.

However, in the last three paragraphs of the poem (¶¶ 7–9, also added in 1862), Baudelaire's narrator sets himself apart from this insanity. Night for him is not "un signal de sabbat," but "le signal d'une fête intérieure" ("[the] signal [of] an inward celebration") heralding the arrival of "la déesse Liberté." The narrator views twilight as a deliverance, and he describes it in the most positive terms. The poem opposes the frenzy of madness to internal peace, both brought about by the coming of night. Yet, different as the beginning and ending of the poem may be, they both take their cue from the "grotesque" opera. The last paragraphs of the poem describe something like a fair—St. Preux's metaphor for the lyric stage. The onset of night is a "fête," involving dancers and at least one goddess ("the goddess Liberty") and marked by fireworks whose name in French, *feu d'artifice,* emphasizes the artifice involved. Furthermore, the poem's ending borrows verbally from St. Preux's description of the Opéra. The "explosion des lanternes," the "feu d'artifice," the "lourdes draperies qu'une main invisible attire" ("heavy draperies drawn by an invisible hand") and the "robes étranges de danseuses, où une gaze transparente et sombre laisse entrevoir les splendeurs amorties d'une jupe éclatante, comme sous le noir présent transperce le délicieux passé" ("strange dancing dress[es], whose transparent and dark gauze reveals a glimpse of the muted splendors of a brilliant skirt") all refer to details of the operatic staging, with its "lanternes," its "pincées de poix-résine qu'on projette sur un flambeau" ("pinch[es] of rosin tossed into a flame"), and especially its backdrop, "un grand rideau . . . presque toujours percé ou déchiré, [qui] représente des gouffres dans la terre ou des trous dans le ciel, selon la perspective" ("a large curtain . . . almost always pierced or torn, which represents chasms in the earth or holes in the Sky, according to the perspective"). But if Baudelaire has captured St. Preux's lighthearted mood, he appears to use it in the service of a far different aesthetic; for in place of a satirical critique, he proclaims the positive benefits of this nightly performance. The end of the poem is a celebration of the "fires of fantasy" ("ces feux de la fantaisie") that run directly counter to the "realist" subject matter and production values propounded by Rousseau.

Like "Le Vieux Saltimbanque," with its light and dark moods, "Le Crépuscule du soir" is structured around a contrast between a positive reaction to twilight and a lugubrious one; and both the poem's literally mad and more reassuring aspects draw on the hyperbolic language of St. Preux's satire. Illustrating

the narrator's observation that "la même cause [peut] engendrer deux effets contraires" ("the same cause [can] beget two opposite effects"), the poem suggests that the grotesque is everywhere, usurping any semblance of the real. If "Le Vieux Saltimbanque" posits a link between the grotesque and the real, "Le Crépuscule du soir" calls into question the very distinction between the two terms. It raises the possibility that the grotesque may not be a style at all, but a principle or structure capable of masquerading in different stylistic guises. In "Le Crépuscule du soir," Baudelaire prepares us to understand allegory as a "machine" capable of the *indiscriminate* generation of serene or mad effects. Baudelaire's idea of allegory runs counter to Rousseau's, while nonetheless building on Rousseau's work. Where Rousseau opposes an ideal ("realistic" and therefore meaningful) form of allegory to the mechanical hijinks of the rococo, Baudelaire sees no fundamental difference between the two.

This discrepancy between the two authors' aesthetic theories is the almost explicit focus of "Une Mort héroïque" ("A Heroic Death"). Baudelaire seems to signal his borrowing from Rousseau (and Rousseau's support of Italian music in the Querelle des Bouffons) by giving the "bouffon" in the poem an Italianate name—Fancioulle.[65] In fact, it is possible to read Fancioulle as another caricature of Rousseau, and the first two paragraphs of the poem as a commentary on Rousseau's participation in the operatic quarrel,[66] as well as on his talents as a comic author (or "histrion"), who mistakes his vocation and becomes "fatally" interested in serious subjects like "la patrie" (the fatherland) and "la liberté." But, most important, through its central figure, the poem foregrounds Rousseau's artistic ideal, a performance that promotes illusion and engages the spectator's emotions by concealing the mechanics that make it work. Fancioulle incarnates this Rousseauist ideal when he successfully hides "l'art, l'effort, la volonté" (the "art, effort, will") that undergird his role. His performance is the opposite of the Opéra's elaborate staging, which produces "small things with a great effort."

If Fancioulle is in some ways Rousseau's double, he also shares many traits with Rousseau's Laberius, the *mimus* (writer of mime plays) who offended Caesar with his satire and was summoned to perform before the ruler as a result.[67] Fancioulle, too, is a mime (a silent actor) accused of plotting to overthrow the despotic government under which he lives, and he is also forced by the prince to go on stage. Fancioulle's life is on the line and, like Laberius, he might be considered "un cadavre, un sépulcre animé" when he performs "at the edge of the tomb" ("au bord de la tombe") and succeeds in "animating" his role: "[il] arrivait à être . . . ce que les meilleures statues de l'antiquité, mirac-

uleusement *animées* . . . seraient relativement à l'idée générale et confuse de beauté" ("[he] succeed[ed] in being . . . what the best statues of antiquity, if miraculously *animated,* . . . might become relative to the general and vague idea of beauty"). Like Laberius, Fancioulle walks the impossible line between life and death. He is captivating because he projects the image of grace and immortality and makes the audience forget his distress. Finally, Fancioulle and Laberius share a similar fate: their powerful performances cause the despots' jealous rage and both are put down for their success. Laberius loses Caesar's patronage and Fancioulle dies, having fallen from the prince's "favor."[68]

Fancioulle may be the embodiment of Rousseau's ideal, an allegory that hides its rhetorical workings and veils the terrifying emptiness that inhabits it. But ultimately this ideal is undone, and inescapable reality (Fancioulle's corpse/death) is exposed. Fancioulle is counterbalanced in the poem by the despot who presides over the mime's performance. Rousseau's aesthetic ideal—"une parfaite idéalisation, qu'il était impossible de ne pas supposer vivante, possible, réelle" ("a perfect idealization, which it was impossible not to accept as living, possible, real"),[69] "un chef-d'oeuvre d'art vivant" ("a master-piece of living art")—is set off against, and finally destroyed by, the prince's grotesque excesses. The extraordinary equilibrium of ideal and real is upset by the discordant sound of a whistle, the sign of disapproval, which interrupts the illusion, like the cacophonous music or obtrusive mechanical devices at the Opéra. The prince, whose face seems to reveal the excessive emotions that motivate this act—"une pâleur nouvelle s'ajoutait sans cesse à sa pâleur habituelle, comme la neige s'ajoute à la neige. Ses lèvres se resserraient de plus en plus" ("a new pallor continuously increased his usual pallor, like snow added to snow. His lips tightened more and more")—applauds "conspicuously" ("ostensiblement"), while the fires of jealousy and rancor (perhaps) burn within. The despot's inscrutability, the difference between his apparent enthusiasm and the fatal act he apparently causes, reintroduces the question of meaning—the imbalance between appearance and essence—which the mime's performance has temporarily obscured. A "monster" whose intentions will forever remain unknown, the prince partakes fully of the grotesque.

Refusing to respect the difference that Rousseau wants to enforce between realism and its grotesque double, Baudelaire interweaves a "realist" allegory with the grotesque it hopes to "overthrow" and shows the impossibility of this artistic insurrection. Indeed, by depicting the conspiring mime and the despotic prince in similar terms, he underscores the fundamental similarity between the two.[70] Reading Rousseau against himself, Baudelaire brings out, in

a way Rousseau would have abhorred, the grotesqueness of all allegory. "Une Mort héroïque," Baudelaire's own fatal whistle, makes clear the vulnerability of Rousseau's ideal.

Naturalizing Allegory: "La Corde"

The poems examined so far, which all borrow rather obviously from Rousseau's satirical letter, either foreground the grotesque as a prominent feature alongside the "real" or underscore the enduring power of the grotesque to unveil allegory's truth. But "La Corde" ("The Rope") stands apart from this group. Unlike the others, none of this poem's characters bears any resemblance to Laberius, and its language and plot owe no obvious debt to Rousseau's delineation of the grotesque. On the contrary, "La Corde" demonstrates how the grotesque can be naturalized and made to disappear. Undoubtedly one of the most instructive of Baudelaire's dialogues with Rousseau, "La Corde" simultaneously produces the grotesque and hides it, in a feat of rhetorical "magic."[71]

Based on an actual event (the suicide of Manet's young model Alexandre) and written in a manner that Robert Kopp terms "precise and cold," the poem seems thoroughly steeped in the real.[72] Even the poem's dedication, "A Edouard Manet," suggests the poet's desire to situate his work in the world. Yet this "cruel story,"[73] with its long quotation of the artist and its almost clinical details, takes its point of departure, too, from the fanciful imagery of St. Preux's satire. Nonetheless, in keeping with its emphasis on the real, "La Corde" eschews the overtly theatrical frame that ties the other Baudelaire poems thematically to Rousseau's work. Instead, the poem draws out the theme of illusion in art from the example of the painter's young model.

The artist uses the boy as a support for his visual allegories. He paints the child frequently, depicting him variously as a mythological Cupid, a bohemian, and an angel carrying the Crown of Thorns and the Nails of the Passion. However, when the youngster commits suicide by hanging himself on a rope ("une corde") from a very *real* nail, he is reduced to a rigid body and is presumably incapable of producing any further illusions. The painter describes in gruesome detail the consequences of the young boy's act. First, the artist has to cut the body down and prepare it, finding the rope in the swollen flesh and snipping it away:

Il était déjà fort roide, et j'avais une répugnance inexplicable à le faire brusquement tomber sur le sol. Il fallait le soutenir tout entier avec un bras,

et, avec la main de l'autre bras, couper la corde. Mais cela fait, tout n'était pas fini; le petit monstre s'était servi d'une ficelle fort mince qui était entrée profondément dans les chairs, et il fallait maintenant, avec de minces ciseaux, chercher la corde entre les deux bourrelets de l'enflure, pour lui dégager le cou.

He was already quite stiff, and I was inexplicably reluctant to let him drop abruptly to the ground. I had to support his whole body with one arm, and, with the hand of the other arm, cut the rope. But that being done, everything was not finished. The little monster had used very fine twine, which had entered deeply into the flesh, and in order to release it from the neck, with fine scissors, I now had to locate the rope between the two folds of the swelling. (Baudelaire, *Parisian Prowler,* trans. Kaplan, 78; trans. modified)

In this account, what appears to be just a detail—the rope used in the suicide—is already mentioned twice; but in the second half of the poem, "la corde" becomes the focus of the narrative. The rope turns into a semi-religious relic, an object of superstition and perverse desire, not unlike the "Nails of [Christ's] Passion" represented in the painter's art.

The little boy's mother contacts the painter, hoping to see her son's body. Ushered into the room where the corpse is laid out, however, she scarcely glances at the youngster and, instead, pointedly asks for the cord on which his body hung. The startled artist interprets the request as a sign of the mother's despair and a displacement of maternal tenderness. Only when he receives letters asking for more pieces of the rope does he grasp the woman's real motivation: she has profited from her son's suicide by selling the cord as an object of veneration, an awful good luck charm.

Manet passes along this anecdote to the narrator as an illustration of how he was taken in by the most natural illusion—"singulièrement mystifié par l'illusion la plus naturelle" ("remarkably duped by the most natural illusion")—his belief in maternal love. And, in fact, the story *is* about the mystification of natural illusion, although it is the reader who is deceived. When the narrator takes up the artist's story, supposedly unchanged, it becomes a demonstration of the mystification of rhetoric.[74] "La Corde" achieves Rousseau's ideal of realistic illusion, by paradoxically putting into play a rather obvious device. Although it boldly displays its mechanics, the poem successfully masks its grotesqueness by taking up an allegory that is, in one sense, "real."

Although the reference to Rousseau's work is far more subtle here than in the other poems that borrow from it, "La Corde" takes its cue from St. Preux's

repeated emphasis on the instrumental ropes used to hang various machines at the Opéra:

> Le Ciel est réprésenté par certaines guenilles bleuâtres, suspendues à des bâtons ou à *des cordes*. . . . Les chars des Dieux et des Déesses sont composés de quatre solives encadrées et suspendues à *une grosse corde*. . . .
> Quand [les Démons] doivent s'élever dans les airs, on leur substitue adroitement de petits Démons de toile brune empaillée, ou quelquefois de vrais ramoneurs, qui branlent en l'air suspendus à *des cordes*. . . . Mais ce qu'il y a de réellement tragique, c'est quand *les cordes* sont mal conduites ou viennent à rompre; car alors les esprits infernaux et les Dieux immortels tombent, s'estropient, *se tuent* quelquefois. (Rouss., *OC*, 2: 283–84; my emphasis)

> The Sky is represented by certain bluish tatters, suspended on sticks or *ropes*. . . . The chariots of the Gods and Goddesses are composed of four beams in a frame and suspended by *a heavy rope*. . . .
> When [the Demons] are to rise into the air, little Demons of stuffed brown canvas are skillfully substituted for them, or sometimes real chimney sweeps who sway in the air suspended on *ropes*. . . .But the really tragic thing is when *the ropes* are badly maneuvered or happen to break; for then the infernal spirits and immortal Gods fall, are maimed, sometimes *killed*. (Rouss., *CW*, 6: 232; my emphasis)

The ropes at the Opéra, which dangle down from the "sky" and lift various "deities" up, are so obvious that they intrude on the illusion they were supposed to produce. Not only do the ropes allow the spectators to see the crude machinery that makes the performance work, but like the rope with which Manet's model hanged himself, they sometimes kill the children (the *ramoneurs,* or chimney sweeps) clinging to them. When this happens, the brutal reality of the youngsters' death puts an end to the idea of immortality they were attempting to portray. Furthermore, their death shows how little bearing the immortal lives of the gods have on the existence of the human beings who act in or attend the performance. Death defies any hope of illusion, in every sense.

Baudelaire has taken this horrific example of the dead child and the broken rope and written it out, with all its implications, in his poem. Rousseau's story is an allegory about the tenuous link between grotesque figures and the ideas they represent, as well as their lack of significance for the real world. Baudelaire's anecdote leaves Rousseau's meaning intact. His story, too, is about the

broken connection between the figural and the real, the artist's idea and the model who embodies it—both in art and in life. As a model for the angel bearing the emblems of Christ's death, the boy may take part in the allegorical representation of the Passion, but there is nothing immortal about him. Furthermore, his love of drink and his tendency to petty thievery do not put him in the company of life's "angels." Indeed, the boy confounds the painter, who has given the youngster a better life and therefore cannot comprehend his irrational behavior and his sadness. The youngster does not fit the artist's expectations. Between the artist and the child, as between the model and the art, there is a gulf. Art and the artist both seem to neglect the real. As J. A. Hiddleston notes:

> The ultimate moral message [of "La Corde"] appears to be that art, whether the painter's or the poet's, is unable to come to grips with reality, which it sidesteps or fails to recognize. Art is a lie, a simulacrum, a comedy, which appeals only to the eye of the spectator or ear of the reader without involving any genuine emotion. . . . It appears, then, that in this deceptively straightforward piece Baudelaire is expressing his despair before what Proust called . . . *the illusory magic of literature,* and is asking the anguished question: what is the value of art if, in veiling the terrors of the abyss, it removes from men's eyes the contemplation of real suffering?[75]

The boy's demise is merely a pretext for Baudelaire's poem, just as the boy, while alive, was an object to be transformed by Manet's art. The child himself is of no consequence. Baudelaire apparently seconds Rousseau's complaint about the inability of grotesque art, at least, to arouse passion and foster identification with others.

But the poem does not stop with the child's death. Whereas, in Manet's story, the painter's work is disrupted by his model's suicide, Baudelaire's poem is propelled forward by this event. The instrument of the boy's death, the rope, becomes the means to *reconnect* the literal (body of the boy) to the divinity he comes to represent (Christ). People who have heard of the child's suicide want to buy pieces of the rope with which he hanged himself, as if it were an instrument of Christ's passion. If in life the boy was asked to play the part of various mythological figures or gods, in death his body becomes even more divine. The "real" little boy is never more thoroughly transfigured than when he is dead.

"La Corde" is a complex reaction to Rousseau's artistic and moral advice. On the one hand, Baudelaire flies in the face of Rousseau's aesthetic theory by

flaunting rather than hiding the grotesque "mechanical" rope that Rousseau finds excessive, meaningless, and intrusive in the Opéra's spectacle. On the other hand, by inserting it in the intimate context of the child's act, in which it is appropriate and tragically meaningful, Baudelaire reclaims the obvious device as a subtle, even understated element of the poem's realism. But Baudelaire then goes one step further: In the story of the mother and the neighbors who want pieces of the rope as quasi-religious objects, he shows how allegory functions as a real part of the everyday world. When they take the instrument of the boy's suicide as a simulacrum of the instruments of Christ's passion, or as an object of superstitious veneration, the mother and her ilk treat allegory as a worthy and integral part of their lives. The rope has become a fetish, but for that very reason, it has special meaning for them. Allegory is the prized possession of true believers.

By taking up allegory in an already allegorical context (by situating it first in the studio where making allegories is the artist's daily occupation, and then by establishing the connection between Christ's passion and popular superstition), Baudelaire naturalizes the allegory and makes it disappear. In this way, he follows the advice of the author of the *Encyclopédie* article "Merveilleux," who argues that

> la poésie est un art d'illusion qui nous présente des choses imaginées comme réelles . . . [et] l'illusion ne peut être complette qu'autant que la poésie se renferme dans la créance commune et dans les opinions nationales: c'est ce qu'Homere a pensé; c'est pour cela qu'il a tiré du fond de la créance et des opinions répandues chez les Grecs, tout le merveilleux, tout le surnaturel, toutes les machines de ses poëmes.

> poetry is an art of illusion that presents imagined things as real . . . [and] the illusion can only be complete in so far as poetry involves itself with a common set of beliefs and national opinions: that is what Homer thought; that is why he drew from the store of widespread beliefs and opinions among the Greeks, all the marvelous, all the supernatural, all the machines of his poems.[76]

Baudelaire takes advantage of Rousseau's "rope," transforming it from a blatant machine into a realist detail, and then into a "realist" allegory. By assimilating the mechanical to the real and thus naturalizing it, Baudelaire accomplishes precisely what Rousseau wished to achieve; he obscures the poem's rhetorical mechanism—by hiding it in plain sight.[77]

This process does not completely resolve the questions surrounding the real and the grotesque, however. If the promise of realism is to make us forget that it's the product of illusion, "La Corde" both does and doesn't keep this promise. By telling us the story of how the mundane cord became a religious artifact and an object of savvy marketing, the poem foregrounds the very transformative processes and seductive techniques that make it work. The poem hovers on the cusp between literal and figural meaning, between real things and their allegorical functions. Of course, by "purport[ing] to illustrate mother love and moraliz[ing] on that theme,"[78] the poem also diverts our attention away from its own rhetorical doings. By setting us up to believe that illusion has been dispelled and "le fait réel" is before us (the first paragraph explicitly philosophizes about the "bizarre sentiment" we experience when this happens), the poem urges us to buy into its own marketing techniques. It wants to trick us into forgetting the very hybrid status that it flaunts.

Baudelaire's poem is not simple, as Hiddleston remarks. Since it demonstrates allegory's functions in art, as well as in life, it cannot be read as simply a commentary on the artist's elitist neglect of the real world. Insofar as Baudelaire uses the rope first as a concrete, meaningful, and appropriate sign, and then shows how it becomes a marketable commodity, he does not overlook the real. On the contrary, he shows precisely that allegory is at home everywhere and is not limited to the domain of art. Although the secondary narrator, Manet, does not condone the crass use that the boy's mother makes of the rope, it is not clear whether his reaction predicts Baudelaire's own. Manet is aghast that commercialism stands in for mother love (or that the rope replaces the boy in the mother's interest), but Baudelaire's point, I think, is different. He is fascinated, I would submit, with the process by which allegory, arising out of death or loss, generates a supposedly meaningful and therefore marketable sign.

Baudelaire's ethics are not easy to discern. "La Corde" implies that all allegories, even Christian allegories like the Passion, amount to superstitions; they are "mere games, amusements, totally devoid of seriousness, for all their power to persuade and move."[79] But allegories are everywhere, and they may even function to relieve the distress and misery of the real world. Should the mother not try to improve her lot by making money from her trade in allegorical signs? Should people not harbor the illusion that a rope can ward off fate? "La Corde" may underscore the superficiality or excesses of allegory, but it does not necessarily condemn them. The poem seems to confirm what "Le Vieux Saltimbanque" presents so overtly: that allegory is a valid escape from

the misery and death that characterize the real. Converting "la corde" from a suicidal instrument into a source of fortune and good luck, allegory appeals to humanity's real, basic needs. Whereas Rousseau pronounces a moral and aesthetic indictment of the grotesque, with its spectacular effects and comic machinery, Baudelaire, I believe, finds welcome relief or solace in the escape it provides.[80] In any case, Baudelaire makes us aware that allegory itself (whether comic or tragic) is inescapable.

6 The Sociopolitical Implications of the Grotesque

"Opéra" and "Les Yeux des pauvres"

Reading Rousseau's writings on opera, Baudelaire came into contact with a theory and practice of allegory that inspired his own. Rousseau's aesthetic musings gave Baudelaire not only an understanding of the mechanical operation and narrative effects of allegory, but a sense of its comic potential as well. Yet, as I have already begun to show, Rousseau's work on opera was more than a literal critique of the rococo's favorite themes and style. In taking aim at French music and particularly the Paris Opéra, Rousseau and his associates were also contesting the absolute monarchy that underwrote the Opéra and perpetuated, through the Opéra's extravagant productions, an image of itself as a lavish and frivolous regime. Rousseau's attack on the Opéra had social and political implications; it represented a strategy for challenging the monarchy without incurring censorship. Given Baudelaire's own personal experience with the repressive practices of the Second Empire, he must have found Rousseau's oppositional stance intriguing. Evidence in the prose poems shows that the poet not only borrowed from the letter on the Paris Opéra in Rousseau's novel *Julie* but also carefully analyzed Rousseau's dictionary article "Opéra" and rewrote it for his own ends.

Although Baudelaire's prose poems make occasional reference to despotism, conspiracy, usurpation, fratricide, and warfare, they have generally been deemed apolitical. Yet, as the preceding analysis of the poems as topical cartoons suggests, the apparent ahistoricity of Baudelaire's poetry is deceptive. Baudelaire's prose poems, like the duplicitous modern texts they are, mobilize behind their mildly provocative surface narratives "a call for a more subversive

reading" and produce a new ("textual") reader, capable of reading the poems' allegorical play.[1] Rather than engaging in overt opposition, then, the prose poems demand to be read differently, against the grain of the habitual categories and classes of the dominant discourse, as something "new."[2] A case in point is "Les Yeux des pauvres," which calls upon the destabilizing force of the grotesque to unsettle the usual categories of analysis and disrupt the dominant conservative discourse from within.

As the generative or transformative force driving allegory, the grotesque disturbs hierarchies and gives rise, indiscriminately, to "real" or artistic effects. In the *Petits Poèmes en prose,* mimes and princes, fairgoers and acrobats, madmen and artists all draw their energy or their inertia from its power. Hidden in plain sight, the grotesque inhabits figures that hint at its own mechanics, as well as those that incarnate its force of law. This chapter explores how Baudelaire harnessed this linguistic power—which can only manifest itself indirectly, through proxies and between the lines—to contravene the repressive practices of Napoléon III's regime.

"Les Yeux des pauvres"

"Les Yeux des pauvres" ("The Eyes of the Poor") is one of several prose poems in which critics have seen a political intention. As its title suggests, it features a poor family depicted in some detail and therefore exemplifies, in Jonathan Monroe's words, "the turn taken by the *Petits Poëmes en Prose* toward more concretely and explicitly social motifs."[3] Its explicit theme—love—extends beyond the solipsistic confines of the couple and includes the altruistic desire to draw other people into a loving family. Put another way, the poem is about the possibility of bringing individuals together into a collective whole. As we shall see, "Les Yeux" contemplates a project not unlike Rousseau's dream of creating a new, more inclusive society through the intermediary of the theater. Baudelaire's poem tells the story of a love that thrives on communication, engendering, in turn, the hope that a whole society might be based on such exchange.

However, "Les Yeux" is not an optimistic poem. The analogy between the two ideals (love and a loving society) is predicated on the simple assumption that people have something in common. The two lovers in the poem make the usual promise that all their thoughts will be held in common and that their two souls will be as one. Since this is a dream "rêvé par tous les hommes [mais] réalisé par aucun" ("dreamed by all men [but] realized by none"), however, finding the common ground on which to base the potential family of man

turns out to be an impossible challenge. The love affair the poem depicts turns sour; and through its narrative of this failure, the poem evokes the corruption of the utopian belief in the universal family frequently associated in the nineteenth century with Rousseau.

However, the meaning of the poem goes well beyond its overt thematic content. The love theme also has implications for the reader, inasmuch as the love relationship (the possibility of a certain kind of communication) is also a figure for reading. The poem is a narrative in the past framed by a direct address in the present to an ambiguous "vous," who is simultaneously the reader and the female lover.[4] By collapsing the two addressees into a single vocative, the frame succinctly sets up a parallel between the interpersonal relationships in the text and the structure of reading and thus makes clear the larger stakes of the poem.[5] Even beyond the anecdotal love story and its extended social meaning, there is a lesson here about how to read. Perhaps the most political message of the poem is not what it has to say about the relations between social classes, but what it has to say about reading class subversively.

In fact, we might say that reading is underscored in the poem. When the couple sit down outside a dazzlingly decorated café, on the corner of one of the new Paris boulevards, the narrator, obviously a man of means who can afford to stop here, encounters the family in rags, which absorbs his attention. The narrator looks into the poor family's eyes, while they look beyond him into the café. This looking leads to reading, as the narrator plumbs the family's eyes and translates their unspoken thoughts into words. Some current of emotion passes into him and a community of sorts is established. But the moment doesn't last. The narrator begins to feel ashamed about the signs of excess consumption at his own table, the glasses and carafes "larger than our thirst." In search of reassurance, he turns to look at his lover, expecting to read his own thoughts in her eyes ("Je tournais mes regards vers les vôtres, cher amour, pour y lire ma pensée"). Searching for the commonly held idea he hoped to find there, he recognizes the signs of capriciousness and "lunacy" instead. The woman is indifferent. She wants nothing more than to have the "maître du café" remove the poor family from the premises. Comparing their eyes to carriage-house doors, she makes it clear that she wants to send them away from her "maison [house or establishment]" and back to the servants' quarters where they belong.[6] Whereas the narrator hoped to extend his almost conjugal bliss by including the poor in their family, the woman will have none of it. She reinforces the class differences that make the idea of a family of man impractical.

The shock of her indifference and the difference it creates between the lovers registers in the frame and, ultimately, throughout the poem. The narrator has learned some hard lessons about the incommunicability of thoughts and about the unlikelihood of creating a workable utopian community, which he sums up in the final lines of his story: "Tant il est difficile de s'entendre . . . et tant la pensée est incommunicable, même entre gens qui s'aiment!" ("How difficult it is to understand one another . . . and how uncommunicable thought is, even among people who love each other!").[7] Presumably it is this devastating discovery in the past that causes the narrator to lash out in the present at his addressee(s), "Ah! vous voulez savoir pourquoi je vous hais aujourd'hui" ("Ah, you want to know why I hate you today"). The last sentence of the poem brings us up to the present moment, when "vous," the lover/reader, has become "le plus bel exemple de l'imperméabilité féminine qui se puisse rencontrer" ("the most beautiful example of feminine impermeability anyone can meet"). Love, the figure of direct and transparent communication, has given way to hatred, which destroys society—and figures the difficulty of reading. But in the very same move, which appears to write off communication and render community impossible, the narrator sets up a new category, "impermeability," to replace the hackneyed and useless categories of "love" and "family." Including the reader in this new class, the narrator ups the stakes for us personally. Even as he excoriates us, he seems to warn us about the importance of choosing our terms, and reading them well.

The Politics and Rhetoric of "Opéra"

The idea that Baudelaire's political poem could be related to an entry on the opera from an eighteenth-century music dictionary seems almost preposterous. At its most literal, Rousseau's article "Opéra" is an essay about musical drama. But read allegorically, or outside the frame of the *Dictionnaire de musique,* as the autonomous essay Rousseau also intended it to be,[8] "Opéra" is not just about the lyric theater, but about texts—the written "opus" or "opera" of an author. In this sense, "Opéra" is a rhetorical treatise with broad aesthetic and political ramifications.[9] Taking its place alongside the other heuristic fictions created by Rousseau (the fictional state of nature and the hypothetical origins of language), it writes out its rhetorical concerns as an aesthetic history, which parallels the creation and evolution of society from the first encounter of primitive men, to the golden age of perfect social harmony, and culminates in the current degraded state of civil society. Read alongside the *Essay on the*

Origin of Language, the article provides us with a fairly comprehensive picture of the aesthetic and political connotations of the opera, according to Rousseau.

Opera is meant to participate in the creation of a new man for the republic Rousseau imagines. The right kind of performance should contribute to establishing a bond of sympathy and identification with others that will, in turn, foster a more cohesive and egalitarian society. Opera will thus generate a new citizen-spectator, on whom a new social and political order may be predicated. We already recognize some of the ideas hinted at, albeit in a very different context, in Baudelaire's poem. But the influence on "Les Yeux des pauvres" of Rousseau's article is not limited to its political undercurrents. For the essay furnishes most of the images and rhetorical strategies, the dramatic framework, and the tripartite structure of Baudelaire's poem as well.

The Rousseau article opens with a definition that furnishes the key terms: opera is a representation of passion (or "action passionnée") that combines poetry, music, and visual art in such a way as to excite the spectator's interest and foster illusion:

> Spectacle dramatique et lyrique où l'on s'efforce de réunir tous les charmes des beaux Arts, dans la représentation d'une action passionnée, pour exciter, à l'aide des sensations agréables, l'intérêt et l'illusion.
>
> Les parties constitutives d'un *Opera* sont, le Poëme, la Musique, et la Décoration. Par la Poésie on parle à l'esprit, par la Musique à l'oreille, par la Peinture aux yeux; et le tout doit se réunir pour émouvoir le coeur et y porter à la fois la même impression par divers organes. (Rouss., *OC,* 5: 948)

> A Dramatic and lyric Spectacle in which one endeavors to bring together all the charms of the fine Arts in the representation of a passionate action in order to arouse interest and illusion with the help of pleasant sensations.
>
> The constituent parts of an *Opera* are: the Poem, the Music, and the Decoration. Through the Poetry one speaks to the mind, through the Music to the ear, through the Painting to the eyes, and the whole should bring them together in order to move the heart and convey to it the same impression simultaneously by the various organs. (Rouss., *CW,* 7: 447–48)

If the immediate goal of the opera is to speak to the heart, its unspoken aim, which we can deduce not only from the article but from other Rousseau texts about language and the theater, is the creation of a community or nation bound by like feelings. As in the contemporaneous *Essai sur l'origine des langues* and the *Lettre à d'Alembert,* "the spectator who is actively engaged in

the creation of meaning through passion [is] an implicit metaphor for the citizen."[10] The opera must produce a "reasonable illusion,"[11] which will move the "man of good taste" ("l'homme de goût") and bind him to his fellow man.[12] The question is how best to achieve these results.

The problem with which the article grapples, then, is finding the proper balance among the opera's three components: music, poetry, and scene design. Although these might appear to be three separate languages, which come together loosely in the lyric drama, Rousseau treats them as three aspects of the single operatic sign, which appeal to emotion, reason, and imagination respectively.[13] Music, poetry, and visual art exist in a supplementary relation to each other such that one is always primary, while the others are either useful or extraneous adjuncts. Thus when Rousseau considers the positive and negative combinatory possibilities of these three, he writes a rhetorical treatise in the guise of an aesthetic history. Baudelaire sees through this conceit, when he condenses, applies, and contests Rousseau's three aesthetic "phases" in "Les Yeux des pauvres."

Three Historical Stages, Three Rhetorical Styles

Tracking the relation between inner meaning ("le coeur") and outward sensation ("les yeux" and "les oreilles"), Rousseau follows the opera's transformation from a hybrid spectacle appealing to the senses, through a moment of perfect but unstable realism, to its present condition, which Rousseau sums up as "pas un tout aussi monstrueux qu'il paraît l'être" (Rouss., *OC*, 5: 956): "not as monstrous a whole as it appears to be" (Rouss., *CW*, 7: 454). Although the article rejects "le merveilleux" and exhibits a preference for transparent language over the figural, the history it relates culminates, not with the realist aesthetic Rousseau prefers, but in a mixed state that is not politically neutral.

Throughout the article, Rousseau emphasizes the role of music, in keeping with the fact that he is writing an entry for his *Dictionnaire de musique,* but also because music has special qualities that Rousseau does not find in poetry and decoration. Music is clearly Rousseau's preferred medium, and he ranks the three "eras" of opera "history" by the degree to which music is uppermost in each. According to Rousseau, opera began in a figural mode. Its depiction of gods, devils, fairies, and other esoteric creatures reflected the incoherence of opera's mission—to bring about the improbable and unnatural union of music and speech, while imitating human life:

A la naissancc de l'Opera, ses inventeurs voulant éluder ce qu'avait de peu naturel l'union de la Musique au discours dans l'imitation de la vie humaine, s'avisèrent de transporter la Scène aux Cieux et dans les Enfers, et faute de savoir faire parler les hommes, ils aimèrent mieux faire chanter les Dieux et les Diables, que les Héros et les Bergers. (Rouss., *OC,* 5: 951)

At the birth of the Opera, its inventors, wanting to avoid what was scarcely natural in the unison of Music with discourse in the imitation of human life, took it into their heads to transport the Scene into the Heavens and into Hell, and, for want of knowing how to make men speak, they preferred to make Gods and Devils sing rather than Heroes and Shepherds. (Rouss., *CW,* 7: 450)

Although, from Rousseau's point of view, it would have been far better to depict "the meanest of mortals" ("le dernier des mortels") or "the valets of Molière" than "the King of the Gods" ("le Roi des Dieux"),[14] the first opera put gods and devils on stage because it was inconceivable that *men* should express their thoughts in music. The marvelous or grotesque was an expedient substitute for the unlikely imitation of human life in song.

Since the opera's founders could not hope to touch the heartstrings with their subject matter or action, they appealed to the senses instead.[15] They relied on every possible visual trick and musical combination to engage the audience: "tous les prestiges de la baguette furent employés à fasciner les yeux, tandis que des multitudes d'Instruments et de voix étonnaient les oreilles" ("all the magic tricks of the wand were employed to fascinate the eyes while multitudes of Instruments and voices astonished the ears") (Rouss., *OC,* 5: 952; Rouss., *CW,* 7: 450). The public was astounded and transfixed, rather than moved. Without any human drama at its core, early opera was "cold" ("l'action restait toujours froide" [*OC,* 5: 952]); it made no connection to the heart. In short, the grotesque style was superficial, sterile and infantile:

[Les contemporains] ne voyoient pas que cette richesse apparente n'étoit au fond qu'un signe de stérilité, comme les fleurs qui couvrent les champs avant la moisson. C'étoit faute de savoir toucher qu'ils vouloient surprendre, et cette admiration prétendue n'étoit en effet qu'un étonnement puérile dont ils auroient dû rougir. (Rouss., *OC,* 5: 952)

[Its contemporaries] did not see that this apparent richness was at bottom only a sign of sterility, like the flowers that cover the fields before the har-

vest. It was for want of knowing how to touch that they desired to surprise, and this pretended admiration was in effect only a puerile astonishment at which they should have blushed. (Rouss., *CW,* 7: 451)

The first opera is figural because it represents mythological or imaginary objects that call forth childish wonderment or fascination, without conveying any meaning: "tous les Chants . . . n'étoient qu'un vain bruit" ("every Song . . . was merely vain noise") (Rouss., *OC,* 5: 955; *CW,* 7: 453). This original, figural stage correlates to the initial use of language described in Rousseau's *Essai sur l'origine des langues,* which was written at about the same time as "Opéra" and borrows from it. There Rousseau tells the fable of the primitive man who meets another man for the first time and, paralyzed by fear, mistakenly calls him "giant." But if that giant was actually an ordinary individual, whom the primitive man misperceived and misnamed, on stage "giant" is the right name for the monster (or chimerical being) who stands in for the *missing* man, opera's proper object. Although the grotesque is not an error based on passion, it nonetheless reproduces the discrepancy between idea and object or sign and thing that passion provokes, and produces the same effect as passion—an illusion that has no basis in the world.[16] Although this is an empty sign, like passion it, too, "fascinates the eyes" and takes the spectator in.

According to Rousseau's telling of the story, this first deplorable stage in opera's history was gradually left behind. Becoming more sophisticated and better able to produce a compelling imitation of human emotions, the lyric drama took on a nobler and less "gigantic" form over time. Putting man on stage instead of monsters, it moved away from the grotesque or marvelous toward a greater realism: "l'intérêt fut substitué au merveilleux, les machines des Poëtes et des Charpentiers furent détruites, et le Drame lyrique prit une forme plus noble et moins gigantesque" ("interest was substituted for *merveilleux,* the machines of the Poets and of the Carpenters were destroyed and lyric Drama took a more noble and less gigantic form") (Rouss., *OC,* 5: 953–54; *CW,* 7: 452). This progress was made possible by music's growing independence. Music gradually assumed a new innerness and no longer functioned as the sensual supplement for the rational or analytical character of poetry or speech. The point of perfection in the opera was reached when music fulfilled its potential for awakening the emotions directly, bypassing poetry altogether.

In this second phase, music dominates poetry to such a degree that it seems to "speak without the help of words" and makes the spectator believe he hears the language of the heart itself: "l'effet de la seule Musique . . . pouvoit aller

jusqu'au coeur" ("the effect of the Music alone . . . could be conveyed all the way to the heart") (Rouss., *OC*, 5: 953; *CW*, 7: 451). This illusion of direct communication is fostered by excluding from the drama anything "cold" and "reasoned": "Toutes les délibérations politiques, tous les projets de conspiration, les expositions, les récits . . . en un mot, tout ce qui ne parle qu'à la raison fut banni du langage du coeur" ("All political deliberations, all conspiratorial plans, expositions, narrations . . . in a word everything that speaks to reason alone was banished from the language of the heart") (Rouss., *OC*, 5: 954; *CW*, 7: 452). Still, despite these exclusions, the illusion is unstable; it can be maintained only as long as the spectator's emotions are engaged. The spectator can never be left alone:

> L'énergie de tous les sentiments, la violence de toutes les passions sont donc l'objet principal du Drame lyrique; et l'illusion qui en fait le charme, est toujours détruite aussi-tôt que l'Auteur et l'Acteur laissent un moment le Spectateur à lui-même. (Rouss., *OC*, 5: 954)

> The energy of every feeling, the violence of every passion are thus the principal object of lyric Drama, and the illusion that produces charm is always destroyed as soon as the Author and the Actor leave the Spectator to himself for an instant. (Rouss., *CW*, 7: 453)

The opera at its high point recapitulates the first social moments leading away from primitive isolation and toward the creation of civil society, as depicted in the *Essai*: "Là se formérent les prémiers liens des familles; là furent les prémiers rendez-vous des deux séxes. . . . Là des yeux accoutumés aux mêmes objets dès l'enfance commencérent d'en voir de plus doux. Le coeur s'émut à ces nouveaux objets, un attrait inconnu le rendit moins sauvage, il sentit le plaisir de n'être pas seul" ("There were formed the first ties between families; there the first meetings between the two sexes took place. . . . There eyes accustomed to the same objects from childhood began to see sweeter ones. The heart was moved by these new objects, an unfamiliar attraction made it less savage, it felt the pleasure of not being alone").[17] This is the period Rousseau called "cet âge heureux où rien ne marquoit les heures" ("that happy age when nothing marked the hours"); at this time, "se firent les prémiéres fêtes, les pieds bondissoient de joye, le geste empressé ne suffisoit plus, la voix l'accompagnoit d'accens passionnés, le plaisir et le desir confondus ensemble se faisoient sentir à la fois. Là fut enfin le vrai berceau des peuples" ("the first festivals took place, feet leaped with joy, eager gesture no longer sufficed, the

voice accompanied it with passionate accents; mingled together, pleasure and desire made themselves felt at the same time. There, finally, was the true cradle of peoples").[18] Indeed, the lyric theater at its best operates rather like "the first fires of love" that marked the origins of society: the spectator is so emotionally involved in the passion represented on stage that he forgets the differences that exist beneath the appearance of unity.[19]

Forgetting difference is the key to social harmony. Therefore, in this ideal phase, the opera relies on music to make the public forget the difference between the conventions of song and the harsh "accents" that accompany life's events.

[L]'on sentit que le chef-d'oeuvre de la Musique étoit de se faire oublier elle-même, qu'en jettant le désordre et le trouble dans l'âme du Spectateur elle l'empêchoit de distinguer les Chants tendres et pathétiques d'une Héroïne gémissante, des vrais accens de la douleur. . . .

Cyrus, César, Caton même, ont paru sur la Scène avec succès, et les Spectateurs les plus révoltés d'entendre chanter de tels hommes, ont bien-tôt oublié qu'ils chantoient, subjugués et ravis par l'éclat d'une Musique aussi pleine de noblesse et de dignité que d'enthousiasme et de feu. L'on suppose aisément que des sentimens si différens des nôtres doivent s'exprimer aussi sur un autre ton. (Rouss., *OC,* 5: 954–55)

[I]t was felt that the Masterpiece of Music was to make itself forgotten, that by plunging the Spectator's soul into disorder and turmoil, it prevented him from distinguishing the tender and pathetic Singing of a moaning Heroine from the true accents of distress. . . .

Cyrus, Caesar, Cato himself have appeared on the Stage with success, and the Spectators most repulsed at hearing such men sing soon forgot that they sang, subjugated and delighted by the brilliance of a Music as full of nobility and dignity as of enthusiasm and fire. One readily supposes that feelings so different from our own should also be expressed in another tone. (Rouss., *CW,* 7: 453; trans. modified)

Music works by causing disorder in the mind. Playing on the emotions, it inhibits critical reason and makes the spectator forget the difference between operatic and street language, between song and speech. At the height of the opera, music promotes communal awareness: "This idealized community—utopian mirror of the origin—is formed by subjects both present to themselves and present to each other within the participatory mimetic experience."[20] Yet, paradoxically, the erasure of difference that permits this mirroring

depends on the acknowledgment of a different difference, the supposed gap between heroes and just plain folks. The moment of greatest immediacy, when the emotions represented are communicated with the least distortion and resistance, depends on difference and otherness.

Although in this second evolutionary phase the operatic sign seems full and adequate ("la plus propre à l'illusion" [Rouss., *OC,* 5: 954]), because man is on stage and man's emotions are represented, this properness is based on engaging the audience's passions and encouraging them to forget the difference between stage and street, while recalling the difference between the heroes and the common man. The spectator now attributes different, nobler feelings to the heroes on stage and thus infers a moral hierarchy that may or may not exist. The drama that brings together man (the hero) and man (the spectator) depends for its effectiveness on a fiction—a suspension of meaning between sameness and difference that can never be decided with certainty one way or the other.[21]

Man may have replaced the giants and monsters, but the hypothetical differences among men stand in the way of the commonality connoted by the noun; "man" is a metaphor, a singular idea referring to a plural (and uncertain) object. Thus the realism of this moment is not the aesthetic equivalent of a nonfigural or literal mode of expression. The illusion of reality is based on passion, which "fascinates the eyes," just as the grotesque did. As Rousseau explains in the *Essai:* "Voila comment le mot figuré nait avant le mot propre, lorsque la passion nous fascine les yeux et que la prémiére idée qu'elle nous offre n'est pas celle de la vérité" ("That is how the figurative word arises before the proper word, when passion fascinates our eyes and the first idea it offers us is not the true one") (Rouss., *OC,* 5: 381; *CW,* 7: 295). In this golden age of the opera, which harks back to the harmonious early society described in the *Essai,* the transmission of fellow feeling depends on the mobilization of the spectator's passions and can easily fall victim to critical distance if the spectator is left "alone."

Predictably, this second era of carefully honed perfection is short-lived ("la perfection est un point où il est difficile de se maintenir"), and in the third and current phase, apparently equivalent to contemporary French opera, the inherent competition between music and poetry becomes an outright conflict: "[La Musique] prend, en quelque sorte, un autre langage, et, quoique l'objet soit le même, le Poëte et le Musicien, trop séparés dans leur travail, en offrent à la fois deux images ressemblantes, mais distinctes, qui se nuisent mutuellement" ("[Music] takes on another language, after a fashion, and although the

object is the same, the Poet and the Musician, too separated in their work, offer at the same time two similar, but distinct images, which work against one another") (Rouss., *OC,* 5: 955; *CW,* 7: 453; trans. modified). Rousseau deems that this crisis can only be resolved by subordinating poetry to music.[22] In his scheme, human emotion and the illusion of sameness among men, represented by music, are the preeminent values. Poetry, which is associated with critical reason and the acknowledgement of differences, interferes with the promotion of fellow feeling and must be kept in check.[23] Otherwise, the forced union of the two arts shocks the ear and destroys the operatic sign: "l'on sent dans l'union forcée de ces deux arts une contrainte perpétuelle qui choque l'oreille et détruit à la fois l'attrait de la Mélodie et l'effet de la Déclamation" ("a perpetual constraint felt in the forced union of these two Arts shocks the ear and destroys at the same time the appeal of the Melody and the effect of the Declamation"). Rousseau comments, "Ce défaut est sans remède" ("This defect is without remedy") (Rouss., *OC,* 5: 956; *CW,* 7: 454).

Given this impossible tension between music and poetry, Rousseau opines that the visual, although it has less in common with music than poetry does, is a better match for melody. Because scene design is truly supplementary (that is, exterior and inferior) to music, it can combine with music more cohesively, resulting in a more effective representation:

> Quoique la Musique . . . ait encore plus de rapport à la Poésie qu'à la Peinture; celle-ci . . . n'est pas aussi sujette que la Poésie à faire avec la Musique une double représentation du même objet; parce que l'une rend les sentimens des hommes, et l'autre seulement l'image du lieu où ils se trouvent, image qui renforce l'illusion et transporte le Spectateur partout où l'Acteur est supposé être. (Rouss., *OC,* 5: 957)

> Although Music . . . has an even closer relationship to Poetry than to Painting, the latter . . . is not, like Poetry, as subject to making a double representation of the same object with the Music, because the first renders the feelings of men and the other only the image of the place where they are found, an image which strengthens the illusion and transports the Spectator everywhere the Actor is assumed to be. (Rouss., *CW,* 7: 455)

If music makes the spectator forget difference, poetry pulls in the opposite direction. Poetry is aligned with doubleness or "duplicité" and therefore must be overcome.[24] Meaning (the transmission of emotion) is disrupted if the sign (in this case, poetry) and the idea (music) fail to coalesce. Then the mind, unwill-

ing to divide its attention, must choose one or the other representation, dividing instead the operatic sign and weakening the force of the illusion. Unlike the shocking combination of song and speech, which conveys difference (the difference between stage and street, for example), the coming together of painting and music unites two distinct (visible and invisible) representations that are only tangentially related. The result is the perfect marriage of sight and sound ("l'accord parfait").

Painting is cold and static—"la peinture est toujours froide"; "tout est dit au premier coup d'oeil" (Rouss., *OC,* 5: 958)—and is limited to the direct representation of objects that appear in the mind's eye. In a kind of Platonic hierarchy, music has greater value, precisely because it "warms" the heart and "excites" the mind without representing its object directly:

> [L]'art du Musicien consiste à substituer à l'image insensible de l'objet, celle des mouvemens que sa présence excite dans l'esprit du Spectateur: il ne représente pas directement la chose, mais il réveille dans notre ame le même sentiment qu'on éprouve en la voyant. (Rouss., *OC,* 5: 959)

> [T]he Musician's art consists in substituting for the imperceptible image of the object that of the movements its presence arouses in the mind of the Spectator; it does not represent the thing directly, but awakens in our soul the same feeling experienced in seeing it. (Rouss., *CW,* 7: 456)

Music is capable of awakening "presence" in the absence of the object itself and thus outstrips painting, which cannot imitate what does not appear, and which is necessarily intermediate between the object and the eye. Painting's function on the lyric stage is therefore not to render into its visual medium the invisible emotions aroused by music, but to create a setting ("la décoration") that allows the invisible to appear. By transporting the spectator into the world of the actor, it effaces the very difference between stage and world that poetry threatens to make clear: "Voilà comment le concours de l'acoustique et de la perspective peut perfectionner l'illusion, flatter les sens par des impressions diverses, mais analogues, et porter à l'âme un même intérêt avec un double plaisir" ("This is how the combination of Acoustics and Perspective can perfect the illusion, flatter the senses by diverse, but analogous impressions, and convey to the soul a single interest with a double pleasure") (Rouss., *OC,* 5: 958; *CW,* 7: 456). The operatic staging or imagery literally replaces one world with another and thus covers up the problematic "duplicité" of the operatic sign.

Visual imagery seems ideally suited for its role because it is not significant

in itself. Rather, it is an empty sign—a mere "place"—ready to be filled up with the emotion that music conveys. However, this union of image and music is, at best, a compromise; and Rousseau's ambivalence about this third phase of operatic history comes through when he concedes that "à certains égards l'*Opera,* constitué comme il est, n'est pas un tout aussi monstrueux qu'il paroît l'être" ("in certain regards *Opera,* constituted as it is, is not as monstrous a whole as it appears to be") (Rouss., *OC,* 5:956; *CW,* 7:454). The problem with the reliance on the visual is that painting and stage design, although they are poor imitations of imaginary constructs, can in turn cause the imagination to take flight and create extraordinary chimeras on its own. The image can acquire an unintended dynamism quite apart from the music, skewing once again the operatic sign and potentially returning opera to the grotesque state in which it began. Despite the prior disappearance of the grotesque from the operatic stage, it continues to haunt the lyric theater:

> Un beau Palais, des Jardins délicieux, de savantes ruines plaisent encore plus à l'oeil que la fantasque image du Tartare, de l'Olympe, du Char du Soleil; image d'autant plus inférieure à celle que chacun se trace en lui-même, que dans les objets chimériques il n'en coûte rien à l'esprit d'aller au-delà du possible, et de se faire des modèles au-dessus de toute imitation. De-là vient que le merveilleux, quoique déplacé dans la Tragédie, ne l'est pas dans le Poëme épique où l'imagination toujours industrieuse et dépensière se charge de l'exécution, et en tire un tout autre parti que ne peut faire sur nos Théâtres le talent du meilleur Machiniste, et la magnificence du plus puissant Roi. (Rouss., *OC,* 5: 957)

> A beautiful Palace, delightful Gardens, clever ruins please the eye still more than the fantastic image of Tartarus, of Olympus, of the Chariot of the Sun—an image all the more inferior to that which everyone can trace for himself, as with chimerical objects it costs the mind nothing to go beyond the possible and to make up models beyond any imitation. From this it follows that *merveilleux,* although out of place in Tragedy, are not so in the epic Poem, in which the imagination, always industrious and spendthrift, sees to the execution and draws from it a completely different component than the talent of the best Machinist and the munificence of the most powerful King could produce in our Theaters. (Rouss., *CW,* 7:455)

The vitality and independence of the imagination are such that the grotesque (that "mauvais supplément") will always be a potential threat to a reasonable or tasteful representation. Insofar as it requires a step beyond the

given, into the realm of images and the imaginary, the figural is always apt to become "excessive." Rousseau acknowledges this fact even as he declares the grotesque inappropriate for tragedy and relegates it to the domain of epic poetry (or the popular fair theaters) instead.[25] The immanent threat of the figural explains why, having declared the grotesque out of place in the lyric drama, Rousseau still has to resort to the language of laws, boundaries, and prohibitions to restrict the use of images on the operatic stage:

> Mais ce transport d'un lieu à un autre doit avoir des règles et des bornes: il n'est permis de se prévaloir à cet égard de l'agilité de l'imagination qu'en consultant la loi de la vraisemblance, et, quoique le Spectateur ne cherche qu'à se prêter à des fictions dont il tire tout son plaisir, il ne faut pas abuser de sa crédulité au point de lui en faire honte. (Rouss., *OC,* 5: 957)

> But this transportation from one place to another must have rules and limits; in this regard it is permissible to take advantage of the agility of the imagination only while consulting the law of plausibility, and, although the Spectator seeks only to lend himself to the fictions from which he derives all his pleasure, his credulity must not be abused to the point of making him ashamed of it. (Rouss., *CW,* 7: 455)

Images ("l'appareil des yeux ou la décoration") require constant surveillance lest they overrun their limits and detract from the effective transmission of emotional meaning. The third stage of opera is a conscious attempt to transport the spectator a little, but not too much.

On the modern opera stage, conditions are carefully controlled. Figuration involves a risk, which must be checked. The prospect of a kind of anarchy underlies the fear of the figure and motivates the policing of the sign. The potential for images to run wild requires the imposition of the law of verisimilitude, which in turn reinforces the status quo. In sum, the opera cannot do without censorship. Critical judgment is suspended through the exclusion of poetry (or critical thought), and limits are applied to painting (or imagery) to curb the freedom of the imagination. Unable to maintain the illusion of spontaneous feeling that characterized its "golden age" and the free society to which it refers, the opera makes a pact with the powers-that-be. It accepts civil society for what it is, a construct that replaces utopian dreams with pragmatic pleasures. Ultimately, the nation fostered by the transmission of emotion across the ramp is a figure limited by the possible and monitored by the powerful.

In the final analysis, although Rousseau's essay manifests many of the same

concerns as the satirical letter in *Julie,* the two works come out in very different places politically. As we saw in the previous chapter, *Julie* makes a point of turning away from the French monarchy and its aesthetic institutions. St. Preux's letter on the Paris Opéra criticizes Louis XIV, the opera's founder; attacks "le faux goût de la magnificence" ("the false taste for magnificence" characteristic of both the opera's productions and the kings who sponsor them); and finally displays Rousseau's political preferences in the example of Laberius, whose dissidence was a stance in favor of republican values. The dictionary entry, on the other hand, ultimately accepts the French status quo. Furthermore, while *Julie* puts forward a certain kind of family life as a model for society,[26] there is no such alternative to the French monarchy in the article "Opéra." In Rousseau's historical account, the opera passes beyond the point of perfection that is the aesthetic equivalent of the harmonious society gathered, like a family, to sing and dance at spontaneous "fêtes." "Opéra," perhaps because it has a pragmatic aim, recognizes the tenuousness of the ideal that *Julie,* as a fiction, can afford to maintain.

Writing his response to Rousseau in "Les Yeux des pauvres," Baudelaire acknowledges the very different political stances Rousseau takes in these two works and refuses them both. Baudelaire proposes the family as a political ideal, only to show how flawed the concept is and how impossible it is to realize. But he does not come out on the side of the powers-that-be. Where Rousseau wavers between two political models, to the point of sometimes contradicting himself, Baudelaire, in his rewriting of Rousseau's essay, single-mindedly pursues his challenge to the dominant discourse.

Dramatizing Rousseau's Theories

Difficult as it may be to discern, "Les Yeux des pauvres" recapitulates the three stages of Rousseau's operatic history. Since music is not a feature of Baudelaire's poem, we can only understand the parallels between the two texts at the level of allegory. Rousseau's three operatic epochs—the primitive period marked by the excessiveness and sensual pleasure of the grotesque, the golden age of so-called transparency and realism, and the current age of authoritarian control and censorship—represent a ranking of three types of figure, judged by the criteria of efficacy and pragmatic possibility. Within this allegory, music serves as a figure for inwardness or meaning, the vehicle for a desired return to a supposedly originary, but lost moment of plenitude when there was free and harmonious communication and a society characterized by love. If we

keep in mind the shifting rhetorical and social paradigm represented by these three eras or moments in Rousseau's article, we shall see how they are taken up and put to use in Baudelaire's poem.

The poem borrows its basic structure and many of its terms from Rousseau's dictionary entry; it strives (in vain) for the fellow feeling among men that is the implicit sociopolitical goal motivating Rousseau's theories; and it tries out the three types of figuration explored by Rousseau. Within the frame of the love/hate relationship, "Les Yeux des pauvres" depicts three distinct (albeit almost simultaneous) moments of theatrical viewing, corresponding to the three stages of the opera and the three kinds of figures set out in Rousseau's article: (1) the poor family in the street gaze at the luxurious café, (2) the narrator and his lover stare at the poor family, and (3) the narrator looks into his lover's eyes. The first moment situates us immediately in the realm of the primitive, which is offensive to good taste. The extraordinary mural decorating the café, described in detail by the narrator, reminds us by its very placement that the *grottesque* derived its name from the decorative art found on the walls of old Roman ruins (or *grotte*).[27] But more important, like the first stage of the opera that Rousseau described, the painting on the café wall throws together pell-mell historical and mythological references, in which, as Maurice Delcroix has observed, "man is missing" ("l'homme fait défaut"). Just as the grotesque in the opera was a poor substitute for opera's proper subject matter (man), these scenes in the new café of pages walking dogs, ladies taming falcons, and mythological gods and goddesses serving fruits, pâtés, and ice cream exclude the adult male and his emotions. In fact, as Marie Maclean argues, "[t]here is nothing human, nothing moving" in this painting: "The depicted women and boys, the Hebes and the Ganymedes, are themselves objects of consumption to the eyes, frozen as they endlessly proffer their wares. They are the equivalent of the fruit, the pâtés and game, the mousse and the ices."[28] The elaborate mural is a feast for the eyes, but it has no other point—or, as the narrator puts it, all of history and all of mythology are here in the service of gluttony ("la goinfrerie").[29] The café's decor—which reduces a whole culture to a commercial package designed to appeal to the nouveaux riches of the Second Empire—is vulgar, "a hyperbolic instance of economic [and aesthetic] excess."[30]

This vulgarity is only visible from a certain point of view, however. Like Rousseau's "homme de goût," Baudelaire's narrator sees and scorns it, whereas the poor family does not.[31] Confronting the fanciful depictions on the café walls, they react just the way the first opera audiences did: they are fascinated.

If in early opera, "tous les prestiges de la baguette furent employés à *fasciner* les yeux" ("all the magic tricks of the wand were employed to *fascinate* the eyes"),[32] the same tricks have the same effect on the poor family, especially the youngest child: "Quant aux yeux du plus petit, ils étaient trop *fascinés* pour exprimer autre chose qu'une joie stupide et profonde" ("As for the eyes of the smallest, they were too *fascinated* to express anything other than a stupid and deep joy").[33] The baby's "stupid joy" literalizes Rousseau's condescending assessment of the opera public's amazement: "cette admiration prétendue n'était en effet qu'un étonnement puérile" ("this pretended admiration was in effect only a puerile astonishment"). The father and his children resemble the spectators of the primitive opera, who failed to see that the apparent riches on stage were only a sign of sterility ("cette richesse apparente n'était au fond qu'un signe de stérilité"). The poor family is taken in by the lavish display and confuses superficial signs for rich meaning. At least this is what the father's eyes seem to say: "on dirait que tout l'or du pauvre monde est venu se porter sur ces murs" ("All the poor world's gold seems to have fallen upon these walls").

In the second theatrical moment, the narrator stares at the individuals in tattered rags who face him. He is the spectator of a different, "realist" spectacle, which corresponds to the high point of the opera in Rousseau's aesthetic history. In place of the aristocratic ladies, nymphs, and other ornamental figures on the café wall, the narrator contemplates a man of such lowly stature that he could easily be "le dernier des mortels"—a far more worthy subject, Rousseau argued, than the kings and gods of the marvelous. Indeed, when the narrator compares the father of this little family to a maid taking the children for a walk—"Il remplissait l'office de bonne" ("He was filling the charge of nursemaid")—he evokes Rousseau's idea that it is better to put "les valets de Molière" on stage than many heros.[34] The poor family, the only element of the poem that does not attract the epithet "beau," gives Rousseau's realism a nineteenth-century spin: the real is not just any man, but a poor man with children, worn out and prematurely grey from hard labor and worry.[35]

If the sight of the poor family is not exactly beautiful, it has an important advantage over the extravagant decor of the café, at least for the narrator. As during opera's golden age, a current of emotion passes from one world to another (from the street to the sidewalk), and the narrator believes he can read the family's thoughts.[36] The narrator becomes emotionally involved in the spectacle before him and says: "Les chansonniers disent que le plaisir rend l'âme bonne et amollit le coeur. La chanson avait raison ce soir-là, relativement à moi" ("Popular singers say that pleasure makes the soul kind and softens the

heart. The song was right that evening, relative to me"). The family speaks to his heart, without ever uttering a sound. In opera, as described by Rousseau, this communal effect was accomplished when music began to "speak without the help of words" ("la symphonie même apprit à parler sans le secours des paroles" [Rouss., *OC,* 5: 953]) and transmitted emotion across the ramp, straight into the spectator's heart ("l'effet de la seule musique . . . pouvait aller jusqu'au coeur"). And, like the audience during the era of operatic perfection, Baudelaire's narrator more or less forgets the difference between himself and the family he observes as he reads the family's eyes. At least his interpretation facilitates the communication of meaning and equality between "men," even as it suggests the differences (of class, age, and number) that divide them.

However, this new "golden age," this momentary suspension of difference via the communication of emotion, is, like its counterpart in Rousseau, a work of fiction. On the one hand, the narrator assumes that the family's innermost feelings are transparently joined with the outward signs of wonder in their eyes. On the other hand, he translates the family's gaze into words, attributing to them sentiments that he can never verify, and substituting speech for their silence. His supposedly literal reading is inseparable from this metaphorical substitution, which makes the narrator an author, writing his actors' lines. The feel-good moment of equality among men, based on shared emotions, depends for its effectiveness on the suspension of meaning between the literal and the figural, which is both produced by the narrator as author and consumed by him as spectator. If the poor family are naïve spectators whose admiration for the café's splendor is unalloyed, the narrator's position as a man, author, and spectator is not so simple.[37]

The moment at which the narrator turns to his lover, in the third scene, is the moment when he acknowledges a quantitative imbalance between himself and the family before him. Feeling a little ashamed ("un peu honteux") of the signs of his own excess consumption ("de nos verres et de nos carafes, plus grands que notre soif"), he averts his gaze and looks to his lover for reassurance instead. This third theatrical moment reflects Rousseau's judgment that perfection is impossible to maintain. As if to demonstrate how illusion is imperiled when the author and the actors neglect the spectator, the female lover, who has been marginalized by the narrator's involvement with the poor family, boldly rejects the illusion of commonality among men in which the narrator wants to believe. In this third moment, the tension between similarity and difference, which lay submerged in his connection to the family, is made explicit by the narrator's female companion.

This third stage takes us back to the third phase of Rousseau's operatic history, where poetry and music find themselves in conflict, with music playing on the emotions to make the spectator forget the differences among men, and poetry aligned with critical reason, which brings differences to the fore. Rousseau worried that the forced union of these two semiotic systems would be too much of a shock and would destroy the carefully honed illusion of transparent communication—and community—promoted by the ideal operatic sign. The creation of understanding and harmony would be disrupted if critical analysis and emotion failed to coalesce. Of course, this is exactly what happens to Baudelaire's narrator when his lover fails to share his sentiments. Instead of fostering his sympathy for the poor family, she shocks him and the reader with her cold indifference: "Ces gens-là me sont insupportables avec leurs yeux ouverts comme des portes cochères! Ne pourriez-vous pas prier le maître du café de les éloigner d'ici?" ("I can't stand those people with their eyes wide open like carriage-house gates! Can't you ask the manager to send them away?"). Instead of seeing eye-to-eye with the narrator, the woman debunks his idealization of the poor. Not only does she read the eyes as empty (open wide "like carriage-house doors"), but with her analogy, she sends the family back to its place—in the servants' quarters. The lover brings forward the class hierarchy that makes the dream of a society based on shared inner qualities appear highly improbable.[38] Her negative reaction to the poor destroys the transmission of meaning and prompts the hatred the narrator expresses at the beginning of the poem. As Rousseau commented, this situation is "without remedy" ("sans remède").

Curiously, however, the woman's critical response enacts the very program that Rousseau condoned in the third phase of his operatic history. Not only does she reject the poor, whose eyes repel her, but she calls on the "maître du café" to remove these visual signs that make her lover dream. In accordance with Rousseau's ultimately pragmatic proposals for the opera, she asks the manager or "master" of this place (Baudelaire's sardonic representation of Napoléon III?) to exercise his role and police the perimeters of the café, keeping unwanted onlookers—and their enticing eyes—away. Acting as a censor, she ensures the stability of the current class hierarchy, the status quo. Through the woman's behavior, the third sequence of the poem showcases the mobilization of the powerful to suppress the disruptive threat inherent in the "wild" visual sign.

The Politics of Rhetoric

"Les Yeux des pauvres" follows Rousseau's model in his article "Opéra" to a surprising degree. Although Baudelaire refashions his predecessor's rhetorical treatise as a narrative of human relations, giving it a topical nineteenth-century setting, a simple plot, and a memorable punch line, Rousseau's work thoroughly informs the poem. Even the political overtones of Rousseau's article are retained. Nonetheless, despite all the signs to the contrary, Baudelaire does not espouse Rousseau's rhetorical program, any more than he accepts Rousseau's political compromise.

By rewriting Rousseau's theories within a different frame, by situating the problem of representation not in the exclusive world of the Paris Opéra but on the city streets, Baudelaire brings forward the underlying issues of class and force that are hidden away in Rousseau's "Opéra." However, Baudelaire does not exactly spell out his own political stance. The poem, like Rousseau's article, is an allegory that offers its political message between the lines. Obliquely, through its own use and problematization of Rousseau's rhetorical ideas, the poem both displays the power of rhetoric to shape political belief, or put ideology into practice, and warns us of the need to read well, if we want to resist this political manipulation. By virtue of its own duplicitous practices, however, the poem hides its warning from those—like the government censors—who read only for the most explicit content. Simultaneously foregrounding and resisting Rousseau's rhetorical and political categories, the poem teaches the importance of reading between the lines, of reading *against* censorship. In order to see how this is so, we must examine Baudelaire's own rhetorical practices in this poem.

In some rather obvious ways, "Les Yeux des pauvres" departs from its Rousseau intertext. Despite its demonstrable adoption of Rousseau's aesthetic categories, the poem does not follow the linear, historical aspect of Rousseau's text. "Les Yeux des pauvres" collapses diachrony into synchrony and at the same time it foregrounds visual signs. Whereas Rousseau calls upon the visual as a necessary but dubious supplement only in the third phase of his narrative, Baudelaire's poem is all about seeing and sight. From the brilliant decor of the café, to the "famille d'yeux" and the capricious eyes of the female lover, the poem takes the visual as its focal point, so to speak. This difference between the Rousseau and Baudelaire texts can lead us to an understanding of the authors' rhetorical and political disagreement. For if, in Rousseau's account, the visual is a supplement with the potential to run wild and obscure meaning, we

must wonder why Baudelaire allows the visual to overrun his poem. Baude-laire's poem brings forward the supplementarity that Rousseau struggles to control and uses it to make a point about reading.

By collapsing the three phases of Rousseau's history into a single event, Baudelaire is able to show rather succinctly how Rousseau's categories leak into each other. Each of the scenes in the love story reaches a point of disequilib-rium, which is tied to the context that frames it. Thus the family's fascination with the café is tied to their exclusion from the premises, which the narrator then "reads" in their faces, and which forms the basis of his empathy. But this assumption of common humanity (based in part on spectatorship) begins to unravel, as the narrator becomes aware of his own excess consumption, which is out of reach of the poor. Expecting to read his own thoughts in his lover's eyes, he is then confronted with the ultimate sign of difference, when her eyes fail to serve as a mirror and return only the idea of his exclusion. Each category tips over into the next, until finally the narrator, in a fourth, framing moment, reacts with animosity and hatred, in the ultimate gesture of excess. The very existence of this fourth moment, which exceeds the three stages of Rousseau's aesthetic "history," can be understood as a patent statement of the supple-mentarity at work in the poem. As we might expect, this supplementarity is borne out by the tropes that Baudelaire uses in each scene, and by reading them now, we can see how the supplement becomes an instrument in the serv-ice of a subversive political strategy.

The poem puts into play a number of key words or phrases that reflect the narrator's desire to bring disparate individuals into a collective whole. These figural expressions both exemplify the rhetorical practices Rousseau describes and convey a variety of subtle political messages. In the example of the "grottesque" café, the play of singular and plural manifests itself in the de-scription of the decorative mural, peopled by various unnamed characters and "les Hébés et les Ganymèdes." These mythological figures, whose names we scarcely recognize, recall the Enlightenment's critique of the marvelous for its reliance on pagan gods whose names meant nothing to contemporary readers. But here Baudelaire takes advantage of their "empty" status to reinvest them with meaning. Hebe and Ganymede were two lesser gods who served their su-periors in the court of Jupiter; in the poem they are taken as figures for the whole category of waiters and servants.[39] This transformation of unique indi-viduals into a class of persons makes an important, if not very obvious point in the poem.[40] It collects together, under a godly name, workers of the lowest social rank, and thereby introduces them into the highest echelons of society

(albeit still in their serving role). Even as it debases the gods by locating them in a vulgar café, the phrase works in the opposite direction by raising the poor to a kind of divine status. The allegory may represent an illusion that has no basis in the world, but it nonetheless hints at a revolutionary idea: the possibility of a society turned upside down.

The use of the mythological figure and the grammatical change from singular to plural, which suggest an unlikely inclusiveness not otherwise connoted by the café, find a well-hidden echo in the second scene of the poem, where the narrator confronts the poor man and his children. In the sixth paragraph, after the narrator has broken the poor family down into its component parts—three faces and six eyes—he gathers these parts up again into another odd collective phrase: "cette famille d'yeux." This expression has always eluded critical attention, although it is rather bizarre (if we imagine disembodied eyes, it is especially disquieting). But when we stop to consider it, it reveals an incredible density of meaning. At the most obvious level, it plays an extremely complex game of substitution, using the plural "eyes" to represent a whole person, and the singular "family" to represent the collection of individuals. At the same time, while each of the two parts collapses singular into plural or vice versa, the entire phrase juxtaposes the individual components ("yeux") and the whole ("famille"). The phrase plays in two directions simultaneously, although we can only begin to appreciate this when we take it apart piece by piece, reading each piece ("famille" and "yeux") on its own.

For an excellent Latin scholar like Baudelaire, "famille" has ancient connotations that the rest of us are apt to miss. Derived from the Latin *famulus*, meaning servant (*serviteur*), the etymological sense of the word is: "The whole group of people (children, servants, slaves, relatives) living under the same roof, under the authority of the paterfamilias."[41] This meaning was recognized in France up through the seventeenth century, and the *Grand Robert* gives an example of this usage drawn from La Fontaine's *Fables.* In the nineteenth century, however, the word *famille* had come to mean, not only the nuclear family, but any group of beings or things having a common origin or common characteristics, which presume analogies among them. For instance, under the influence of certain bourgeois ideologies, one might speak of "la grande famille humaine" or, to designate relations between boss and worker, "une grande famille" (which "connotes participation in the paternalistic discourse of the employer or boss").[42] The narrator is clearly one of the bourgeois individuals who think along these lines. His inappropriate reference to the poor father as a "maid" ("il remplissait l'office de bonne") borrows from a bourgeois

idea of family life, which is supported by a serving class, and suggests the narrator's inability to wrench himself loose from that frame of reference. His discourse is paternalistic, even if his sympathy for the poor is sincere. Without modifying the class hierarchy, he wants to fold the poor man and his children into his own potential family, in the manner of an old-style paterfamilias. He would translate the confusion of aristocrats and servants depicted as superficial ornaments on the café wall into a more meaningful or real family group, loosely based on the idea of the great family of man.

At least, this is one set of meanings connoted by "la famille d'yeux." When we turn our attention to the other part of the expression, the "eyes," a very different and opposite set of meanings appears. In this poem, "yeux" are multiply figural. Not only are they a synecdoche for the whole person of whom they are a part, they are also a figure for the visual sign—a figure for rhetorical figures. As such, they exemplify the advantages and dangers of the visual, which were underscored by Rousseau. The "famille d'yeux," in particular, brings these lessons together in condensed form. For if we read this phrase only with our eyes, instead of reading the "eyes" aloud, we tend to miss the pun it conceals. "Famille d'yeux" sounds like "famille dieu"—but because of the difference in spelling, we are apt to overlook this similarity.[43] Baudelaire's play on words, depending as it does on a homophony hidden by the written word, is an extraordinary example of how the visual can foster illusion, by covering over the sign's duplicity. Not only does the written (visually perceived) sign prevent us from recognizing the aural homonym, but the visual image (of disembodied eyes) is disconcerting enough to prevent us from "hearing" the other meaning it conveys. The image hides the difference, allowing the easy transmission of a single meaning or emotion to occur. It effectively captures the readers' attention and "transports" us into the scene, as if we were there. On the other hand, by calling attention to itself (to its own unsettling quality, for instance) and turning the imagination loose, the visual can be dangerous. As Rousseau predicted, it may skew the sign away from its apparent meaning and carry us into uncharted, uncontrolled territory. In this case, making the poor family into gods can upset the social hierarchy represented by the paterfamilias, his lover, and the "maître." The image gives rise to two diametrically opposed meanings, one of which predicts the radical revolutionary practices that the other seeks to repress.

Baudelaire has written into a single expression two competing ideologies of the mid-nineteenth century: the revolutionary notion of the people as "gods" (which Michelet attributes to Rousseau),[44] and the self-satisfied notion of the

powers-that-be that the servants or workers are just part of the family and that no change needs to occur in this family of man.[45] Baudelaire's humor, in creating through the "famille d'yeux" a parody of the "grande famille des hommes," marks his critical stance relative to the conservative bourgeois ideology, the dominant discourse of his day, even as the punning phrase covers over his ennobling intent.

The supplementary nature of the pun ("d'yeux/dieu"), which sets the sensory (visual and auditory) signs at odds, disrupts the simple transmission of inner meaning that the narrator purports to carry out. The sensorial surface of the sign, as it were, intrudes upon our awareness and brings critical analysis into play. This is reflected both in the woman's reading of the eyes as empty (too full of meaning, they convey no single meaning clearly) and in the "capriciousness" of her own "impenetrable" gaze. Yet it is only in this third instance of "lunacy" that the threat of the visual is brought under control. Through the play on the grammatical categories of singular and plural, the first two visual figures put forward (albeit surreptitiously) the idea of a new society that would incorporate and even deify the poor. But the third visual sign—the woman's beautiful green eyes, "inhabited by Capriciousness and inspired by the Moon" ("habités par le Caprice et inspirés par la Lune")—runs directly counter to the first two. Although the "inhabitants" of the woman's eyes recall the mythological figures on the café walls ("la Lune" being another name for the virgin goddess Diana), and although the woman claims the café as her own (it is she who wants to stop there and who behaves as if it were her "home"), the gods of the café and those associated with the woman are actually quite different. If the proper names stand out in both cases as mythological or allegorical figures, "le Caprice" and "la Lune," unlike "les Hébés et les Ganymedes," are not collective nouns representing a class of persons. Rather they are common nouns transformed into exclusive names—personifications only of the woman's eccentric character. As singular nouns, "le Caprice" and "la Lune" do not become categories; they do not open themselves up, like the servant gods, to include others.

In place of the fellow feeling or reassuring sameness the narrator expected from his lover, he finds only difference in his partner's gaze. This difference is "capricious" or wild precisely because it falls outside and thus reveals the limits of the narrator's reading of the poor. But this wildness does not go very far. Paradoxically, as he evokes "capriciousness" and "lunacy," two attributes that raise havoc between the lovers, the narrator uses names that exclude any turbulence of meaning. Although they are allegorical, "le Caprice" and "la Lune"

are abstract and impersonal. They may "transport" us, as all figures do, but only a very little. In fact, they conform nicely to Rousseau's warning that images must be carefully monitored and restricted.

It is only in this third case, which features controlled figuration, that the threat of social upheaval is contained. A certain appropriate rhetorical balance (the infinitesimal difference between the literal and figural meanings, that is, between the woman's capricious behavior and its personification) and a correspondingly "balanced" political result (the realization of class homogeneity, albeit at the expense of the poor) are finally brought about. This cohesion or closeness between the figure, the behavior it designates, and the political consequences it implies prompts the narrator to refer to the woman, in the frame of the poem, as the most impermeable, or closed, person he knows—"le plus bel exemple de l'imperméabilité féminine."

The woman's impermeability, and the near-suppression of figural difference associated with it, would seem to give a certain closure to the poem. But as we have seen in other Baudelaire prose poems, the enunciation of the moral lesson is in fact another figural turn, one that opens up the text to the full implications of supplementarity. It is part of the incredible genius of Baudelaire's poem that each of the three theatrical moments it depicts demonstrates not only the practical application of Rousseau's rhetorical theories but the political connotations of rhetoric as well. However, as we noted earlier, the poem goes beyond Rousseau's essay on the Opéra to include a fourth, framing moment, which both exceeds its model and brings out, in a most unlikely manner, the political ramifications of the supplement.

Like the three other figures examined, the first paragraph of the poem subtly trades on the permeability of grammatical categories. The possible confusion of singular and plural is brought out in the very first sentence, when the narrator addresses his interlocutor(s) with an ambiguous "vous" ("Ah! vous voulez savoir pourquoi je vous hais aujourd'hui"). As we have already noted, the sentence leaves open the question of whether a singular person is being addressed in the formal manner or whether more than one person is designated. Coming at the beginning of the poem, with no prior referent, "vous" first appears to be the implied reader—already a figure for a larger group, the real readers of the poem.[46] After all, Baudelaire was not known for being indulgent to his public, whom he treated as "dogs" in "Le Chien et le flacon," so the hatred the narrator expresses here might well be another instance of the poet's animosity towards "us." The second sentence seems to clarify the matter, by specifying "vous" as "le plus bel exemple d'imperméabilité *féminine*" and thus

preparing the anecdote about the woman that follows. But coming here, in the first paragraph of the poem, the doubt is not entirely lifted. First of all, a feminine trait need not be confined to women; addressed to men, the epithet "feminine" could function as a hateful insult, in keeping with the tone of these lines. We may even wonder whether the woman in the poem is yet another caricature of that "femmelin," Rousseau. Furthermore, the fact that "vous" is a superlative example ("le plus bel") keeps the concept of a group of individuals alive, if only as a foil for this singularity. "Le plus bel exemple" suggests hierarchy within a class of people or things; as a superlative, "vous" stands out as a singularly apt member of a larger group. In other words, the statement condemning "vous" for being so exclusive and closed paradoxically leaves the door open to inclusivity. It seems that more is going on here than meets the eye.

This is precisely the problem Rousseau so feared; the imbalance between appearance and essence, between sign and idea, which he deemed grotesque, caused him to accept exclusion and call for the policing of boundaries in an attempt to contain the waywardness of meaning. But Baudelaire parts company with Rousseau at this point. Whereas Rousseau accepts the status quo and concludes, perhaps reluctantly, that the opera of his day—and the repressive government that sponsors it—is "not as monstrous as it seems," Baudelaire's poem does not leave matters there. By framing his little drama with a "definite" conclusion, Baudelaire actually destabilizes the carefully controlled language of the third and final scene, as well as the authoritarian civil society that requires it. And he tries to help his reader do the same. By making the female lover the prime example of a "bad reader," while creating uncertainty about the implied reader's inclusion in that category, he tries to discourage us from identifying with the illustration.[47] If we refuse this representation of ourselves, if we reject our own categorization, we may find ourselves reading the other categories or classes in the poem differently. It is only by looking beyond the most visible signs of (rigid) class hierarchy in the poem and noticing the signs of instability or upheaval instead, that we can avoid being "bad readers" of "Les Yeux"—and any text about categories or class. By insulting us, Baudelaire urges us to see double, to see what the emphasis on visual signs tends to cover up. He tries to call attention, backhandedly, to his poem's duplicity.

Baudelaire has written a poem opposing the politics of inclusion and exclusion that is the subtext of Rousseau's aesthetic treatise. However, his opposition is nowhere stated as such. Instead, Baudelaire refuses to authorize any of the three vantage points proposed in this poem. Interpretation is a matter of point of view in "Les Yeux des pauvres," but no single point of view holds

sway. None of the readers in the poem is advanced as an ideal; all of them (the family, the narrator, the lover) are presented as flawed, and their interpretations subjected to doubt.[48] Even a close examination of the rhetorical examples in the poem fails to resolve the problem, since each one undermines the meaning (of exclusion, inclusion, or capriciousness) it is meant to illustrate. The imbalance between meaning and signs or the lack of correlation between statements and examples foils interpretation. Meaning in "Les Yeux des pauvres" is excessive and out of control. This point is made everywhere and nowhere; it cannot be pinned down. In this poem, where "impermeability" connotes its opposite, Baudelaire suggests the futility of the controlling and repressive practices of Napoléon III's discursive regime.

Thus, although the usual approaches to interpretation are foreclosed in the poem, Baudelaire offers his readers a different possibility, not embodied by any character (except perhaps the ambiguous "vous"). He proposes that we eschew representation altogether and read instability, or the force of the grotesque, instead.[49] Unlike Rousseau, Baudelaire adopts the grotesque wholeheartedly. For Baudelaire, the inherently unstable grotesque—"the antithesis of representation"[50]—is a welcome subversive force in oppressive times.

7 Rousseau, Trauma, and Fetishism
"Le Vieux Saltimbanque"

Baudelaire once referred to Rousseau as an "obscene charlatan."[1] The disparaging remark, aimed at Rousseau's false candor, would seem to bespeak Baudelaire's antipathy toward his literary forefather and confirm the received negative idea of the relationship between the two. Yet the word "charlatan" was not necessarily a pejorative term for Baudelaire, who also used it to describe one of his true literary heroes, Edgar Allan Poe. "[I]l sera toujours utile," Baudelaire asserts in the preamble to "La Genèse d'un poème,"

> de faire voir aux gens du monde quel labeur exige cet objet de luxe qu'on nomme Poésie.
>   Après tout, *un peu de charlatanerie est toujours permis au génie, et même ne lui messied pas.* C'est, comme le fard sur les pommettes d'une femme naturellement belle, un assaisonnement nouveau pour l'esprit.

> [I]t will always be useful . . . to show the worldly people what labor is required by this object of luxury we call Poetry.
>   After all, *the genius is always allowed a little charlatanism, and indeed it is not unbecoming to him.* Like rouge on the cheekbones of a naturally beautiful woman, it's a new seasoning for the mind.[2]

As the previous chapters make clear, Baudelaire's reservations about Rousseau did not prevent him from admiring Rousseau's genius. Rousseau may have been obscene, in Baudelaire's view, but the idea that Rousseau was a charlatan —a peddler of quack remedies, a deceitful orator, a mountebank—was no reason to dismiss him.

It appears, in fact, that Baudelaire was thinking of Rousseau's charlatanism when he took up the language and ideas of Rousseau's satirical letter on the Paris Opéra in his notes for a late preface to *Les Fleurs du mal*.[3] The passage occurs in the context of Baudelaire's musings about how to exculpate himself following the government's judgment against his work of verse. He rejects his editor's suggestion that he explain his aims and methods. Such a statement might amuse "those minds who love deep rhetoric" ("les esprits amoureux de la rhétorique profonde"), but it would be superfluous, since those readers already know or guess at his rhetorical approach, while others would never understand it:

> Mène-t-on la foule dans les ateliers de l'habilleuse et du décorateur, dans la loge de la comédienne? Montre-t-on au public affolé aujourd'hui, indifférent demain, le mécanisme des trucs? Lui explique-t-on les retouches et les variantes improvisées aux répétitions, et jusqu'à quelle dose l'instinct et la sincérité sont mêlés aux rubriques et au *charlatanisme indispensable* dans l'amalgame de l'oeuvre? Lui révèle-t-on toutes les loques, les fards, les poulies, les chaînes, les repentirs, les épreuves barbouillées, bref toutes les horreurs qui composent le sanctuaire de l'art?

> Do you take the crowd into the workrooms of the dresser and the stage designer, or into the dressing room of the actress? Do you show the public, crazy today, indifferent tomorrow, how the stage effects work [*le mécanisme des trucs*]? Do you explain to them the little changes and the variants improvised during rehearsal, and the degree to which instinct and sincerity are mixed with ruses and *indispensable charlatanism* in the amalgamation of the work? Do you reveal to them all the tatters, the makeup, the pulleys, the chains, the changes of heart, the scribbled proofs, in short all the horrors that make up the sanctuary of art?[4]

"Charlatanism" is the poet's metaphor for rhetorical acumen, the ability to juggle words and play acrobatic tricks that dazzle and fool the reader. Poetry is like a theater, where the actor's craft—the key to a successful performance— must be carefully hidden. By borrowing from Rousseau's writings on opera to discuss his own poetic enterprise, Baudelaire associates Rousseau's rhetorical finesse, or theatricality, with his own art.

A similar link between Rousseau's rhetoric and Baudelaire's poetics underlies the complex personal and allegorical poem "Le Vieux Saltimbanque," in which Rousseau plays the role of the eponymous figure. The poem has a strong autobiographical cast. It delivers up a story about the relationship between generations, which seems to encapsulate Baudelaire's ambivalence

toward his predecessor. Building on Rousseau's autobiographies, as well as contemporary caricatures, the poem presents Rousseau as a broken-down gymnast (or mountebank) who has outlived his admiring public. Yet this old acrobat, who recalls the grotesque's traditional ties to street theater and the commedia dell'arte, is simultaneously a modern type, an outcast who poignantly reflects the Second Empire's mistreatment of itinerant actors (or poets) and elicits the narrator's sympathy.[5]

"The Old Acrobat" gives us a familiar rococo theme and carnivalesque setting, but with a new, somber twist. Intertwining a relic of an earlier era with a contemporary drama, it depicts the carefree present as haunted by a past that it willfully shuns, but can never completely forget. The present generation, caught up in the desire to escape misery and avoid death, finds itself bound to the past, which not only shadows but underwrites the here and now. What makes the poem particularly intriguing is that the entanglement of present and past finds its cause and its expression in a textual encounter. Ultimately, the autobiographical or intergenerational narrative makes a larger point. In fact, the poem's story of generations is also a story about the (rhetorical) generation of texts. "Le Vieux Saltimbanque" not only links the spirit of mid-nineteenth-century France to the traumatic legacy of Rousseau, but locates this trauma in the act of reading.

Past and Present in the Poem

At the most immediate level, "Le Vieux Saltimbanque" is the story of an old tumbler who is no longer able to perform. In a run-down booth on the outer edge of a Paris street fair, he looks on, mute and immobile, as the bright costumes and extraordinary feats of the fair's strong men, dancers, and magicians lure the crowd their way. The narrator's poignant description of the old man's decaying body and squalid hut attests to his plight:

> Au bout, à l'extrême bout de la rangée de baraques, comme si, honteux, il s'était exilé lui-même de toutes ces splendeurs, je vis un pauvre saltimbanque, voûté, caduc, décrépit, une ruine d'homme, adossé contre un des poteaux de sa cahute; une cahute plus misérable que celle du sauvage le plus abruti; et dont deux bouts de chandelles, coulants et fumants, éclairaient trop bien encore la détresse.

> At the end, at the extreme end of the row of booths, as if, ashamed, he had exiled himself from all those splendors, I saw a pitiful acrobat, stooped, bro-

ken, decrepit, a ruin of a man, backed against one of the posts of his hut; a hut more wretched than that of the most abject savage, and whose distress was illumined all too well by two burned-down candles, dripping and smoking.[6]

The old entertainer is the opposite of the high-spirited rococo aesthetic that his profession connotes.[7] Unlike other acrobats, whose tumbling calls to mind the spirals of the arabesque, he stands still, defeated, and shunned by the crowd.

Only the narrator moves toward the old man, but even he cannot think how to act. Struck by the acrobat's "profound, unforgettable gaze" ("quel regard profond, inoubliable, il promenait sur la foule et les lumières"), he claims to feel the "terrible hand of hysteria" grip him, and he wonders what to do. He can't ask the man to perform, knowing that the old acrobat has nothing to show ("A quoi bon demander à l'infortuné quelle curiosité, quelle merveille il avait à montrer . . . ?"). He has just decided to leave some money on the acrobat's boards, when, unexpectedly "swept away" by the milling throng, he too turns his back on the outcast performer. "Obsessed" by what he has seen, the narrator is reduced to interpreting his vision:

Et, m'en retournant, obsédé par cette vision, je cherchai à analyser ma soudaine douleur, et je me dis: Je viens de voir l'image du vieil homme de lettres qui a survécu à la génération dont il fut le brillant amuseur; du vieux poète sans amis, sans famille, sans enfants, dégradé par sa misère et par l'ingratitude publique, et dans la baraque de qui le monde oublieux ne veut plus entrer!

And, turning around, obsessed by that vision, I tried to analyze my sudden sorrow, and I told myself: I have just seen the image of the old man of letters who has survived the generation he brilliantly entertained; of the old poet without friends, without family, without children, debased by his wretchedness and the public's ingratitude, and whose booth the forgetful world no longer wants to enter!

With this culminating metaphor, which aligns the mute acrobat with an outmoded author forgotten by modern readers, the narrator turns the poem into an allegory of reading. In this same moment, he positions himself as a reader too, indeed the only reader who takes an interest in the old author, even though he finds himself drawn away from the man's dusty work. This final

statement effectively rewrites the poem as the story of the public's negative reaction to Rousseau under the Second Empire, while hinting at Baudelaire's positive, albeit tentative stance.

This interpretation is more than speculation. In fact, Baudelaire draws on Rousseau's own self-portraits (in book 12 of the *Confessions* and the first and ninth *Rêveries*) for his depiction of the "vieux saltimbanque." The image of the solitary soul "alone on earth, [with] no brother, neighbor, friend, or society other than [him]self" ("seul sur la terre, n'ayant plus de frère, de prochain, d'ami, de société que moi-même") is familiar from the opening paragraph of the *Rêveries,* where Rousseau explains how he has been misunderstood and cast out by the rest of humanity ("proscrit par un accord unanime").[8] And the paradoxical immobility of the "saltimbanque," which contradicts his name, "jump-on-the-bench" ("saute-en-banc"), combines the idea of renunciation explored in the first *rêverie* with Rousseau's description of his misery and inactivity at social gatherings. When Baudelaire writes:

> [I]l ne riait pas, le misérable! Il ne pleurait pas, il ne dansait pas, il ne *gesticulait* pas, il ne *criait* pas; il ne *chantait* aucune chanson, ni gaie ni lamentable, il n'implorait pas. Il était muet et immobile. (my emphases)

> He was not laughing, the wretched man! He was not crying, he was not dancing, he was not *gesturing,* he was not *shouting;* he was *singing* no song, neither jolly nor woeful, he was not beseeching. He was mute and motionless. (my emphases)

he is repeating what Rousseau says:

> Il faut que je reste là cloué sur une chaise ou debout planté comme un piquet, sans remuer ni pied ni patte, n'osant ni courir, ni *sauter,* ni *chanter,* ni *crier,* ni *gesticuler* quand j'en ai envie, n'osant pas même rêver.[9]

> I must stay there nailed to the chair or standing planted like a stake, moving neither foot nor paw, daring neither to run, nor *jump,* nor *sing,* nor *cry out,* nor *gesture* when I wanted to, not even daring to dream.

Baudelaire combines details of Rousseau's self-portrait with the received idea of Rousseau as a "charlatan" and creates the image of Rousseau as a lonely old "saltimbanque."[10]

This stylized portrait or caricature of Rousseau lends itself to a political in-

terpretation that does not completely follow the conservatives' condemnation of Jean-Jacques. Of course, the narrator does portray the mute performer as an author who has nothing to offer "the people."[11] This idea, which runs directly counter to Michelet's sympathetic reading of Rousseau as the people's champion, suggests the demystification or vilification that "Rousseau" has undergone under Napoléon III's regime. The once godlike Rousseau is now outdated, and no one looks up to him anymore. By dramatizing this shift, the poem emphasizes the hostile caricature of Rousseau as a mountebank, which was common currency in 1861 when the poem was first published.[12] As we saw in Chapter 3, Nisard used the word "charlatan" with all the virulence it can convey to sum up his view of "Jean-Jacques" as a utopianist or hypocrite. According to Nisard, Rousseau was a liar who made a pretense of expertise in areas about which he knew nothing; like Baudelaire's performer, Nisard's Rousseau had "nothing to show." Proudhon, too, underscored Rousseau's lack of substance, albeit from a very different political perspective, when he attacked Rousseau as "the Genevan charlatan" and called the *Social Contract* a "masterpiece of oratory juggling." However, the empathy and pain of the poem's narrator, as well as the identification implied in his vision of the performer as an "old man of letters," attenuate the negativity of the caricature.[13] "Le Vieux Saltimbanque" resembles far more the sympathetic images of downtrodden acrobats produced by Honoré Daumier, one of Baudelaire's favorite artists, than the disdainful critique of the ideologues.

If there is a political point in this poem, then, it has more to do with the contemporary antagonism between the government of Napoléon III and the street performers of the time. Under the Second Empire, the saltimbanques had significant political connotations, which extended well beyond the negative caricatures of Rousseau. Throughout the period leading up to the Revolution of 1848, they had been the "entertainers of the People," itinerant tumblers and singers who drew crowds in the provinces, and in the streets of Paris as well.[14] Although even in their heyday, they were the objects of police attention and brutality (as Baudelaire's early poem "A une Jeune Saltimbanque" makes clear),[15] their situation became more precarious when, in 1849, the government "declared war" on them. As T. J. Clark explains, "they had become, at least in the Ministers' and Prefects' fantasy, . . . teachers of subversion, . . . singers of Socialist ballads and sellers of Communist broadsheets."[16] The official campaign against them peaked in 1853 when their performances were effectively, if indirectly, banned.[17] Where they had once been outcasts by profession, the popular performers became outcasts in fact:

A rococo theme updated: *Les Saltimbanques.* Honoré Daumier, ca. 1860–65. Charcoal, pen and ink, wash, watercolor, and conté crayon. Victoria and Albert Museum, London, Ionides Collection (120).

> Once [the saltimbanque] acted as a critic and mocker of the social conventions because that was the role society gave him; he was the accepted, professional outsider. [After 1853] he is outcast in fiction and fact; society takes its revenge on his mockery, wags its finger at his naked children and his dirty songs, and hustles him off the street. The clown is both artist and worker . . . and that mixture, once tolerated, is now too dangerous to be allowed.[18]

Thus when Baudelaire calls on the figure of the saltimbanque, he displays a certain nostalgia for the politics of his youth.

Baudelaire's poem, like Daumier's saltimbanque series, hinges on the street performer's status as a pariah under the government of Napoléon III. The popular entertainer associated with the ambiance and attitudes of 1848 has lost his public. The increased governmental suspicion of the saltimbanques'

political sympathies and of their influence among the people perhaps explains why the word "charlatan" came to mind when Nisard and Proudhon sought to damn the "utopianist" Rousseau. Viewed in the light of Second Empire politics, Baudelaire's saltimbanque recalls Rousseau's status as a man "of the people" and the much-admired patron saint of the February revolution,[19] who since the failure of that uprising has fallen out of favor. The public, and particularly the conservative critics comforted by Napoléon III's regime, have deliberately and happily rejected Rousseau. They would have others believe that the decrepit old "charlatan" means nothing to them—his work is irrelevant to their times.

With his saltimbanque, Baudelaire has condensed into one figure an image of both distant and contemporary artists, and a reminder of politics both current and past. While Baudelaire's saltimbanque refers to a concrete individual familiar to the nineteenth-century reader, who encountered him on the street and read about him in the newspaper, he simultaneously recalls another "performer" or author (Rousseau), who operates in the poem as a sad hold-over from the politics of 1848. This historical character functions, in turn, as a double for the contemporary artist who has been cast out by society and by the government; he connotes the poet's marginalization in an era when journalism prevailed over the arts and political censorship was rife.[20] The image of the defeated performer allows Baudelaire, like Daumier, to reflect, in T. J. Clark's words, on "the place of art in the city and society: the space allowed to art, its different guises and its very different publics, its perversion in the courts and its suppression on the streets."[21] By merely allowing for this reflection in his poem, Baudelaire takes his distance from the ideological cant of his day. He does not gleefully dismiss Rousseau, the very prototype of the outcast artist. In fact, his poem reflects not only on the role of the poet in society, but also on the part poetry plays in the preservation or suppression of the past. This reflection is carried out, or dramatized, in the narrator's behavior toward "the old man of letters."

The Poet's Obsession

If "Le Vieux Saltimbanque" is a poem about Rousseau and his complicated reception history, it is also a poem about the poet's relationship to the literature and ideas of the past. When the narrator conjures up the final metaphor of the poem and equates the mute acrobat with an outmoded writer, he positions himself not only as a sometime reader of musty texts but as a poet too.

As he summons up the image of the old man of letters, the narrator's troping turns him into a "faiseur de tours"—"a turner of tricks [or tropes]"—like those who take part in the fair. With this one metaphor, then, he does what the old acrobat can no longer do: he becomes the "brillant amuseur" of his generation. Obsessed with the old man's impotence, he speaks in the old man's place, restoring fullness to this empty sign. The narrator's final speech can be read as the gesture of a thoroughly modern poet filling up his predecessor's "mute" text with a new imagery, style, and meaning all his own.

In fact, the poem not only tells a fictional story about an intergenerational encounter at a fair, but also a verifiable story about an intertextual encounter which contributes to the poem's generation. For just as the narrator/poet has displaced the old acrobat/author, Baudelaire has taken the most important features of Rousseau's ninth *rêverie* and written them out with a new style and imagery in this poem. "Le Vieux Saltimbanque" is thick with borrowings from Rousseau. While the letter on the Paris Opéra in *Julie* provides the idea and the verbal materials for the description of the fair and the acrobat's hovel (as we saw in Chapter 5), and the twelfth book of the *Confessions* furnishes key traits for the old acrobat's portrait, Rousseau's ninth *rêverie*, the poem's most important intertext, gives Baudelaire all the rest: not only the anecdote of the old man and the theme of intergenerational relations, but even the emphasis on forgetting and the unforgettable, which underlie the allegory of reading at the core of the poem.[22]

Baudelaire has repeated much of his predecessor's work, taking up its form and its most important characters. Yet he makes one all-important change in his intertext: he puts himself (or his surrogate, the first-person narrator) in Rousseau's place and makes "Rousseau" the would-be recipient of his charity. Not only does Baudelaire have his narrator speak for the mute "Rousseau," but he actually casts the autobiographer out of his own first-person role! Indeed, although Baudelaire may be giving the mute text of the ninth *rêverie* a "voice," that voice—not surprisingly—has never been attributed to Rousseau. If Baudelaire has taken Rousseau's place in the very structure of Rousseau's own autobiography, has he not definitively supplanted him? "Le Vieux Saltimbanque" is both a contemporary history of Rousseau's demise as an influential writer and an apparently personal statement of the poet's ambition to displace his literary father.

In a sense, "Le Vieux Saltimbanque" continues Rousseau's autobiography beyond the grave—and serves as Baudelaire's own. Baudelaire's ambition to write an autobiography that would make "the *Confessions* of J[ean]-J[acques]

appear pale" by comparison seems to have found its way into Baudelaire's multilayered poem.[23] "Le Vieux Saltimbanque" is the nearest thing we have to the poet's literary confession. Of all Baudelaire's "stories of Rousseau," it comes closest to revealing the psychological dynamic—the "obsession"—that evidently motivates the hidden but insistent presence of Rousseau in Baudelaire's poems. In the poem, Baudelaire admits, albeit indirectly, the power Rousseau has over him. In the terrible hand of hysteria gripping the narrator's throat ("ma gorge serrée par la main terrible de l'hystérie"), the poem registers the shock to Baudelaire's system brought about by his encounter with Rousseau's work. It is understandable, then, that the poet would conjure up the image of Rousseau as a bankrupt author incapable of affecting the world, to help him forget his perception of Rousseau as a force still able to elicit fear.

As "Le Vieux Saltimbanque" demonstrates, Baudelaire views Rousseau as a kind of living cadaver whose appearance in the most unlikely places—even in the midst of festive circumstances—has the capacity to traumatize or shock.[24] Baudelaire's Rousseau is neither successfully relegated to the past as a safely forgotten author nor completely buried as an unconscious source of uncanny effects. Rather, he exists for Baudelaire in a liminal state, somewhere between the two.[25] A "dead" author who refuses to die, Rousseau lingers on in the margins, or just beneath the surface, of Baudelaire's poetic activity, where he plays an overlooked but very important role. We might say that "Rousseau" is Baudelaire's fetish object, who holds the key to the trauma that threatens the poet and yet allows him to parry that threat.[26] Just as a fetish is at once a sign of and a protection against trauma, a present and perceptible object that both stands for and allows the fetishist to disavow a repressed event, so Baudelaire toys with "Rousseau" as a way of recalling and facing down his forefather's immanence in his work. Baudelaire is at once fascinated and perturbed by the massive (albeit largely negative) reaction Rousseau can still engender in the nineteenth-century public and by the *necessary* rhetorical charlatanism that drives Rousseau's work—and his own.

"Forgetting" the Unforgettable

The image of the forgotten, but unforgettable, "old man of letters" reflects this complex dynamic, which plays itself out not only in the anecdote of "Le Vieux Saltimbanque" but in the poem's rhetorical structure as well. The primary theme of "Le Vieux Saltimbanque" is "l'oubli" (forgetting).[27] The fair that serves as a backdrop for the action takes place on a date set aside in the

church calendar for a "solennité." Of course, this solemn religious occasion has been forgotten by the people in the joy of a day off ("le peuple en vacances"). In fact, joy and forgetfulness are allied in the text. Only by overlooking life's miseries for a day can the crowd enjoy itself in the fair's atmosphere of plenitude and bustle. The pain of work and the horror of school must be forgotten in order for the fun to begin: "En ces jours-là, . . . le peuple oublie tout, la douleur et le travail; il devient pareil aux enfants" ("On such days as these, . . . the people forget everything, [their] pain and work; they become like children").

"Oubli" and "vacances" are also the operative rhetorical principles of the first half of the poem; they name the vacating of the sign that allows metaphoric substitution to take place. Examples of this process abound in the description of the fair. First, the "vacancy" of the original religious meaning of "solennité" leaves a simple opening in the calendar, so that "solennité" becomes synonymous with the purely temporal "vacances." This "vacation" then prepares the ultimate conversion of "solennité" to "jubilé" ("ce jubilé populaire"), whose own religious significance is also overlooked in the jubilation of the day.[28] The "vacances," in the double sense of semantic vacancy and temporal vacation, have made possible a new comic "jubilé," which fills up the void with extraordinary activity and life. The atmosphere of abundance, stylistically rendered by increasingly long descriptions and explicit similes ("comme celui de Molière," "comme les orang-outangs," "comme des fées ou des princesses") and placed under the aegis of dramatic literature, exemplifies the metaphoricity of this moment.

Marginalized but still present, the "saltimbanque" reintroduces into this dynamic scene everything that was forgotten. Cast out of the fair's "frenzied explosion of vitality," neglected by the carefree throng, the immobile "ruin of a man" ("une ruine d'homme") is the concretization of the misery and horror overlooked by the crowd. Nonetheless, the forgotten acrobat on the far edge of the fair cannot be entirely separated from the action. The elimination of misery, incarnated by the miserable performer, is what makes the joy possible. As a figure for forgetting, the forgotten acrobat is unforgettable; in a sense, the fair's very existence depends on him. Thus he lingers at the edge of the fun, where his immobility and his empty booth acquire metaphorical significance in turn. The "saltimbanque" is a sign whose failure to participate in the "fair" plays an important role in the economy of the poem, that is, in the textual system as a whole. In other words, meaning (or value) accrues to the acrobat precisely because he has none; he is an empty sign. Despite his inactivity, the textual economy circulates around and through this immobile figure, as both the

beginning and the ending of the poem make clear. For just as the vacating of the sign opens the way for the lively metaphoricity of the first part of the text, with its proliferation of images, comparisons and similes, the acrobat who has "nothing to show" calls forth the ultimate metaphor of the "old man of letters" that concludes the poem.

When the narrator, "turning around," utters his interpretation of what he has seen, he represents the endless and inevitable process of re-covering the void. The narrator's statement, like the lively scene to which he returns, displays the rhetorical necessity and generative effects of the empty sign. Thus the description of the acrobat's clothing is also a statement about the rhetoric at work in the poem: "Ici la misère absolue, la misère affublée, pour comble d'horreur, de haillons comiques, où la nécessité, bien plus que l'art, avait introduit le contraste" ("Here absolute wretchedness, wretchedness rigged out, most horrible, in comic rags, where necessity, far more than art, had introduced the contrast"). The deictic "here" points to the *mise-en-abyme* of the poem's structure. Here—figured by the acrobat's patched and motley rags—is the necessary juxtaposition and contrast of metaphors and vacant signs that structures the poem. The narrator acknowledges the rhetorical determinism that governs the text, as he plays down the freedom of artistic or authorial choice: "necessity, far more than art, introduced the contrast." The mute and immobile acrobat, whose tattered Harlequin coat sums up the shocking tensions operative in Baudelaire's poem, is an allegory for the production of this text. A dual sign representing both the evacuation and restoration of meaning, he figures the process by which metaphor is produced, disfigured, and produced again. Both worthless and invaluable, both excluded and essential, the inert performer is a grotesque figure, the personification of the rhetorical force of language that generates "Le Vieux Saltimbanque."

Rhetorical Charlatanism: Rousseau's "Oublies"

The Rousseau figure in Baudelaire's poem is an example of the logical impasse characteristic of the modern grotesque. Like the beautiful woman in the verse poem, "Le Masque," he is a figure for figuration who never yields a simple or original meaning. And yet, as we have come to understand, the Rousseau figure does denote the presence of Rousseau's work in the poem. The figure "Rousseau" stands in for the author Rousseau and seems to bring the interpretation around to an original model and meaning, after all. Although Rousseau retains his reputation for rhetorical "charlatanism," both as a figure

in "Le Vieux Saltimbanque" and as the author of the ninth *rêverie* on which it is predicated, it is nonetheless true that Rousseau's rhetorical sleight-of-hand does generate Baudelaire's poem. However, even this close proximity of the two texts does nothing to stabilize the meaning of the sign.

The ninth *rêverie* is a text about reading and writing autobiography that engages in an examination of the nature of signs.[29] Rousseau's immediate aim is to determine whether we can know a person by reading the outward signs of his emotion. Because this broad question is pursued through a series of anecdotes drawn from Rousseau's own experience, it becomes evident that he has a personal stake in the outcome of the inquiry. As someone who has been misread and misunderstood by others, Rousseau hopes to clear his name by making his good nature known. Charged with inhumanity for having abandoned his children, Rousseau wants to prove that he is not a monster, but a loving and honest man. The success of this venture hinges, then, on the readability of the *rêverie* itself. Inasmuch as it explores the possibility of acquiring knowledge (or truth) through reading, the text reflects on its own ability to transmit knowledge about Rousseau. Since we cannot read the man's eyes, posture, accent, or gait ("les yeux," "le maintien," "l'accent," "la démarche") to get a sense of his inner being, we are called upon to compare the *rêverie*'s statements about signs with its own signifying practices.[30] Ultimately, we need to know whether the ninth *rêverie* is a transparent text that can give us insight into the "real" Rousseau. The answer to this question turns out to be no, and the repercussions of this discovery are felt even in Baudelaire's poem.

The *rêverie* begins by asserting that inner emotion *can* be transmitted and known by outward signs. However, subsequent examples reveal the failure of this ideal and threaten the narrative of self-justification. In fact, many of the examples Rousseau proposes suggest a discrepancy between outward signs and (putative) inner truth. The problem becomes acute midway through the text in an episode Rousseau remembers about buying sweet wafers, or "oublies," for a group of schoolgirls. This anecdote engenders, albeit in a very different guise, the problem of forgetting the unforgettable, which is explored in Baudelaire's poem.

In this crucial story, Rousseau describes how he rigged the outcome of a game of chance normally used to determine who will win the "oublies" and who will lose. Paying the "oublieur" (the wafer seller) to put his "usual skills" to work in an unusual way, in order to distribute as many winning lots as possible, Rousseau ensured that all the girls received at least one "oublie." Everyone was happy—the girls, their chaperone, and Rousseau himself: "Ce mot

[his offer to treat everyone to a cookie] répandit dans toute la troupe une joye qui seule eut plus que payé ma bourse quand je l'aurois toute employée à cela." ("This word [his offer to treat everyone to a cookie] spread a joy through the whole group, which alone would have more than reimbursed me even if I had used up all my money").[31]

The story carries the message that Rousseau has recouped the loss of pleasure he suffered when his old face (his "figure caduque") began to frighten children away. Difference—the age difference between Rousseau and the children he adores, or the difference between Rousseau's frightening face and his loving soul—is forgotten, thanks to the skillful manipulation (the "adresse en sens contraire") of the "oublieur." Yet, in terms of the underlying relation of sign to referent that is central to Rousseau's project, the sought-after balance has hardly been achieved. For even as the anecdote claims to provide a model of how to overcome difference, it offers up an example of how different values can attach to the same sign. By emphasizing the tricks of the "oublieur," Rousseau alerts us to the trickiness of the word "oublies."

Although, in Rousseau's context, "oublie" names the insignificant treat he offered to the schoolgirls, the word also designates the highly symbolic wafer of the Eucharist. "Oublie" derives its religious meaning from "oblata," the ritual offering served to the faithful as a memorial or anamnesis of Christ's sacrifice on the cross.[32] Anamnesis supposes an identity between the memorial object (the host) and that to which it refers;[33] but, oddly, the sign ("oublie") that refers to the absolute identity of a sign and its referent does not exhibit such an identity. For one thing, of course, the word *oublie* refers to two kinds of wafers, functioning in two very different cultural contexts. Received as a snack to be purchased and consumed in a city park, an "oublie" bears little resemblance to a religious offering; used in this setting, the word entails not an anamnesis but a kind of amnesia—it forgets, so to speak, the religious memorial it connotes. Indeed, through its homonym, "oublie" may easily be taken to mean "forgetting;" uttered aloud, the word *oublie* recalls *oubli.* Not only is the sign not transparent, but it actively engenders confusion by conflating remembering and forgetting, identity and difference. And yet the text proceeds as if the referential complexity of signs has been forgotten.

The anecdote of the "oublieur" and his "oublies" is an allegory for the epistemological problem and the rhetorical sleight of hand (or "adresse") that are at work in the ninth *rêverie.* The word *oublies,* on the one hand, makes obvious the disjunction that can occur between a sign and its referent, even as it points to the putative unity or indistinction between the two. The "oublieur,"

on the other hand, raises the possibility that the uncertainty governing signs can be addressed, in order to arrive at a solution that does not depend on chance. The "oublieur" suggests the potential for "fixing" the problem. Indeed, the story of the "oublies" is a turning point in the *rêverie*, the locus of a transfer or exchange that allows Rousseau to arrive at an illusory resolution of his epistemological dilemma.

Embedded in a series of anecdotes that have to do with the relation between external signs and internal states or essences, the story of the "oublies" calls our attention away from inner spiritual phenomena to focus on material conditions and "accidents" alone. The anecdote emphasizes the process of producing and distributing the cookie, which effectively erases inequalities of wealth among the young recipients and renders the age difference between Rousseau and the girls meaningless. In this story, the significance of the sweet wafer has nothing to do with inherent value; it is, after all, a trivial object rather than a useful or necessary one. Instead, it is the act of distribution that counts. The inwardness or spiritual "substance" of the host is forgotten in Rousseau's self-serving manipulation of the "oublies."

The anecdote gives us to understand that value may not always inhere in the sign itself, but may rather derive from the way empty signs are circulated or distributed. We need not see through the sign to some putative innerness, or inherent value, as long as we can identify differences in the way signs are put into play. Thus Rousseau puts forward an example contrasting his respectful distribution of apples to children with the reprehensible way his rich friends toss cake into the dirt for young peasants to fight over.[34] The observable difference between these acts invariably acquires significance, however, and redounds to Rousseau's credit. Subtly, by attaching moral value to such gestures (usually in inverse proportion to the monetary expenditure involved), Rousseau invests these outward signs with new meaning. The less they cost (in monetary terms), the more they are worth (in human terms). By pointing to the elimination of excess, Rousseau suggests that the gap between sign and referent (between simple gift and simple decency) has been closed; his true character has been established.

Forgetting the sign's referential complexity and trading on its external aspects alone has allowed innerness to return. Displacing difference "outward," so that it no longer appears as a problem of value affecting the individual sign, and emphasizing instead the difference between the ways signs are circulated, allows for the progressive trivialization of external signs and the reassertion of inner worth. Thus, gradually, Rousseau seems to acquit himself of the charge

of inhumanity and, by the end of the *rêverie*, he speaks with the voice of moral authority. Despite all the textual evidence to the contrary, Rousseau asserts that he, at least, uses transparent signs—he can be read and trusted.

And yet it is impossible to forget the story of forgetting that allowed this transformation and recuperation to take place. As Cynthia Chase remarks, Rousseau *recalls* the incident as "one of his fondest memories," while he tells "of engaging an *oublieur*":

> Rousseau celebrates a memory and writes a word that sounds like forgetting. The reader is forced to forget the meaning of the word's sound in order to follow its function in the syntax of the anecdote. What the reader is forced to forget is forgetting. But at the same time the dual sign forces forgetting on the reader: *e* or no *e,* "oubli(e)" forces forgetting down our throat.[35]

We might say that, in both the *rêverie* as a whole and its pivotal anecdote, memory clings to forgetting and vice versa. Signs have a memory of their own.

Not surprisingly, then, the dithyrambic ending of the ninth *rêverie* is punctuated and undermined by several plays on words, especially a telling mention of a trip to the Isle aux Cignes [swans], which phonically recalls the complexity and unreliability of signs [*signes*] at the very moment when Rousseau is writing the problem off. Rousseau's effort at self-disclosure founders on a problem of reference that he both acknowledges and tries to forget. Even as Rousseau asserts the opposite, his text suggests that getting to know him or any man by reading his signs is an uncertain undertaking at best. In the end, the *rêverie* raises the question that threatens it: "[N]'est-ce rien de se dire je suis homme?" ("[I]s it nothing to say to oneself: I am a man?"). What is the value of the sign "man" (or the name "Rousseau") when its ability to refer to a knowable entity is in doubt?

The Ruin of Man

Rousseau's *rêverie*, with its emphasis on the relationship between generations and its pivotal story of forgetting and remembering, furnishes both the themes and the rhetorical structure of "Le Vieux Saltimbanque." Rousseau's central anecdote of the "oublies," which dramatizes a forgetting that both enables and threatens his autobiographical narrative, is adopted—with a different look but a similar effect—in Baudelaire's poem. Instead of focusing on a trivial cookie, however, "Le Vieux Saltimbanque" goes right to the heart of

Rousseau's project and asks what it means to forget *man*. Baudelaire's old acrobat—"une ruine d'homme"—is not so much a "ruin of a man," a man disfigured by age, as the "ruin of man," a figure for the emptiness or unknowability of "man" revealed by Rousseau. Baudelaire knowingly builds his poem around the referential instability of the autobiographical project.

This instability plays itself out in "Le Vieux Saltimbanque" in the double posture of Baudelaire's narrator, who is at once reader and poet. The narrator's ultimate vision, which simultaneously transforms the poem into an allegory of reading and makes him into an author figure, turns him into a dual sign. When the narrator delivers up the analogy between the immobile acrobat and the old man of letters, he produces a statement that reinterprets all the events he has described—including his own actions—as different kinds of reading. But in producing the statement that reveals him to be a reader, the narrator at the same moment becomes a poet. Although the narrator's two identities are narrated as a before and an after (the narrator first has the experience of his encounter with the acrobat and then understands or interprets it), they are both brought into being in the poem by the final metaphor. Conflating the narrator/*reader*'s discovery of the referential instability of language and the ruin of "man" with the narrator/*poet*'s attempt to stabilize and understand that event by infusing it with meaning, the final paragraph of the poem sets up a contradiction that it cannot resolve. These two events cannot be held in the mind and understood simultaneously; otherwise, the very act of imputing meaning to an empty sign would be vitiated as it occurs. Therefore the poem encourages us to read the narrator's two identities as two separate and successive states of being, *forgetting* that they are produced together, at the very same time. We can always say that the reader reading the empty sign "man" is the prior event that produces the final metaphor and thus the poet; but we can just as accurately say that the ultimate metaphor produces the reader reading. The putative disjunction of two supposedly separate "moments" represents the divergence of reference within the same text and makes us aware again that reading, which is remembering, involves a necessary forgetting. Baudelaire has written out as a personal, psychological narrative a story about the traumatic dissociation of a sign or event from its understanding[36]—that is, a story about the aporia of reading. Of course, this aporia is precisely the epistemological problem that the poem would have us forget. By writing a poem that can be convincingly understood as "his own" autobiography, Baudelaire produces a meaning that covers over the referential instability that threatens it.

Reading the ninth *rêverie*, Baudelaire learns a lesson about the impossibil-

ity of controlling language's memory effects. As Rousseau's *rêverie* shows, signs, through their etymology or their phonic resemblance to other signs, or even by virtue of their circulation, have a way of disrupting meaning and forcing multiple and often contradictory ideas on the reader. The evacuation of meaning, the process by which one meaning comes to take the place of another, cannot completely eradicate the traces of the sign's constitutive otherness. This referential instability plays itself out even in the "persons" or personifications (such as Rousseau's "Rousseau" or Baudelaire's "poet") that are meant to concretize and stabilize meaning.

Nonetheless, personification—by which Baudelaire converts "Rousseau" into a series of collectible figures or fetish objects—is his best line of defense against the trauma of language's referential uncertainty and its generative force. Baudelaire defends against the traumatic fact that "man" is an empty sign by reproducing and "animating" the vacant sign in his own poetry. Using the old acrobat to personify the emptiness of "Rousseau," Baudelaire fixes the problem, in a way, by concretizing the empty sign and giving it a meaning in his poem. By exposing both the empty sign ("man") and the way it attracts new meaning ("the old man of letters"), Baudelaire makes this metamorphosis the hallmark of his own modern poem. If fetishism kills the object and makes the sign live,[37] Baudelaire's reading brings Rousseau's work to life, as it were, while emphasizing its near-death. Making "Rousseau" the personification of his poetic allegories, Baudelaire underscores both the emptiness and endless creativity of the allegorical sign.

Baudelaire's Modernity

As "Le Vieux Saltimbanque" suggests, Baudelaire's perspicuity regarding Rousseau's intractable effect on the present and future puts him at variance with his conservative contemporaries. Whereas most of those who debate the meaning of France's traumatic past for the nation's identity are determined to will away Rousseau's influence on both nineteenth-century political theory and current events, Baudelaire recognizes the futility of his contemporaries' efforts. In contrast to conservatives like Nisard, who characterize Rousseau as "mad" and deliberately write him out of their narratives of "true French" history as an "illness" of the French mind, Baudelaire understands the impossibility of forgetting Rousseau. (To be sure, even Nisard could not actually leave Rousseau out of his history, given the factual importance of Rousseau's contri-

bution to the evolution of events; but he did everything he could to make it clear that Rousseau was an anomaly and should not be counted among France's great authors, the anchor of her present and future identity.) Whereas the dominant discourse of the Second Empire attempts "to place the past of remembered events in a stable relation to the present of their interpretation, [so as to] shelter the present from the past,"[38] Baudelaire does not share the conservatives' smug certainty that, thanks to their efforts, Rousseau can be contained. Nor does he concur with the idea that Rousseau is passé. On the contrary, he takes seriously the continuing power of Rousseau's ideas and his masterful rhetoric, even acknowledging their capacity to shock. Baudelaire does not try to write Rousseau out of the present, in a sweeping gesture of condemnation. For him, Rousseau is less a historical being or a set of writings whose essence can be understood and set aside than the permanent trace of a trauma that no effort of will can overcome.

Baudelaire is thus also at odds with his mentor, Sainte-Beuve, who published the third and last of his articles on Rousseau on two subsequent Mondays in July 1861. In this essay, as in his two earlier ones, Sainte-Beuve makes little reference to the political events and ideologies with which Rousseau's name had come to be linked. In 1861, Rousseau was once again a subject of attack, as we have seen, and although Sainte-Beuve claims (paradoxically) that no one reads Rousseau anymore, he expresses the wish that his contemporaries would judge the eighteenth-century author "as he was," without letting polemics influence their appreciation. Sainte-Beuve wants them to cut through the countless disputes Rousseau's doctrines have engendered; otherwise, "we shall never find him again as he was [*tel qu'il fut*]":

> Sa figure, comme celle de tous les puissants mortels qui ont excité enthousiasme et colère, ainsi aperçue de loin à travers un nuage de lumière et de poussière, se transformerait à nos yeux; nous le ferions trop grand, trop beau ou trop laid, trop génie ou trop monstre. . . . replaçons-nous de l'autre côté du nuage, voyons-le de près . . . c'est encore le moyen de nous faire de lui la plus juste idée.

> His figure, like that of all the powerful mortals who have excited enthusiasm and anger, thus glimpsed from afar through a cloud of light and dust, would be transformed in our eyes: we would make him too big, too handsome, or too ugly, too much a genius or too much a monster. . . . let us place ourselves again on the other side of the cloud, let us see him up close . . . that is still the way to do him justice.[39]

Sainte-Beuve clings to the vain hope that there can be a "just" reading of Rousseau—an even-handed and accurate reading that would reveal Rousseau's essence. But Baudelaire, ever the rhetorically savvy reader, knows that Rousseau is doomed to be eternally a "figure," a rhetorical construct whose shape changes according to one's point of view. Baudelaire has the acuity to recognize that Rousseau can never be captured with the fullness of being and meaning to which Sainte-Beuve aspires. Perhaps that is why he proposed "La Lueur et la fumée" ("Glimmer and Smoke") as another possible title for his prose poems, realizing that his own work—with its double stance toward Rousseau—was resolutely positioned on the "wrong" side of the "light and dust."[40]

Conclusion

Throughout this book I have tried to make clear that Baudelaire's relationship to Rousseau is not a simple matter of literary influence. Although Baudelaire may from a certain point of view be seen as Rousseau's heir and rival in the nineteenth century, and although his poems and letters do manifest some of the oedipal impulses often associated with the relationship between literary generations, the impetus behind Baudelaire's prose poems is not primarily a private, psychological one. If Baudelaire revels in his ability to match Rousseau's rhetorical prowess and occasionally enjoys himself at Rousseau's expense, this personal pleasure by no means explains the complex use the poet makes of Rousseau, not only as a reference for understanding allegory and the grotesque, but as a political figure and contemporary cliché. There is much more to the Rousseau–Baudelaire relationship than the hackneyed features of a father–son pair.

Rousseau is Baudelaire's *poncif*—his "cliché," or commonplace. Both a device for generating multiple images and a means of capturing the shifting shapes of the present, Baudelaire's Rousseau is the modern equivalent of the metamorphoses so prevalent in rococo art. Adopting "Rousseau" as a generative motif in the *Petits Poèmes en prose,* Baudelaire updates the look or style of the grotesque while personifying its transformative function. For Baudelaire, "Rousseau" is both a modern man and an allegorical figure; like a modern-day Venus in the Luxembourg Gardens, he is a way of bringing out the allegorical in everyday life.[1]

Baudelaire understands that Rousseau is one "face" of nineteenth-century

France, the personification of his contemporaries' fascination with and fear of the past. Rousseau both haunted and repulsed the French ideologues of Baudelaire's day, and their discourse about Rousseau and his legacy marks the political debates of the mid-nineteenth century. "Rousseau" is a sign of Baudelaire's times. When the poet uses "Jean-Jacques" as a type and trades on the caricatures of Rousseau put into circulation by the political discourse, he relies on the figure of Rousseau to capture the ethos of the "present." "Rousseau" marks the nineteenth-century's obsession with the past, its need to work through the trauma of the French Revolution and the difficulty it had in defining itself as something new.

Yet, even as he is a time-bound character, "Rousseau" also serves as Baudelaire's point of entry into the timelessness of the grotesque. The Rousseau figure in the prose poems points to the persistent and uncontrollable (grotesque) effects that are liberated in Baudelaire's reading of his predecessor's works. Inasmuch as Rousseau's texts are the site of an unresolvable tension between allegory as a restricted figure and allegory as an open-ended and inevitable play of language that threatens authorial control, "Rousseau" names the slippage and resistance of allegory, its inability to coalesce into a stable and transparent meaning. Reading Baudelaire reading Rousseau thus delivers us up to a perpetually regressive and disorienting world, which resembles nothing so much as a painted arabesque. The visual twists and turns of the rococo that inspire Baudelaire disappear in his poems, becoming instead the imperceptible spiraling of the poems' tropes. In *Le Spleen de Paris,* the rococo's "decorative allegorism" gives way to the unrepresentable play of allegory, which might be called the "most spiritual" of designs and "most ideal of all."[2]

Baudelaire's poems take their place, not in a present that can be separated out as the future of Rousseau's work, but within the rhetoric of Rousseau's texts. The prose poems put into play the doubleness, duplicity, and unassimilatable excess that are "Rousseau." Like the beheaded Pierrot in "De l'essence du rire" or the two-faced statue in "Le Masque," "Rousseau" is simultaneously one, double, and capable of the endless generation of extraordinary effects. Representative of a present unable to let go of the terrible past, figure for the timeless but ineffable play of language, "Rousseau" is anything but a stable ground or point of origin for Baudelaire's poems. For all these reasons, the Baudelaire–Rousseau relationship cannot be construed as a linear history, a progression in which the new generation replaces or eclipses the old.

This book, then, is not a literary history in the usual sense. And yet it does make a contribution to aesthetic history by exploring something like a turn-

ing point in the way the grotesque is understood and used. Although both Rousseau and Baudelaire acknowledge the grotesque as a phenomenon of language, they experience it and deal with it very differently.

Writing in the context of a bankrupt and ineffective monarchy in the decades leading up to 1789, Rousseau looks forward to the possibility of social and political change. He views the excesses of the grotesque with suspicion. He wants to sweep aside allegory's morally unsavory and politically dubious dominion in favor of a more sober use of language, consonant with his hopes for man and his republican aspirations. Writing in the aftermath of the French Revolution and the revolution of 1848, Baudelaire cannot subscribe to Rousseau's reformist ideals. Instead, he welcomes the grotesque as the appropriate aesthetic for a generation still coping with the wreckage of the Terror. Baudelaire accepts the pervasiveness of the grotesque in everyday life and the way it challenges closely held beliefs in the ultimate powers of man and creation. Despite the poet's intermittent utopian yearnings, the world of *Le Spleen de Paris* is essentially marked by the demise of man and the fall of God.[3]

Baudelaire embraces the excesses that Rousseau despised. For Baudelaire, language is not a tool for mastering the demons, but the exhilarating, overpowering, even "comic" medium in which they are met. Thus by making the "ruin of man" the locus of his allegory and adopting "Rousseau" as its personification, Baudelaire both exposes his own pessimism about the human condition in post-Revolutionary France and "laughs" at what he knows. What is new and modern in the prose poems is not Baudelaire's understanding of the grotesque, but his now giddy, now ironic acceptance of its *inevitability* in life and art.

Notes

Introduction

1. Baud., *OC,* 2: 54 and 1: 709. *Vitam impendere vero* was Rousseau's motto.

2. "Notes nouvelles sur Edgar Poe," in Baud., *OC,* 2: 327.

3. Letter to Armand Fraisse, Aug. 12, 1860, in Baudelaire, *Nouvelles lettres,* ed. Claude Pichois (Paris: Fayard, 2000), 30–32.

4. "Fusées VI," *OC,* 1: 654, and "Hygiène VI," ibid., 672.

5. Letters to Madame Aupick, Apr. 1, 1861, July 25, 1861, and June 3, 1863, in Baud., *Corr.,* 2: 141, 182, and 302.

6. For a preliminary overview, see Robert Kopp's notes to Baudelaire, *Petits Poëmes en prose* (Paris: José Corti, 1969). Discoveries made since Kopp's edition appeared will be noted as appropriate throughout this book.

7. Jean Starobinski, "From the Solitary Walker to the *Flâneur*: Baudelaire's Caricature of Rousseau," in *Approaches to Teaching Rousseau's "Confessions" and "Reveries of the Solitary Walker,"* ed. John C. O'Neal and Ourida Mostefai (New York: MLA, 2003), 115.

8. In his seminal book *The Grotesque in Art and Literature,* trans. Ulrich Weisstein (Bloomington: Indiana University Press, 1963), 53, Wolfgang Kayser quotes Friedrich Schlegel as calling the French Revolution the "most awe-inspiring grotesque of the age, where its profoundest prejudices and its most violent anticipations result in a terrible chaos, a bizarre mixture, a colossal tragicomedy of all mankind." This view is also reflected in Victor Hugo's call for the grotesque to become "the new principle, the modern principle" that would embody "the truth proper to [post-Revolutionary] times." Hugo, Preface to *Cromwell,* in *Oeuvres complètes,* ed. Jean-Pierre Reynaud et al. (Paris: Robert Laffont, 1985), 12: 10.

9. Mikhail Bakhtin, *Rabelais and His World,* trans. Helene Iswolsky (Cambridge, Mass.: MIT Press, 1968), 9; 4; 11; 34.

10. Ibid., 38.

11. Kayser, *Grotesque in Art and Literature,* 188; 184–85; 187; 188.

One   The Grotesque: Definitions and Figures

1. "Cet élément transitoire, fugitif, dont les *métamorphoses* sont si fréquentes, vous n'avez pas le droit de le mépriser ou de vous en passer" ("This transitory, fugi-

tive element, the *metamorphoses* of which are so frequent, you do not have the right to scorn it or do without it"). "Le Peintre de la vie moderne," in Baud., *OC*, 2: 695; my emphasis. All translations of "Le Peintre de la vie moderne" in this book are mine.

2. Frances Barasch notes that the earliest of the French commentators to employ the term *grotesques* to designate a category of poetry was André Dacier in his translation and commentary of *La Poétique d'Aristote* (1692). Dacier attacked the contemporary taste for what he called "'Tragedies in music': 'For the Operas, are, if I dare say, *the grotesques* of Poetry, and Grotesques that are all the more unbearable because people want to pass them off as regular works.'" His critique was quoted in full by the abbé Jean Baptiste Dubos in *Réflexions critiques sur la poésie et sur la peinture* (published in 1719, reprinted several times before 1760), so that "the habit of regarding opera as a grotesque form was well established [in France] during the early half of the [eighteenth] century." Barasch, *The Grotesque: A Study in Meanings* (The Hague: Mouton, 1971), 119; my translation of Dacier, quoted in French by Barasch. However, it was the campaign of the philosophes that had the most direct transformational effect on the aesthetics of the time.

3. In this chapter, in addition to Barasch, I draw on Bakhtin, *Rabelais and His World*; Kayser, *Grotesque in Art and Literature*; Geoffrey Golt Harpham, *On the Grotesque: Strategies of Contradiction in Art and Literature* (Princeton, N.J.: Princeton University Press, 1982); André Chastel, *La Grottesque* (Paris: Le Promeneur, 1988); Bernard McElroy, *Fiction of the Modern Grotesque* (New York: St. Martin's Press, 1989); and Yvonne Bargues Rollins, *Baudelaire et le grotesque* (Washington, D.C.: University Press of America, 1978). Recent work of interest focuses on the "female grotesque" and testifies to the ongoing relevance of this aesthetic category for contemporary art and feminism. See, e.g., Mary Russo, *The Female Grotesque: Risk, Excess and Modernity* (New York: Routledge, 1994).

4. McElroy, *Fiction of the Modern Grotesque*, 16–17.

5. Kayser, *Grotesque in Art and Literature*, 24.

6. Bakhtin, *Rabelais and His World*, 23.

7. Chastel, *Grottesque*, 25, says that the painted grotesque conveys "un double sentiment de libération, à l'égard de l'étendue concrète, où règne la pesanteur, et à l'égard de l'ordre du monde, que gouverne la distinction des êtres" ("a double feeling of liberation, with regard to concrete space, where weight reigns, and with regard to the order of the world, governed by the distinction between beings"). So, too, I would argue, does the literary grotesque.

8. Bakhtin, *Rabelais and His World*, 48.

9. Kayser, *Grotesque in Art and Literature*, 59.

10. Chastel, *Grottesque*, 25.

11. Bakhtin, *Rabelais and His World*, 24. For an example of the foundational role of time in a nineteenth-century grotesque narrative, see Harpham's reading, in *On the Grotesque*, of Edgar Allan Poe's story "The Masque of the Red Death."

12. Harpham, *On the Grotesque*, 11, referencing Gaston Bachelard, *The Poetics of Space* (New York: Orion Press, 1964).

13. Ibid., 11.

14. Ibid., 18, 13.

15. Where Bakhtin sees the joyous and liberating aspect of the grotesque, Kayser views it as intellectually and emotionally disturbing. Friederich Schlegel, on the other hand, defines the grotesque as "the unstable mixture of heterogeneous elements, the explosive force of the paradoxical, which is both ridiculous and terrifying." Schlegel, *Athenäum,* fr. 389, cited by Kayser, *Grotesque in Art and Literature,* 53.

16. Kayser, *Grotesque in Art and Literature,* 183.

17. For a thorough overview of the European history of the term, and its development in England, see Barasch, *Grotesque.*

18. Harpham, *On the Grotesque,* xvi.

19. In quoting Kayser (*Grotesque in Art and Literature,* 184), I take his meaning out of context. However, his formulations capture particularly well the linguistic or rhetorical phenomena I discuss.

20. The art historian André Chastel uses the term "graphic play" in his description of "the style without a name": "[C'est] un monde vertical entièrement défini par le jeu graphique" ("[It's] a vertical world entirely defined by graphic play") (Chastel, *Grottesque,* 25). "Painter's dream" is the phrase that appears repeatedly in works from the sixteenth through the eighteenth centuries to describe the grotesque.

21. Harpham, *On the Grotesque,* 4: "'grotesque' is another word for nonthing."

22. Bakhtin, *Rabelais and His World,* 24.

23. See, e.g., Patrick Labarthe's extraordinary study *Baudelaire et la tradition de l'allégorie* (Geneva: Droz, 1999) and Walter Benjamin, *Charles Baudelaire: Un Poète lyrique à l'apogée du capitalisme,* trans. Jean Lacoste (Paris: Petite Bibliothèque Payot, 1974), esp. "Zentralpark: Fragments sur Baudelaire," 209–51. On the subject of allegory, its structure and its thematic associations, I am indebted to Angus Fletcher, *Allegory: The Theory of a Symbolic Mode* (Ithaca, N.Y.: Cornell University Press, 1964); Joel Fineman, "The Structure of Allegorical Desire," in *Allegory and Representation,* ed. Stephen Greenblatt (Baltimore: Johns Hopkins University Press, 1981), 26–60; Paul de Man, *Blindness and Insight,* 2d ed. (Minneapolis: University of Minnesota Press, 1983), 187–228; and Maureen Quilligan, *The Language of Allegory* (Ithaca, N.Y.: Cornell University Press, 1979).

24. César Chesnau Du Marsais, *Des tropes* (1818), reprint (Geneva: Slatkine, 1967), cited in Tzvetan Todorov, *Théories du symbole* (Paris: Seuil, 1977), 94; my translation.

25. Todorov, *Théories du symbole,* 94; my emphasis and translation.

26. De Man, *Blindness and Insight,* 207.

27. Nicolas Beauzée, "Allégorie," *Encyclopédie méthodique* (1782), 1: 123; cited in Todorov, *Théories du symbole,* 96.

28. See Richard Stamelman, *Lost Beyond Telling: Representations of Death and Absence in Modern French Poetry* (Ithaca, N.Y.: Cornell University Press, 1990), 49–69, and Fineman, "Structure of Allegorical Desire," for insightful accounts of allegory's futile search for the lost object that would supposedly render it whole.

29. McElroy, *Fiction of the Modern Grotesque,* 1, remarks that "in its colloquial usage, it can mean almost anything unseemly, disproportionate, or in bad taste" and can be applied to "everything from a necktie to a relationship."

30. The earliest commentaries on the grotesque in art refer to it as "l'ornement sans nom"; see Chastel, *Grottesque,* 12.

31. Baud., *OC,* 2: 535 ff.

32. Baudelaire sometimes makes laughter the only distinctive mark of the grotesque, writing, for example: "Il n'y a qu'une vérification du grotesque, c'est le rire, et le rire subit" ("There is only one verification of the grotesque, laughter, sudden laughter"), but we can legitimately say that there are other diagnostic signs of the grotesque in which laughter is lacking, which may be the meaning of Baudelaire's statement: "Le rire n'est qu'une expression, un symptôme, un diagnostic" ("Laughter is only one expression, one symptom, one diagnostic sign") (*OC,* 2: 536, 534). Moreover, as J. A. Hiddleston demonstrates in *Baudelaire and the Art of Memory* (Oxford: Clarendon Press, 1999), 101–33, laughter is not the ultimate subject of "De l'essence du rire," despite its title. Of course, although there is a link between laughter and the surprise or shock so important in Baudelaire's aesthetic theory, one may have the surprise or shock without having the laughter itself, as Walter Benjamin points out in *The Arcades Project,* trans. Howard Eiland and Kevin McLaughlin (Cambridge, Mass.: Harvard University Press, Belknap Press, 1999), 325 (J53a, 4) and 383 (J90, 2).

33. According to the *Petit Robert,* the word "fetish" (from the Latin *facticius*— by way of the Portuguese *feitiço*—made by art, artificial, skillfully contrived) has been in use in French since 1669, well before psychoanalysis gave it the meaning by which we generally know it today. Although originally it designated, in the words of the *Oxford English Dictionary,* "any of the objects used by the negroes of the Guinea coast and neighboring regions as amulets or means of enchantment, or regarded by them with superstitious dread," "fetish" came to be used in the wider sense of "an inanimate object worshipped . . . on account of its supposed inherent magical powers, or as being animated by a spirit; [or] figuratively, something irrationally reverenced."

34. Walter Benjamin argues similarly that "[i]f the church had not been able . . . to banish the gods from the memory of the faithful, allegorical language would never have come into being." Yet allegory also preserves the pagan world: "the words and the names [of the Olympian gods] remain behind [in the Christian world], and, as the living contexts of their birth disappear, so they become the

origins of concepts, in which these words acquire a new content, which is predisposed to allegorical representation; such is the case with Fortuna, Venus (as Dame World) and so on. The deadness of the figures and the abstraction of the concepts are therefore the precondition for the allegorical metamorphosis of the pantheon into a world of magical, conceptual creatures." Benjamin, *The Origin of German Tragic Drama,* trans. John Osborne (London: NLB, 1977), 223; 225–26.

35. John W. MacInnes picks up on this idea when he relates Pierrot to the thyrsus, "that jubilant object that figures for Baudelaire [in his prose poem "Le Thyrse"] the very figurality of writing." MacInnes, *The Comical as Textual Practice in Les Fleurs du Mal* (Gainesville: University Press of Florida, 1988), 45. Other comparisons might be the carriages that Constantin Guys paints or the complex lines in space drawn by the mast and rigging of a sailing ship, cited by de Man, *Blindness and Insight,* 142–65.

36. No doubt, as J. A. Hiddleston remarks, laughter is not the only nor always the most appropriate response to the grotesque, as outlined by Baudelaire. Baudelaire observes, however, that "le rire causé par le grotesque a en soi quelque chose de profond, d'axiomatique et de primitif qui se rapproche beaucoup plus de la vie innocente et de la joie absolue que le rire causé par le comique de moeurs" ("the laughter caused by the grotesque contains something profound, axiomatic and primitive that comes much closer to innocent life and absolute joy than the laughter caused by the comic of manners"). By virtue of its spontaneity and its proximity to a fundamental law (of language), the grotesque is "innocent." It is not an intentional phenomenon, the effect of a social or individual will, and in this sense it precedes and eludes moral judgment. Hiddleston, *Baudelaire and the Art of Memory*; Baud., *OC,* 2: 535.

37. Stamelman, *Lost Beyond Telling,* 63–64.

38. A third example in "De l'essence du rire," a synopsis of E. T. A. Hoffmann's story *Daucus Carota,* also ties impotence to the grotesque. In Baudelaire's retelling of the story, allegory is conceived from two diametrically opposite points of view: it is either a charming, childish dream that makes us forget the isolation and routine of life or a dangerous and evil illusion that must be eradicated. Baudelaire's summary of the plot emphasizes the negative analysis of the dreamer's father and his radical intervention, which destroys the child's illusion. The father's violent action, carried out in the name of reason and truth but in opposition to the dreamer's wishes, raises again the specter of the dreamer/poet's "castration."

39. *OC,* 2: 536.

40. Friedrich Schlegel, *Atheneum,* XVIII, IV.666, quoted in French in Todorov, *Théories du symbole,* 230; my translation.

41. My reading of "Le Masque" is informed by the brilliant analysis of Richard Stamelman in "L'Anamorphose baudelairienne: L'Allégorie du 'Masque,'" *Cahiers de l'Association internationale des études françaises* 41 (1989): 251–67.

42. Fletcher, *Allegory,* 18.

43. It is also possible that the main speaker and his companion (whom he alternately exhorts in the first person plural and addresses as "tu") represent an internal dialogue within the "poet," in which case they would be just as inseparable as the two faces of the single statue.

44. Stamelman calls allegory "a mask behind which innumerable signifying faces are hidden, and from which erupts at every moment the deforming reality of alterity. By multiplying the meaning through an indefinite proliferation of signifiers, allegory becomes a decentered writing." ("Anamorphose," 265; all translations of this essay are mine). See also Nathaniel Wing's comments on the poem in *The Limits of Narrative* (Cambridge: Cambridge University Press, 1986), 8–18.

45. Giglio Fava, the hero of Hoffmann's *Princess Brambilla,* another illustration in "De l'essence du rire," also brings out this paradoxical structure. The example once again underscores the relationship of the singular and the plural within a single figure and suggests the unstoppable whirligig that is allegory: "Ce personnage *un* change de temps en temps de personnalité, et, sous le nom de Giglio Fava, il se déclare l'ennemi du prince assyrien Cornelio Chiapperi; et quand il est prince assyrien, il déverse le plus profond et le plus royal mépris . . . sur un misérable histrion qui s'appelle, à ce qu'on dit, Giglio Fava" ("This *indivisible* character changes personality from time to time, and, under the name of Giglio Fava, he is the sworn enemy of the Assyrian prince Cornelio Chiapperi; and when he is the Assyrian prince, he heaps the most profound and royal scorn . . . on a miserable two-bit actor whose name is, so they say, Giglio Fava") (*OC,* 2: 542; my translation). Although this peculiar behavior might be an extension of the role-playing associated with an actor such as Fava, the boundary between life and art in this case is transgressed so thoroughly that the two worlds merge and become indistinct. Giglio Fava and Cornelio Chiapperi insult each other in a way that actor and character do not; the "actor" and the "role" he intermittently incarnates exist in the same register, and there is never any question of an ontological difference between them. What makes the story fantastic or marvelous is precisely the lack of a distinction between truth and illusion, original and copy. The "chronic dualism" of Giglio Fava escapes hierarchical ordering. See de Man, *Blindness and Insight,* 217–18.

46. Stamelman, "Anamorphose," 260, 265. Wing remarks in a similar vein in *Limits of Narrative,* 3–4, that in "Le Cygne," "Les Sept Vieillards," and "Le Tonneau de la haine," "allegory momentarily effects a recuperation of sense, hidden and controlled by the figural system, only to be caught in a vertiginous and virtually limitless multiplication of meaning in an open displacement. . . . there is an irresistible imperative to contain meaning, to fill the figure with its own sense, yet meaning always exceeds the limits of containment."

47. Calling the painted grotesque "graphic play," Chastel, *Grottesque,* 25, sets up, perhaps unintentionally, a parallel with the linguistic play outlined by Jacques Derrida in "Structure, Sign and Play in the Human Sciences," in *The Languages of Criticism and the Sciences of Man: The Structuralist Controversy,* ed. Richard Mack-

sey and Eugenio Donato (Baltimore: Johns Hopkins University Press, 1969), 247–265; id., *Of Grammatology,* trans. Gayatri Chakravorty Spivak (Baltimore: Johns Hopkins University Press, 1998); *Writing and Difference,* trans. Alan Bass (London: Routledge & Kegan Paul, 1978); and other essays. This is more systemic and more far-reaching than the "wordplay" that Maureen Quilligan terms "the basic mechanism of allegory," although not totally unrelated to it (*Language of Allegory,* 34).

48. As Stamelman, "Anamorphose," 265, states: "Allegory always takes aim at an image or a figure, lost or absent, existing beyond the horizon of writing. Discourse never can catch hold of it because it is only allegory's mask. Meaning is always elsewhere."

49. *OC,* 2: 540. Baudelaire clearly gives full weight to the term *merveilleux,* for he later reiterates the importance of the mimes' "oeuvre fantastique . . . sur la frontière du merveilleux" ("fantastic work . . . on the edge of the marvelous"). His reference to the marvelous functions as a reminder of the rococo, and his choice of the commedia dell'arte as an example recalls the Regency of Philippe d'Orleans, when Italian comedy was the favorite entertainment of Parisian high society. By choosing a contemporary production that is overtly indebted to eighteenth-century aesthetics, Baudelaire simultaneously evokes the history of the grotesque and its relevance to his theory of modernity.

50. Baud., *OC,* 2: 540: "[Une fée] promène avec un geste mystérieux et plein d'autorité sa baguette dans les airs. . . . Aussitôt le vertige est entré, le vertige circule dans l'air; on respire le vertige; c'est le vertige qui remplit les poumons et renouvelle le sang dans le ventricule" ("[A fairy] moves her wand through the air with a mysterious and authoritative gesture. . . . At once vertigo enters, vertigo circulates through the air; you breathe in vertigo; it's vertigo that fills the lungs and renews the blood in the ventricles"). According to Michele Hannoosh, *Baudelaire and Caricature: From the Comic to an Art of Modernity* (University Park: Pennsylvania State University Press, 1992), 47–63, who consulted the original scenario for this performance, the fairy was a scripted part and Baudelaire was accurately recounting what he had seen; but this in no way alters the allegorical implications of the example.

51. Baudelaire was eager to "create" a cliché (*poncif*), which he took to be the soul of genius. In his private journal, he wrote this note to himself: "Créer un poncif, c'est le génie. Je dois créer un poncif. Le concetto est un chef-d'oeuvre" ("Creating a cliché is genius. I must create a cliché. The *concetto* [conceit] is a masterpiece") ("Fusées," XIII, in *OC,* 1: 662). And he praises the beauty of the commonplace, even in prose: "Sois toujours poète, même en prose. Grand style (rien de plus beau que le lieu commun)" ("Hygiène," III, in *OC,* 1: 670). For him, the commonplace ("le lieu commun") was "le lieu de rencontre de la foule, le rendezvous public de l'éloquence" ("the meeting place of the crowd, the public rendezvous of eloquence") (*OC,* 2: 79).

52. "Rousseau" is a concrete manifestation of what Benjamin calls "rememoration": "the key figure of late allegory is 'rememoration' [. . . that is,] the metamor-

phosis of merchandise into a collector's item." Benjamin, *Charles Baudelaire,* fr. 44, p. 250; my translation; see also fr. 32a: pp. 239–40.

53. Quilligan, *Language of Allegory,* 26.

Two   Rococo Rhetoric: Figures of the Past in "Le Poème du hachisch"

1. "From 1500 to 1700 more than fifteen works were written concerning opium and its marvelous effects. Interest in the drug increased noticeably from 1700 to 1800, as more than forty full length studies appeared concerning its effects and possible therapeutic uses. . . . After 1800 there is, on the average, more than one full length study a year. For the most part these works concern only the medical aspects of the drug. . . . Hashish, on the other hand, was rarely mentioned and there are few studies on it before 1800," according to Emanuel J. Mickel Jr., *The Artificial Paradises in French Literature* (Chapel Hill: University of North Carolina Press, 1969), 58. Apparently, the marquis des Alleurs gave Mme du Deffand some expert advice about how to smoke opium, and Turkish pipes were quite common in France in the eighteenth century, but Mickel (59) does not in any way suggest that recreational smoking of opium was prevalent in the eighteenth century. In this regard, the nineteenth century was distinct.

2. "Le Poème du hachisch," pt. 1 of Charles Baudelaire, *Les Paradis artificiels,* in *OC,* 1: 399–441. The anecdote I have paraphrased here is recounted in the middle chapter of the "Poème," "Le Théâtre du Séraphin," 421–26. There are at least two translations of this work, that of Arthur Symons, in Charles Baudelaire, *Les Fleurs du mal, Petits Poèmes en prose, Les Paradis artificiels* (London: Casanova Society, 1925), 241–88, and "The Poem of Hashish," in *My Heart Laid Bare, and Other Prose Writings,* trans. Norman Cameron, ed. Peter Quennell (London: G. Weidenfeld & Nicolson, 1950), 75–123. However, all translations of the "Poème" in this book are my own.

3. As Baudelaire readily admits, only the "Poème" is his creation; the second part of the *Paradis artificiels* is an abridged translation of Thomas de Quincey's *Confessions of an English Opium-Eater* (1822), into which Baudelaire occasionally inserts some personal reflections (*OC,* 1: 519).

4. Richard Sieburth, "Gaspard de la Nuit: Prefacing Genre," *Studies in Romanticism* 24 (Summer 1985): 246.

5. One of the verse poems in Baudelaire's *Les Fleurs du mal,* "Spleen" ("J'ai plus de souvenirs. . ."), contains a similar but much less elaborate reference to this aesthetic in its description of the "vieux boudoir plein de roses fanées, / Où gît tout un fouillis de modes surannées, / Où les pastels plaintifs et les pâles Boucher, / Seuls, respirent l'odeur d'un flacon débouché" ("the old boudoir full of faded roses, / Where a whole pile of outdated fashions lies dead, / Where the plaintive pastels and the pale paintings of Boucher, / Alone, breathe in the odor of an uncorked perfume bottle").

6. There have been a few studies relating Baudelaire and the baroque, in par-

ticular Walter Benjamin's *Charles Baudelaire* and Christine Buci-Glucksmann's *La Raison baroque: De Baudelaire à Benjamin* (Paris: Galilée, 1984), as well as a smattering of articles and books on Baudelaire's relation to Rousseau, but they make up only a small fraction of the scholarship on Baudelaire to date.

7. In *Blindness and Insight*, 190, de Man calls the rococo "decorative allegorism." Vernon Hyde Minor explains: "The term Rococo also was used at first with some distaste, and the study of that period still remains mired in controversy and prejudice. . . . Like the Baroque, the Rococo [with its 'incongruous combinations, bristling surfaces, profuse ornament, strange or broken curves or lines'] is deviant—perhaps demented. Nineteenth-century critics have also commented on an old-fashioned quality to Rococo, perhaps because it was associated with the taste of the *ancien régime* in France (before the Revolution). The period—and the style—still appears to many as archaic and strange." *Baroque and Rococo* (New York: Harry N. Abrams, 1999), 14.

8. Paul de Man's famous article, "The Rhetoric of Temporality," first published in 1969, and reprinted in *Blindness and Insight*, is largely responsible for this now-standard interpretation.

9. Hoffmann took the idea and many of the images for his novella *Princess Brambilla* from the grotesque drawings of the seventeenth-century French artist Jacques Callot. Théophile Gautier, one of Baudelaire's mentors, uses rococo backdrops in his stories "Omphale: Histoire rococo" and "La Cafetière." Both stories actually blur the distinction between decorative setting and narrative action, when an element of the rococo decor, a painting or tapestry, comes to life and invades the present space and time of the protagonist. For a fascinating discussion of ornament in Gautier's stories, see Rae Beth Gordon, *Ornament, Fantasy, and Desire in Nineteenth-Century French Literature* (Princeton, N.J.: Princeton University Press, 1992), chs. 3 and 4.

10. Baud., *OC,* 2: 533.

11. Baudelaire is speaking specifically of the arrival of the troop of Carrots at the farm in *Daucus Carota,* but he similarly declares that Hoffmann's most supernatural stories "ressemblent souvent à des *visions* de l'ivresse" ("often resemble intoxicated *visions*") (*OC,* 2: 541, 542, my emphasis).

12. "The ornaments we call *grottesques* in painting, we also call *arabesques*" ("Grottesques," in C.-H. Watelet and P.-C. Lévesque's *Dictionnaire des arts de peinture, sculpture et gravure* [Paris: Prault, 1792], 1: 630; all translations of this text here are mine). Although *grottesque* was the original name for the style, *arabesque* and *grotesque* were interchangeable terms well before the eighteenth century. The semantic confusion stems from the discovery of the arabesques in the cavelike ruins, or "grotte," of Rome and Pompeii. *Grotesque* therefore names the style with reference to its point of origin. See Bruno Pons, "Arabesques ou nouvelles grotesques," in *L'Art décoratif en Europe: Classique et baroque,* ed. Alain Gruber (Paris: Citadelles & Mazenod, 1992), 161–62. There is some disagreement about the history of the genre. Although Antoine Furetière's *Dictionnaire universel* (2d ed., rev.,

The Hague: Leers, 1702) and Diderot et al.'s *Encyclopédie* both relate the arabesque to Moorish ornament (the *Encyclopédie*'s rubric is "Arabesque ou Moresque, s. m. ouvrage de peinture ou de sculpture"), this derivation is regularly set aside in histories of the genre, which trace the arabesque in France to its Roman roots. And whereas Pons sees the genre continuing into the nineteenth century (without offering any evidence for this view), Chastel (*Grottesque,* 82) believes that the arabesque per se died out in the late eighteenth century, to be replaced by caricature, the free-spirited genre that proliferated in the French press in the nineteenth century.

13. "Between the arabesques of the Renaissance and those of neoclassicism, other arabesques take their place, and from the seventeenth century until the first third of the eighteenth especially, they renewed the genre. [The] arabesques of Jean Berain and of Antoine Watteau more or less constitute the generic model of these 'new arabesques,'" Pons says ("Arabesques ou nouvelles grotesques," 159; all translations of Pons here are mine). Pons (176) also believes that it was no coincidence that the arabesque flourished during the Regency (1715–23): "It is not immaterial to note that the Regency, with its tendency to derisiveness [*la dérision*] and its passion for freedom, is the moment when the arabesque flourished in France."

14. Vitruvius quoted in ibid., 159. For a rather different translation of this passage, see Vitruvius, *On Architecture,* ed. and trans. Frank Granger (London: Heinemann; New York: Putnam, 1931–34), 2: 105. Pons argues that the new arabesques no longer referred back to antiquity, but took Raphael and Renaissance Italian ornamentalists as their models. Much depends, however, on which artist's work one chooses as an example of the new arabesques. Jean Berain, the artist whose experiments with the genre constitute the pivot between old and new styles, incorporates many elements of the old "grottesque" into his designs; and we continue to find the defiance of gravity, the admixture of surreal and real elements, and the trellises, consoles, and chimeras of the old style even in Watteau's new arabesques. See Pons, "Arabesques ou nouvelles grotesques," 166 and 168, for an account of the transition between the older grotesque style and the "nouvelles arabesques."

15. Chastel, *Grottesque,* 12.

16. Ibid., 25.

17. Kayser, *Grotesque in Art and Literature,* 22.

18. "But the essential aspect of the reform lies in the thematic unification of any panel of grotesques: one program—the seasons, the gods, the arts . . . must tie together all the elements," Chastel explains. "Fillets made up of leaflike scrolls [*filets rinceaux*], platforms [*étages*] are the paradoxical supports of a coherent imagery; the crazy, disordered expansion has come to an end—at least in appearance" (*Grottesque,* 65; all translations of Chastel in this book are mine).

19. Chastel, *Grottesque,* 49–52.

20. Pons, "Arabesques ou nouvelles grotesques," 174; and see 176: "the arabesques seem essentially tied to changes in one's condition or state of being [*des changements d'état*]."

21. Ibid., 174. Watelet and Lévesque's *Dictionnaire* (92–93) confirms this relationship to metamorphosis and pagan mythology: "Does the painter of arabesques have in mind to distance himself from nature in order to enrich and characterize his compositions? He immediately recalls to memory the ingenious metamorphoses sung by the poets. He reproduces their sirens, their sphinxes, their dryades, the fauns, the genies, and those celestial children, who, flying about, caress and wound mortals according to their whim. These educated artists also people their compositions with chimerical or real animals; they recall the bizarre cults that have sometimes been established around them, as well as around the divinities who are so celebrated by all the arts; and near statues of Diana, of Venus, of Flora, or of Hebe, they suspend garlands, crowns, musical instruments and trophies; they erect altars, tripods bearing little dishes, from which perfumed smoke emanates."

22. For the political and social contexts in which the rococo evolved, see Thomas Crow, *Painters and Public Life in Eighteenth-Century Paris* (New Haven, Conn.: Yale University Press, 1985), and Katie Scott, *The Rococo Interior* (New Haven, Conn.: Yale University Press, 1995).

23. Pons, "Arabesques ou nouvelles grotesques," 174.

24. Watelet and Lévesque, *Dictionnaire,* 90–91. This reference to opium sheds new light on the illustration of the man smoking; is it possible, in fact, that eighteenth-century arabesques of men or monkeys smoking refer to drugs? In that case, the art of the time would be ahead of the literature in acknowledging recreational drug use.

25. "Another of the favorite themes . . . is that of madness. The arabesque is associated rather naturally with dreams, an ensemble of strange apparitions and fleeting impressions that are difficult to truly memorize, the apparent logic at the moment of perception taking a burlesque turn when one tries to understand them" (Pons, "Arabesques ou nouvelles grotesques," 176). As we shall see, this comic logic or lack of logic is equally characteristic of the drug experiences that Baudelaire describes in the "Poème du hachisch."

26. In his article on the "Grotesque" for the *Encyclopédie,* Watelet willingly allowed the grotesque to have a place in art, as an enjoyable respite from more serious pursuits, but he no longer welcomed it in 1792. If he had once believed that it was possible to contain the grotesque, to relegate it to an "ornamental" role, a few decades later, he had apparently learned to distrust the grotesque as a style capable of "infinite" permutations that kept transgressing its bounds: "He who looks at an object lacking any support, a weight that does not appear sufficiently upheld, an assemblage of unbalanced parts, feels an uneasy and painful sensation" (Watelet and Lévesque, *Dictionnaire,* 94). And Kayser, *Grotesque in Art and Literature,* 21, observes: "By the word *grottesco* the Renaissance . . . understood not only something playfully gay and carelessly fantastic, but also something ominous and sinister in the face of a world totally different from the familiar one."

27. Kayser, *Grotesque in Art and Literature,* 18, 59.

28. Baud., *OC*, 1: 441: "un jardin de vraie beauté," "le seul miracle dont Dieu nous ait octroyé la licence!"

29. Paradise is "cet état charmant et singulier, où toutes les forces s'équilibrent, où l'imagination, quoique merveilleusement puissante, n'entraîne pas à sa suite le sens moral dans de périlleuses aventures, où une sensibilité exquise n'est plus torturée par des nerfs malades" ("that charming and singular state, where all the forces balance each other, where the imagination, although marvelously powerful, does not drag the moral sense into perilous adventures, where an exquisite sensitivity is no longer tortured by diseased nerves") (*OC*, 1: 402).

30. In addition to presenting the opposition, the first chapter anticipates the last ("Morale"), by noting the "chastisements" and "immorality" attendant on the use of drugs.

31. "On dit que l'enthousiasme des poètes et des créateurs ressemble à ce que j'ai éprouvé . . .; mais si le délire poétique ressemble à celui que m'a procuré une petite cuillerée de confiture, je pense que les plaisirs du public coûtent bien cher aux poètes" ("They say that the enthusiasm of poets and creators resembles what I experienced . . . ; but if poetic delirium resembles the delirium that a little teaspoon of [hashish] jam produced in me, I think that the public's pleasures cost poets dearly") (Baud., *OC*, 1: 424). The anecdote illustrates the free play of imagination, which authorizes the analogy between intoxication and poetic creation, according to Claude Pichois (see, e.g., his "Notice" in ibid., 1365); and the narrator's presentation of the story reinforces this analogy between the poet's creative enthusiasm and the woman's experience of being high by making it clear that she has arranged her experience into a very poetic narrative for a female friend's consumption. The woman is a kind of poet in her own right. But I submit that her story (and its contextualization) supports the analogy of the woman and the reader even more.

32. In his article, "Baudelaire et le théâtre d'ombres," in *Le Lieu et la formule: Hommage à Marc Eigeldinger* (Neuchâtel: La Baconnière, 1978), Michel Jeanneret explains that the Théâtre du Séraphin, named after its creator, the director Séraphin, in 1776, very quickly acquired great popularity among the people, and especially the children of Paris, which it retained throughout the nineteenth century. It was famous for its puppet shows and magic lantern performances and other illusionist presentations. The theater had been through some ups and downs, but it was in vogue in 1858, the year "Le Poème du hachisch" appeared, when it moved from the Palais-Royal to the boulevard Montmartre (124).

33. The way Baudelaire frames the grotesque in the "Poème" recalls the way he reframed Poe's tale "The Oval Portrait" in "Un Fantôme." See Mary Ann Caws, "Insertion in an Oval Frame: Poe Circumscribed by Baudelaire," in *Charles Baudelaire*, ed. Harold Bloom (New York: Chelsea House, 1987), 101–23.

34. In the nine paragraphs that make up chapter 2 ("Qu'est-ce que le hachisch?"), Egypt, Algeria, and "l'Arabie Heureuse" are all named individually at

least twice, and three times they are collapsed into the collective "les Arabes": "comme si les Arabes avaient voulu définir en un mot l'*herbe*"; "L'*extrait gras* du hachisch, tel que le préparent les Arabes"; "les Arabes mettent l'extrait gras sous la forme de confitures" (Baud., *OC*, 1: 406).

35. See, e.g., Furetière's definition of "Arabesque, adj." in his *Dictionnaire universel*: "Which is made in the manner of the Arabs. The curious go to see the Palace of Granada, because of the *Arabesque* ornaments, which are marvelous. Paintings and ornaments where there are no human figures are called *Grotesque, Moresque*, and *Arabesque*" (my translation). It appears that Baudelaire was familiar with this definition, since he makes a similar statement about the title of Poe's *Tales of the Grotesque and Arabesque*: "titre remarquable et intentionnel, car les ornements grotesques et arabesques repoussent la figure humaine, et l'on verra qu'à beaucoup d'égards la littérature de Poe est extra ou suprahumaine" ("remarkable and deliberate title, for grotesque and arabesque ornaments shun the human figure, and we shall see that in many respects, the literature of Poe is extra- or superhuman") (Baud., *OC*, 2: 304).

36. Alexandra K. Wettlaufer, "Paradise Regained: The *Flâneur*, the *Badaud*, and the Aesthetics of Artistic Reception in *Le Poème du haschisch*," *Nineteenth-Century French Studies* 24 (Spring–Summer 1996): 388. Jeanneret ("Baudelaire et le théâtre d'ombres," 132–33; all translations of this text here are mine) puts it another way: "Two voices, in fact, overlap, one manifest, the other discreet, and the tension between them gives the text its ambiguity: a normative and patent discourse, which, in order to try the case against drugs, draws on an ethical and religious model; a subversive and latent discourse, which insinuates the charms of the fantasmatic vision and suggests its relationship with poetic creation. . . . And it's undoubtedly precisely because the attraction of the shadows is so powerful, because the mirror sends back such captivating reflections, that the normative discourse occupies so much space in *Le Poème du Hachisch*." Others who discuss the tensions within the "Poème" and the challenge they pose to readers include Hannoosh, *Baudelaire and Caricature*, esp. ch. 4, and Claire Lyu, "'High' Poetics: Baudelaire's *Le Poème du hachisch*," *MLN* 109 (1994): 698–740.

37. Although the "Poème" itself urges us to do this rereading in two consecutive moments, the double reading need not be spaced out over time. The two readings—literal and figural—can be carried out more or less simultaneously. That is, we may be aware of the coexistence of two levels of meaning at various points in the text, although it is impossible to expand upon them at the same time.

38. Curiously, Symons translates this passage as if the narrator were speaking, not directly *to* the reader in the text ("you"), but *about* him (e.g., "Here is the drug before his eyes") (Baudelaire, *Fleurs du mal* . . . , 254–55).

39. Baud., *OC*, 1: 411; my emphasis.

40. This analogy refutes the notion that the rococo should be understood as pure "decorative allegorism." If the story of the woman in the rococo boudoir is

"decorative," in the sense that it is an elaborate illustration, it nonetheless establishes poetry *as* decoration. The anecdote casts doubt on the common belief that surface aspects of a text are necessarily superficial or meaningless, and that rhetoric is always a deep structure. In the woman's fantasies, at least, ornament is nothing if not rhetoric, and the distinction between surface and depth is irrelevant. Baudelaire's work bears out Fletcher's observation in *Allegory,* 128, that "[t]he history of rhetoric shows a gradual generalization of the term *ornament,* until ornament includes all the figures of speech and all tropes."

41. In chapter 1 already, the narrator announces his method: he will choose "une âme, facile d'ailleurs à expliquer et à définir, comme type propre aux expériences de cette nature" ("a soul, easy to explain and to define, as the proper type for experiments of this nature").

42. Baud., *OC,* 1: 430.

43. Baudelaire even goes so far as to imagine that Fourier and Swedenborg are incarnated in the vegetable and animal designs of the rococo decor! "Fourier et Swedenborg, l'un avec ses analogies, l'autre avec ses correspondances, se sont *incarnés* dans le végétal et l'animal qui tombent sous votre regard, et au lieu d'enseigner par la voix, ils vous endoctrinent par la forme et par la couleur" ("Fourier and Swedenborg, the one with his analogies, the other with his correspondences, are *incarnated* in the vegetable and the animal that appear under your gaze, and instead of teaching orally, they indoctrinate you through the use of form and color") (*OC,* 1: 430; my emphasis). Baudelaire later calls attention to the role of personification in allegory when he says, "Il est facile de saisir le rapport qui existe entre les créations sataniques des poètes [les allégories] et les créatures vivantes qui se sont vouées aux excitants [les personnifications de l'allégorie]" ("It is easy to grasp the relationship that exists between the satanic creations of the poets [allegories] and the living creatures who have devoted themselves to stimulants [the personifications of allegory]") (*OC,* 1: 438).

44. For example, the woman in the rococo boudoir floats at the boundary between wakefulness and sleep, unable to say for sure whether she has actually slept or simply experienced a delicious insomnia.

45. For example, rereading the second chapter, the most apparently literal of all, we can find allegory even in the driest exposition of the botanical plant. The poet anticipates the development of the figure when he focuses on the (rhetorical) flowers of hashish: "c'est quand [le hachisch] est en fleur qu'il possède sa plus grande énergie; les sommités fleuries sont, par conséquent, les seules parties employées dans les différentes préparations dont nous avons à dire quelques mots" ("it's when [the hashish] is in flower that it possesses its greatest energy; the flowering tips are, consequently, the only parts employed in the different preparations about which we are going to say a few words").

46. See Ulrich Baer, *Remnants of Song: Trauma and the Experience of Modernity in Charles Baudelaire and Paul Celan* (Stanford, Calif.: Stanford University

Press, 2000), 76–81, for a pertinent discussion of figure/ground issues in "Le Peintre de la vie moderne."

47. Baudelaire, *The Parisian Prowler,* trans. Edward K. Kaplan (Athens: University of Georgia Press, 1989), 86. Translations of Baudelaire's prose poems are from this edition, unless otherwise indicated.

48. Kayser, *Grotesque in Art and Literature,* 187, expresses the risks inherent in the grotesque in similar terms: "the grotesque is a play with the absurd. It may begin in a gay and carefree manner. . . . But it may also carry the player away, deprive him of his freedom, and make him afraid of the ghosts which he so frivolously invoked."

49. Richard Klein, "Straight Lines and Arabesques: Metaphors of Metaphor," *Yale French Studies* 45 (1970): 68. For other insightful rhetorical readings of the poem, see Barbara Johnson, *Défigurations du langage poétique* (Paris: Flammarion, 1979), 62–65, and Suzanne Guerlac, *The Impersonal Sublime: Hugo, Baudelaire, Lautréamont* (Stanford, Calif.: Stanford University Press, 1990), 78–85. The threat of the poet's emasculation is embodied also by Pierrot, the star of the English mime troop, whom Baudelaire proposes as an example of the grotesque in "De l'essence du rire." See Chapter 1 above.

50. Although the last chapter speaks only about hashish, and not about allegory, the connection is signaled by the reference to "magic" and "witchcraft," two words that characterize allegory in the "Poème"—for instance in the description of grammar, coming to life under allegory's influence, as "la sorcellerie évocatoire" (Baud., *OC,* 1: 431).

51. Ibid.

52. "[M]an must not, on pain of decline and intellectual death, upset the primordial conditions of his existence and disrupt the equilibrium between his faculties and the environment in which they are destined to operate; in a word, he must not disrupt his destiny in order to replace it with a fatality of a different sort" ("[I]l est défendu à l'homme, sous peine de déchéance et de mort intellectuelle, de déranger les conditions primordiales de son existence et de rompre l'équilibre de ses facultés avec les milieux où elles sont destinées à se mouvoir, en un mot, de déranger son destin pour y substituer une fatalité d'un nouveau genre") (ibid., 438).

53. "La hideuse nature, dépouillée de son illumination de la veille, ressemble aux mélancoliques débris d'une fête." As Walter Benjamin says, "L'allégorie s'attache aux ruines" ("Allegory attaches itself to ruins") ("Zentralpark: Fragments sur Baudelaire," in *Charles Baudelaire,* fr. 13, p. 222; see also fr. 5, p. 215, and fr. 7, p. 216).

54. In the first three instances, the verb is in the third person, and either in the form of a question or an implied negation: "Se figure-t-on un Etat dont tous les citoyens s'enivreraient de hachisch?"; "En effet, il est difficile de se figurer le théoricien de la *volonté* . . . consentant à perdre une parcelle de cette précieuse *substance*"; "Se figure-t-on le sort affreux d'un homme dont l'imagination paralysée ne saurait plus fonctionner sans le secours du hachisch ou de l'opium?" But in the

fourth instance, the narrator-poet takes it up in his own name and produces the image in question: "*Je me figure* un homme (dirai-je un brahmane, un poète, ou un philosophe chrétien?)." The verb *se figurer* can only be translated by the English "to imagine," which makes these quotations impossible to render appropriately in this context.

55. Jeanneret, "Baudelaire et le théâtre d'ombres," 133–34; my emphasis.

56. Ibid., 134.

57. The poet refers to this artificial means of creation as "une espèce de machine à penser, un instrument fécond" ("a kind of thinking machine, a fertile instrument").

58. Hannoosh, *Baudelaire and Caricature,* 281, also views the "Poème" as ambiguous: "Baudelaire seems to undermine the morality of the work in the very act of affirming it. . . . The problem is especially evident in the final lines of the *Poème du Hashisch.*" But Hannoosh concludes, and I agree, that this tension is an example of comic art at its best, *le comique absolu:* "The irony signals not the falsity of the passage but its metaphoricity, just as in the essay on the comic. . . . More important, ironizing the metaphor makes the ending—and the work itself—an example of comic art in the best sense" (283).

59. On the other hand, Claude Pichois very appropriately remarks that "the ties that he [Baudelaire] has with Rousseau are much stronger than he wants to believe" (Baud., *OC,* 2: 1107, n. 2), and Melvin Zimmerman notes that the attraction Rousseau exerts over Baudelaire "is doubled and troubled by an even stronger repulsion. This dichotomy with regard to Rousseau is often unacknowledged, and we have the right to think that it sometimes operated without Baudelaire's awareness, or very nearly so." Zimmerman, *Visions du monde: Baudelaire et Cie* (Paris: A.-G. Nizet; Toronto: GREF, 1991), 8; my translation.

60. In the same essay, which was composed and published during the same few years as the "Poème du hachisch" and a number of the prose poems, Baudelaire wrote: "La poésie moderne tient à la fois de la peinture, de la musique, de la statuaire, de l'art arabesque, de la philosophie railleuse, de l'esprit analytique. . . . Aucuns y pourraient voir peut-être des symptômes de dépravation" ("Modern poetry derives at once from painting, music, sculpture, arabesque art, mocking philosophy, the analytical mind. . . . Some might see in it symptoms of depravity") (Baud., *OC,* 2: 167). In contrast to this admixture, Théodore de Banville represents for Baudelaire the classical ideal—"un retour très volontaire vers l'état paradisiaque" ("a very deliberate return to the state of paradise").

61. "[L]'art moderne a une tendance essentiellement démoniaque. Et il semble que cette part infernale de l'homme, que l'homme prend plaisir à s'expliquer à lui-même, augmente journellement, comme si le Diable s'amusait à la grossir par des procédés artificiels."

62. See Paul de Man, "Rhetoric of Temporality," in *Blindness and Insight,* 216: "the ironist invents a form of himself that is 'mad' but that does not know its own madness; he then proceeds to reflect on his madness thus objectified."

63. One indicator of Baudelaire's interest in Rousseau during this period is the number of times he mentions him in his letters, essays, and poems. In the period between 1838 and 1857 (as much as imprecise dating will allow us to judge), Rousseau's name comes up explicitly only five times; in contrast, Baudelaire mentions him in twelve different texts, and sometimes more than once in a text, in the next eight years (1857–63).

64. In *The Enlightenment Against the Baroque: Economics and Aesthetics in the Eighteenth Century* (Berkeley: University of California Press, 1992), 28, Rémy G. Saisselin succinctly states the centrality of Rousseau in this repudiation of the baroque: "This great change in French thought began about 1750, and its most eloquent spokesman, the most devastating and thorough critic of baroque society in its advanced state of luxury and hence corruption, was the citizen of Geneva, the capital of Protestantism, Jean-Jacques Rousseau. His eloquence was such as to raise the problem to a universal plane."

65. See, e.g., Letter 2.23, of *Julie; ou, La Nouvelle Héloïse,* the great satirical letter on the Paris Opéra. Rousseau's critique of the opera (or the grotesque) is discussed in Chapters 5 and 6 of this book.

66. See Rouss., *OC,* 5: 650.

67. Baud., *OC,* 1: 430.

68. De Man, "Rhetoric of Temporality," in *Blindness and Insight,* 205, suggests that Rousseau was not the only European author of the period between 1760 and 1800 to rediscover "an allegorical tradition beyond the sensualistic analogism of the eighteenth century." Nonetheless, by taking up Rousseau as his primary example, de Man implicitly credits Rousseau with a seminal role.

*Three   Identity Politics: "Rousseau" and "France" in the
Mid-Nineteenth Century*

1. At the end of the first chapter of the "Le Poème du hachisch," the narrator announces that he will choose "une âme, facile d'ailleurs à expliquer et à définir, comme *type* propre aux expériences de cette nature" ("a soul, one that is easy to explain and define, as the proper *type* for experiments of this sort") (Baud., *OC,* 1: 404; my emphasis).

2. See Baudelaire, *Petits Poëmes en prose,* ed. Kopp, 173, 419–22 ("Publications préoriginales"). Cf. Baud., *Corr.,* 2: 207.

3. Most critics who have commented on the discarded title agree that it points to Rousseau, but as in any search for sources, now and again a slight doubt creeps in. Kopp reports Jacques Crépet's belief that the title might recall another volume of prose poems, the now-forgotten *Livre du promeneur; ou, Les Mois et les jours* (Paris: Amyot, 1854) by Jules Le Fèvre-Deumier (1797–1857); or it might simply be a generic name, like "Le Rôdeur parisien." See Baudelaire, *Petits Poëmes en prose,* ed. Kopp, xlv, n. 47. For reasons that I hope to make clear, I cannot agree.

4. Baudelaire, *Petits Poëmes en prose,* ed. Kopp, 420.

5. Jean Starobinski, "Sur Rousseau et Baudelaire: Le Dédommagement et l'irréparable," in *Le Lieu et la formule: Hommage à Marc Eigeldinger* (Neuchâtel: La Baconnière, 1978), 53–54; my translation. Robert Kopp (Baudelaire, *Petits Poëmes en prose,* xlv) also dismisses the connection. Baudelaire undoubtedly chose the title, he says, "thinking of Rousseau, as an antiphrasis: the poet of the capital responding to the poet of the countryside." Marcel Gutwirth goes so far as to assert that the current tendency to compare the *Rêveries* and the prose poems is wrongheaded: "It is perilous to juxtapose [to Baudelaire's work] the Rêveries of that Jean-Jacques Rousseau for whom Baudelaire professed only execration. . . . Therefore it is entirely *a contrario* that people have sought recently to bring these two authors together." "A propos du 'Gâteau': Baudelaire, Rousseau et le recours à l'enfance," *Romanic Review* 80 (1989): 75.

6. Marc Eigeldinger, *Mythologie et intertextualité* (Geneva: Slatkine, 1987), 127–28, says: "It is a question of a religious and ethical conflict that, by its unresolvability, helps to legitimate Baudelaire's hostility, his tendency to consider Rousseau the author of an erroneous and pernicious system. Nonetheless, it was certainly with reference to Rousseau that Baudelaire planned to entitle his future *Spleen de Paris Le Promeneur solitaire,* and that he set the title aside as an homage deemed illegitimate" (my translation).

7. Richard Terdiman, *Present Past: Modernity and the Memory Crisis* (Ithaca, N.Y.: Cornell University Press, 1993), 3, 6.

8. Pierre Nora, "Between Memory and History: *Les Lieux de mémoire,*" *Representations* 26 (Spring 1989): 8.

9. Ibid., 10.

10. Raymond Trousson, *Défenseurs et adversaires de J.-J. Rousseau: D'Isabelle de Charrière à Charles Maurras* (Paris: Honoré Champion, 1995), 238; my translation.

11. V. N. Volosinov, *Marxism and the Philosophy of Language,* trans. Ladislav Matejka and I. R. Titunik (New York: Seminar Press, 1973; Cambridge, Mass.: Harvard University Press, 1986), 23. Although we could say with equal justification that "Rousseau" was a "lieu de mémoire," the emphasis in these pages falls on the dispute that raged around the name, the tendentious process of "codify[ing], condens[ing] and anchor[ing] France's national memory," rather than its outcome (Nora, "Between Memory and History," 25 n).

12. I submit that when Baudelaire wrote Rousseau's name—"De Jean-Jacques—auteur sentimental et infâme" ("About Jean-Jacques—sentimental and loathsome author")—on a list of topics he wanted to address under the enigmatic title "De quelques préjugés contemporains," he acknowledged his awareness of "Rousseau"'s important ideological status (Baud., *OC,* 2: 54). Pichois believes that this list (the date of which is uncertain) testifies to Baudelaire's abandonment of the principles that nourished the Revolution of 1848. He also argues that Baudelaire's mention of Rousseau is his "first stand, as brutal as it is unjust, with regard

to Rousseau. By this condemnation, it seems, Baudelaire liquidates a part of his socialist past. But the ties he has to Rousseau are much stronger than he wants to believe" (ibid., 1107 n. 2). Although the phrase certainly appears to be a vitriolic attack on Rousseau, the heading that precedes it leaves the interpretation of this statement wide open. It is impossible to know whether Baudelaire meant this characterization of Rousseau as a wrong received idea to be refuted or as a popular truth to be upheld. The most we can say is that when Baudelaire thought of contemporary biases—or clichés—he thought of "Rousseau."

13. See Ross Chambers, *The Writing of Melancholy: Modes of Opposition in Early French Modernism,* trans. Mary Seidman Trouille (Chicago: Chicago University Press, 1993), 7–13, and Terdiman, *Discourse/Counter-discourse: The Theory and Practice of Symbolic Resistance in Nineteenth-Century France* (Ithaca, N.Y.: Cornell University Press, 1985), 342: "the counter-discourse emerges as [modernity's] crucially repressed secret, as the alternative whose exclusion defines the apparent stability of the social formation itself."

14. Linda Orr, *Headless History: Nineteenth-Century French Historiography of the Revolution* (Ithaca, N.Y.: Cornell University Press, 1990), 18.

15. Nora, "Between Memory and History," 11.

16. The careers of Michelet and Nisard, both eminent teachers and scholars, follow symmetrically opposite courses between the mid-1840s and the end of their lives. Born eight years apart, Michelet and his younger colleague were rising stars at about the same time, and they saw their careers sidetracked or propelled by the same political events. Both began their teaching at the Ecole normale, and both quickly rose to positions of prominence in the field of education.

Already chef de section at the Archives nationales, Michelet was named to the chair of "histoire et morale" at the Collège de France in 1838, where his (and Quinet's) popular lectures on Voltaire and Rousseau created a scandal in 1844 and caused the Catholic clergy to protest their teaching. The polemical character of Michelet's course at the Collège de France and his great popularity with the students prompted the government of Louis-Philippe to order an indefinite suspension of the course in January 1848, but Michelet fought back by publishing the lectures he was unable to teach, including two (dated Jan. 17 and Feb. 3) dealing with Rousseau. The course was reinstated by the provisional government that proclaimed the Second Republic on February 24, and Michelet was able to finish his year. Later, under the presidency of Louis-Napoléon, Michelet was again suspended from all teaching responsibilities; and in 1852, having refused to support the new imperial regime, he was expelled from the Archives de France and went into semi-exile. Lionel Gossman, *Between History and Literature* (Cambridge, Mass.: Harvard University Press, 1990), 166, calls this one of "the most visible episodes in an important process by which the teaching of history was transformed in the course of the nineteenth century."

Nisard, meanwhile, made his way up the ranks of the educational administra-

tion within the government of Louis-Philippe. He became a conservative deputy in 1842 and remained in the Assembly until the events of 1848. Like Michelet, he wrote and published actively during this entire period, making his name first with a controversial essay condemning "la littérature facile" and following up with a *Précis de l'histoire de la littérature française* (1840) and a collaborative edition of classical Latin texts, the multivolume *Collection des auteurs latins* (1838–50) that bears his name. Nisard was hostile to the republic and suffered as a result in 1848, losing his government jobs and his seat in the Assembly. The publication of his *Histoire de la littérature française* was broken off. However, his career was not disrupted for long. He became a member of the Académie française in 1850, was named Inspecteur général de l'enseignement and played a large role in the reorganization of the curriculum at the Ecole normale, and finally took over the chair of French eloquence at the Faculté des Lettres from Villemain. "Michelet, Jules" and "Nisard, Désiré," in Robert Laffont and Valentino Bompiani, eds., *Dictionnaire biographique des auteurs de tous les temps et de tous les pays* (Paris: S.E.D.E., 1957–58).

17. Jules Michelet, *Histoire de la Révolution française* (Paris: Gallimard, 1952), 1: 1; all translations of this text here are mine.

18. Ibid., 3.

19. Ibid., 52.

20. Ibid., 57.

21. Ibid., 59.

22. Désiré Nisard, *Histoire de la littérature française* (Paris: Firmin Didot, 1844–61), 1: v (Préface de la première édition). All the translations of Nisard in this book are mine.

23. Ibid., 40: Nisard adopts the list of authors that French readers themselves preferred, leaving the "dead" for dead and extolling only the survivors. Ibid., 9.

24. Ibid., 13; 10–11. Cf. 4: 451 and 497.

25. Ibid., 4: v; vi.

26. Ibid., 1: 26; 2: 44 ff.

27. Ibid., 4: 477; 555; 453; 441 and 443; 465; 454.

28. Ibid., 498; cf. 496.

29. Raymond Trousson, *Rousseau et sa fortune littéraire* (Bordeaux: Ducros, 1971), 72; my translation. Despite the rampant hostility toward this "mauvais génie" throughout the first half of the nineteenth century, as many as twenty-five editions of Rousseau's works appeared in print between 1817 and 1846 (ibid., 84).

30. See lessons 7 and 8 of Michelet's *L'Etudiant* (Paris: Seuil, 1970), the hastily published transcripts of the lectures he was prevented from giving at the Collège de France.

31. "June 1848 and the aftermath of the counterrevolution shattered [the] idealized image of a 'free market' of ideas" (Terdiman, *Discourse/Counter-discourse*, 71). Writers expressed their opposition to the dominant discourse only while there was a belief in the authentic competition for control of the structure of events.

Following the revolution of 1848 and the coup d'état in December 1851, the struggle between the dominant discourse and dissident discourses to determine "the system of meaning by which the social formation is reproduced" went underground (ibid., 339).

32. See Jean Garrigues, *La France de 1848 à 1870* (Paris: Armand Colin, 1995), 156–60. For general historical background on political currents and events in mid-century, I have also consulted F. W. J. Hemmings, *Culture and Society in France, 1789–1848* (Leicester, Eng.: Leicester University Press, 1987), and Theodore Zeldin, *France, 1848–1945* (Oxford: Clarendon Press, 1973), vol. 1. In 1861, Sainte-Beuve makes the curious claim that no one cares anymore about "Rousseau." He begins his *Causerie* of Monday, July 15, 1861—a review of the *Correspondance de Voltaire* and Georges Streckeisen-Moultou's *Oeuvres et correspondance inédites de J.-J. Rousseau*—with this observation: "Again a little Voltaire, again a little Rousseau! There was a time when this announcement alone would have stirred up emotions in the public, divided into a double row of enthusiastic admirers. Today this public is dissolved, and we have had our fill." Sainte-Beuve, *Causeries du lundi,* 4th ed. (Paris: Garnier frères, n.d), 15: 219; all translations of this text here are mine. His statement was either wishful thinking or perhaps a modest attempt to quiet the republican winds that were ruffling tempers around him, for in the intellectual milieux to which Sainte-Beuve and Baudelaire were primarily attuned, Rousseau continued to elicit strong emotions.

33. For the political ins and outs of the time as they may have affected Baudelaire's sympathies, see Richard D. E. Burton, *Baudelaire and the Second Republic: Writing and Revolution* (Oxford: Clarendon Press, 1991).

34. Baud., *Corr.* 1: 188, letter to Narcisse Ancelle, Mar. 5, 1852: "LE 2 DÉCEMBRE m'a *physiquement dépolitiqué.*"

35. Ibid., 578–79, letter to [Félix Tournachon, *dit*] Nadar, May 1859. In this same letter (579), Baudelaire also extols Jules Favre's "admirable discourse" to the legislative body, in which Favre "a posé nettement la nécessité, la fatalité révolutionnaires" ("clearly pointed to the absolute necessity of revolution").

36. Ibid., 2: 220, letter to Sainte-Beuve, January 1862; see my subsequent discussion of this correspondance. In *Baudelaire and the Second Republic,* Burton refers to "the 'Utopian' ethical theory that underpins the Salon [of 1846]" as "essentially a Rousseauistic belief in the intrinsic goodness of man and nature" (51), and he agrees with F. W. Leakey that throughout the 1840s, "Baudelaire's thinking was dominated by a 'Utopian' view of nature as beneficent and of man as intrinsically good" (52). But, Burton argues, this view could not "permanently suppress and conceal—and still less could it explain—the underside of nature which, with truly explosive force, intermittently imposes itself on Baudelaire's consciousness" (52). This pessimism drove Baudelaire's reactionary attitude in the 1850s. However, Burton concludes, Baudelaire's ultraconservatism did not completely eradicate his passion; ultimately, at any stage of his career, Baudelaire was "simultaneously

dandy, radical, *and* reactionary, with now one now another 'tendency' apparently in the ascendant, but always divided, always in conflict" (52). Burton puts his finger on the difficulty of establishing the exact content of Baudelaire's political views.

37. Garrigues, *La France de 1848 à 1870*, 156–60. In July 1861, article 32 of the decree of February 1852 was repealed. Article 32 required the automatic suppression of newspapers that had been condemned twice in two years. Regarding the repressive measures of 1852–53, see also ibid., 77–79.

38. Ibid., 157.

39. In *Alphonse de Lamartine: A Political Biography* (London: Croom Helm; New York: St. Martin's Press, 1983), 239, William Fortescue refers to Lamartine in the post-1848 years as a moderate republican, "in so far as a political label can be attached to him." As minister of foreign affairs in its provisional government, Lamartine had for a time been the Second Republic's figurehead and virtual ruler. However, as he aged, his politics became less clear. He shared many of Louis-Napoléon's positions until the coup d'état, which he abhorred; thereafter, he looked back nostalgically on the restoration of the Bourbon monarchy. The article on Rousseau in the *Cours familier* "illustrates Lamartine's political conservatism since the June Days," Fortescue notes (265).

40. Alphonse de Lamartine, *Lettres des années sombres, 1853–1867*, intro. Henri Guillemin (Fribourg: Librairie de l'Université, 1942), 162, letter to M. Bertucat, Feb. 25, 1861; my emphasis. The translations of Lamartine here are mine.

41. Ibid., 162, letter to M. Dubois, Apr. 1861; my emphasis.

42. Alphonse de Lamartine, "LXVe Entretien: J.-J. Rousseau. Son faux contrat social et le vrai contrat social," in *Cours familier de littérature* (Paris, 1861), 11: 346–47. Albert Schinz, in his *Etat présent des travaux sur J.-J. Rousseau* (Paris: Les Belles Lettres; New York: MLA, 1941), completely misses this moment in Rousseau's reception, subsuming it under "Quatrième vague: Aux environs de 1850" and giving 1856–57 as the dates of the *Cours familier*.

43. Nisard, *Histoire de la littérature française*, 4: 477.

44. Ibid., 452. As we saw in Chapter 2, in the "Poème du hachisch," Baudelaire utilizes this idea about Rousseau's intoxication to condemn him as a would-be "man-God."

45. Ibid., 454.

46. Ibid., 495–96; my emphasis.

47. In contrast to Lamartine, Nisard, and their ilk, Baudelaire never engages in the vitriolic assault on the "utopian Rousseau" that was characteristic of conservative writing in the early 1860s. Baudelaire once or twice refers to Rousseau and utopianism in the same phrase, but these references (from 1863 and 1865) have little in common with the extraordinary antipathy expressed by Lamartine and Nisard just two years earlier. Reading between the lines of *L'Oeuvre et la vie de Delacroix*, one can pick up a link between "Jean-Jacques" and "les utopistes et les furibonds," but it is understated and open to nuance (Baud., *OC*, 2: 756–60, esp.

757). And in his obituary notice for his good friend the actor Rouvière (written in October 1865), Baudelaire seems more fascinated than repulsed by Rouvière's little-known "love of utopia" and "cult of Jean-Jacques" (ibid., 241–43). Although the name "Jean-Jacques" clearly functions in these texts as the ideological sign it had become, the reference does not carry the virulent tone usually reserved for reactionary mythologizing about Rousseau.

48. Baudelaire had read Proudhon's theories closely and with respect in the late 1840s. In 1851, in his "Notice sur Pierre Dupont," Baudelaire states his ongoing attraction to Proudhon: "Quand je parcours l'oeuvre de Dupont, je sens toujours revenir dans ma mémoire, sans doute à cause de quelque secrète affinité, ce sublime mouvement de Proudhon" ("When I skim through the work of Dupont, I am always reminded, undoubtedly because of some secret affinity, of the sublime movement of Proudhon") (Baud., *OC,* 2: 34). There follows a gap of some years when Baudelaire never mentions Proudhon's name; but in 1858, at the instigation of Sainte-Beuve, Baudelaire picked up Proudhon's work again, and in the 1860s, he speaks of Proudhon quite often. In a letter to Narcisse Ancelle, Feb. 8, 1865 (*Corr.* 2: 453), he leaves no doubt that he still finds Proudhon's "utopian" economics compelling.

49. The second number (Mar. 1, 1848) of *Le Salut public,* a newspaper Baudelaire briefly edited with two friends, cites Lacordaire's presence at the barricades as a model for all priests: "Prêtres, n'hésitez pas: jetez-vous hardiment dans les bras du peuple. . . . Jésus-Christ, votre maître, est aussi le nôtre; il était avec nous aux barricades, et c'est par lui, par lui seul que nous avons vaincu. . . . Prêtres, ralliez-vous hardiment à nous; Affre et Lacordaire vous en ont donné l'exemple" ("Priests, don't hesitate: throw yourselves boldly into the arms of the people. . . . Jesus Christ, your master, is also ours; he was with us on the barricades, and it's through him, through him alone that we were victorious. . . . Priests, rally boldly to our cause; Affre and Lacordaire have set an example for you") (Baud., *OC,* 2: 1035).

50. On February 10, 1853, Lacordaire preached publicly in Paris for the last time. With Saint-Roch "bristling with policemen," he condemned the emperor's uncle, Napoléon I, and supposedly finished his sermon with the words, "Moi aussi, je suis une liberté, il faut que je disparaisse" ("I too, I am a liberty, I must disappear"). José Cabanis, *Lacordaire et quelques autres: Politique et religion* (Paris: Gallimard, 1982), 330.

51. Cabanis resumes Lacordaire's political leanings in 1848 as follows: "Lacordaire was not one of those who accepted the republic provisionally, to take it over and restore the threatened order; he saw in it a point of departure, and once he had become the representative of the people, he sat very naturally on the left, among those who wanted to go farther, and not hold back the movement of History" (ibid., 311; my translation). Cabanis notes of Lacordaire's election to the French Academy: "That it was a manifestation of hostility toward the regime that had been prepared well in advance, there is no doubt" (ibid., 409). Voting for the

priest were Guizot, Thiers, Victor Cousin, Villemain, Lamartine, and the "parti des ducs" (at least de Noailles and Broglie)—united by their disapproval of the coup d'état and the war in Italy. Sainte-Beuve, Vigny, and Nisard voted against the nomination. See Daniel Oster, *Histoire de l'Académie française* (Paris: Vialetay, 1970), 120.

52. Garrigues, *La France de 1848 à 1870,* 159.

53. Baud., *Corr.,* 2: 222, letter to Vigny, Jan. 26, 1862. Baudelaire also explains why he wants to succeed Lacordaire in a letter to Sainte-Beuve, ibid., 220, Jan. 24[?], 1862.

54. Oster, *Histoire,* 132; Sainte-Beuve's emphasis.

55. Baud., *Corr.,* 2: 222; his emphasis. Marcel Ruff, who argues that Baudelaire manifested his republican sympathies during this period, cites the poet's letter to Victor de Laprade (Dec. 23, 1861), in which Baudelaire presents himself as a Catholic-republican, at the opposite pole from Laprade's royalism. Ruff, "La Pensée politique et sociale de Baudelaire," in *Littérature et société: Recueil d'études en l'honneur de Bernard Guyon* (Paris: De Brouwer, 1973), 72.

56. Baud., *Corr.,* 2: 220; his emphasis. Sainte-Beuve's article calls for the French Academy to institute reforms aimed at keeping (a certain) political influence out of the elections and promoting more opportunity for "contemporary and living literature" or "la Bohême littéraire." Sainte-Beuve devotes more space to Baudelaire than to any of the other candidates, but his comments are not entirely laudatory. See Sainte-Beuve, *Les Nouveaux Lundis* (Paris: Michel Lévy, 1879–95), 1: 394.

57. Baudelaire, "Une Réforme à l'Académie," in *OC,* 2: 189.

58. Ibid., 242. Peter S. Hambly, in "Baudelaire et l'utopie," *Bulletin baudelairien* 6, no. 1 (Aug. 31, 1970), argues that utopia is "one of the constants" in Baudelaire's thought. As an example, Hambly cites Baudelaire's statement: "C'est une grande destinée que celle de la poésie! Joyeuse ou lamentable, elle porte toujours en soi le divin caractère utopique. Elle contredit sans cesse le fait, à peine de ne plus être" ("What a great destiny is poetry's! Joyous or lamentable, poetry always bears within itself the divine utopian character. It ceaselessly contradicts the factual, on pain of no longer existing"); Baudelaire, "Notice sur Pierre Dupont" (1851) *OC,* 1: 614.

59. According to Dolf Oehler, the Latin epigraphs Baudelaire submitted to his editor about the same time (probably in July 1861) for use in the definitive edition of *Les Fleurs du mal* evoked the rhetoric of 1848 and had the same polemical content as "Le Promeneur solitaire." These were phrases like "Morte libertati provisuerunt" ("Through death they saved [their] liberty"), which recalls the republican cry "La liberté ou la mort" ("Liberty or death"). Moreover, Baudelaire proposed to add a visual emblem that would have reinforced the republican character of the phrase: "Une tête de mort, avec les attributs de la Liberté, coiffée de bonnet phrygien" ("A death's head, with the attributes of Liberty, wearing the phrygian bonnet"). Baud., *Corr.,* 2: 179, cited in Oehler, *Le Spleen contre l'oubli, Juin 1848:*

Baudelaire, Flaubert, Heine, Herzen, trans. Guy Petitdemange (Paris: Payot & Rivages, 1996), 294.

60. Arsène Houssaye was a regular commentator on the eighteenth century. His reputation was made in large part by a book of history and criticism, *Galerie de portraits du XVIIIe siècle,* first published in 1844 and often revised and reprinted in the years following (even into the 1870s). This book lent its title and its weight to Houssaye's ongoing column "Galerie du XVIIIe siècle" in *L'Artiste,* a periodical of which he was the editor. Under this title, or sometimes without it, Houssaye painted portraits of eighteenth-century luminaries, commented on new publications of eighteenth-century texts, and editorialized about eighteenth-century authors in the politically charged context of the Second Empire. For example, in November 1861, a few weeks before Baudelaire wrote him the letter about the publication of his prose poems, Houssaye published a recently discovered piece by Rousseau, "Fiction sur la révélation," in the column immediately preceding his "Galerie" (*L'Artiste,* n.s., 12, no. 16 [Nov. 15, 1861], 217–21). He also included an article on Rousseau's youth in the 1858 (or sixth) edition of the *Galerie de portraits;* and he subsequently published *Les Charmettes: Jean-Jacques Rousseau et Madame de Warens* (Paris: Didier, 1863). In other words, Houssaye was an established specialist on the eighteenth century. Not only was he well placed to pick up on the textual presence of Rousseau, which is woven like a thread through the poems he published, but his name in Baudelaire's dedication may be part of the poet's strategy for suppressing the most overt evidence of his dialogue with Rousseau, while leaving scattered traces of it behind.

Four Baudelaire's Physiologie: *Rousseau as Caricature and Type in the Prose Poems*

1. Ainslie Armstrong McLees, *Baudelaire's "Argot Plastique": Poetic Caricature and Modernism* (Athens: University of Georgia Press, 1989), 79, 83.

2. However, in *The World Viewed: Reflections on the Ontology of Film,* enlarged ed. (Cambridge, Mass.: Harvard University Press, 1979), 33, 36, Stanley Cavell makes a relevant distinction between the two: types, he asserts, eventually ramify into various subtle individualities, whereas stereotypes (such as those in which black people were cast in films until recently—"mammies, shiftless servants, loyal retainers, entertainers") do not. This distinction is tantamount to the difference between "particular *ways* of inhabiting a social role" and "only the role." Nonetheless, when Cavell lists examples, he unwittingly suggests the difficulty of differentiating between the comic type, the social, and the famous individual: "the original types ramified into individualities as various and subtle, as far-reaching in their capacities to inflect mood and release fantasy as any set of characters who inhabited the great theaters of our world. We do not know them by such names as Pulcinella, Crispin, Harlequin, Pantaloon . . . ; we call them the Public Enemy, the

Priest, James Cagney, Pat O'Brien, the Confederate Spy, the Army Scout, Randolph Scott, Gary Cooper."

3. Werner Hofmann, *Caricature from Leonardo to Picasso* (New York: Crown, 1957), 15, 9, 26, traces the evolution of caricature from its creation by the Caracci brothers in the late sixteenth century in Italy to its development in England in the eighteenth century and finally its apogee in France in the work of Daumier. Hofmann argues that the term "caricature" was unknown in France before 1665, and that the Enlightenment viewed caricature as "a dangerous violation of the rules," a "libertinage d'imagination." Arsène Alexandre, *L'Art du rire et de la caricature* (Paris: Librairies-Imprimeries Réunies, n.d.), 95 argues that caricature in the eighteenth century was not the same "frank" genre that became so popular in the nineteenth. According to him, it was only after the Revolution that real caricature flourished: "True caricature is more accentuated in periods of passion and violence" (my translation).

4. Chastel, *Grotesque,* 79, 82.

5. Kayser, *Grotesque in Art and Literature,* 53, quoting Schlegel's fr. 396.

6. Werner Hofmann, "Baudelaire et la caricature," *Preuves* 207 (1967): 38–43; my translation. Rollins, *Baudelaire et le grotesque, 28,* remarks that Baudelaire uses a semantic triptych of interchangeable terms: "caricature,—grotesque,—comique absolu." Although this statement needs nuancing, it is not fundamentally wrong.

7. Baudelaire explains why Daumier, whom he greatly admired, is not an example of the grotesque: "Comme il aime très passionnément et très naturellement la nature, il s'élèverait difficilement au comique absolu. Il évite même avec soin tout ce qui ne serait pas pour un public français l'objet d'une perception claire et immédiate" ("As he loves nature passionately and very naturally, it would be difficult for him to rise to the absolute comic. He even carefully avoids anything that would not be immediately and clearly perceptible to the French public") (*OC,* 2: 557). On the other hand, Baudelaire deems George Cruikshank's particular merit to be "une abondance inépuisable dans le grotesque. . . . le grotesque coule incessamment et inévitablement de la pointe de Cruikshank, comme les rimes riches de la plume des poètes naturels. Le grotesque est son habitude" ("an inexhaustible abundance in the grotesque. . . . the grotesque drips incessantly and inevitably from the tip of Cruikshank's engraving tool, just as *rimes riches* flow from the pen of natural poets. The grotesque is his custom"). Baudelaire defines Cruikshank's grotesque as "la violence extravagante du geste et du mouvement, et l'explosion dans l'expression" ("the extravagant violence of gesture and movement, and the explosiveness of expression"), and he makes the telling connection between Cruickshank's characters and "des acteurs de pantomime" (*OC,* 2: 566).

8. In "Arcimboldo; *ou,* Rhétoriqueur et magicien," in *L'Obvie et l'obtus* (Paris: Seuil, 1982), Roland Barthes analyzes some of Arcimboldo's baroque paintings in rhetorical terms. Callot is systematically cited as an early practitioner of the grotesque, as we have seen. Hofmann, *Caricature from Leonardo to Picasso,* 19, 37–38, outlines Arcimboldo's and Callot's relation to caricature.

9. Barbara Maria Stafford, "The Eighteenth-Century: Towards an Interdisciplinary Model," *Art Bulletin* 70, no. 1 (Mar. 1988): 15.

10. In saying that the events of 1848 were charming "par l'excès même du Ridicule" ("because of the very excess of Ridiculousness") (*OC*, 1: 680), Baudelaire may have had in mind the *Encyclopédie*'s definition of *charge,* a synonym for caricature in French, which begins: "[I]t is the representation on canvas or on paper, by means of colors, of a person, of an action, or more generally of a subject, in which precise truth and exact resemblance are altered only by *an excess of ridiculousness* [ne sont altérées que *par l'excès du ridicule*]" (my emphasis and translation).

11. Hofmann, *Caricature from Leonardo to Picasso,* 28.

12. See Judith Wechsler, *A Human Comedy: Physiognomy and Caricature in Nineteenth-Century Paris* (Chicago: University of Chicago Press, 1982), 161 (fig. 148).

13. Gérald Froidevaux, in *Baudelaire: Représentation et modernité* (Paris: José Corti, 1989), 111, calls caricature, along with fashion engraving or the *croquis de moeurs,* two other minor genres that Baudelaire favored, "allegorical arts." Alexandre, *Art du rire et de la caricature,* 94, includes some of Baudelaire's favorite eighteenth-century artists, the Saint-Aubin brothers and Debucourt, in his study of caricature. Debucourt's work, says Alexandre, sums up "much of the spirit of the eighteenth century" (94). "He incarnates the decadence of the eighteenth century, recalling in a attenuated and softened manner all its elegance, all its affectations, all its precious discourse. That's why, in his work, we read more readily and more ingenuously its vices and its faults; little by little all that was exaggerated as it was passed along. And that's also why Debucourt, arriving the last, is the most decidedly caricatural" (95).

14. Wechsler, *Human Comedy,* 23–38.

15. Ibid., 34. Wechsler states that "The term *physiologie* suggested objective observation of a *type* rather than of an individual." Professional types included doctor, lawyer, investor, soldier, traveler, student, poet, musician, and tailor; there were also classifications by class or lifestyle, such as the bluestocking, the bachelor or spinster, the bourgeois, and the salesgirl. However, with few exceptions, the aristocracy and "le peuple" were excluded. See Richard Sieburth, "Same Difference: The French Physiologies, 1840–1842," *Notebooks in Cultural Analysis* 1 (1984): 163–200.

16. See, e.g., the illustrations in Wechsler, *Human Comedy,* and McLees, *Baudelaire's "Argot Plastique."*

17. Caricature "reshap[es] an individual as a type," Ernst Kris and E. H. Gombrich assert in "The Principles of Caricature," in Kris, *Psychoanalytic Explorations in Art* (New York: International Universities Press, 1952), 191.

18. Fletcher, *Allegory,* 28.

19. Ibid.

20. Erich Auerbach, *Mimesis,* trans. Willard R. Trask (Princeton, N.J.: Princeton University Press, 1953), 116. Auerbach is speaking about the use of types in the

medieval French epic the *Chanson de Roland,* but his analysis is equally applicable to caricature in mid-nineteenth-century France.

21. Auerbach, *Mimesis,* 116.

22. This is not to say that types come into play for the first time only in the nineteenth century or that abstract allegories no longer had meaning for Baudelaire or his contemporaries. The political cartoons of the early 1830s could hardly have done without the allegorical figure of Liberty, for example, and Baudelaire's own poems certainly contain many allegorical abstractions.

23. Goya is "le véritable artiste, toujours durable et vivace même dans ces oeuvres fugitives, pour ainsi dire suspendues aux événements, qu'on appelle *caricatures*" ("the true artist, always durable and lively even in these fugitive works, suspended as it were from events, that we call *caricatures*"), Baudelaire says in his essay on foreign cartoonists (*OC,* 2: 568).

24. James A. Hiddleston, "Les Poèmes en prose de Baudelaire et la caricature," *Romantisme* 74 (1991): 58; my translation.

25. My examples are drawn from ibid., 57.

26. In fact, Baudelaire had initially hoped to write a series of short poems to accompany some engravings of Paris by Charles Meryon. When that project collapsed, it seems that he retained the idea of visual inspiration, but in another form.

27. Hiddleston, "Poèmes en prose de Baudelaire et la caricature," 57–58.

28. James Sherry, "Four Modes of Caricature: Reflections upon a Genre," *Bulletin of Research in the Humanities* 87, no. 1 (1987): 50.

29. One could add to this list the use of animals to represent people, such as the dog standing in for the reading public in "Le Chien et le flacon," or the donkey representing the downtrodden laborer in "Un Plaisant."

30. For Baudelaire's transposition of visual art into verse, see David Scott, *Pictorialist Poetics: Poetry and the Visual Arts in Nineteenth-Century France* (Cambridge: Cambridge University Press, 1988).

31. Froidevaux, *Baudelaire,* 24, comments that caricature "retained Baudelaire's particular attention, not only because it chooses in the historical present the object that it wants to invest with an artistic essence, but because it exemplifies the subversive logic of modernity: it snatches the sublime from the vulgar and expresses beauty through ugliness."

32. McLees, *Baudelaire's "Argot Plastique,"* 96, 101.

33. Citing Baudelaire's "Notice sur Pierre Dupont," Ruff ("La Pensée politique et sociale de Baudelaire," 73) argues that the poet was extremely sensitive to the misery of the working classes. He cites this statement from the "Notice," which I quote from "Pierre Dupont [I]" (*OC,* 2: 31): "Il est impossible, à quelque parti qu'on appartienne, de quelques préjugés qu'on ait été nourri, de ne pas être touché du spectacle de cette multitude maladive respirant la poussière des ateliers, avalant du coton, s'imprégnant de céruse, de mercure et de tous les poisons nécessaires à la création des chefs-d'oeuvre, dormant dans la vermine, au fond des quartiers où

les vertus les plus humbles et les plus grandes nichent à côté des vices les plus endurcis et des vomissements du bagne" ("It is impossible, regardless of the political party to which one adheres, regardless of the prejudices with which one has been nourished, not to be touched by the spectacle of that unhealthy multitude breathing in the dust of the workshops, swallowing cotton, absorbing ceruse [white lead], mercury, and all the poisons necessary to the creation of masterpieces, sleeping among the vermin, in the heart of those neighborhoods where the humblest and greatest virtues lodge next to the most hardened vices and the vomit of the slave laborers") (my translation).

34. For political or "social" readings of "Assommons les pauvres!" "Les Yeux des pauvres," and "Le Joujou du pauvre," see Terdiman, *Discourse/Counter-discourse,* ch. 7; Jonathan Monroe, *A Poverty of Objects: The Prose Poem and the Politics of Genre* (Ithaca, N.Y.: Cornell University Press, 1987), ch. 3; Gretchen van Slyke, "Dans l'intertexte de Baudelaire et de Proudhon: Pourquoi faut-il assommer les pauvres?" *Romantisme* 45 (1984): 57–77; and Geraldine Friedman, "Baudelaire's Theory of Practice: Ideology and Difference in 'Les Yeux des pauvres,'" *PMLA* 104, no. 3 (May 1989): 317–28. For a political reading of "Une Mort héroïque" and "La Fausse Monnaie," see Nathaniel Wing, "Poets, Mimes and Counterfeit Coins: On Power and Discourse in Baudelaire's Prose Poetry," *Paragraph* 13, no. 1 (Mar. 1990): 1–18.

35. See Chapter 3. On the subject of Baudelaire and the Italian revolution, see Richard D. E. Burton, "'Jésuite et révolutionnaire': Baudelaire, Nadar and the 'Question italienne,'" *Studi francesi* 113, xxxviii–2 (1994), 241–50. Burton characterizes the emperor's Italian policy and the republican reaction to it in France as "at most, a subject of ephemeral, if intense, interest" to Baudelaire (245).

36. Wechsler, *Human Comedy,* 14. Wechsler makes a sharper distinction between social and allegorical caricature than I would. In fact, I find her comments on allegorical caricature extremely pertinent to Baudelaire's (superficially) "social" poems.

37. Different translators of the prose poems have provided different English titles for "L'Etranger." In Baudelaire, *The Poems in Prose with "La Fanfarlo"* (London: Anvil Press Poetry, 1989), Francis Scarfe titles it "The Outsider," whereas William H. Crosby (Baudelaire, *The Flowers of Evil and Paris Spleen* [Brockport, N.Y.: BOA Editions, 1991]) and Edward Kaplan (Baudelaire, *Parisian Prowler*) both use "The Stranger." My reasons for proposing the variant "The Foreigner" will appear later.

38. Wechsler, *Human Comedy,* 15.

39. In this way, Baudelaire's prose poems conform to Ross Chambers's assessment of the necessary, constitutive duplicity—the doubleness and deceitfulness—of the early modernist texts. See Chambers, *Writing of Melancholy,* 1–23, and also Terdiman, *Discourse/Counter-discourse,* 342.

40. Wechsler, *Human Comedy,* 14–15.

41. Like J. A. Hiddleston in *Baudelaire and Le Spleen de Paris* (Oxford: Clarendon Press, 1987) and "Les Poèmes en prose de Baudelaire et la caricature," Sonya Stephens's *Baudelaire's Prose Poems: The Practice and Politics of Irony* (Oxford: Oxford University Press, 1999), 120, identifies many of these same figures as caricatures; but she considers them to be so many "anonymous others (representing generalized types)." The failure of critics today to identify the specific reference to "Rousseau" confirms the tendency of portrait caricatures, in particular, to lose their meaning and become enigmas over time.

42. The terms are drawn from Fletcher (*Allegory,* 35), who describes the allegorical hero as "not so much a real person as . . . a generator of other secondary personalities, which are partial aspects of himself."

43. Critics have found reminiscences or repetitions of Rousseau's expressions and themes in I: "L'Etranger", II: "Le Désespoir de la vieille," III: "Le *Confiteor* de l'artiste," V: "La Chambre double," IX: "Le Mauvais Vitrier," XII: "Les Foules," XV: "Le Gâteau," XIX: "Le Joujou du pauvre," XXIII: "La Solitude," as well as in the slightly later poems "La Fausse Monnaie" (XXVIII) and "Enivrez-vous" (XXXIII), but these are not the only poems that allude to Rousseau, as we shall see. To my knowledge, no one has discussed these references in relation to the midcentury polemics about "the spirit of France" or as caricatures of "Rousseau."

44. See Victor Cousin's article on *Emile* in the *Journal des Savants,* Nov. 1848, 664. Frayssinous is quoted by Trousson, *Défenseurs et adversaires de J.-J. Rousseau,* 234; my translation. Trousson goes on: "The grievances that counterrevolutionary thinkers will repeat ad nauseam are already noticeable here . . . Rousseau is the man of paradoxes, both enchanting and corrupting, the *foreigner* come to falsify the French spirit [*l'esprit français*], the barbarous negator of civilization" (my emphasis). Even Proudhon, hardly a conservative but no admirer of Rousseau's either, points to the role of Rousseau's ideas in legitimating the bloody struggles of the Terror as an example of the nefarious "influence des étrangers." See *Idée générale de la Révolution au XIXe siècle,* in Proud., *OC,* 2: 195.

45. In his first *rêverie,* Rousseau describes himself as "alone on earth, no longer having any brother, neighbor, friend, or society other than myself," and he hopes that rereading these *rêveries* later will revive the past and enable him to "double [his] existence" and "live with [his] earlier self as [he] might with a younger friend." Jean-Jacques Rousseau, *Reveries of the Solitary Walker,* trans. Peter France (New York: Penguin Books, 1979), 34. I would argue that Baudelaire rewrites Rousseau's self-doubling as the dialogue in "L'Etranger."

46. See Baud., *Corr.,* 1: 62, letter to Madame Aupick, Aug. 23, 1838, and Abel-François Villemain, *Cours de littérature française,* vol. 2: *Tableau de la littérature au XVIIIe siècle,* new ed. (Paris: Didier, 1858–59), 236, 254, 291. At the beginning of his twenty-sixth lesson (310), as he prepares to move on to another subject, Villemain cites critics who have reproached him for extolling "ce *vil* . . . cet *infâme* Rousseau." This reference could be the basis for Baudelaire's own elliptical citation of Rousseau as "infâme" in "De quelques préjugés contemporains" (*OC,* 3: 54).

47. "After [Rousseau] had . . . written, under the deceptive title of *Social Contract,* the code book of capitalist and mercantile tyranny, the Genevan charlatan concluded by arguing for the necessity of the proletariat, the subalternization of the worker, dictatorship, and inquisition," Proudhon says in *Idée générale de la Révolution au XIXe siècle*; and, cementing the link to the old acrobat, he goes on to call the *Contrat social* Rousseau's "chef d'oeuvre de jonglerie oratoire" (Proud., *OC,* 2: 194, 195).

48. Louis Blanc, *Histoire de la Révolution française* (1847), 3: 1, quoted in Schinz, *Etat présent des travaux sur J.-J. Rousseau,* 19.

49. See Sainte-Beuve, "Madame de la Tour-Franqueville et Jean-Jacques Rousseau" (Apr. 29, 1850), in *Causeries du lundi,* 4th ed., 2: 63–84. Sainte-Beuve also declares that Rousseau's sanity was profoundly at risk: "he was beginning, not only to appear mad [*paraître fou*] in the vague and general sense of the word, but to be really mad [*l'être trop réellement*] in the precise and medical meaning of the term" (78).

50. Michelet, *L'Etudiant,* 131: "et cela, chose merveilleuse, dans un coeur de femme."

51. Proudhon, *De la justice dans la Révolution et dans l'église,* IV, in Proud., *OC,* 8: 217; Proudhon's emphasis. Baudelaire reveals his awareness of Proudhon's attitude and his disagreement with it when he uses Proudhon's pejorative term *femmelin* to compliment Sainte-Beuve (Baud., *Corr.,* 1: 505).

52. Baudelaire, "Fusées," XIII, in *OC,* 1: 662; cf. "Hygiène," III, in ibid., 670. Baudelaire also called the commonplace "le lieu de rencontre de la foule, le rendezvous public de l'éloquence" ("the meeting place of the crowd, the public rendezvous of eloquence") (*OC,* 2: 79).

53. The standard references for the theory of caricature are Ernst Kris, "The Psychology of Caricature" and Kris and E. H. Gombrich, "Principles of Caricature," in Kris, *Psychoanalytic Explorations in Art,* 189–203; Gombrich and Kris, *Caricature* (Harmondsworth, Eng.: Penguin Books, 1940); and Gombrich, "The Experiment of Caricature," in idem, *Art and Illusion: A Study in the Psychology of Pictorial Representation* (New York: Pantheon Books, 1960), 330–58. See also Gombrich, "The Cartoonist's Armoury," in idem, *Meditations on a Hobby Horse and Other Essays on the Theory of Art* (London: Phaidon, 1963), 127–42, and Sherry, "Four Modes of Caricature."

54. These are the goals of caricature outlined by Kris, "Psychology of Caricature," 175, 179. Caricature reduces a person's features "to an easily remembered formula. . . . 'Look here,' the artist seems to say, 'that is all the great man consists of'" (Kris and Gombrich, "Principles of Caricature," 191).

55. Baud., *OC,* 2: 549: Baudelaire calls Charlet a "fabricant de niaiseries nationales, commerçant patenté de proverbes politiques . . . il connaîtra prochainement la force de l'oubli" ("manufacturer of nationalist stupidities, patented merchant of political proverbs . . . he will soon feel forcefully what it is to be forgotten").

56. Baudelaire calls caricature "les oeuvres destinées à représenter à l'homme sa propre laideur morale et physique" (*OC,* 2: 526).

57. Terdiman, *Discourse/Counter-discourse,* 210, explains that "rather than involuntarily adding one's own authority" to an idiocy by proffering it in turn, "the very fact of citing a cliché—rather than simply uttering it mindlessly—signals that the 'citing subject is an eccentric one' with respect to the cited discourse" (211).

58. Baudelaire, *Petits Poëmes en prose,* ed. Kopp, xliii. In February 1860, Baudelaire accepted an invitation to write this text to accompany the works of Charles Meryon, an artist he greatly admired (see *Salon de 1859,* in *OC,* 2: 666–67; and also "Peintres et aquafortistes," in *OC,* 2: 740–41). But Meryon rejected Baudelaire's ideas, and the project was dropped. On this episode, see Rémi Labrusse, "Baudelaire et Meryon," *L'Année Baudelaire* 1 (Paris: Klincksieck, 1995): 106.

59. Baudelaire, *Petits Poëmes en prose,* ed. Kopp, xlvii.

60. Labrusse, "Baudelaire et Meryon," 106, 112 ff., argues that the Meryon etchings of Paris could never have formed the basis of *Le Spleen de Paris* because the poetic ideas of the two men were incompatible, especially where allegory was concerned. Meryon practiced what Labrusse, following Michel Thévoz, calls "pseudo-allegory," which made the image unreadable and therefore did not allow for any real interpretation.

61. For a very informative account of these little books, see Richard Sieburth, "Same Difference," 163–200.

62. Ibid., 167–69, and fig. 2, 169.

63. According to Sieburth (ibid., 167), the very "topicality and ephemerality" of the "cheap, throwaway" *physiologies* appealed to the modern reader.

64. Ibid., 175, 176.

65. Baudelaire, "Les Foules," in *Petits Poèmes en prose* (*OC,* 1: 291). The explicit theme of the "promeneur" is also an element in "Les Projets" (which opens: "Il se disait, en se promenant dans un grand parc solitaire . . ."), "Le Tir et le cimetière," and "Mademoiselle Bistouri." Although the "promeneur" is not always the narrator, there is a definite slippage toward a "je" in these poems. As Stephens, *Baudelaire's Prose Poems,* 62–63, notes, "because there is a unifying identity behind the different voices [of the prose poems], we are more inclined to read the *Je* and its fictions as the voice of the poet, despite the preponderance of narrative texts." She cites "Les Foules" and "Les Veuves," "where the protagonist is referred to in the third person as *le poète, le promeneur solitaire,* and *le philosophe*," as two cases in point.

66. Baudelaire, "Mon coeur mis à nu," XXXVI, in *OC,* 1: 700. Cf. "Mon coeur mis à nu," VII (*OC,* 1: 680): "Sentiment de solitude, dès mon enfance. Malgré la famille,—et au milieu des camarades, surtout,—sentiment de destinée éternellement solitaire" ("Feeling of solitude, since my childhood. Despite the family,—and in the midst of friends, especially,—feeling of an eternally solitary destiny").

Charles Mauron, *Le Dernier Baudelaire* (Paris: José Corti, 1966), 44, thinks the theme and the proposed titles, "Le Promeneur solitaire" and "Le Rôdeur parisien," constitute a link between Baudelaire, his father ("an artist full of curiosity and a great walker"), and the eighteenth century: "Through him, the son still participated somewhat in the eighteenth century and in its mocking objectivity" (my translation).

67. All in all, the tone and preoccupations that accompany the allusion to the "solitary walker" are dark and tormented, a fact reflected by Benjamin's remark (*Charles Baudelaire*, 101–3). Baudelaire makes it clear that the goals and attitude of the modern artist distinguish him from the mere "flâneur": "[il] a un but plus élevé que celui d'un pur flâneur, un but général, autre que le plaisir fugitif de la circonstance. Il cherche ce quelque chose qu'on nous permettra d'appeler la *modernité*" ("[he] has a higher goal than that of a pure 'flâneur,' a general goal, other than fleeting circumstantial pleasure. He is looking for that something that we may be permitted to call *modernity*") (*OC*, 2: 694).

68. Baud., *OC*, 2: 694: "ce solitaire doué d'une imagination active, toujours voyageant à travers le grand désert d'hommes" ("this solitary man endowed with an active imagination, always traveling across the great desert of men").

69. For example, Villemain asserts that Rousseau "steeped literature in his colors for more than a half-century, and through the greatest of social revolutions, he prepared, in France and in Europe, what constitutes the poetry of our time, this melancholic contemplation of man." And he thinks that Chateaubriand's René retains "some traces of the melancholy of the *Promeneur solitaire*" (*Cours de littérature française*, 2: 293, 305).

70. Paul Verlaine, quoted in McLees, *Baudelaire's "Argot Plastique,"* 151.

71. Théodore de Banville, quoted in McLees, *Baudelaire's "Argot Plastique,"* 151.

72. Baud., *OC*, 2: 695.

73. Ibid., 707.

74. Discussing the importance of fashion for representing the moment, Baudelaire insists that "les modes ne doivent pas être, si l'on veut bien les goûter, considérées comme choses mortes. . . . Il faut se les figurer *vitalisées, vivifiées* par les belles femmes qui les portèrent" ("if you want to really get a taste for them, fashions must not be considered dead objects. . . . You must imagine them as they were *given vitality and life* by the beautiful women who wore them") (*OC*, 2: 716; my emphasis).

75. "Nous avons parlé déjà de l'idiotisme de beauté particulier à chaque époque, et nous avons observé que chaque siècle avait, pour ainsi dire, sa grâce personnelle. La même remarque peut s'appliquer aux professions; chacune tire sa beauté extérieure des lois morales auxquelles elle est soumise. Dans les unes, cette beauté sera marquée d'énergie, et, dans les autres, elle portera les signes visibles de l'oisiveté. C'est comme l'emblème du caractère, c'est l'estampille de la fatalité. Le militaire, pris en général, a sa beauté, comme le dandy et la femme galante ont la leur, d'un goût essentiellement différent" ("We have already spoken about the id-

iomatic language of beauty peculiar to each epoch, and we have observed that each century had, so to speak, its personal grace. The same remark can be made about the professions; each one draws its external beauty from the moral laws to which it is subject. In some professions, this beauty will be characterized by energy, and in others, it will wear the visible signs of leisure. It's like the emblem of character; it's the little stamp of fatality. The military man, in general, has his beauty, just as the dandy and the woman of easy virtue have theirs, reflecting an essentially different taste") (*OC,* 2: 707).

76. Baudelaire criticizes Ingres, for example, for making his types too perfect, and therefore classical (*OC,* 2: 696). In this area, Baudelaire takes after Hugo, who argued in the Preface to *Cromwell,* 12: 26, that "the poet must *choose* not what is beautiful in things, but what is *characteristic.* . . . Every figure must be brought back to its most salient, most individual, most precise trait. Even the vulgar and the trivial should have an accent. Nothing must be overlooked. Like God, the true poet is present everywhere at once in his work. The genius resembles the die that stamps the royal effigy on copper coins and gold pieces alike."

77. According to the *Oxford English Dictionary,* a type may be a pattern or model after which something is made, a general idea that is the standard of comparison by which we judge various instantiations of that idea, or a character distinguishing a particular group or class of beings. Conversely, it may be a "person or thing that exhibits the characteristic qualities of a class; a representative specimen; a typical example or instance"; or, in the same vein, a "person or thing that exemplifies the ideal qualities or characteristics of a kind or order; a perfect example or specimen of something; a model, pattern, exemplar."

78. Charles Nodier, "Des Types en littérature" (1830) in *Romans* (Paris: Bibliothèque Charpentier, 1900), 8.

79. Ibid., 6, 7, 15.

80. "Rousseau appeared: the day he bared himself totally to himself, he revealed in the same moment to his century the writer best able to express with newness, with vigor, with a logic mixed with passion, the confused ideas that were fermenting and waiting to be born," wrote Baudelaire's sometime mentor Sainte-Beuve (*Causeries,* 3: 79).

81. In the same way, "goddesses, nymphs and beautiful sultan's wives" were not common in the early eighteenth century, but they accurately reflected the spirit of the rococo, the love of costumes and masquerades: "les déesses, les nymphes et les sultanes du XVIIIe siècle sont des portraits *moralement* ressemblants" ("the goddesses, nymphs, and sultanas of the eighteenth century are *moral* likenesses") (Baud., *OC,* 2: 695).

82. Benjamin, *Charles Baudelaire,* 170.

83. Patrick Labarthe takes note of Baudelaire's attraction to "le Type et le cliché" (*Baudelaire et la Tradition de l'Allégorie,* 401), and he calculates that Claude Pichois's "Index of the Allegories and Personifications in *Les Fleurs du mal*" (*OC,* 2: 1673–76) cites 665 instances in those poems alone!

84. Aloysius Bertrand, "Préface," in id., *Gaspard de la Nuit: Fantaisies à la manière de Rembrandt et de Callot,* ed. Max Milner (Paris: Gallimard, 1980), 79.

85. Baud., *OC,* 2: 549.

86. Edward Lucie-Smith, *The Art of Caricature* (Ithaca, N.Y.: Cornell University Press, 1981), 78.

87. Wechsler, *Human Comedy,* 82.

88. Honoré Daumier, *Les Gens d'affaires (Robert Macaire),* ed. Jean Adhémar (Paris: Editions Vilo, 1968), 14. See also Daumier, *Les Cent et un Robert-Macaire,* with accompanying texts by Maurice Alhoy and Louis Huart (Paris: Aubert et Cie, 1839).

89. McLees, *Baudelaire's "Argot Plastique,"* 40.

90. Quoted by Wechsler, *Human Comedy,* 86. Baudelaire singles out the Macaire series for comment in his essay "Quelques caricaturistes français" (*OC,* 2: 555).

91. Lucie-Smith, *Art of Caricature,* 80, also observes that certain imaginary types "became recognizable symbols of Louis Napoleon's regime" in French caricature after overtly political subjects were forbidden by the government's censorship laws. According to Lucie-Smith, the appearance of these types in a series of lithographs "was welcomed with increasing public delight."

92. Portrait caricature has this tendency to become indecipherable over time. "If the connections and allusions forming its content are obscure . . . the hieroglyphic nature of caricature becomes a reality. . . . the caricature has changed into a rebus," Kris, "Psychology of Caricature," 176, asserts. On the other hand, as Wechsler explains, social caricature "dispenses with allegory and personal allusion" and is therefore "more lasting and accessible" to the public over the years. "Editor's Statement: The Issue of Caricature," *Art Journal* 43, no. 4 (Winter 1983): 317.

93. Wechsler, *Human Comedy,* 82. T. J. Clark has observed that Daumier "was many different things to Baudelaire: the man who blasphemed and spat upon mythology in the series of caricatures *Ancient History;* the great draughtsman . . .; the friend whom one visited when times were bad (after the *coup d'état,* for example, with Poulet-Malassis). But above all he was the anti-bourgeois. He was the one critic whose laughter could not be ignored, who loved and hated the bourgeois in ways that had nothing to do with artistic fashion. The disdain of the studios for the bourgeois was futile, self-congratulating; Baudelaire wanted nothing to do with it. . . . It was Daumier who suggested an alternative—a style which could be hostile but not petulant, which could mock the bourgeois without carping. By the end of 1851, Baudelaire the journalist was producing his own kind of caricature." Ultimately, Clark asserts, "Daumier taught Baudelaire to look at 'all that a great town contains of living monstrosities'. He was one of the forces that made Baudelaire a poet of the city." T. J. Clark, *The Absolute Bourgeois: Artists and Politics in France, 1848–1851* (Berkeley: University of California Press, 1999), 144, 161.

94. Benjamin, *Charles Baudelaire,* fr. 32a, p. 240: "L'allégorie est l'armature de la modernité" ("Allegory is the structural framework of modernity").

95. Regarding the relationship between "La Chanson du Vitrier" by Houssaye

and "Le Mauvais Vitrier," see Steve Murphy, "'Le Mauvais Vitrier'; ou, La crise du verre," *Romanic Review* 82, no. 3 (1990): 339–49. For the relevance of Poe's story, see Alain Toumayan, *La Littérature et la hantise du mal* (Lexington, Ky.: French Forum, 1987), ch. 4; and also Arnaldo Pizzorusso, "Le Mauvais Vitrier; ou, L'Impulsion inconnue," in *Etudes baudelairiennes* 8 (Neuchâtel: La Baconnière, 1976), 147–71.

96. The "pot de fleurs" that the narrator deliberately drops on the glazier has been read both as Baudelaire's renunciation of beautiful verse (his *Fleurs du mal*) and also as a flowery weapon against the crude portrayal of reality, a denunciation of a certain idea of realism. See the readings of "Le Mauvais Vitrier" by Jérôme Thélot, in *Baudelaire: Violence et poésie* (Paris: Gallimard, 1993), 100–11, and Francis S. Heck, in "'Le Mauvais Vitrier': A Literary Transfiguration," *Nineteenth-Century French Studies* 14, nos. 3–4 (1986): 260–68. Another current of thought takes the "vitrier" as a reference to certain participants in the political events of 1848 and 1851 and, beyond them, to the dubious politics of Arsène Houssaye, whose poem about "vitriers" Baudelaire references in the letter-preface to the prose poems. See Richard D. E. Burton, "Destruction as Creation: 'Le Mauvais Vitrier' and the Poetics and Politics of Violence," *Romanic Review* 83, no. 3 (May 1992): 297–322; Sonya Stephens, *Baudelaire's Prose Poems,* 64–70; and Murphy, "'Le Mauvais Vitrier'; ou, La Crise du verre."

97. Baud., *OC,* 2: 540. "Le souffle merveilleux qui va les faire se mouvoir extraordinairement n'a pas encore soufflé sur leurs cervelles" ("The breath of the marvelous that will make them move in extraordinary ways has not yet wafted over their brains"). Baudelaire clearly gives full weight to the term *merveilleux,* for he later reiterates the importance of the mimes' "oeuvre fantastique . . . sur la frontière du merveilleux" ("fantastic work . . . on the edge of the marvelous"). His reference to the marvelous functions as a reminder of the rococo, and his choice of the commedia dell'arte as an example recalls the Regency of Philippe d'Orleans, when the Italian comedy was the favorite entertainment of Parisian high society. By choosing a contemporary production that is overtly indebted to eighteenth-century aesthetics, Baudelaire simultaneously evokes the history of the grotesque and its relevance to his theory of modernity.

98. Baud., *OC, 2:* 540: "ils se sentent introduits de force dans une existence nouvelle." The agent of this transformation is said to be a fairy: "[Une fée] promène avec un geste mystérieux et plein d'autorité sa baguette dans les airs. . . . Aussitôt le vertige est entré. . . . Qu'est-ce que ce vertige? C'est le comique absolu; il s'est emparé de chaque être."

99. Baudelaire cites one of these double souls who "would light a cigar next to a powder keg" ("allumera un cigare à côté d'un tonneau de poudre"), thus recalling Proudhon's statement about Rousseau: "Rousseau's influence was immense however: why? *He set fire to the powder that had been accumulating among the literate French for two centuries.* It's something to have sparked such a conflagration in

people's souls: that is the force and the virility of Rousseau; for all the rest, he is a woman [*pour tout le reste il est femme*]." *De la justice dans la Révolution et dans l'église,* IV, in Proud., *OC,* 8: 219; my emphasis and translation.

100. Sainte-Beuve, *Causeries,* 3: 84: "il a de ces longues timidités qui se retournent tout d'un coup en effronteries de *polisson* et de *vaurien* comme il s'appelle." Having underscored the words, Sainte-Beuve remarks that *polisson* and *vaurien,* and other words like them (for example, *gueux* and *fripon*), are signs of poor taste, which reveal Rousseau's lower-class origins and his difference from more aristocratic authors whose lexicon reflects their breeding.

101. Sainte-Beuve, *Causeries,* 3: 88: "un coin malade, trop d'ardeur mêlée à l'inaction et au désoeuvrement, une prédominance de l'imagination et de la sensibilité qui se replient sur elles-mêmes et se dévorent."

102. Some of the poem's individual characters—in particular, the timid man who hardly dares enter a café or a theater—also resemble Rousseau. See Baudelaire's description of "Jean-Jacques"'s timidity in "Fusées" (*OC,* 1: 654).

103. In this Baudelaire joins up with critics like Nisard.

104. Rouss., *OC,* 1: 1084; id., *Reveries,* trans. France, 134 (all translations of the eighth *rêverie* are taken from this edition unless otherwise indicated).

105. These interpretations come from Murphy and Burton, who think Baudelaire is criticizing Arsène Houssaye for his false humanitarianism and false aesthetic. Without changing much in their readings of the poem, the substitution of "Rousseau" for "Houssaye" produces compelling results. See esp. Murphy, "'Le Mauvais Vitrier'; ou, La Crise du verre," 340, 346, 348–49. The idea of Rousseau's "realism" (touted by Sainte-Beuve) is discussed in Chapter 5.

106. For a more detailed discussion of the theory and function of personification in the eighth *rêverie,* see my article "The Mechanics of Language: Personification in Rousseau's *Rêveries,*" in *Approaches to Teaching Rousseau's "Confessions" and "Reveries of the Solitary Walker,"* ed. John C. O'Neal and Ourida Mostefai (New York: Modern Language Association, 2003), 90–95.

107. Rouss., *OC,* 1: 1078; id., *Reveries,* trans. France, 127; translation modified.

108. Rouss., *OC,* 1: 1078; my translation.

109. Baudelaire takes up these ideas and images when he has his narrator drop the flowerpot from his top-floor window onto the poor glazier below.

110. Rouss., *OC,* 1: 1078; id., *Reveries,* trans. France, 128; translation modified.

111. Rousseau's eighth *rêverie* is an excellent, if somewhat more complicated, example of Donald Davie's observation that "[w]e may in our considered opinion reject a view of Nature thus at the mercy of largely inscrutable energies running wild; but [. . . our very language] impels us to a 'Nature' conceived in this way. . . . I am forced to the conclusion that a whole-heartedly nominalist or mechanistic view of Nature, if it tries to express itself in our language, will find itself obstructed by the ingrained bent of that language." Davie, "Personification," *Essays in Criticism* 31, no. 2 (1981): 103.

112. According to *Le Petit Robert, engin* has the general meaning of "tool, instrument or machine." *Engin de guerre,* a term dating from the twelfth century, formerly designated "any weapon launching projectiles (except the cannon)"; in the age of rocketry, it specifically means missiles.

113. According to E. H. Gombrich, the humorist and draughtsman Rodolphe Töpffer (credited with having invented and propagated the comic strip), in a pamphlet on physiognomics published in 1845, states that "any drawing of a human face, however inept, however childish, possesses, by the very fact that it has been drawn, a character and an expression." Gombrich goes on: "Discover expression in the staring eye or gaping jaw of a lifeless form, and what might be called 'Töpffer's law' will come into operation—it will not be classed just as a face but will acquire a definite character and expression, will be endowed with life, with a presence." "The Experiment of Caricature," in *Art and Illusion,* 339–40; 342. This law of caricature seems to me to express perfectly the "personal" effects of personification.

114. I suspect that Baudelaire meant to flag this flaw in Rousseau's logic. When his narrator observes that the glazier must have experienced some difficulty in "operating his ascension" ("à opérer son ascension"), this stilted expression for "climbing the stairs" seems to call attention to another, more metaphysical idea: to wit, the logical problems Rousseau encountered when he tried to raise himself above the level of his impulsive enemies.

115. My reading amply confirms Rosemary Lloyd's argument that Baudelaire "takes the same pleasure in experimenting with [the methods of those he discusses] as he does in working out for himself the themes a work develops or the problems it raises." It is clear, as Lloyd asserts, that "Baudelaire's interest in rhetoric and prosody as 'une collection de règles réclamées par l'organisation même de l'être spirituel' [a collection of rules called for by the very organization of (man's) spiritual being] (II, 627), made him sensitive . . . to what he calls 'toutes les ruses du style' [all the ruses of style] (II, 3)." Lloyd, *Baudelaire's Literary Criticism* (Cambridge: Cambridge University Press, 1981), 278, 279.

116. "In the eighteenth century the term 'demon' is a common one for allegorical agency, and in neoclassic odes and preromantic verse, as well as in the gothic novel, it is openly accepted and understood for what it is, a means of developing romantic plots by giving miraculous power to heroes and heroines," Fletcher writes. He also relates the demonic to "allegorical 'machines'": "Constriction of meaning, when it is the limit put upon a personified force or power, causes that personification to act somewhat mechanistically. The perfect allegorical agent is not a man possessed by a daemon, but a robot" (Fletcher, *Allegory,* 51–52, 55). Cf. Kayser's observations that "[a]mong the most persistent motifs of the grotesque we find human bodies reduced to puppets, marionettes, and automata"; "it is as if an impersonal force, an alien and inhuman spirit, had entered the soul" (*Grotesque in Art and Literature,* 183, 184).

Five   Machines, Monsters, and Men: Realism and the Modern Grotesque

1. *OC,* 2: 685; my translation.

2. In the fourth part of the "Poème," the poet says, "J'assiste à son raisonnement comme au jeu d'un mécanisme sous une vitre transparente" (*OC,* 1: 435).

3. De Maistre's manuscript on Rousseau, written in the 1790s, was not published until after Baudelaire's death, so he could not have known it. However, there is no denying that in the 1850s, he came under the influence of the ultramontane royalist critic, who treated Rousseau with the utmost scorn in his *Considérations sur la France* (Paris: Société typographique, 1814), saying that he displayed "an equal ignorance in matters of language, metaphysics, and history" and calling him "perhaps the man of all men who was most often wrong" (96–97; 61). De Maistre finds fault with Rousseau's political philosophy (he criticizes Rousseau's definition of the word "citizen"), his educational theory (he heaps sarcasm on the proposal that Emile should only begin thinking about God at twenty), and even his style (he inveighs against Rousseau's improper use of abstract terms). But Baudelaire disregards all of these criticisms and retains just two of the "wrongs" underscored by de Maistre: the question of Rousseau's truthfulness and the notion and status of "l'homme sauvage" in Rousseau's thought. Baudelaire gave both issues serious consideration. For a more complete account of the relationship between the two authors, see Daniel Vouga, *Baudelaire et Joseph de Maistre* (Paris: José Corti, 1957), and Bernard Howells, *Baudelaire: Individualism, Dandyism and the Philosophy of History* (Oxford: Legenda / European Humanities Research Centre, 1996). "There is little justification for the opinion which persists in holding Maistre responsible, even indirectly, for Baudelaire's increasing pessimism after 1852," Howells believes (125–26), but he does subscribe to the idea that Baudelaire gravitated to de Maistre's work because of their "common hostility to Rousseau" (130). Marcel Ruff, on the other hand, notes that although Baudelaire admired de Maistre, calling him "le grand génie de notre temps" ("the great genius of our times"), he never referred to de Maistre's political arguments (Ruff, "La Pensée politique et sociale de Baudelaire," 71).

4. Baud., *OC,* 1: 669.

5. References to "Jean-Jacques" first appear in Baudelaire's own writing in the period between 1846 and 1857 (it is impossible to pinpoint the date more exactly). Sometime after he attempted to take his life in 1845, Baudelaire expressed his disagreement with Rousseau's views on suicide ("Titres et canevas, XII," in Baud., *OC,* 1, 592–93), which appeared in excerpts from *Julie* reprinted in François Joseph Michel Noël, *Leçons françaises de littérature et de morale* (Paris: Le Normant père, 1830, and many other editions), the two volumes of which were in Baudelaire's possession; and sometime after 1848, in a cryptic note entitled "De quelques préjugés contemporains," he wrote: "De Jean-Jacques—auteur sentimental et infâme." It is in the decade following the Revolution of 1848, when Baudelaire was

the most influenced by de Maistre, that his asides about Rousseau are the most clearly deprecating.

6. "Vous avez, plus que jamais, l'air d'un confesseur et d'un accoucheur d'âmes" ("More than ever, you have the air of a confessor and a midwife of souls"), Baudelaire wrote Sainte-Beuve (*Corr.,* 2: 563, letter dated Jan. 2, 1866). In *Baudelaire's Literary Criticism* (270), Rosemary Lloyd also concludes that Sainte-Beuve, along with Théophile Gautier, especially influenced Baudelaire's thinking and expression. Indeed, Sainte-Beuve could have been responsible for Baudelaire's interest in de Maistre: "Joseph de Maistre" was one of Sainte-Beuve's *Portraits littéraires* in 1843.

7. In 1844 or 1845, Baudelaire took note of Sainte-Beuve's influence in a lengthy poem of praise (Baud., *Corr.,* 1: 116–18).

8. Robert Kopp attributes Baudelaire's interest in Aloysius Bertrand's *Gaspard de la Nuit* to Sainte-Beuve's influence (in fact, Sainte-Beuve edited and wrote a preface for Bertrand's work). Kopp reviews the relationship between the critic and Baudelaire in the introduction to his critical edition of the *Petits Poëmes en prose,* xxv–xxvi.

9. It would be naïve to take Sainte-Beuve's apparent neutrality regarding Rousseau at face value. His approach was undoubtedly motivated by political expediency. By underscoring the writer's artistic achievements, he meant to diminish or obscure the Rousseau of the Revolution and his revolutionary thought. In this way, he subtly promoted a return to order, while seeming to sidestep politics altogether. See Trousson, *Défenseurs et adversaires de J.-J. Rousseau,* 244. "In 1850, Sainte-Beuve's situation is analogous to Villemain's at the end of the Restoration. He can only speak about Rousseau if he underscores Rousseau's errors and his madness and if he dwells only on his talent as a writer and a poet," Roger Fayolle writes in *Sainte-Beuve et le XVIIIe siècle; ou, Comment les révolutions arrivent* (Paris: Armand Colin, 1972), 103 (my translation); cf. 228.

10. The dates of these influential columns suggest that Baudelaire was thinking about Rousseau even during the period between 1848 and the mid-1850s, when he was silent on the subject, and that he weighed de Maistre's heated condemnation against his mentor's rather more benign, although not uncritical, reading of the eighteenth-century author.

11. Sainte-Beuve, *Causeries,* 2: 83; my translation. This passage could also have inspired "Le Fou et la Vénus." All the translations of Sainte-Beuve's *Causeries* here are mine.

12. Sainte-Beuve, *Causeries,* 3: 78, "Les *Confessions* de J.-J. Rousseau" (Nov. 4, 1850).

13. Ibid.: "rudesses d'accent," "crudités de terroir" (82); "détails de mauvais ton où il parle de volerie et de *mangeaille*" (83).

14. Ibid., 85.

15. Ibid., 91.

16. The passage is from book 4 of the *Confessions* (Rouss., *OC,* 1: 169; *CW,* 5:

142). Pieces of six whites were coins of little value; the total sum would have been about two and a half "sous."

17. Sainte-Beuve, *Causeries*, 3: 96.

18. "His free *rêverie* often expresses things that decorum [*la bienséance*] prevented other eighteenth-century authors from saying," but "he nonetheless produced *a new art* [*un art nouveau*] of pleasing and drawing in [the reader]," Villemain observes, anticipating Sainte-Beuve's comments (*Cours de littérature française*, 2: 300–301; my emphasis).

19. Hiddleston, *Baudelaire and Le Spleen de Paris*, 93, enumerates the different "daring intrusions" of "gross and vulgar vocabulary" in the *Petits Poèmes en prose* as follows: "references to spit, soot, excrement, rats, 'sauteuses', soup, henpecked husbands, broken teeth, blacked eyes, together with a variety of oaths and expletives. Some expressions could come only from the totally uneducated like 'Vénustre' for Vénus, while others, though not slang or uneducated, have at once a comic and a conversational tonality." Graham M. Robb, "Les Origines journalistiques de la prose poétique de Baudelaire," *Lettres romanes* 44 (1990): 1–2: 15–25, points out the parallel between certain types of journalistic language and the prose poems' mixture of up-to-the-minute allusions and classical references, of commonplaces and deformed maxims, of slang and preciosity, of familiar expressions and erudite language. Robb argues that Baudelaire set out to create a kind of slang, a subversive language based on bourgeois expressions, the full meaning of which would only be available to other marginalized members of Bohemia. See also Johnson, *Défigurations du langage poétique*, 38–39, 103 ff., on Baudelaire's "disgusting" mixture of poetic and novelistic language or codes.

20. Baudelaire apparently also lifted at least one passage from Sainte-Beuve's commentary and worked it into "Le Gâteau." Sainte-Beuve describes Rousseau's painterly style in terms of gradations of light and warmth, where the "warm light and the clarity of Italy or Greece" represent the best moments. Sometimes Rousseau fails to achieve this ideal, Sainte-Beuve notes, but he adds: "if, as around that beautiful lake in Geneva, the breeze sometimes comes to cool the air, and if some cloud suddenly throws a greyish tint over the flanks of the mountains, there are also days and hours of a perfectly limpid serenity" (*Causeries*, 3: 96). Sainte-Beuve's commentary mediates between Rousseau's text (*Julie*, 1: 23) and Baudelaire's rendition of it by making Rousseau's style as much the subject of Baudelaire's poem as the theory of the sublime in Rousseau's text. Incorporated into Baudelaire's poem, Sainte-Beuve's cloud is likened to the "manteau d'un géant aérien volant à travers le ciel" ("cloak of an aerial giant flying through the air"), a reflection perhaps of Baudelaire's own unease as he confronts Rousseau's giant shadow, his lingering challenge to the modern artist.

21. Among other things, Baudelaire told his mother in April 1861 that he was writing an autobiography that would make Rousseau's *Confessions* pale by comparison (Baud., *Corr.*, 2: 141).

22. According to Claude Pichois, Baudelaire was wary of the word *réalisme*:

"The word *realism* was the muddied banner that those who had been Baudelaire's friends picked up. Baudelaire sensed that it posed a threat to his work, which, indeed, will be condemned for its *realism,* a word loaded with implied immorality" (Baud., *OC,* 2: 1110). Pichois cites the tribunals that judged Flaubert (for "the vulgar and often shocking realism of his character depictions") and Baudelaire (guilty of "a crude realism that was offensive to decency") (ibid., 80 n. 1).

23. Ibid., 58.

24. The two texts on which I focus here, and which Baudelaire obviously read with care, presumably also led the poet to Rousseau's related, contemporaneous works on language and the theater, *L'Essai sur l'origine des langues* and *La Lettre à d'Alembert,* which figure too, albeit much less prominently, in Baudelaire's poems. *La Lettre à d'Alembert* was composed and published in 1758, following the publication in the *Encyclopédie* of d'Alembert's article "Genève," in which he faulted Geneva for not having a theater. According to Jean-Jacques Eigeldinger, in his introduction to the *Dictionnaire de musique,* Rousseau had finished the dictionary entries that related to the *Essai sur l'origine des langues* (among them "Opéra") before he submitted the *Essai* to Malesherbes at the end of September 1761; and apparently he had finished the letter "O" of the *Dictionnaire* even earlier, by the end of 1759 (Rouss., *OC,* 5: cclxxvii). *Julie* was published in 1761.

25. For the complete texts of the pamphlets that make up this Querelle, see *La Querelle des Bouffons: Texte des pamphlets,* ed. Denise Launay (Geneva: Minkoff Reprint, 1973). For the history of the quarrel, see Louisette Reichenburg, *Contribution à l'histoire de la "querelle des bouffons": Guerre de brochures suscitées par le "Petit prophète" de Grimm et par la "Lettre sur la musique française" de Rousseau* (diss., University of Pennsylvania, 1937; reprint, New York: AMS Press, 1978).

26. Saisselin, *Enlightenment,* 43.

27. See Chastel, *Grottesque,* 52. The Italian players of the commedia dell'arte performed in fair theaters.

28. Ibid., 34.

29. Friedrich Melchior Grimm, "Poëme lyrique," in *Encyclopédie,* 12: 828.

30. Ibid., 829.

31. *Encyclopédie,* s.v. "Machine (Littér.)": ". . . in a dramatic poem, refers to the artifice by which the poet introduces on stage some divinity, genie, or other supernatural being, to bring about some important plan, or to surmount some difficulty that exceeds the power of men." Stage machines were in prominent use in the seventeenth century in "la tragédie à machines," or "machine tragedy," that inspired the newly created opera. Each tragedy was set in a variety of fictional locales, which might include a garden, a cave, Hades, a fortress, the Sun and Jupiter on clouds, or Circe in a flying chariot, and each set change or arrival of a god on high required the intervention of machines. See Jacques Scherer, *La Dramaturgie classique en France* (Paris: Nizet, 1950), 165–66.

32. Fletcher, *Allegory,* 56–57, remarks: "It has long been traditional to use the

word 'machine' in a technical sense, to mean the theatrical or rhetorical device by which daemonic agency was introduced onto the stage, so that the action could be resolved by fiat, by sheer force. The 'god from the machine' enters upon action blocked by an impasse and breaks this impasse in a manner beyond human strength. . . . [Eighteenth-century writers] organize the so-called 'sublime poem' according to a plan of allegorical agents which are often called 'machines,' or less frequently 'engines.' In this sense the term 'machine' does not, however, connote a scientific ordering of thought . . . while allegory employs 'machinery,' it is not an engineer's type of machinery at all."

33. Thus the author of the article "Merveilleux" in the *Encyclopédie* begins his review by defining the marvelous as a "term devoted to epic poetry, by which is meant certain bold, but nonetheless plausible fictions, which being outside the circle of common ideas astonish the mind. Such is the intervention of the gods of paganism in the poems of Homer and Virgil. Such are the metaphysical beings personified in modern writings, such as Discord, Love, Fanaticism, etc. These are what we otherwise call *machines*."

34. Grimm, "Poëme lyrique," 829, remarks on the poor taste of the Italian poet, who dared to include magicians alongside Christian warriors and who called up Hatred from hell. When Quinault made Tasso's poem into an opera, Grimm notes, Hatred appeared on stage wearing "his wig made of snakes, with another passel of serpents in his right hand, and his red gloves and stockings sparkling with silver sequins."

35. Another sign of their affinity is the occasional presence in grotesque painting of fairies, imported from the marvelous literary genre of fairy tales; or conversely, the presence in fairy tales, such as Madame de Villeneuve's *La Belle et la bête (Beauty and the Beast),* of the monkeys and birds so often depicted in arabesque works.

36. Because of its popularity, the abbé Batteux's *Les Beaux-Arts réduits à un même principe* was reprinted in 1753, along with his *Cours de belles-lettres* (1747–48), under the title of *Cours de belles-lettres; ou, Principes de la littérature.*

37. Charles Batteux, *Les Beaux-Arts réduits à un même principe* (1746), ed. J.-R. Mantion (Paris: Aux Amateurs de Livres, 1989), 85; my translation.

38. Ibid., 206. The Latin quotation is from Horace, *Ars poetica,* v. 188.

39. Batteux, *Beaux-Arts,* 175–76.

40. Ibid., 211.

41. "To fill its long schedule, [the Opéra] was forced to keep operas in the repertory for periods of time most unnatural by the norms of musical taste. . . . The old operas, most importantly those of Lully, came to be a symbol of the state. . . . In these operas France displayed the glories of its past, and Frenchmen took pleasure in both a social and political nostalgia." William Weber, "*La musique ancienne* in the Waning of the Ancien Régime," *Journal of Modern History* 56 (1984): 63–64.

42. The classic work on the royal spectacles and the king's successive roles as "machinist" and "machine" is Jean-Marie Apostolidès, *Le Roi-machine: Spectacle et politique au temps de Louis XIV* (Paris: Minuit, 1981). See also Charles Mazouer, *Molière et ses comédies-ballets* (Paris: Klincksieck, 1993), and Jean-Pierre Néraudau, *L'Olympe du Roi-Soleil: Mythologie et idéologie royale au Grand Siècle* (Paris: Les Belles Lettres, 1986).

43. Weber, *"La musique ancienne,"* argues that the modern era of the Paris Opéra began in 1774, and his table 1 (70–71) shows the complete elimination of Lully's works from the program around this time.

44. Ibid., 79. See also Saisselin, *Enlightenment,* 44: "Taste could not be divorced from politics. Indeed, taste *was* politics."

45. On the revolutionary implications of the Querelle des Bouffons, see Robert Wokler, *"La Querelle des Bouffons* and the Italian Liberation of France: A Study of Revolutionary Foreplay," *Studies in the Eighteenth Century* 6, special issue of *Eighteenth-Century Life* 11, no. 1 (1987), 94–116, and Charles B. Paul, "Music and Ideology: Rameau, Rousseau, and 1789," *Journal of the History of Ideas* 32, no. 3 (1971): 395–410.

46. Saisselin, *Enlightenment,* 28. On the reception accorded the partisans of Italian music and Rousseau in particular, see "De la liberté de la musique," d'Alembert's postscript to the Querelle, in his *Oeuvres complètes* (Paris, 1821), 1: 515–46. The French side viewed the whole Querelle as "a kind of international conspiracy against France," Wokler notes, and they became increasingly political in their attacks, writing essays like Rochemont's "Réflexions d'un patriote" (*"La Querelle des Bouffons,"* 100).

47. *Julie, or the New Heloise,* trans. Philip Stewart and Jean Vaché, in *The Collected Writings of Rousseau,* ed. Roger D. Masters and Christopher Kelly (Hanover, N.H.: University Press of New England, 1997), 6: 230. All English translations are from this edition.

48. Rouss., *OC,* 2: 284; *CW,* 6: 232.

49. Ibid., 2: 281; *CW,* 6: 230.

50. Ibid., 2: 282; *CW,* 6: 231; translation modified.

51. Ibid., 2: 288; *CW,* 6: 235. See also "Ballet," in *Dictionnaire de musique,* in Rouss., *OC,* 5: 648–50. Unfortunately, this article is not included in the selections from the *Dictionary of Music* translated by John Scott.

52. Rouss., *OC,* 2: 284; *CW,* 6: 232; translation modified.

53. Rouss., *OC,* 5: 956; *CW,* 7: 454, s.v. "Opéra."

54. *Encyclopédie,* 10: 393–95, s.v. "Merveilleux": "Minerve et Junon, Mars et Venus, qui jouent de si grands rôles dans l'Iliade et dans l'Enéide, ne seraient aujourd'hui dans un poème épique que des noms sans réalité, auxquels le lecteur n'attacherait aucune idée distincte" ("Minerva and Juno, Mars and Venus, who played such important roles in the *Iliad* and in the *Aeneid,* would be just names without reality in an epic poem today, and the reader would attach no clear idea to them").

55. *Encyclopédie,* s.v. "Merveilleux": "Une règle qu'on pourrait proposer sur cet article, ce serait de ne jamais entrelacer des êtres réels avec des êtres moraux ou métaphysiques; parce que de deux choses l'une, ou l'allégorie domine et fait prendre les êtres physiques pour des personnages imaginaires, ou elle se dément et devient un composé bizarre de figures et de réalités qui se détruisent mutuellement" ("A rule that one might propose [regarding the use of allegory] would be never to interweave real beings with moral or metaphysical beings; because one of two things will happen: either the allegory will dominate and make us interpret physical beings as imaginary characters, or else the allegory will belie itself and become a bizarre composite of figures and realities that destroy one another").

56. These misplaced elements resemble the rococo architectural ornaments and decorative paintings Louis de Jaucourt fulminates against in his *Encyclopédie* article "Ornement." Lamenting the depraved taste implicit in these "grotesques," he points to the example of the sculpted images on the doors of the basilica of St. Peter in Rome of Ganymede and the eagle and Jupiter and Leda, which are out of place there. De Jaucourt compares the corrupted taste in architecture and in painting and concludes: "on ne se propose ordinairement d'autre but, que celui de couvrir des places vides . . . l'horreur du vide remplit les murs de peintures vides de sens" ("they ordinarily pursue no other goal than that of covering empty spaces . . . a fear of the void [or vacuum] fills the walls with paintings empty of meaning") (my translation).

57. Rouss., *OC,* 2: 284; *CW,* 6: 232.

58. St. Preux complains: "Il semble que les esprits se roidissent contre une illusion raisonnable, et ne s'y prêtent qu'autant qu'elle est absurde et grossiere; ou peut-être que des Dieux leur coûtent moins à concevoir que des Héros" ("It seems their minds brace themselves against a reasonable illusion, and give in to it only insofar as it is absurd and crude; or perhaps Gods are easier for them to imagine than Heroes") (Rouss., *OC,* 2: 281–82; *CW,* 6: 230).

59. For example, St. Preux says sarcastically, "jamais on n'entendit parler à Rome avec tant de respect de la majesté du peuple romain qu'on parle à Paris de la majesté de l'Opéra" ("never was the majesty of the Roman people invoked with such respect in Rome as the majesty of the Opéra is in Paris") (ibid., *OC,* 2: 283; *CW,* 6: 231).

60. In Macrobius's *Saturnalia* 2.7, Avienus presents Laberius as "a Roman knight, a blunt and outspoken man, whom Caesar for a fee of five hundred thousand sesterces invited to appear on the stage and act in person in the mimes which it was his practice to write." Macrobius, *The Saturnalia,* trans. Percival Vaughan Davies (New York: Columbia University Press, 1969), 180.

61. Rousseau mistakenly cites "Aulu-Gèle" (i.e., Aulus Gellius) rather than Macrobius as the source of this material. The error was corrected in the 1763 edition of *La Nouvelle Héloïse,* but the original mistake is retained in most subsequent editions, with the correction appended in a note.

62. Baudelaire, *Parisian Prowler,* trans. Kaplan, 27–28: "dancing girls, lovely as

fairies"; "a magician dazzling like *a god*" (my emphases); "muscle men [Baudelaire uses the word *Hercules*], proud of the hugeness of their limbs."

63. Rouss., *OC,* 2: 285; *CW,* 6: 233; my emphases. Rousseau's article "Opéra" explains this analogy. Because he expects the opera to embody a certain realism, which is the antithesis of the grotesque, he relegates the extravagant scenery and broad acting to the popular fair theaters, which derive from the zany comedy of the commedia dell'arte and make no pretense of realism: "Nous avons vu que, voulant offrir aux regards l'intérêt et les mouvements qui manquoient à la Musique, on avoit imaginé les grossiers prestiges des machines et des vols. . . . Il est donc très-naturel que la musique, devenue passionnée et pathétique, ait renvoyé sur *les Théâtres des Foires* ces mauvais suppléments dont elle n'avoit plus besoin sur le sien" ("We have seen that, wanting to offer to view the interest and the movements the Music lacked, crude tricks of machines and flights were devised. . . . It is therefore quite natural that music, having become passionate and pathetic, would have sent back those poor supplements, which it no longer needed in its own, to *the Theaters of the Fairs*") (Rouss., *OC,* 5: 956; *CW,* 7: 454; my emphasis;)

64. For a more complete reading of this poem and "Une Mort héroïque," see my article "The Legitimation Crisis: Event and Meaning in Baudelaire's 'Le Vieux Saltimbanque' and 'Une Mort héroïque,'" *Romanic Review* 73 (1982): 452–62. When I wrote that essay, I had not yet seen the relation to Rousseau that informs the two poems.

65. Furthermore, Baudelaire utilizes almost verbatim a phrase from a letter by St. Preux adjacent to the satire on the Paris Opéra. St. Preux writes: "la plume échappe à ma main tremblante; mes larmes inondent le papier" (Rouss., *Julie,* 2: 26); and the narrator of "Une Mort héroïque" reiterates: "Ma plume tremble, et des larmes d'une émotion toujours présente me montent aux yeux pendant que je cherche à vous décrire cette inoubliable soirée."

66. The opening of the poem describes Fancioulle's participation in "une conspiration formée par quelques gentilshommes mécontents" ("a conspiracy formed by some disgruntled gentlemen") and ranks him among "ces individus d'humeur atrabilaire qui veulent déposer les princes et opérer, sans la consulter, le déménagement d'une société" ("those hot-tempered individuals who try to depose princes and to operate, without consulting it, the dismantling of a society").

67. The "mime" (in Latin *mimus*) in Macrobius's day designated both a specific theatrical genre and an actor in plays of this type, rather than the mute pantomimist denoted by the term today. Baudelaire tracked down Macrobius's original version of chapter 7 of *The Saturnalia* (he found a few more details there for the delineation of his own "histrion"), and he simply updated Macrobius's "mimus" to resemble the pantomime artists of the popular theater of his own day, of which he was fond.

68. The conclusion of Laberius's story is not in St. Preux's letter but in the letter's source. Chafing against "the constraint put upon him by Caesar," Macrobius

says, Laberius took revenge in his acting. He included in his roles provocative challenges to the emperor, crying out, for instance: "On, Citizens of Rome, we lose our liberty" and "Many he needs must fear whom many fear." Laberius put the audience on his side, and this was more than Caesar could bear: "[At] those last words the audience as one man turned and looked at Caesar, thus indicating that this scathing gibe was an attack on his despotism. It was for this reason that Caesar transferred his patronage to Publilius" (Macrobius, *Saturnalia,* trans. Davies, 180–81).

69. Baudelaire, *Parisian Prowler,* trans. Kaplan, 65; translation modified.

70. As I point out in my article on this poem (cited in n. 64 above), the mime exercises the same "toute-puissante domination" over the audience that the prince exercises over his state; and the prince, conversely, is a "véritable artiste lui-même."

71. "La Corde" demonstrates that language and writing (or rhetoric) are, as Baudelaire knew, truly "magical operations" ("[des] opérations magiques") (*OC,* 1: 658).

72. In his notes on the poem, Kopp gives the background to this true story (Baudelaire, *Petits Poëmes en prose,* 302–5), as well as a rundown of Manet's art around the time of the poem's composition and publication.

73. Ibid., 302.

74. Since, of course, the whole point is to create a deceptive illusion of "reality," this difference is not directly stated in the poem. In fact, the narrator's presence is limited to four words ("—me disait mon ami—") inserted in the first sentence of an otherwise uninterrupted quotation. This parenthetical note is sufficient, however, to establish a double reading, corresponding to the "énoncé" and the "énonciation" of the poem, and to displace the mystification from the level of the painter's experience to the level of the poet's address to the reader.

75. Hiddleston, *Baudelaire and the Art of Memory,* 249; my emphasis.

76. My translation. The author therefore argues, as did many eighteenth-century critics of the marvelous, that pagan gods have no place in contemporary epic poetry. Instead, taking the ancients as their models, the moderns should incorporate (if they must) only Christian figures, such as angels, saints, and demons—or, at the limit, "certaines traditions ou fabuleuses ou suspectes, mais pourtant communément reçues" ("certain traditions, whether fabulous or suspect, which are nonetheless commonly received").

77. Baudelaire works the same "magic" with the grotesque idea of "monsters." In this poem, for instance, the passing reference to the painter's model as "le petit monstre" stands out very little or not at all. In Baudelaire's poem, the monster is no longer one of the Paris Opéra's gauche beasts, the dragons and fat toads animated by silly peasants, but the real boy behind the artistic rendering. By transferring the term from the role to the person who incarnates it, and by incorporating the reference in a lengthy description of the swollen and stiffened body of the dead boy, Baudelaire naturalizes the figure. It passes unnoticed as an everyday epithet used to describe little boys who misbehave.

78. Marie Maclean, *Narrative as Performance: The Baudelairean Experiment* (London: Routledge, 1988), 58.

79. Hiddleston, *Baudelaire and the Art of Memory*, 248.

80. Hiddleston reads "La Corde" as just such an indictment, which would suggest that Baudelaire is in complete agreement with Rousseau. But if I am right that the opening paragraphs of "Une Mort héroïque" are a commentary on Rousseau's talent as a comic author, it seems that Baudelaire loved the satirical letter as much as the eighteenth-century public loved the "false magnificence" of the Paris Opéra.

Six   The Sociopolitical Implications of the Grotesque: "Opéra" and "Les Yeux des pauvres"

1. Chambers, *Writing of Melancholy*, 2.

2. Ibid., 7: the duplicitous modern text "raises the question of *nouveauté* or 'newness' . . . in a universe so rigidly structured that everything is always already *classé*, that is, *identified by class*." Indeed, Chambers locates this moment of "newness" in a specific historical universe, under the repressive control of the Second Empire. Baudelaire seems to have decided, as Nathaniel Wing argues, that the most effective opposition to power is not direct confrontation (which in 1848 resulted in the repression of the opposition and the imposition of tighter censorship) but the use of "evasive strategies" to disrupt the dominant narrative (Wing, "Poets, Mimes and Counterfeit Coins," 10).

3. Monroe, *Poverty of Objects*, 103.

4. Underscoring the ambiguity, not only of the addressee (lover or reader), but of that addressee's number (singular or plural), Maclean, *Narrative as Performance*, 114, notes: "For a brief but important moment until the interlocutor is identified, the reader or readers tend to be assimilated by the deictic *you* and to read the message ambiguously. The receiver is felt both to be the unknown *you and* the readers themselves who partially experience [the first sentence] as a message to them."

5. Friedman, "Baudelaire's Theory of Practice," 321, makes this larger connection: "the speaker's opening remark about feminine impermeability could well stand as a warning about the difficulties of reading Baudelaire's prose poems. . . . the critic is often in the position of the obtuse woman."

6. The café is referred to as an exclusive "house [or establishment]" where, as even the poor child knows, "only people who are not like us can enter" ("c'est une maison où peuvent seuls entrer les gens qui ne sont pas comme nous"). The term "porte cochère" has sometimes been translated as "entrance gate" (see, e.g., Baudelaire, *Parisian Prowler*, trans. Kaplan, 60–61), but that translation does not retain the idea of the horse-drawn coach ("coche") and the coachman ("cocher"), which are both contained within "cochère," and it therefore eliminates the idea of service and servants from this part of the text.

7. Except where noted, translations of "Les Yeux des pauvres" are by Kaplan, ibid.

8. The dictionary entry was so complete and important that Rousseau thought of publishing it as a stand-alone piece. In his introduction to the *Dictionnaire de Musique* (Rouss., *OC,* 5: cclxxxvii–cclxxxviii), Jean-Jacques Eigeldinger makes this point: "Moreover, the author considered the articles 'Music' . . . and 'Opera' as writings like any others [des écrits à part entière], worthy of appearing in the collection of his general works, projected for the beginning of 1765" (my translation).

9. I particularly like Downing Thomas's formulation that opera, in general, is "rhetoric *in musica.*" *Music and the Origins of Language: Theories from the French Enlightenment* (Cambridge: Cambridge University Press, 1995), 146.

10. Ibid., 10. For an insightful reading of the *Lettre à d'Alembert* and its political project, see Patrick Coleman, *Rousseau's Political Imagination: Rule and Representation in the Lettre à d'Alembert* (Geneva: Droz, 1984).

11. In the satirical letter, St. Preux complains, "Il semble que les esprits se roidissent contre une illusion raisonnable, et ne s'y prêtent qu'autant qu'elle est absurde et grossière" ("It seems their minds brace themselves against a reasonable illusion, and give in to it only insofar as it is absurd and crude") (Rouss., *OC,* 2: 281–82; *CW,* 6: 230).

12. For the emphasis on the "man of taste," see e.g., Rouss., *OC,* 5: 951; *CW,* 7: 450: "l'homme de goût rebute [cette Mélodie enchanteresse] au Théâtre, quand on le flatte sans l'émouvoir" ("the man of taste rebuffs [that enchantress Melody] at the Theater when it flatters him without moving him").

13. Rousseau's formulations are misleading if taken literally, instead of in the sense of the allegory, for he typically refers to music and poetry as separate languages. That opera is a language unto itself is made clear almost from the beginning of the article when, in a discussion of Greek forms, Rousseau specifies the need to unite music and speech or poetry on the lyric stage: "il fut ensuite question d'appliquer la Musique à la parole, et de la lui rendre tellement propre sur la Sçène lyrique, que *le tout pûr* [sic] *être pris pour un seul et même idiôme*" ("it was then a question of applying the Music to the speech and of making it so appropriate for the lyric Scene that *the whole could be taken for a single and identical idiom*") (Rouss., *OC,* 5: 950; *CW,* 7: 449); my emphasis. This ideal governs his entire piece.

14. Rouss., *OC,* 5: 952; *CW,* 7: 451: " comme s'il y avoit plus de mérite à faire parler platement le Roi des Dieux que le dernier des mortels, et que les Valets de Molière ne fussent pas préférables aux Héros de Pradon" ("as if there were more merit in making the King of the Gods speak as insipidly as the lowest of mortals, and as if Molière's Valets were not preferable to Pradon's Heroes!").

15. Rouss., *OC,* 5: 951; *CW,* 7: 450: "nous sommes forcés de chercher dans la sensation le plaisir que le sentiment nous refuse" ("we are forced to seek in sensation the pleasure which feeling denies us"). As Downing Thomas notes, "the visible was a touchy subject within neo-classical codes of *bienséance,* or propriety [because it made available what should be sublimated in poetic discourse]" (*Music and the Origins of Language,* 147). The philosophes agreed with Boileau, for whom the interest of drama should lie in the plot, not in the visual.

16. Rouss., *OC,* 5: 953; *CW,* 7: 452: "quel meilleur usage pouvoit-on faire au Théâtre d'une Musique qui ne savoit rien peindre, que de l'employer à la représentation des choses qui ne pouvoient exister, et sur lesquelles personne n'étoit en état de comparer l'image à l'objet?" ("what better use could be made in the Theater of a Music that didn't know how to portray anything than to employ it for the representation of things that could not exist and of which no one was in a position to compare the image to the object?").

17. Rouss., *OC,* 5: 405–6; *Essay on the Origin of Languages,* trans. and ed. John T. Scott, in Rouss., *CW,* 7: 314.

18. Rouss., *OC,* 5: 406; *CW,* 7: 314.

19. See Thomas, *Music and the Origins of Language,* 120: "Rousseau is describing an inaugural (and final) moment of plenitude in which the musical accents of language are made to express a state of being free from the troubles of work, repressed sexuality, and social constraint. Rousseau uses music to represent this liminal, pre-linguistic state that is nonetheless inhabited by unrepressed signification and social practices."

20. Ibid., 175.

21. I rely here on Paul de Man's reading of the *Essai sur l'origine des langues* in *Allegories of Reading* (New Haven, Conn.: Yale University Press, 1979), 135–59.

22. My very condensed formulation here belies the importance of this point, which is at the heart of Rousseau's critique of the French opera in the "Lettre sur la musique française" and of his position in the Querelle des Bouffons.

23. "The divorce between language and music . . . also carried within it implications for the history of culture, politics, and social vitality," Downing Thomas observes; "the development of languages contributes to the disaffection of individuals within society and even to oppression" (*Music and the Origins of Language,* 55, 90).

24. "Sur quoi l'on doit remarquer que les Langues les plus propres à fléchir sous les loix de la Mesure et de la Mélodie sont celles où la duplicité dont je viens de parler est le moins apparente" ("Concerning this it should be noted that the Languages most suited to yield to the laws of Meter and of Melody are those in which the doubleness of which I have just been speaking is least apparent") (Rouss., *OC,* 5: 956; *CW,* 7: 454; translation modified). In the *Essai,* Rousseau makes it clear that, unlike music, language separates men from other animals and from each other—speech differentiates : "La parole distingue l'homme entre les animaux: le langage distingue les nations entre elles; on ne connoit d'où est un homme qu'après qu'il a parlé" ("Speech distinguishes man from the animals. Language distinguishes nations from each other; one does not know where a man is from until after he has spoken") (Rouss., *OC,* 5: 375; *CW,* 7: 289).

25. "Nous avons vu que, voulant offrir aux regards l'intérêt et les mouvements qui manquoient à la Musique, on avoit imaginé les grossiers prestiges des machines et des vols. . . . Il est donc très naturel que la musique, devenue passionnée et pathétique, ait renvoyé sur les Théâtres des Foires ces mauvais supplémens dont

elle n'avoit plus besoin sur le sien" ("We have seen that, wanting to offer to view the interest and the movements which the Music lacked, crude tricks of machines and flights were devised. . . . It is therefore quite natural that music, having become passionate and pathetic, would have sent back those poor supplements which it no longer needed in its own to the Theaters of the Fairs") (Rouss., *OC,* 5: 956; *CW,* 7: 454).

26. The second half of the novel develops at length the values and successes of the extended family gathered around Julie and her husband on their estate at Clarens.

27. Chastel, *Grottesque,* 12, cites Benvenuto Cellini's explanation of the origins of the name.

28. Maurice Delcroix, "Un Poème en prose de Charles Baudelaire: *Les Yeux des pauvres,*" *Cahiers d'analyse textuelle* 19 (1977): 55; Maclean, *Narrative as Performance,* 116–17.

29. The narrator uses a vulgar, slangy term, *la goinfrerie,* to mirror the inappropriateness of this excessive decor.

30. Friedman, "Baudelaire's Theory of Practice," 325.

31. Delcroix's very rich reading in "Un Poème en prose de Charles Baudelaire" furnishes many of my insights, although he does not develop his analysis according to the stylistic or rhetorical categories I want to emphasize.

32. Even the "baguette" turns up in the café's decorations, in "les ors des baguettes et des corniches" ("the gilding of the moldings and cornices")!

33. My translation and emphasis.

34. Rouss., *OC,* 5: 952; *CW,* 7: 451.

35. As Delcroix helpfully points out ("Un Poème en prose de Charles Baudelaire," 57), the effects of realism in this segment include the approximate age of the father, the revealing detail of his prematurely grey beard, and mention of the man's fatigue.

36. Maclean suggests a further correspondance when she assimilates the sidewalk to a stage and the street to the audience in a theater (*Narrative as Performance,* 117). I would argue that this allocation of space is reversed when the narrator looks at the family before him.

37. Friedman's reading of the poem in "Baudelaire's Theory of Practice" is particularly acute concerning the various divisions *within* the different subject positions, not just among them.

38. This utopian dream was often associated with Rousseau in nineteenth-century France, but it is important to bear in mind that in his article, Rousseau recognizes the inherent instability or unattainability of this dream.

39. Hebe, Juno's daughter and the goddess of youth, was cup-bearer to the gods. Ganymede was a Trojan boy whom Jupiter, disguised as an eagle, carried off to heaven and installed as Hebe's successor. *Bulfinch's Mythology,* ed. Bryan Holme (New York: Viking Press, 1979), 180.

40. One of the distinguishing features of a proper noun is that it does "not

freely allow determiners or number contrasts." There is some latitude in this usage, of course; for instance, we refer to "the two Koreas," and we might speak of "the Baudelaires of this world." Nonetheless, the pluralization of a proper noun is distinctive and calls for interpretation. See Sylvia Chalker and Edmund Weiner, *The Oxford Dictionary of English Grammar* (Oxford: Clarendon Press, 1994), s.v. "proper noun."

41. Robert, *Dictionnaire de la Langue française:* "L'ensemble des personnes (enfants, serviteurs, esclaves, parents) vivant sous le même toit, sous la puissance du *pater familias*"*;* my translation.

42. *Ibid.:* "est connoté comme faisant partie du discours patronal et paternaliste"*;* my translation.

43. Baudelaire gives us a hint about how to read his poem when his narrator sums up the problem of communication (*s'entendre*) as a problem of hearing (*entendre*)—"tant il est difficile de s'entendre"—but there is no evidence that anyone has ever heeded this clue.

44. Michelet claims that Rousseau's message was "'Votre volonté collective, c'est la Raison elle-même.' Autrement dit: Vous êtes Dieux" ("'Your collective will is reason itself.' In other words: You are gods") (*Histoire de la Révolution française*, 1: 58).

45. Baudelaire may have had in mind a recent case of such paternalism: in 1859, one André Godin, a disciple of Charles Fourier's, created a cooperative industrial establishment which he named "Familistère" after Fourier's "phalanstères" (Robert, *Dictionnaire de la Langue française*).

46. Margery Evans, *Baudelaire and Intertextuality* (Cambridge: Cambridge University Press), 53, observes that the poem "casts doubt on its own power to communicate with the reader, who is aggressively stigmatised along with the poet's insensitive companion."

47. Friedman, "Baudelaire's Theory of Practice," 320, notes that "the man's condemnation of the woman's callousness ultimately charges her with being a bad reader," and she goes on to suggest (321) that "the critic is often in the position of the obtuse woman."

48. It seems clear enough that Baudelaire wants to discourage readers who, like the woman, have no tolerance for difference or otherness. But Baudelaire does not suggest, either, that we identify with the narrator, himself a monological reader, whose bourgeois discourse permits diversity within the "family," while repressing revolution. I agree with Friedman ("Baudelaire's Theory of Practice," 323) that the text "dramatizes the difficulty of taking either character as a positive alternative to the other's blindness." As for the family, they are depicted as naïve, even infantile, in their inability to see figures for what they are.

49. Wing has astutely demonstrated ("Poets, Mimes and Counterfeit Coins," 10, 12) that Baudelaire's politics come across in his prose poems not as direct opposition to power but as "an explosive interruption" of the master narrative that

maintains social agents in subject positions. By destabilizing, rather than partici-
pating in the dichotomies underlying power, Wing argues, Baudelaire both eludes
censorship and makes clear "the precarious discursive equilibrium by which power
is articulated."

50. Chastel, *Grottesque*, 25: "Le domaine des grottesques est donc assez exacte-
ment l'antithèse de celui de la représentation" ("The domain of grotesques is thus
quite exactly the antithesis of the domain of representation").

Seven   Rousseau, Trauma, and Fetishism: "Le Vieux Saltimbanque"

1. In a letter to Armand Fraisse dated Aug. 12, 1860, Baudelaire states: "J'ai une
très profonde horreur de la candeur dans l'exercice du métier littéraire, parce que
le genre humain n'est pas un confesseur, et qu'infailliblement l'homme de lettres
candide sera dupe, à moins qu'il ne soit *un charlatan obscène comme J.-J. Rousseau*
ou George Sand" ("I have a very deep horror of candor in the exercise of the literary craft, because humankind is not a confessor, and because infallibly the candid
man of letters will be a dupe, unless he is *an obscene charlatan like J.-J. Rousseau* or
George Sand"). Charles Baudelaire, *Nouvelles lettres* (Paris: Fayard, 2000), 30; my
emphasis and translation. Baudelaire appears to reinforce the scurrilous epithet
brandished by conservatives such as Désiré Nisard. However, interpreting Baudelaire's remarks is not easy, given the political climate of the time and the fact that
Fraisse was a journalist for *Le Salut Public* in Lyon, whom Baudelaire had never
met. See *Armand Fraisse sur Baudelaire, 1857–1869,* ed. Claude Pichois and
Vincenette Pichois (Gembloux, Belgium: J. Duculot, 1973). As Claude Pichois has
noted, Baudelaire had a habit of expressing very different opinions about an author in public and in private, and there may be just such a dichotomy in his views
in this case. Claude Pichois, *Baudelaire,* trans. Graham Robb (London: Hamish
Hamilton, 1989), 298.

2. Baud., *OC,* 2: 343–44; my emphasis and translation.

3. Pichois surmises that this preface was first drafted in 1862–63 and reworked
as late as 1864–66, when the poet was in Brussels. See Baud., *OC,* 1: 1170, notes to
page 185. The passage, in particular the reference to "le mécanisme des trucs,"
compares to Rousseau's critical statements about the Opéra's machines, which became a code word for allegory.

4. Baud., *OC,* 1: 185; my emphasis and translation.

5. Jean Starobinski makes this point in his article, "Sur quelques répondants allégoriques du poète," *Revue d'histoire littéraire de la France* 67 (1967): 404 (my
translation): "The saltimbanques will appear in a series of resolutely modern poems ["La Muse vénale"; "Le Vieux Saltimbanque"; "Les Vocations"; "Les Bons
Chiens"], although they have their precursors in Callot's universe."

6. Baudelaire, *Parisian Prowler,* trans. Kaplan, 29; translation modified.

7. Chastel, *Grottesque,* 49, remarks on the similarity between arabesque foliage

(*rinceaux*) and acrobatics: "The figures lend themselves to contortions that may make one think of gymnasts elaborating with their bodies who knows what decorative curves."

8. Rouss., *OC*, 1: 995.

9. Ibid., 640; my translation and emphasis.

10. Baudelaire also picks up on Rousseau's depiction of his aging face as "ma figure caduque" in the ninth *rêverie* (Baud., *OC*, 1: 1088) and writes this into the portrait of "le vieux saltimbanque" as well: "un pauvre saltimbanque, voûté, *caduc*, décrépit."

11. The word *peuple*, used so often in the nineteenth-century debate over Rousseau's political legacy, is repeated three times in the poem, in paragraphs one, two, and nine.

12. The poem first appeared in the *Revue fantaisiste*, Nov. 1, 1861; see Hiddleston's chronology of the prose poems' publication in *Baudelaire et le Spleen de Paris*, 114–16, and Baudelaire, *Petits Poëmes en prose*, ed. Kopp, 419–20.

13. It is widely agreed that Baudelaire's acrobats, jugglers, and mimes are avatars of the alienated artist, if not of Baudelaire himself. See, in particular, Starobinski, "Sur quelques répondants allégoriques du poète" and *Portrait de l'artiste en saltimbanque* (Geneva: Albert Skira, 1970).

14. Clark, *Absolute Bourgeois*, 120.

15. Baud., *OC*, 1: 221: "tu couvais de l'oeil . . . Quelque athlète en maillot, . . . que la police écharpe."

16. Clark, *Absolute Bourgeois*, 120–21.

17. The government drafted a law requiring the performers to obtain licenses and submit their songs to the appropriate prefect for approval, and they could not perform during the early evening hours, although that was the only time of day when they made money. See ibid., 122.

18. Ibid.

19. See, e.g., Michelet's lessons on Rousseau published in *L'Etudiant*.

20. Starobinski, *Portrait de l'artiste en Saltimbanque*, 96, remarks that in both "Une Mort héroïque" and "Le Vieux Saltimbanque," "l'artiste, en opposition au pouvoir (incarné par le prince ou par le peuple), n'est pas assez fort pour survivre à la condamnation passée contre lui par le pouvoir."

21. Clark, *Absolute Bourgeois*, 122.

22. The ninth *rêverie* presents itself very directly as a story of intergenerational relations. The text falls neatly into two parts, with opposing but interconnected themes. The first part describes the pleasure Rousseau derives from children and their games and seeks to justify his notorious abandonment of his own offspring; the second narrates his encounters with the elderly inhabitants of the Invalides. Both emphasize the change in Rousseau's relationships with others over time. Whereas children used to accept him as their equal and playmate, they are now frightened away by his collapsing face (*figure caduque*), and the old men, too, view

him differently now. They used to approach him with a courteous salute, but since they have learned who he is, their civility has given way to open animosity. This bipartite structure, and the theme of intergenerational relations, are obvious elements in Baudelaire's poem. Baudelaire also writes out at length, in the description of the fair, a remark about feast days that opens the ninth *rêverie*: "Est-il une jouissance plus douce que de voir un peuple entier se livrer à la joie un jour de fête, et tous les coeurs s'épanouir aux rayons suprêmes du plaisir qui passe rapidement, mais vivement, à travers les nuages de la vie?" And the encounter with the old acrobat takes up, in some of the same terms, Rousseau's chance meeting with a "vieux invalide" at the end of Rousseau's text. (Rousseau meets the old veteran on an outing, and finds him so moving that he wants to give him some money, but ultimately, out of shame, he refrains from putting a coin in the man's hand.)

23. Baudelaire had a keen interest in autobiography, and in 1861, the year of the poem's initial publication, he was trying to write his own, tentatively titled "Mon coeur mis à nu" (My heart laid bare). In a letter to his mother written on April 1, 1861, he discussed his autobiographical project and declared: "Ah! si jamais ['Mon coeur mis à nu'] voit le jour, les *Confessions* de J[ean]-J[acques] paraîtront pâles. Tu vois que je rêve encore" ("Ah! if ever ['Mon coeur mis à nu'] sees the light of day, Jean-Jacques' *Confessions* will appear pale. You see I'm still dreaming") (Baud., *Corr.*, 2: 141; my translation). Two years later, he told his mother again that "'Mon coeur mis à nu' qui est devenu la vraie passion de mon cerveau, . . . sera autre chose que les fameuses *Confessions* de Jean-Jacques" ("'Mon coeur mis à nu,' which has become the true passion of my brain, . . . will be quite unlike the famous *Confessions* of Jean-Jacques") (Baud., *Corr.* 2: 302, letter to Madame Aupick, June 3, 1863). Unfortunately, Baudelaire never completed the autobiography he envisioned, and it exists today only in the form of fragments, the ultimate shape of which we cannot know.

24. The same may be said of the Rousseau figure, Fancioulle, in "Une Mort héroïque."

25. Freud explains that "when the fetish is instituted some process occurs which reminds one of the stopping of memory in traumatic amnesia. As in this latter case, the subject's interest comes to a halt half-way, as it were; it is as though the last impression before the uncanny and traumatic one is retained as a fetish." "Fetishism," trans. Joan Riviere, in *The Standard Edition of the Complete Psychological Works of Sigmund Freud,* ed. James Strachey et al. (London: Hogarth Press and the Institute of Psycho-Analysis, 1961), 21: 155.

26. In Freud's theory, the fetish holds in abeyance the trauma of the mother's castration. Froidevaux, *Baudelaire,* 105, explains: "The fetishist thus represses an observed fact thanks to a symbolic operation that allows two incompatible things to come together: the fact (the absence of the feminine penis) and the desire (the feminine penis exists, if only in the form of a substitute). The fetish is the bearer of two perfectly contradictory meanings" (my translation).

27. For further details about the poem, and an earlier version of this analysis, I refer the reader to my article "The Legitimation Crisis."

28. The solemn ritual lingers only in a comic allusion: the fair is dominated by "une odeur de friture qui était comme *l'encens* de cette fête" ("an odor of fried food, which was like that festival's *incense*").

29. For a more complete analysis of the ninth *rêverie*, see my article, "'La Neuvième Rêverie': On Reading a 'Man's' Autobiography," *Studies in Romanticism* 26, no. 4 (Winter 1987): 573–90.

30. The first paragraph of the *rêverie* discusses the difference between happiness, which has no outward signs and therefore would have to be discerned in a man's heart ("il faudroit lire dans le coeur de l'homme heureux"), and contentment, which can be read in a person's face and attitude ("le contentement se lit dans les yeux, dans le maintien, dans l'accent, dans la démarche, et semble se communiquer à celui qui l'apperçoit"). After this prelude, Rousseau recalls a visit he had from Mr. P., who insisted on reading aloud d'Alembert's piece in memory of Madame Geoffrin. In this example, Rousseau claims to discern not only the motivations of the author in writing certain statements about the recently deceased *salonnière,* but also the motivations of his visitor in reading him these passages. This heavy emphasis on reading from the outset of the *rêverie* makes Rousseau's subject clear; and the insistence that one can know an author's motivation by reading his text puts us on notice concerning our role as *active* readers.

31. Rouss., *OC,* 1: 1091; *CW,* 8: 82; translation modified.

32. E. O. James, "Rites and Ceremonies: Sacrament," and Raymond Firth, "Rites and Ceremonies: Sacrifice," in *The New Encyclopedia Britannica: Macropaedia,* 15th ed. (1991).

33. Firth, "Rites and Ceremonies: Sacrifice."

34. As Jean Starobinski has shown, this example is one basis for Baudelaire's prose poem, "Le Gâteau." "Rousseau, Baudelaire, Huysmans (les pains d'épices, le gâteau, et l'immonde tartine)," in *Baudelaire, Mallarmé, Valéry: New Essays in Honour of Lloyd Austin,* ed. Malcolm Bowie et al., (Cambridge: Cambridge University Press, 1982), 128–41.

35. Cynthia Chase, "Paragon, Parergon: Baudelaire Translates Rousseau," *Diacritics* 11 (1981): 44.

36. See Kevin Newmark, "Traumatic Poetry: Charles Baudelaire and the Shock of Laughter," *Trauma: Explorations in Memory,* ed. Cathy Caruth (Baltimore: Johns Hopkins University Press, 1995), 240. Newmark's brilliant reading of "De l'essence du rire" exposes another version of the problem of reading and remembering with which I am dealing here.

37. Froidevaux, *Baudelaire,* 104.

38. E. S. Burt, *Poetry's Appeal: Nineteenth-Century French Lyric and the Political Space* (Stanford, Calif.: Stanford University Press, 1999), 192. In her insightful chapter on Baudelaire, Burt defines memory (in opposition to remembrance) as

"an experiencing for the first time of left-out impressions." In other words, memory is not the storehouse of events already experienced and recorded as over and done. Rather, in memory, the past "has not taken place until it emerges, shattering the stability of the present, in the act of recollection" (191). This is the liminal temporality (neither exactly past nor fully present) that attaches to Baudelaire's Rousseau.

39. Sainte-Beuve, *Causeries,* 15: 230 (15–22 July, 1861).

40. In his notice regarding *Le Spleen de Paris* (Baud., *OC,* 1: 1298–1301), Pichois reviews the various titles Baudelaire proposed over the years, including "La Lueur et la fumée."

Conclusion

1. Baudelaire expressed his idea of the modern use of allegory when he commented that "Même dans la poésie idéale, la Muse peut, sans déroger, frayer avec les vivants. Elle saura ramasser partout une nouvelle parure. Un oripeau moderne peut ajouter une grâce exquise, un mordant nouveau . . . à sa beauté de déesse. . . . Vénus, qui est immortelle, peut bien, quand elle veut visiter Paris, faire descendre son char dans les bosquets du Luxembourg" ("Even in ideal poetry, the Muse can, without overstepping her rights, rub elbows with the living. She will pick up new finery everywhere. Some modern flashy dress can add an exquisite grace, a new bite . . . to her divine beauty. . . . Venus, who is immortal, can perfectly well, when she wants to visit Paris, bring down her chariot in the shrubbery of the Luxembourg [Gardens]") (*OC,* 2: 167; my translation).

2. Baud., *OC,* 1: 652. Baudelaire was describing the arabesque.

3. Indeed, Baudelaire acknowledged that the grotesque repels the human. In his essay "Edgar Poe, sa vie et ses oeuvres," he cites Poe's *Tales of the Grotesque and the Arabesque* and comments that "les ornements grotesques et arabesques repoussent la figure humaine" ("grotesque and arabesque ornaments refuse the human figure") (Baud., *OC,* 2: 304). Compare Benjamin's observation that the grotesque is associated with "the creaturely world of things, the dead, or at best the half-living" and that "man does not enter its field of vision" (Benjamin, *Origin of Tragic Drama,* 227).

Select Bibliography

Adams, James Luther, and Wilson Yates, eds. *The Grotesque in Art and Literature: Theological Reflections.* Grand Rapids, Mich.: William B. Eerdmans, 1997.

Adatte, Emmanuel. *Les Fleurs du mal et le Spleen de Paris: Essai sur le dépassement du réel.* Paris: José Corti, 1986.

Alexandre, Arsène. *L'Art du rire et de la caricature.* Paris: Librairies-Imprimeries Réunies, n.d.

Apostolidès, Jean-Marie. *Le Roi-machine: Spectacle et politique au temps de Louis XIV.* Paris: Minuit, 1981.

Auerbach, Erich. *Mimesis.* Translated by Willard R. Trask. Princeton, N.J.: Princeton University Press, 1953.

Bachelard, Gaston. *The Poetics of Space.* Translated by Maria Jolas. New York: Orion Press, 1964.

Baer, Ulrich. *Remnants of Song: Trauma and the Experience of Modernity in Charles Baudelaire and Paul Celan.* Stanford, Calif.: Stanford University Press, 2000.

Bakhtin, Mikhail. *Rabelais and His World.* Translated by Helene Iswolsky. Cambridge, Mass.: MIT Press, 1968.

Barasch, Frances K. *The Grotesque: A Study in Meanings.* The Hague: Mouton, 1971.

Barthes, Roland. "Arcimboldo; ou, Rhétoriqueur et magicien." In id., *L'Obvie et l'obtus.* Paris: Seuil, 1982.

Batteux, Charles. *Les Beaux-Arts réduits à un même principe.* Edited by J.-R. Mantion. Paris: Aux Amateurs de Livres, 1989.

Baudelaire, Charles. *Correspondance.* Edited by Claude Pichois and Jean Ziegler. 2 vols. Bibliothèque de la Pléiade. Paris: Gallimard, 1973.

———. *Les Fleurs du mal, Petits Poèmes en prose, Les Paradis artificiels.* Translated by Arthur Symons. London: Casanova Society, 1925.

———. *The Flowers of Evil and Paris Spleen.* Translated by William H. Crosby. Brockport, N.Y.: BOA Editions, 1991.

———. *My Heart Laid Bare, and Other Prose Writings.* Translated by Norman Cameron. Edited by Peter Quennell. London: G. Weidenfeld & Nicolson, 1950.

———. *Nouvelles Lettres.* Edited by Claude Pichois. Paris: Fayard, 2000.

———. *Oeuvres complètes.* Edited by Claude Pichois. 2 vols. Bibliothèque de la Pléiade. Paris: Gallimard, 1976.

————. *The Painter of Modern Life, and Other Essays.* Translated and edited by Jonathan Mayne. London: Phaidon, 1964.

————. *The Parisian Prowler.* Translated by Edward K. Kaplan. Athens: University of Georgia Press, 1989.

————. *Petits Poëmes en prose.* Edited by Robert Kopp. Paris: José Corti, 1969.

————. *The Poems in Prose with "La Fanfarlo."* Vol. 2 of *Baudelaire.* Translated and edited by Francis Scarfe. London: Anvil Press Poetry, 1989.

Benjamin, Walter. *The Arcades Project.* Translated by Howard Eiland and Kevin McLaughlin. Cambridge, Mass.: Harvard University Press, Belknap Press, 1999.

————. *Charles Baudelaire: Un Poète lyrique à l'apogée du capitalisme.* Translated by Jean Lacoste. Paris: Petite Bibliothèque Payot, 1974.

————. *Illuminations.* New York: Schocken Books, 1969.

————. *The Origin of German Tragic Drama.* Translated by John Osborne. London: NLB, 1977.

Berman, Marshall. *All That Is Solid Melts into Air: The Experience of Modernity.* New York: Simon & Schuster, 1982.

Bernard, Suzanne. *Le Poème en prose de Baudelaire jusqu'à nos jours.* Paris: Nizet, 1959.

Bersani, Leo. *Baudelaire and Freud.* Berkeley: University of California Press, 1977.

Bertrand, Aloysius. *Gaspard de la Nuit: Fantaisies à la manière de Rembrandt et de Callot.* Edited by Max Milner. Paris: Gallimard, 1980.

Blanc, Louis. *Histoire de la Révolution française.* Paris, 1847.

Buci-Glucksmann, Christine. *La Raison baroque: De Baudelaire à Benjamin.* Paris: Galilée, 1984.

Bulfinch, Thomas. *Bulfinch's Mythology.* Edited by Bryan Holme. New York: Viking, 1979.

Burt, E. S. *Poetry's Appeal: Nineteenth-Century French Lyric and the Political Space.* Stanford, Calif.: Stanford University Press, 1999.

Burton, Richard D. E. *Baudelaire and the Second Republic: Writing and Revolution.* Oxford: Clarendon Press, 1991.

————. *Baudelaire in 1859: A Study in the Sources of Poetic Creativity.* Cambridge: Cambridge University Press, 1988.

————. "Bonding and Breaking in Baudelaire's *Petits poèmes en prose.*" *Modern Language Review* 88 (1993): 58–73.

————. "Destruction as Creation: 'Le Mauvais Vitrier' and the Poetics and Politics of Violence." *Romanic Review* 83 (1992): 297–322.

————. "'Jésuite et révolutionnaire': Baudelaire, Nadar and the 'Question italienne.'" *Studi francesi* 113 (1994): 241–50.

Cabanis, José. *Lacordaire et quelques autres: Politique et religion.* Paris: Gallimard, 1982.

Cavell, Stanley. *The World Viewed: Reflections on the Ontology of Film.* Enlarged ed. Cambridge, Mass.: Harvard University Press, 1979.

Caws, Mary Ann. "Insertion in an Oval Frame: Poe Circumscribed by Baudelaire." In *Charles Baudelaire,* edited by Harold Bloom, 101–23. New York: Chelsea House, 1987.

Chalker, Sylvia, and Edmund Weiner. "Proper Noun." *The Oxford Dictionary of English Grammar.* Oxford: Clarendon Press, 1994.

Chambers, Ross. "L'Art sublime du comédien." *Saggi e ricerche di letteratura francese* 11 (1971): 191–260.

———. "Frôler ceux qui rôdent: Le Paradoxe du saltimbanque." *Revue des Sciences humaines* 44 (1977): 347–63.

———. *Story and Situation: Narrative Seduction and the Power of Fiction.* Minneapolis: University of Minnesota Press, 1984.

———. *The Writing of Melancholy: Modes of Opposition in Early French Modernism.* Translated by Mary Seidman Trouille. Chicago: University of Chicago Press, 1993.

Chase, Cynthia. "Paragon, Parergon: Baudelaire Translates Rousseau." *Diacritics* 11 (1981).

Chastel, André. *La Grottesque.* Paris: Le Promeneur, 1988.

Clark, T. J. *The Absolute Bourgeois: Artists and Politics in France, 1848–1851.* Berkeley: University of California Press, 1999.

Coleman, Patrick. *Rousseau's Political Imagination: Rule and Representation in the "Lettre à d'Alembert."* Geneva: Droz, 1984.

Cousin, Victor. "Du Manuscrit del'*Emile,* conservé à la bibliothèque de la Chambre des Représentants. Premier article." *Journal des Savants* (September 1848): 517–28.

———. "Du Manuscrit del'*Emile,* conservé à la bibliothèque de la Chambre des Représentants. Deuxième article." *Journal des Savants* (November 1848): 658–72.

Crow, Thomas. *Painters and Public Life in Eighteenth Century Paris.* New Haven, Conn.: Yale University Press, 1985.

D'Alembert, Jean LeRond. "De la liberté de la musique." In *Oeuvres complètes,* 1: 515–46. Paris: 1821.

Daumier, Honoré. *Les Cent et un Robert Macaire.* Texts by Maurice Alhoy and Louis Huart. Paris: Aubert et compagnie, 1839.

———. *Les Gens d'Affaires (Robert Macaire).* Edited by Jean Adhémar. Paris: Editions Vilo, 1968.

Davie, Donald. "Personification." F. W. Bateson Memorial Lecture. *Essays in Criticism* 31, no. 2 (1981): 91–104.

Delcroix, Maurice. "Un Poème en prose de Charles Baudelaire: *Les Yeux des pauvres.*" *Cahiers d'analyse textuelle* 19 (1977): 47–65.

De Maistre, Joseph. *Considérations sur la France.* New rev. ed. Paris: Société typographique, 1814.

———. *Essai sur le principe générateur des constitutions politiques.* Lyon, 1874.

———. *St Petersburg Dialogues, or, Conversations on the Temporal Government of*

Providence. Translated and edited by Richard Lebrun. Montréal: McGill-Queen's University Press, 1993.

De Man, Paul. *Allegories of Reading.* New Haven, Conn.: Yale University Press, 1979.

———. *Blindness and Insight.* 2d ed. Minneapolis: University of Minnesota Press, 1983.

Derrida, Jacques. *Of Grammatology.* Translated by Gayatri Chakravorty Spivak. Baltimore: Johns Hopkins University Press, 1998.

———. "Structure, Sign and Play in the Human Sciences." In *The Languages of Criticism and the Sciences of Man: The Structuralist Controversy,* edited by Richard Macksey and Eugenio Donato, 247–65. Baltimore: Johns Hopkins University Press, 1969.

———. *Writing and Difference.* Translated, with an introduction and additional notes, by Alan Bass. London: Routledge & Kegan Paul, 1978.

Dubos, Jean Baptiste. *Réflexions critiques sur la poésie et sur la peinture.* 1719. Paris: Ecole nationale supérieure des beaux-arts, 1993.

Eigeldinger, Marc. *Mythologie et intertextualité.* Geneva: Slatkine, 1987.

Encyclopédie; ou, Dictionnaire raisonné des sciences, des arts et des métiers. 17 vols. Paris, Briasson, 1751–80.

Evans, Margery A. *Baudelaire and Intertextuality.* Cambridge: Cambridge University Press, 1993.

Fayolle, Roger. *Sainte-Beuve et le XVIIIe siècle; ou, Comment les révolutions arrivent.* Paris: Armand Colin, 1972.

Fineman, Joel. "The Structure of Allegorical Desire." In *Allegory and Representation,* edited by Stephen Greenblatt, 26–60. Baltimore: Johns Hopkins University Press, 1981.

Firth, Raymond. "Rites and Ceremonies: Sacrifice." In *The New Encyclopedia Britannica,* 15th ed. (1991), *Macropaedia.*

Fletcher, Angus. *Allegory: The Theory of a Symbolic Mode.* Ithaca, N.Y.: Cornell University Press, 1964.

Fortescue, William. *Alphonse de Lamartine: A Political Biography.* London: Croom Helm; New York: St. Martin's Press, 1983.

Franklin, Ursula. "The Saltimbanque in the Prose Poems of Baudelaire, Mallarmé and Rilke." *Comparative Literature Studies* 19 (1982): 335–50.

Freud, Sigmund. "Fetishism." Translated by Joan Riviere in *The Standard Edition of the Complete Psychological Works of Sigmund Freud,* edited by James Strachey et al., 21: 152–57. London: Hogarth Press and the Institute of Psycho-Analysis, 1961.

Friedman, Geraldine. "Baudelaire's Theory of Practice: Ideology and Difference in 'Les Yeux des pauvres.'" *PMLA* 104, no. 3 (May 1989): 317–28.

Froidevaux, Gérald. *Baudelaire: Représentation et modernité.* Paris: José Corti, 1989.

———. "L'Ivresse comme 'chose moderne' chez Baudelaire." *Neophilologus* 71 (1987): 335–42.

Furctière, Antoine. "Arabesque." *Dictionnaire universel.* 2d ed., rev. The Hague: Leers, 1702.

Garrigues, Jean. *La France de 1848 à 1870.* Paris: Armand Colin, 1995.

Gombrich, E. H. *Art and Illusion: A Study in the Psychology of Pictorial Representation.* Bollingen Series XXXV.5. New York: Pantheon Books, 1960.

———. *Meditations on a Hobby Horse and Other Essays on the Theory of Art.* London: Phaidon, 1963.

Gombrich, E. H., and Ernst Kris. *Caricature.* Harmondsworth, England: Penguin Books, 1940.

Gordon, Rae Beth. *Ornament, Fantasy, and Desire in Nineteenth-Century French Literature.* Princeton, N.J.: Princeton University Press, 1992.

Gossman, Lionel. *Between History and Literature.* Cambridge, Mass.: Harvard University Press, 1990.

Guerlac, Suzanne. *The Impersonal Sublime: Hugo, Baudelaire, Lautréamont.* Stanford, Calif.: Stanford University Press, 1990.

Gutwirth, Marcel. "A propos du 'Gâteau': Baudelaire, Rousseau et le recours à l'enfance." *Romanic Review* 80 (1989): 75–88.

Hambly, Peter S. "Baudelaire et l'utopie." *Bulletin baudelairien* 6, no. 1 (August 31, 1970): 5–7.

Hannoosh, Michele. *Baudelaire and Caricature: From the Comic to an Art of Modernity.* University Park: Pennsylvania State University Press, 1992.

Harpham, Geoffrey Golt. *On the Grotesque: Strategies of Contradiction in Art and Literature.* Princeton, N.J.: Princeton University Press, 1982.

Heck, Francis S. "'Le Mauvais Vitrier': A Literary Transfiguration." *Nineteenth-Century French Studies* 14, nos. 3–4 (1986): 260–68.

Hemmings, F. W. J. *Culture and Society in France, 1789–1848.* Leicester, England: Leicester University Press, 1987.

Hiddleston, J. A. *Baudelaire and Le Spleen de Paris.* Oxford: Clarendon Press, 1987.

———. *Baudelaire and the Art of Memory.* Oxford: Clarendon Press, 1999.

———. "Les Poèmes en prose de Baudelaire et la caricature." *Romantisme* 74 (1991): 57–64.

Hofmann, Werner. "Baudelaire et la caricature." *Preuves* 207 (1967): 38–43.

———. *Caricature from Leonardo to Picasso.* New York: Crown, 1957.

Holland, Eugene W. *Baudelaire and Schizoanalysis.* Cambridge: Cambridge University Press, 1993.

Houssaye, Arsène. *Les Charmettes: Jean-Jacques Rousseau et Madame de Warens.* Paris: Didier, 1863.

———. *Galerie de portraits du XVIIIe siècle.* N.p., 1844.

———. "Oeuvres inédits de Jean-Jacques." *L'Artiste,* n.s., 12, no. 16 (November 15, 1861): 217–21.

Howells, Bernard. *Baudelaire: Individualism, Dandyism and the Philosophy of History.* Oxford: Legenda / European Humanities Research Centre, 1996.

Hugo, Victor. Preface to *Cromwell.* In *Oeuvres complètes,* edited by Jean-Pierre Reynaud et al., vol. 12. Paris: Robert Laffont, 1985.

James, E. O. "Rites and Ceremonies: Sacrament." In *The New Encyclopedia Britannica,* 15th ed. (1991), *Macropaedia.*

Jeanneret, Michel. "Baudelaire et le théâtre d'ombres." In *Le Lieu et la formule: Hommage à Marc Eigeldinger,* 121–36. Neuchâtel: La Baconnière, 1978.

Johnson, Barbara. *Défigurations du langage poétique.* Paris: Flammarion, 1979.

Kaplan, Edward K. *Baudelaire's Prose Poems: The Esthetic, the Ethical, and the Religious in "The Parisian Prowler."* Athens: University of Georgia Press, 1990.

Kayser, Wolfgang. *The Grotesque in Art and Literature.* Translated by Ulrich Weisstein. Bloomington: Indiana University Press, 1963.

Kintzler, Catherine. *Poétique de l'opéra français de Corneille à Rousseau.* Paris: Minerve, 1991.

Klein, Richard. "Straight Lines and Arabesques: Metaphors of Metaphor." *Yale French Studies* 45 (1970): 64–86.

Kris, Ernst. *Psychoanalytic Explorations in Art.* New York: International Universities Press, 1952.

Labarthe, Patrick. *Baudelaire et la tradition de l'allégorie.* Geneva: Droz, 1999.

Labrusse, Rémi. "Baudelaire et Meryon." *L'Année Baudelaire* 1 (1995): 99–132.

Lacoue-Labarthe, Philippe. *Portrait de l'artiste, en général.* Paris: Christian Bourgeois, 1979.

Laffont, Robert, and Valentino Bompiani, eds. *Dictionnaire biographique des auteurs de tous les temps et de tous les pays.* 2 vols. Paris: S.E.D.E., 1957–58.

Lamartine, Alphonse de. *Cours familier de littérature.* Vol. 11. Paris, 1861.

———. *Lettres des années sombres, 1853–1867.* Fribourg: Librairie de l'Université, 1942.

Launay, Denise, ed. *La Querelle des Bouffons: Texte des pamphlets.* 3 vols. Geneva: Minkoff Reprint, 1973. "Réimpression des éditions de Paris, La Haye, 1752–1754."

Lloyd, Rosemary. *Baudelaire's Literary Criticism.* Cambridge: Cambridge University Press, 1981.

———. *Baudelaire's World.* Ithaca, N.Y.: Cornell University Press, 2002.

———. *Selected Letters of Charles Baudelaire.* Chicago: University of Chicago Press, 1986.

Lucie-Smith, Edward. *The Art of Caricature.* Ithaca, N.Y.: Cornell University Press, 1981.

Lyu, Claire. "'High' Poetics: Baudelaire's *Le Poème du hachisch.*" *MLN* 109 (1994): 698–740.

MacInnes, John W. *The Comical as Textual Practice in Les Fleurs du Mal.* Gainesville: University Press of Florida, 1988.

Maclean, Marie. *Narrative as Performance: The Baudelairean Experiment.* London: Routledge, 1988.

Macrobius. *The Saturnalia.* Translated and edited by Percival Vaughan Davies. New York: Columbia University Press, 1969.

Maillard, Robert, et al. *Dictionnaire universel de l'art et des artistes.* Paris: Hazan, 1967.

Marder, Elissa. *Dead Time: Temporal Disorders in the Wake of Modernity.* Stanford, Calif.: Stanford University Press, 2001.

Mauron, Charles. *Le Dernier Baudelaire.* Paris: José Corti, 1966.

Mazouer, Charles. *Molière et ses comédies-ballets.* Paris: Klincksieck, 1993.

McElroy, Bernard. *Fiction of the Modern Grotesque.* New York: St. Martin's Press, 1989.

McLees, Ainslie Armstrong. *Baudelaire's "Argot Plastique": Poetic Caricature and Modernism.* Athens: University of Georgia Press, 1989.

Michelet, Jules. *Histoire de la Révolution française.* Edited by Gérard Walter. 2 vols. Bibliothèque de la Pléiade. Paris: Gallimard, 1952.

———. *L'Etudiant.* Paris: Seuil, 1970.

Mickel, Emanuel J., Jr. *The Artificial Paradises in French Literature.* Chapel Hill: University of North Carolina Press, 1969.

Minor, Vernon Hyde. *Baroque and Rococo.* New York: Harry N. Abrams, 1999.

Monroe, Jonathan. *A Poverty of Objects: The Prose Poem and the Politics of Genre.* Ithaca, N.Y.: Cornell University Press, 1987.

Murphy, Steve. "'Le Mauvais Vitrier'; ou, La Crise du verre." *Romanic Review* 82 (1990): 339–349.

Néraudau, Jean-Pierre. *L'Olympe du Roi-Soleil: Mythologie et idéologie royale au Grand Siècle.* Paris: Les Belles Lettres, 1986.

Newmark, Kevin. "Traumatic Poetry: Charles Baudelaire and the Shock of Laughter." In *Trauma: Explorations in Memory,* edited by Cathy Caruth, 236–55. Baltimore: Johns Hopkins University Press, 1995.

Nisard, Désiré. *Histoire de la littérature française.* 4 vols. Paris: Firmin Didot, 1844–61.

Nodier, Charles. "Des Types en littérature." *Revue de Paris* 18 (September 1830): 187–96.

———. *Romans.* Paris: Bibliothèque Charpentier/Fasquelle, 1900.

Nora, Pierre. "Between Memory and History: *Les Lieux de mémoire.*" *Representations* 26 (1989): 7–25.

Oehler, Dolf. *Le Spleen contre l'oubli, Juin 1848: Baudelaire, Flaubert, Heine, Herzen.* Translated by Guy Petitdemange. Paris: Payot & Rivages, 1996.

Orr, Linda. *Headless History: Nineteenth-Century French Historiography of the Revolution.* Ithaca, N.Y.: Cornell University Press, 1990.

Oster, Daniel. *Histoire de l'Académie française.* Paris: Vialetay, 1970.

Owens, Craig. "The Allegorical Impulse: Toward a Theory of Postmodernism." *October* 12 (1980): 67–86.

Pachet, Pierre. *Le Premier Venu: Essai sur la politique baudelairienne.* Paris: Denoël, 1976.

Paul, Charles B. "Music and Ideology: Rameau, Rousseau, and 1789." *Journal of the History of Ideas* 32, no. 3 (1971): 395–410.

Pichois, Claude. *Baudelaire.* Translated by Graham Robb. London: Hamish Hamilton, 1989.

———. *Baudelaire: Etudes et témoignages.* Neuchâtel: La Baconnière, 1967.

Pichois, Claude, and Vincenette Pichois, ed. *Armand Fraisse sur Baudelaire, 1857–1869.* Gembloux, Belgium: J. Duculot, 1973.

Pietz, William. "The Problem of the Fetish, I." *Res* 9 (Spring 1985): 5–17.

———. "The Problem of the Fetish, II: The Origin of the Fetish." *Res* 13 (Spring 1987): 23–45.

———. "The Problem of the Fetish, IIIa: Bosman's Guinea and the Enlightenment Theory of Fetishism." *Res* 16 (Autumn 1988): 105–23.

Pizzorusso, Arnaldo. "*Le Mauvais Vitrier;* ou, L'Impulsion inconnue." In *Etudes baudelairiennes* 8, 147–71. Neuchâtel: La Baconnière, 1976.

Pons, Bruno. "Arabesques ou nouvelles grotesques." In *L'Art décoratif en Europe: Classique et baroque,* edited by Alain Gruber, 159–209. Paris: Citadelles & Mazenod, 1992.

Prendergast, Christopher. *Paris and the Nineteenth Century.* Oxford: Blackwell, 1992.

Proudhon, P.-J. *Oeuvres complètes.* Edited by C. Bouglé, H. Moysset, et al. Paris: Librairie Marcel Rivière, 1923–59.

Quilligan, Maureen. *The Language of Allegory.* Ithaca, N.Y.: Cornell University Press, 1979.

Reichenburg, Louise. *Contribution à l'histoire de la "querelle des bouffons": Guerre de brochures suscitées par le "Petit prophète" de Grimm et par la "Lettre sur la musique française" de Rousseau.* Reprint of diss., University of Pennsylvania, 1937. New York: AMS Press, 1978.

Robb, Graham M. "Les Origines journalistiques de la prose poétique de Baudelaire." *Lettres romanes* 44 (1990): 15–25.

Rollins, Yvonne Bargues. *Baudelaire et le grotesque.* Washington, D.C.: University Press of America, 1978.

Rousseau, Jean-Jacques. *The Collected Writings of Rousseau.* Edited by Roger D. Masters and Christopher Kelly. 10 vols. to date. Hanover, N.H.: Published for Dartmouth College by the University Press of New England, 1990–.

———. *The Confessions.* Translated by Christopher Kelly. Vol. 5 of *The Collected Writings of Rousseau.* Hanover, N.H.: University Press of New England, 1995.

———. *Essay on the Origin of Languages and Writings Related to Music.* Translated and edited by John T. Scott. Vol. 7 of *The Collected Writings of Rousseau.* Hanover, N.H.: University Press of New England, 1998.

———. *Julie, or the New Heloise.* Translated and annotated Philip Stewart and Jean Vaché. Vol. 6 of *The Collected Writings of Rousseau.* Hanover, N.H.: University Press of New England, 1997.

———. *Oeuvres complètes.* 5 vols. Bibliothèque de la Pléiade. Paris: Gallimard, 1959–95.

————. *Reveries of the Solitary Walker.* Translated by Peter France. New York: Penguin Books, 1979.

Ruff, Marcel. "La Pensée politique et sociale de Baudelaire." In *Littérature et société: Recueil d'études en l'honneur de Bernard Guyon,* 65–75. Paris: De Brouwer, 1973.

Russo, Mary. *The Female Grotesque: Risk, Excess and Modernity.* New York: Routledge, 1994.

Sainte-Beuve, Charles-Augustin. *Causeries du lundi.* 3d ed. Paris: Garnier frères, 1857–72. 4th ed. Paris: Garnier frères, n.d.

————. "Les Confessions de J.-J. Rousseau." In *Causeries du lundi,* 3d ed., 3: 78–97.

————. "Mme de la Tour-Franqueville et Jean-Jacques Rousseau." In *Causeries du lundi,* 3d ed., 2: 63–84.

————. *Les Nouveaux Lundis.* Vol. 1. Paris: Michel Lévy, 1879–95.

————. "Voltaire et J.-J. Rousseau." In *Causeries du lundi,* 4th ed., 15: 219–45.

Saisselin, Rémy G. *The Enlightenment Against the Baroque: Economics and Aesthetics in the Eighteenth Century.* Berkeley: University of California Press, 1992.

Scherer, Jacques. *La Dramaturgie classique en France.* Paris: Nizet, 1950.

Schinz, Albert. *Etat présent des travaux sur J.-J. Rousseau.* Paris: Les Belles Lettres; New York: MLA, 1941.

Scott, David. *Pictorialist Poetics. Poetry and the Visual Arts in Nineteenth-Century France.* Cambridge: Cambridge University Press, 1988.

Scott, Katie. *The Rococo Interior: Decoration and Social Spaces in Early Eighteenth-Century Paris.* New Haven, Conn.: Yale University Press, 1995.

Sherry, James. "Four Modes of Caricature: Reflections upon a Genre." *Bulletin of Research in the Humanities* 87, no. 1 (1987): 29–62.

Sieburth, Richard. "Gaspard de la nuit: Prefacing Genre." *Studies in Romanticism* 24 (1985): 239–55.

————. "Une Idéologie du lisible: Le Phénomène des 'physiologies.'" *Romantisme* 15 (1985): 39–60.

————. "Same Difference: The French Physiologies, 1840–1842." *Notebooks in Cultural Analysis* 1 (1984): 163–200.

Stafford, Barbara Maria. "The Eighteenth-Century: Towards an Interdisciplinary Model." *Art Bulletin* 70, no. 1 (1988): 6–24.

Stamelman, Richard. "L'Anamorphose baudelairienne: L'Allégorie du 'Masque.'" *Cahiers de l'Association internationale des études françaises* 41 (1989): 251–67.

————. *Lost Beyond Telling: Representations of Death and Absence in Modern French Poetry.* Ithaca, N.Y.: Cornell University Press, 1990.

Starobinski, Jean. "From the Solitary Walker to the *Flâneur*: Baudelaire's Caricature of Rousseau." In *Approaches to Teaching Rousseau's "Confessions" and "Reveries of the Solitary Walker,"* edited by John C. O'Neal and Ourida Mostefai, 115–20. New York: Modern Language Association, 2003.

————. *Portrait de l'artiste en saltimbanque.* Geneva: Albert Skira, 1970.

————. "Rousseau, Baudelaire, Huysmans (les pains d'épices, le gâteau, et l'im-

monde tartine)." In *Baudelaire, Mallarmé, Valéry: New Essays in Honour of Lloyd Austin,* edited by Malcolm Bowie et al., 128–41. Cambridge: Cambridge University Press, 1982.

———. "Rousseau et Baudelaire (Les enfants effrayés)." *Nouvelle Revue française* 338 (1981): 37–50.

———. "Sur quelques répondants allégoriques du poète." *Revue d'histoire littéraire de la France* 67 (1967): 402–12.

———. "Sur Rousseau et Baudelaire: Le Dédommagement et l'irréparable." In *Le Lieu et la formule: Hommage à Marc Eigeldinger,* 47–59. Neuchâtel: La Baconnière, 1978.

———. "Windows: From Rousseau to Baudelaire." *Hudson Review* 40 (1988). 551–60.

Stephens, Sonya. *Baudelaire's Prose Poems: The Practice and Politics of Irony.* Oxford: Oxford University Press, 1999.

Swain, Virginia E. "The Legitimation Crisis: Event and Meaning in Baudelaire's 'Le Vieux Saltimbanque' and 'Une Mort héroique.'" *Romanic Review* 73 (1982): 452–62.

———. "The Mechanics of Language: Personification in Rousseau's *Rêveries.*" In *Approaches to Teaching Rousseau's "Confessions" and "Reveries of the Solitary Walker,"* edited by John C. O'Neal and Ourida Mostefai, 90–95. New York: Modern Language Association, 2003.

———. "'La Neuvième Rêverie': On Reading a 'Man's' Autobiography." *Studies in Romanticism* 26, no. 4 (Winter 1987): 573–90.

Terdiman, Richard. *Discourse/Counter-discourse: The Theory and Practice of Symbolic Resistance in Nineteenth-Century France.* Ithaca, N.Y.: Cornell University Press, 1985.

———. *Present Past: Modernity and the Memory Crisis.* Ithaca, N.Y.: Cornell University Press, 1993.

Thélot, Jérôme. *Baudelaire: Violence et poésie.* Paris: Gallimard, 1993.

Thomas, Downing A. *Music and the Origins of Language: Theories from the French Enlightenment.* Cambridge: Cambridge University Press, 1995.

Todorov, Tzvetan. *Théories du symbole.* Paris: Seuil, 1977.

Toumayan, Alain. *La Littérature et la hantise du Mal.* Lexington, Ky.: French Forum, 1987.

Trousson, Raymond. *Défenseurs et adversaires de J.-J. Rousseau: D'Isabelle de Charrière à Charles Maurras.* Paris: Honoré Champion, 1995.

———. *Rousseau et sa fortune littéraire.* Bordeaux: Ducros, 1971.

Valéry, Paul. "Situation de Baudelaire." In *Oeuvres,* edited by Jean Hytier, vol. 1. Bibliothèque de la Pléiade. Paris: Gallimard, 1957.

Van Slyke, Gretchen. "Dans l'intertexte de Baudelaire et de Proudhon: Pourquoi faut-il assommer les pauvres?" *Romantisme* 45 (1984), 57–77.

Villemain, Abel-François. *Cours de littérature française: Tableau de la littérature au XVIIIe siècle.* New ed. Vol. 2. Paris: Didier, 1858.

Vitruvius Pollio. *On Architecture.* Edited and translated by Frank Granger. 2 vols. Loeb Classical Library. London: Heinemann; New York: Putnam, 1931–34.

Volosinov, V. N. *Marxism and the Philosophy of Language.* Translated by Ladislav Matejka and I. R. Titunik. New York: Seminar Press, 1973. Cambridge, Mass.: Harvard University Press, 1986.

Vouga, Daniel. *Baudelaire et Joseph de Maistre.* Paris: José Corti, 1957.

Watelet, C.-H., and P.-C. Lévesque. *Dictionnaire des arts de peinture, sculpture et gravure.* 5 vols. Paris: Prault, 1792. Reprint. Geneva: Minkoff, 1972.

Weber, William. "*La musique ancienne* in the Waning of the Ancien Régime." *Journal of Modern History* 56 (1984): 63–64.

Wechsler, Judith. "Editor's Statement: The Issue of Caricature." *Art Journal* 43 (1983): 317–18.

———. *A Human Comedy: Physiognomy and Caricature in Nineteenth-Century Paris.* Chicago: University of Chicago Press, 1982.

Wettlaufer, Alexandra K. "Paradise Regained: The *Flâneur,* the *Badaud,* and the Aesthetics of Artistic Reception in *Le Poème du haschisch.*" *Nineteenth-Century French Studies* 24 (1996): 388–97.

Wing, Nathaniel. *The Limits of Narrative.* Cambridge: Cambridge University Press, 1986.

———. "Poets, Mimes and Counterfeit Coins: On Power and Discourse in Baudelaire's Prose Poetry." *Paragraph* 13, no. 1 (1990): 1–18.

Wokler, Robert. "*La Querelle des Bouffons* and the Italian Liberation of France: A Study of Revolutionary Foreplay." *Studies in the Eighteenth Century* 6, special issue of *Eighteenth-Century Life* 11, no. 1 (1987): 94–116.

Zeldin, Theodore. *Emile Ollivier and the Liberal Empire of Napoleon III.* Oxford: Clarendon Press, 1963.

———. *France, 1848–1945.* Vol. 1. Oxford: Clarendon Press, 1973.

Zimmerman, Melvin. *Visions du monde: Baudelaire et Cie.* Paris: A.-G. Nizet; Toronto: GREF, 1991.

Index

Italicized numbers correspond to illustrations in the text.

French identity, Rousseau's political and artistic
legacy, the aesthetic and political significance of
the rococo, and the presence of the grotesque
in the modern.

Virginia E. Swain is a professor of French at
Dartmouth College.

PARALLAX Re-visions of Culture and Society

*Stephen G. Nichols, Gerald Prince,
and Wendy Steiner*
SERIES EDITORS